HIGH TARTARY

BY
OWEN LATTIMORE
Author of "The Desert Road to Turkestan"

WITH ILLUSTRATIONS

AND
A NEW INTRODUCTION BY THE AUTHOR

AMS PRESS
NEW YORK
1975

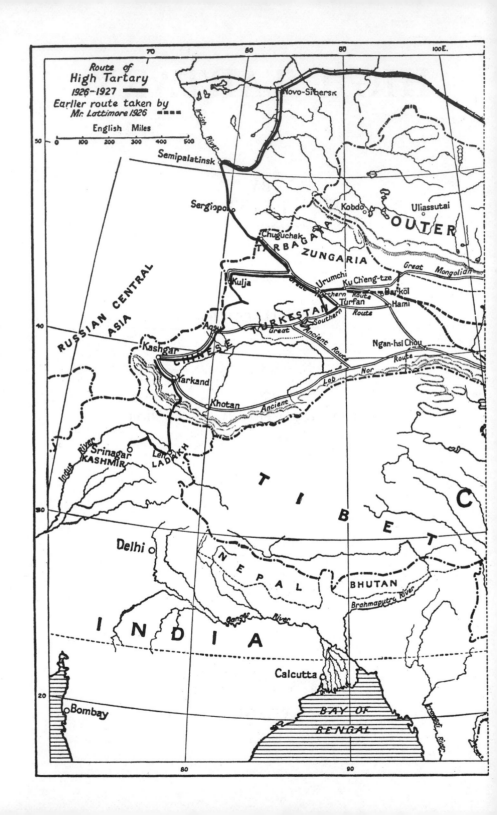

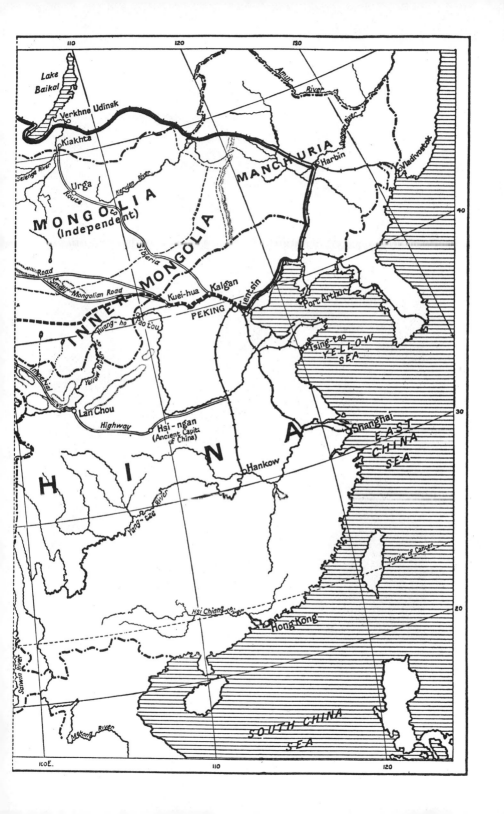

Moses on the left. O.L. with
Celtic fringe.
Eleanor is the Dark Lady

Sui-ting, Chinese Turkestan,
(Ili valley) May 1927

OWEN LATTIMORE AND THE FAITHFUL MOSES

CHINESE TURKESTAN

HIGH TARTARY

BY
OWEN LATTIMORE
Author of " The Desert Road to Turkestan "

WITH ILLUSTRATIONS

BOSTON
LITTLE, BROWN, AND COMPANY
1930

Library of Congress Cataloging in Publication Data

Lattimore, Owen, 1900-
High Tartary.

Reprint of the 1930 ed. published by Little, Brown,
Boston; with new introd.
Includes index.
1. Sinkiang—Description and travel.   I. Title.
DS793.E2L16   1975   915.1'6'044   72-4433

Library of Congress Catalog Card Number: 72-4433

International Standard Book Number: 0-404-10630-7

Manufactured in the United States of America

INTRODUCTION TO THE AMS EDITION

In preparing an introduction for this reprinted edition of *High Tartary*, I had the great advantage of being able to revisit Sinkiang briefly in September, 1972. As I had previously revisited the province—or rather, its capital—in 1944, when accompanying Vice President Henry A. Wallace, who had been sent by President Roosevelt on a special mission to Siberia, Soviet Central Asia, and China (and also Mongolia, although that was not "official"), I had now three marks by which to adjust my sights for a fresh look at China's position in Central Asia.

In 1927 the province had been ruled, as described in *High Tartary*, by a man who was unlike any other warlord of the China of the 1920's. He was, rather, a hold-over from the Manchi-Chinese bureaucracy which had administered Sinkiang ever since its reconquest at the end of the great Moslem rebellions. He was murdered the year after my wife and I were there, and succeeded by Chin Shu-jen, the kindly old gentleman mentioned in this book as the "Tas-yin" of Aksu. After a brief time of troubles, which included an invasion of Chinese Moslems (T'ungkan or Dungan) from Kansu, he gave up the reins of power; they were taken over for the first time by a professional soldier, Sheng Shih-ts'ai, who was governor when I visited Uninichi in 1944.

Sheng Shih-ts'ai was an interesting man. He came from Manchuria, which is now officially not Manchuria (indeed, neither the Chinese nor the Manchus themselves ever used that name), but the Northeast. Some say that he was in fact a Manchu, not a Chinese. He served under a general, Kuo Sung-lin, who tried to overthrow Chang Tso-lin, the "Old Marshal" of the Northeast (whose son, Chang Hsueh-liang, the "Young Marshal," was later to kidnap Chiang Kai-shek at Sian in 1936, and then to become Chiang's prisoner). After the defeat and death of Kuo Sung-lin, Sheng Shih-ts'ai fled to Nanking, where he took service with Chiang Kai-shek's faction of the Kuomintang.

I have described in this book how the policy of Sinkiang was

to hold aloof from the central government of China and the civil wars of Chinese provinces. During the time of troubles under the interim government of Chin Shu-jen, however, an appeal for help had to made to Nanking. Sheng Shih-ts'ai was sent up as a staff-officer to reorganize the provincial forces. He beat off the invading Kansu Moslems—and then, once in power, began to develop his independence of Chiang Kai-shek's government. He revived the old policy of virtually independent relations with the Soviet Union. In 1931, when the Japanese, following the "Mukden incident," occupied the Northeast, a number of defeated Chinese troops retreated into Siberia, and were eventually repatriated by the Soviet authorities; but, since they could not be repatriated to the Japanese-created "Manchukuo," they were repatriated to Sinkiang. This gave the governor, himself a Northeasterner, a body of Northeastern troops who were all the more likely to be loyal to him because they had no other local political connections.

I mention all this in some detail because *High Tartary* is in large part a "geopolitical" book as well as a narrative of travel. Scattered all through the book, but notably in Chapter VIII, "A Frontier of Inner Asia," the reader will find remarks which prove that in 1927, when the journey was made, and 1929-30, when the book was written, I assumed that Sinkiang was drifting into the Soviet orbit, and that I even said (page 78) that "the Soviets are developing, almost unaltered, the old forward policy, the *Drang nach Osten*, of Imperial Russia."

At about the same time, and a little later, I developed these themes even more strongly, in a paper called "The Chinese as a Dominant Race," published in *Journal of the Royal Central Asian Society* (XV, part III, London, 1928), and also in *Asia* (New York, June, 1928), and in a paper called simply "Sinkiang," written at the request of the great Sinologue Berthold Laufer, and published in *The Open Court* (XLVII, No. 921; Chicago, March 1933). Both these papers are reprinted in my *Studies in Frontier History, Collected Papers, 1928-1958* (Paris-La Haye, 1962).

In the first of these papers I wrote that "The price, in fact, of Chinese dominion [in Sinkiang] is acquiescence in Russian economic expansion." Since, however, I was in this paper primarily discussing Chinese imperialism, my concluding sentence was that "...wherever the Chinese have secured (if only for a few days) some measure of power and initiative, they have made it clear (even to their Russian 'advisers'), in spite of all the conflictions of domestic politics, that to their minds one of the chief functions of Chinese power is to assert Chinese domination—domination, not equality—over every race that comes within the scope of Chinese action." (In writing these words in 1928 I had in mind, of course, the breaking of the Kuomintang-Chinese Communist United Front by Chiang Kai-shek in 1927, and the expulsion of the Soviet advisers.)

In the second paper I asked and answered a question: "What, then, is the present state of Chinese Turkestan? The Chinese, after prolonged contact, have not amalgamated with the native population. Nor has Chinese culture penetrated deeply. It remains an alien veneer, affecting only a limited number of activities and a small proportion of the people. Chinese political and military supremacy, long a fiction, but a fiction handled with eminent skill and functioning well as a working theory, is in danger of collapse. The province is an insecure salient in the line of the frontier; and China itself, in the eyes of many of the subject peoples, appears to be crumbling inward on its own centre."

Later in the same paper I added: "In Russian Central Asia, on the other hand, the drift toward Chinese Turkestan is inexorable. The political-economic and social-economic movements there demand extension into Chinese Turkestan if they are to fulfill themselves."

The point of rehashing these "geopolitical" notions is that I do not believe in hiding my mistakes, but in pondering on them and trying to learn from them. After all, they were not mistakes that sprang from frivolous thinking. In fact, my thinking was formed by talking, in the course of travel, with a great diversity of people, very few of whom had intellectual pretensions, and by observing Chinese, Russians, Uighurs (whom in the book I called Turki), T'ungkan or Dungan (who are now officially called Hui Min), Mongols, Kazakhs, Kirghiz, and others. Books influenced me less. I doubt if at that time I even knew the word "geopolitics." Books of course did also influence me, but more in other fields of thought—like Ellsworth Huntington's *Pulse of Asia*, with its theories of dessication and "climatic pulsation"—but in a very few years I recovered from that.

There were two main reasons why the real Sinkiang diverged from the future that I predicted for it—the War, and the Chinese Revolution. They account for the fact that instead of

Sinkiang being "an insecure salient in the line of the frontier," and instead of "China itself...crumbling inward on its own centre," the situation has been entirely turned around. Sinkiang has never been more firmly attached to China in all its history, and even a brief visit is enough to make sure that relations between the Han Chinese and the other peoples are for the first time in history really good. It is true, of course, that nationalism lingers a long time, and that with a frontier that divides Kazakhs on the Chinese side from those on the Soviet side, and Chinese Uighurs from their close kinsmen the Soviet Uzbeks, there is bound to be a kind of competition between the Chinese and the Soviet policies on nationality.

Enough, for now, of the "geopolitical" themes in *High Tartary*. They are taken up again, in a deeper perspective in my retrospective introduction to the reprint edition of *Pivot of Asia: Sinkiang and the Inner Asian Frontier of China* (first published in 1950).

The strong point of *High Tartary* is that it remains, among the Sinkiang travel books of its time, the one most copiously based on a fluent command of the Chinese language, which made possible an easy, friendly, sometimes even intimate contact with all kinds of people: a handful of high officials and any number of carters, horse-handlers, innkeepers, soldiers, rich merchants and small traders. (Part of my exaggerated emphasis on the supposed menace of Soviet expansionism was an echo of the talk of people I met. It is obvious, looking back, that the Russians had in fact no territorial ambitions. If they had been headed for either old-fashioned or new-fashioned imperialism, they could have taken over Sinkiang rather easily.)

I do look back with discomfort, however, on the way in which a great deal of this book was written—the knowingness (a kind of boastfulness), the repeated suggestion that the cocky young traveller had special inside knowledge. Musing about it now, I am sure that I was a young man who was in fact not too sure of himself, who had not long been married, and who was trying to impress his wife. With the extraordinary generosity and wisdom that were hers all her life, she just let me work it out of my system.

There are a number of explanations of names and words in this book that are quite worthless. I did not at the time know Mongol, and on the journey the amount of Central Asian Turkish that I learned was inadequate for such speculations. On page 80, for example, in the footnote, "Chuguchak," whatever it may mean, probably does not mean "a bowl;" nor does "Kukuirgen" mean "blue cloth." In Mongol "kuku" (a better transliteration is "kohkh") does mean "blue," and is a frequent element in place names, but "irghen" (preferably, "irgen") does not mean "cloth." It means "people," and also had two specific meanings, "civilian" and "Chinese."

There is one of my "folk-etymologies," however, which is rather interesting. On pages 5 and 6, describing a man whom the caravan men called the "Bastard of Barkol," I translated "Erh-hun-tze" as a Chinese word for "bastard." That was certainly what it meant to the caravan men, but I am now sure that "Erh-hun-tze" is the Chinese pronunciation of "Erke'un," plural "Erke'ut," the mediaeval Mongol name for Nestorian Christians. It survives as a clan name here and there in Mongolia, and is at the basis of the place-name of Irkutsk, in Siberia. Most interesting of all, Father Antoine Mostaert, the great Belgian Mongolist, discovered among the Ordos Mongols a small community of surviving "crypto-Nestorians." One may recall that Marco Polo, in his account of the Nestorians of the same general region in his time, got the notion (just like the Chinese caravan men) that they were a mixed race, or bastards. How close I came, in my young ignorance, to stumbling on a discovery of real importance! The discovery and, if possible, the straightening out of early mistakes, is one of the pleasures of old age.

Owen Lattimore
Levallois Perret
France
1973

To
PAN TSILU
WHOSE FRIENDSHIP ADDED SO MUCH TO OUR
ENJOYMENT OF CHINESE TURKESTAN

PREFACE

THE name High Tartary is not to be looked for on modern maps. It is a survival from the geography of Asia before international boundaries were determined as they now stand. The name Tatar or Tartar has been used of all the barbarian hordes that in successive waves broke through the barriers of Central Asia to harry both the West and the remoter East. The whole empire of Jenghis Khan was Tartary. Different portions of it ruled by his descendants were likewise called Tartary. Manchuria has been called Eastern or Manchu Tartary; Mongolia has been called Tartary; the commanding heights of the Pamirs and T'ien Shan have been called High Tartary. The name Tatar or Tartar, above all other words, is a link between the geography and history of Central Asia.

The High Tartary through which my wife and I traveled in 1927 stretches from the Altai to the Pamirs. Within it lies the province of Hsin-chiang, including Zungaria, on the north, and Chinese Turkestan proper, on the south, of the T'ien Shan or Heavenly Mountains. In one region or another are to be found peoples as diverse as the Mongols, T'ung-kan, Qazaqs, Qirghiz, and Turki, and their Chinese rulers, besides such minor communities as the Dulani and such visitors as Indian and Afghan traders, and the Ladakhi caravan men who come in from the Five Great Passes of the Karakoram route.

"High Tartary," moreover, recalls the Middle Ages and the names of such courageous Western travelers as William of Rubruck, who penetrated into High Tartary at a time when the affairs of remotest Central Asia and its nomadic hordes were of grave moment to all Christendom. To my mind, the traveler cannot bring back from Central Asia anything of more value than a sense of the continuity of history, and the persistence into our own day of forces that once swept all Asia and all Europe.

In *The Desert Road to Turkestan* I wrote the account of a caravan journey through Mongolia, on the way from China to Chinese Turkestan. At Ku Ch'eng-tze, the end of the sixteen-hundred-mile Gobi route, I parted from the Eldest Son of the House of Chou, and all my other friends among the camel owners and camel pullers. Thus the name of Moses is the only one that survives from *The Desert Road to Turkestan* all the way through *High Tartary*. All I need say here is that Moses is the other name of Li Pao-shun, who although a servant earning wages was throughout the journey rather friend than servant.

The first chapter of this book, then, describes Ku Ch'eng-tze and the borders of Northern Chinese Turkestan. From Ku Ch'eng-tze I went on to Urumchi and after some delay got a message through to my wife, who had been waiting in Peking for the news that I had crossed Mongolia. Within a few days after hearing from me, she started out to travel alone through Siberia to join me, and succeeded in doing so after a journey so difficult and uncertain that it required far more enterprise and hardihood than a man would need to travel through Mongolia. I have not said anything about her experiences at Kuei-hua, where we had parted when I set out into Mongolia, and have given only the barest sketch of her journey through Siberia, with its culminating seventeen days by sled across four hundred miles of snow, because she has described some of these things herself,[1] and will describe them all.

When we had met at Chuguchak we turned once more into Chinese Central Asia and traveled for eight months by routes of trade and routes of nomadic migration through High Tartary; for in this part of the journey, as in Mongolia, my chief interest was in a comparison of the routes that are now used with those anciently in use. In the autumn of 1927 we came down through the Himalayas to enter Kashmir, having both of us traveled over-

---

[1] "By Sledge to the Middle Ages," by Eleanor Lattimore. Boston, the *Atlantic Monthly*, January and February, 1928.

land from Peking to India.   My wife, I think, is the only woman to have traveled from Peking to India through Chinese Turkestan.

I cannot thank personally all the people who contributed to the success of our journey; but I am glad that I can express here our gratitude to the Chinese authorities.   The officials of the province everywhere aided us, and the Chinese Postal Service very kindly provided us with facilities for remitting our funds.   The British authorities also went out of their way to help us, though we had not made the usual applications in advance for permission to use the Ladakh and Kashmir routes.   Major and Mrs. Gillan, in Kashgar, not only entertained us for a long stay, but Major Gillan, as Consul-General, helped us to secure excellent transport for the Karakoram route.   The Russian authorities, for their part, granted my wife the permits and courtesies which alone made it possible for her to travel so far from the regular trans-Siberian' route; and that at a time when permits were by no means freely granted.   M. Bystrov, Consul-General in Urumchi, also put himself out to help us.

Above all, I am glad of the opportunity to recall once more our indebtedness to our friend Mr. Pan Tsilu, of the Chinese Civil Service in Hsin-chiang.

CONTENTS

ILLUSTRATIONS

ILLUSTRATIONS

MAPS

HIGH TARTARY

I

CARAVANSERAI

Riding out of the bleak and windy snow-levels that concluded the caravan journey through Mongolia, I slipped from my riding camel and led him by a cord under a towered gateway of Ku Ch'eng-tze, the Ancient City; thus confirming my entry into Chinese Turkestan — or, if you will, Zungaria, its outlying northern territory. Within two hundred yards a man hailed me; it was Lai-ts'ai-ti (his real name I never knew, and this one, which is caravan slang, would hardly do in English print), none other than the camel puller whom I had kneaded and drenched for the colic, when all his comrades thought him ghost-possessed. He was of the House of Chou, from whom I had parted at the Oasis of the Third Stage, when I was held there in pawn to High Policy, and he had come from caravan camp to shop in the streets.

"Ha, Le Ying-ts'ai!" he cried. "You have come, at last! Have you come well on this last road; this —— freezing road? But go straight to the Vinegar Shop of Chang; there you will find Chou the Big-head, and others of Our People. Go well!"

He was the only one to give me friendly greeting at this my first entry. No one looked at my camel, for camels are of Mongolia and Ku Ch'eng-tze lives by the business of Mongolia and the caravans. No one looked at my single companion, for he was a young Chih-li man, dressed like a Mongol, which is quite proper in a border trader. He and I, leaving our caravans in the snow, had ridden ahead to Ku Ch'eng-tze, each to make sure how he stood with officialdom. He was a good man, the Chih-li youngster, who had stood by Moses and me to help us work our triumph on my own evil camel puller, whom we had cast in the snow.

I was the one that drew notice. All stared at me, because of my beard, which marked me for no Chinese, and because I was dressed poorly and dirtily. Here and there a man would shout *"Oross!"* ("Russian") to himself; which is a way the coolie has of proving to himself that his mind has noticed something. Here and there a mocking child would call *"Drass!"*—the Chinese mutilation of a Russian greeting. Undoubtedly this was no longer the caravan life, where no man remarks on the seat of his fellow's trousers before patching his own.

Once at the Vinegar Shop of Chang, however, I was among my own again. "Bring a carton of the most expensive cigarettes, for which the foreign gentleman will pay, and then we will talk." So spake Big-head, or Liu-tze, or Lao-ta, or the Eldest Son of the House of Chou, to a scuttling apprentice, in his most opulent manner. I found the cigarettes to be Ruby Queens, of which there was a scarcity in Ku Ch'eng-tze, at a price of rather more than four silver dollars for a carton of five hundred. Neither the foreign nor the Chinese tobacco companies have their own agents in the extreme West. Thus the cigarettes being all chance-come, ordered by Chinese traders trying to buy at the cheapest and sell at the dearest, or brought on a venture in cases by caravan owners or in cartons by camel pullers, there is a great play of fashion among them. This year the favorites were Ruby Queens and the Thumbs Up brand called on the packet "Number One" and here in the West "Jade Hand."

"And now," said Chou, "we had thought of preparing, against your coming, a room in a trading firm, where you could spread yourself and have your food sent in and be proud. Then we thought that you had lived with us and like us in Mongolia, and perhaps would rather be with us and like us in Ku Ch'eng-tze. Also you will not be here for long, and we should like to have you. A few of us have the private room here, next to the office, and if you care to bunk in — well, there you are."

We made it so. The private room was about twenty feet long and twelve deep, with a door opening into the hall which lay on the long side of it, between it and the office. More than half the space was taken up by the *k'ang,* the sleeping platform, which was heated by flues. The paper windows were hermetic and the air opaque. Here slept six of us; or seven, at times. In the morning we rolled up our bedding against the back wall, and the *k'ang* was free for society. Next to the windowed end lay Moses; beside him I unrolled my *p'u-kai;* then came Chou. Beyond him were two caravan owners, Westerners of the same name and clan, but not related; then the Bastard of Barköl. At the far end lay sometimes, but more often not, a Shan-hsi trader who was devotedly casting all that he had of substance and prospects into the lap of a woman of the town. She used to send him home at seven or eight in the morning, red rimmed of eye and sour of temper, with wine-soiled silken finery, short of one or two more of the false diamond rings which had originally studded every finger. He had the art of cursing while cleaning his teeth, and after doing so would roll up and sleep out the rest of the morning.

To the Bastard of Barköl I have given his generic, not his particular name. He was the most swaggering blade of all, with his lambskins faced with silk, his hat of sable fur, his eighteen-inch imitation-amber cigarette holder studded with glass brilliants, and one of the showiest ambling ponies out of all the famous Bar Köl herds. His young, thin, eager face was tanned but not yet wrinkled; a deep wooden brown in color. He commanded in a soft, low voice a range of foul language which gave pause even to the caravan men, and he was concentrating for a few days the whole of a forceful character on gambling, drink, opium, women, and any other indulgence that came to hand.

Men called him, behind his back, the Bastard, because he came of a strange, new, mixed race, the *Erh Hun-tze,* who hold the mountains that stand over Barköl and Ku Ch'eng-tze. *Erh* is for "the second generation," and *hun* is for "mixture," "confusion." They are the descendants of Chinese, usually Shan-hsi ne'er-do-wells, offscourings of the caravans, who rather than work for a living have gone into the mountains with Mongol wives taken from the Torguts, or women of the Taghliks, the indigenous mountainy folk.

A careless beginning has made a thrifty end. The fusion of Chinese and Mongol blood begot a bilingual race trained up to the nomadic life, but inheriting the Chinese instinct for money and affairs. "There are no bad Erh Hun-tze," say the Chinese; though the name itself is a revilement, or at least contemptuous. It means at the worst a bastard and at the best a half-breed, someone carelessly begotten. On the Coast, it is a pejorative term for Eurasians.

The Erh Hun-tze are bolder and have more personal independence than the average of either parent race. In every *yurt* is a good rifle, — usually an old-style Russian single-shot weapon, — and, while they stand no nonsense from either Mongol or Qazaq raiders, they are not robbers themselves. More than once on the road I heard tales of Erh Hun-tze, who for half a load of tea had ridden off single-handed after armed parties of Qazaqs that had stolen camels or ponies from caravans; and had brought back the animals. Managing their stock like Mongols and selling the produce of them like Chinese, they have become an established, wealthy class. In their yurts they live and dress like Mongols, but when they come to town they get themselves up like Chinese; they bury their dead, like Chinese, instead of exposing the bodies in the Mongol way; take their brides home in carts, like Chinese, and keep the surnames of their Chinese fathers. For the most part they are only half nomadic, having substantial houses in the lowland winter grazing grounds, from which they move with the Mongol part of their gear when they set up their summer yurts in the mountains. One of the most charming things about them is their divided religious inheritance — a thing that goes delightfully with the tolerance and easy manners of the confused races of Central Asia. In their summer pastures they entertain wandering Mongol lamas, who are recognized as the most proper spiritual advisers for herd masters; but in winter quarters they subscribe to the shrines and temples of the settled Chinese. As for the youngster on our k'ang, he was, for all his dissipation, a sound and prosperous man, spending no more than he could afford. He held a part interest in a caravan firm, and made very comfortable money besides in buying broken-down camels, reconditioning them on his own pastures, and selling them back to caravans.

Thus when the dogged Moses followed me to town in a couple of days, bringing my gear, he found me gathered to a whole k'angful of bosoms. The inn, or rather caravanserai, was called the Vinegar Shop of Chang, because the original manager, whose name was Chang, had worked up his business until from selling vinegar to East-bound caravans he became a chandler of other supplies; and at last he and his partners found themselves running a caravan of their own and a caravanserai at which put up the owners and men of other caravans. The daily terms included two full meals, with free *shao-chiu* (distilled grain spirit); camel owners and camel pullers messing in common at four man tables in the huge kitchen, in a snug frowst of steaming men warmed by the roaring ovens. From the smoke-blackened rafters, glistening like dark enamel in the gloom overhead, depended strings of garlic, and the cooks breathed equality, fraternity, and garlic as they rushed from table to table with renewed platters of garlic-laden *chiao-tze* — steamed meat-patties — and saucers of grilled sliced mutton and fried onions, dishes of sauce and vinegar, and stacks of puffy steamed white-flour rolls.

"No spirits for you," they said to that long-suffering plutocrat the Eldest Son of the House of Chou; "we all know you, Big-head; your turn comes when the opium lamp is lit." At which he would grin the slow grin that we all knew well, and push back the round felt cap from his beaded brow, indicating me with a wily elbow to turn the laugh. "I am a laggard at eating and a sluggard at drinking, no good except at the pipe; but here is my friend and the friend of camel pullers; let everyone drink with Our Foreigner, and Our Foreigner drink double."

Chou had a brother in a handsome shop contiguous to our warren of buildings, manager of the chiefest among the Shan-hsi firms in Ku Ch'eng-tze, with branches and correspondents all through the province. He was as different as could be from the torpid, uncouth caravan man; a huge man in stature, small-headed, deep-jowled, monumentally paunched, with a cultivated voice and a suave unction of manner. He in turn introduced his managing director, the most charming Shan-hsi man I have ever met, tall, frank-featured, and handsome. Though his education and philosophy were Chinese in every expression, and he had spent his life (he was little more than thirty) in the interior provinces of Shan-hsi and Chinese Turkestan, he had a friendly understanding of the processes of foreign civilization that seemed less a forced growth than the overseas culture of most "returned students." This was because his interest was the natural activity of a mind in itself interesting. He was well read in translations of foreign history, economy, geography, and—in a general way—philosophy; and he liked nothing better than to astound a provincial company by turning lightly from the history of Chinese relations with the Mongols to the mediæval ideas of geography which made it so difficult for Columbus to find financial backing.

This was a weirder group of Shan-hsi men than I had ever thought would discuss with me the more delicate ways of cooking fish; the men of Shan-hsi not being distinguished for letters or cultivation. Yet on the same board of directors was a walrus-faced old boy who, though he probably thought that the voyages of Columbus and the exploits of Ts'ao-ts'ao belonged in the same region of mirabilia, could write one of the most delicately schooled hands in the province, and had an easy acquaintance among officials in occasional need of a classical quotation.

In China generally the polite morning salutation between acquaintances meeting on the street is "Have you eaten?" In Ku Ch'eng-tze it is "Have you drunk tea?" Between eight and eleven all the world throngs the restaurants, where "tea" covers everything from half a dozen styles in mutton to the formal "dinners" which are always held in the morning, in a private room at the back; but where even the least ostentatious camel man brings his own somewhat superior brand of tea in a twist of paper. In China anywhere it is delicate manners to take your own tea to tea-shop or restaurant; but in Ku Ch'eng-tze there is an extra emphasis on this, because the public brew is always the harsh brick tea of the caravans. Brick tea is all very well on the caravan road, but in Turkestan it is a mark of the "native."

Every morning I would be stirred up in my bedding on the k'ang and hauled forth to tea. Now it would be the Old Man whom, in his destitution, on his lopsided camel, I had befriended for a few weeks in Mongolia, and who had now found in Ku Ch'eng-tze his nephew, his camels, and a shave, wash, and new sheepskins in which I failed at first to recognize him. Then it would be a group of camel pullers come to show they had not forgotten the friendship of the road; or the handsome managing director, in flowered pale blue satin. In the long public rooms of the restaurants — all Shan-hsi cooking — horse copers, caravan owners, camel pullers, rich business men, and clerks hardly out of their apprenticeship dodged back and forth to each other's tables, with riotous challenges to drink. In the big square private rooms in hinder courtyards, groups of eight or ten solid men nibbled melon and sunflower seeds and talked more decorously while waiting for the principal guest to make a formally late appearance; but from the time the first of a dozen courses came on they showed themselves in no way behind the commonalty. They eat and they drink very stoutly in Ku Ch'eng-tze, where every fashionable dish from China, up to and including sharks' fins and sea-slugs, but stopping short of bird's-nest soup, which is rarely to be tasted in these outlands, can be had at amazingly cheap prices, being just delivered in gross from the caravans. In return for all the hospitality I shared, I gave the most splendid feed of all (Moses ordered it) to about fifteen men, at a cost of less than twenty silver dollars, including tips. At their cups these men were more unflagging, and held their drink better, than the men of any city in China that I know. I have never drunk such strong, high-proof shao-chiu as they distill in Ku Ch'eng-tze, with never a headache in it. Then there is *tai-chiu*, distilled I think from some kind of millet, which tastes like a mild, very sweet white wine, drunk warm; and a grape wine from Turfan which is also drunk warm, like a thick, sweetish, heavy brandy, that would be admirable if aged.

In the caravanserai, those not surfeited with "tea" could take plain cooking a little before noon. In the evening they served another meal, which few of the superior guests attended. We went out by turns, or sent out the apprentices who skivvied for us, to fetch in roast pork, hot or cold, which we ate on the k'ang with sour and salt vegetables, off six-inch-high tables, by candlelight. Everything bought in this way was rated common without invitation, as were cigarettes and tobacco; but anything left rolled up in one's bedding was inviolable.

Then we would play *ma-chiang* (spiritually different from the game which foreigners call mah-jong), the Bastard and I and a caravan owner and one or other of the clerks of the caravan-caravanserai-malting-distilling firm. Had I no other reason for remembering Ku Ch'eng-tze with affection, I should do so because it is the only place at which I ever took in money at ma-chiang. That was because all these Western men are slow at the game, lacking "singsong girls" and brothel play to keep them sharp. I won enough to cover all the expenses of my stay. Alas the boast! The night before I left we were one short, and, Moses being called in to play, he lost me at one sitting all my gains and five or six dollars more.

"This gambling is no good," drawled the Eldest Son of the House of Chou from the corner to which he had taken pipe and lamp. "If you stick to opium, at least you know what your expenses are."

After all my months of travel with Chou, in which he had so often urged me to the pipe, I did at last inhale opium in Ku Ch'eng-tze; I having a slight colic and opium being supposedly the best alleviation. I lay comfortably padded and pillowed, while Chou himself at the lamp twirled and roasted the fat lump of *yen-t'u*, sizzling on the metal pin. When it was ready he patted it deftly into place over the pin-hole in the bulb of the pipe, leaving a draught-hole. I held it over the steady flame of the shielded lamp while Chou squatted ready with the pin to keep the draught free. I took the slow, greasy smoke freely into my lungs; it had heavy, sweet, cloying components, but was easily stomached after all the scents and effluvia with which all my breathing channels were by that time imbued. The trick at which I failed was the true smoker's way of keeping up a steady circulation of the smoke; taking it in from the pipe, dispersing a supply through lungs and stomach, and expelling the residue gently through the nostrils, all in a mild, continuous flow. I smoked several biggish nodules, but felt neither beatified nor gratified, nor yet ordinarily drugged

eved of my ache. So I sat up again to the gaming table
y pains passed off of themselves.

 in the luxury of the private room did not lose touch with
amel pullers, the backbone of the good caravan trade. The
vans were all in winter camp, snugged down in the snow out
the town; but the men had leave by turns, and often their
ployers stood them treat for a day or two. They bunked in
nnumbered swarms in little rooms about the courtyard, where
by no more than sticking their heads out of doors they could see
the bales and cordage, the water butts, cases, sacks, tent-poles,
red-tasseled spears, and flung-down felts of the familiar life of
the road; with now and then a moaning cow camel and her bleating calf, born last month and not yet resigned to the gloom that
falls over a camel's life when it has to look after its own feeding.

For the most part the camel pullers were pathetically clumsy in
taking the celebrated joys of Ku Ch'eng-tze. They ate a few
enormous meals and gambled away the rest of the few taels they
had earned in months of hardship. Then they wagged their heads,
testifying that Ku Ch'eng-tze was a wild, wild place, and shuffled
off to whatever snow-buried plain it was that had swallowed their
tents and their thin camels until the spring. A few of them bar-
tered cannily for lambskins and fox pelts the bits of goods they
had brought with them from the East, and a few earned the mur-
murous admiration of their fellows for their performances among
the women.

Throughout this province the brothels, which add so mu
to the adventurous restlessness of night life in most Chinese citi
are positively discouraged by officialdom; but no amount of s
pression could prevent the existence of a few houses of resor
such a city as this, at the end of such a caravan route. In
Ch'eng-tze, however, prices are so high and results so meagr
most men are content with the more easy society and less
bitant demands of Turki or Mongol women, whose idea
bosom of the family is very cordial. Yet Chinese womer
scarce that, in the natural tendency to make them go ro
rigid Chinese standard of decorum for married womer
among the lower and even middle classes. Many a cara

talks knowingly of the matron he has *hung-lo -*
was in town and her husband was not. Some.
nese gives himself over to a really thoroughgoing
not halt this side of tragedy. Out in the desert I ha
van which was taking home a cousin of the House of
had come a cropper over a woman. He had sold his mo
hundred camels, run through the money, and was at the
of his friends for a passage home. Again, at a God-forg
military post I was told of a broken opium sot who had once be
wealthy and was now servant to soldiers for the scrapings of thei1
pipes. He had not only sold his camels, but mortgaged land
and property in Kuei-hua for a light love in Ku Ch'eng-tze. For
some technical reason the creditors could not foreclose unless
he returned to Kuei-hua, so that his wife continued to live there
comfortably and bring up his children respectably, while he
wore out the butt end of his life on the desert fringe of the Golden
West.

But, as I have said, most of the camel pullers were shy of town
women. After talking for the whole journey of the streets, restaurants, women, and shops of Ku Ch'eng-tze, they ducked un-
easily through the bustle for two or three days. Then they sighed
and went back to the wind of the open and the smoke of the tents.
As for wenching, " So-and-so," they said, " and Such-an-one, who
talk so much of their exploits, they don't really have more fun than
we do, who can spend the whole night in a Mongol yurt for one
paper *tael,* which is forty cents of silver money. With the
Mongols — dogs defile them — when the light is out no one minds
anyone."

When free of hospitality I went out a great deal in the streets,
which were full of life and swagger. The central part of the
Ancient City is a street of the bigger Chinese businesses, and on
it also front the guilds of the different Shan-hsi traders — Tai
Chou, Kuei-hua, and so on — who are lords of the town. These
guilds keep up a rivalry of ornate tiling, fretted brickwork, temples, and pagodas; and the general Shan-hsi Guild is the pride of
them all. The great city temple is the Lao-yeh Miao, tended by
Taoist priests; and there are also the mosques of the Turki immi-

grants from Turkestan proper, — mostly from Hami (Qomul) and Turfan, — who live chiefly in one suburb. In front of the Lao-yeh Miao is a common gambling ground, one of the sights of Ku Ch'eng-tze, frequented by all kinds of tricksters; and this is the camel pullers' exchange, the centre for which they all make.

The core of the town is the caravan trade, but the fringes of it deal in the border trade among the nomads, both Qazaq and Mongol. A great many Qazaqs, of the Eastern Kirei tribe, winter in the dune belt near Ku Ch'eng-tze, and they and the Mongols ride in to loiter, stare, barter skins and pelts, or the meat and hide of wild asses; and, in the invariable upshot, to get drunk. The Qazaq knee-boot has a high wooden heel which makes awkward walking, so that they almost never dismount from their ponies, camels, or riding oxen; they will ride half into the open street-front of a shop, lean from their saddles clear across the counter, and so bargain.

The headgear of the Torgut Mongols hereabouts is a close-fitting cap of felt, trimmed with gold braid; it has rounded ear-panels, very snug, and a ridge of squirrel fur, or the tail of a squirrel, sewn to the top for a crest. The Qazaqs go them one better; their winter bonnets look to be modeled on an ancient style of helmet, of a somewhat Saracenic shape, the kind that went with chain mail. These bonnets or soft helmets rise in a point at the top and descend past the ears and well down on the back of the neck in flaps or skirts, like a camail. The inside is white lambskin, with black lambskin showing at the edges, and the outside is gay flowered chintz, quilted on to the skins. From the peak flutters a tuft of the breast feathers of the eagle owl. This, it appears, must anciently have been the badge of the full warrior, because it continues, as I was told, a mark of the youth who has shown himself a man. Tiny children wear it, but a youth may not until he has proved himself a horse thief. Most of them do, which bears out their universal Chinese name of *tsei Ha-sa,* the thieving Qazaqs.

Things like this, however, — streets and houses, temples, markets, and mingling peoples, — I was not yet really competent to observe. I had still to be shaken out of the long dream of caravan days; mind and speech continued to run by the caravan habit, though Moses had already begun persuasively to school me for new attitudes and a new deportment. After another journey and the feel of another city, I could look back to Ku Ch'eng-tze and see it better.

II

THE SNOW ROAD TO URUMCHI

On leaving Ku Ch'eng-tze I left also the Shan-hsi men with whom I had been so long that I had now even to guard my speech from taking the turn of theirs. The big Shan-hsi firms, rooted in the caravan trade at Ku Ch'eng-tze, have branches or agents in many of the large towns farther on in the province; but from now on, with other connections in Urumchi, my way fell among the Chih-li men.

So far as the men of the caravans are concerned, their wandering life makes them easy to pass among — if you have the right approach — and easy to part from. I found one fine fellow among them, in my friend of the House of Chou, and I liked his brother the merchant in Ku Ch'eng-tze and the charming managing director of the firm, who came not from Kuei-hua but from Shan-hsi proper. Of the common run of Shan-hsi men it is hard to say much good. They are mean and cunning, and though by relentlessly skinning fleas for the hide and tallow they often become wealthy, they remain to the end ignorant and narrow. Only the easy money of Ku Ch'eng-tze makes them free-spending and careless. It is well known that they are the pawnbrokers of all North China; and at one time they monopolized banking (they are still cash-shop dealers) and were the proprietors of the letter-courier firms that the Chinese Post Office has in our time disestablished. For these reasons they have been involved in comparison with the Jews, which is a little hard on them perhaps — but then it must be said on the other side that they have not the flair for art and opulence which gilds the Jews.

A great crowd of them came down to the posthouse to see me off when, my Ku Ch'eng-tze affairs all happily disposed and my transport to Urumchi bespoken, I turned away from the caravan life and the caravan city, it being then the second week in January 1927. Unhappily, my friends had an arrogance in their way of chaffing the driver of the cart which put him in a savage humor. He denied all knowledge of Chinese, and said in Turki, through a young linguist of the Vinegar Shop of Chang, that his job was to deliver me at the next posthouse, not to be nice about it. My heart sank. Was I, after getting rid of the worst camel puller in Mongolia, to be left in this cold of Central Asia with an intractable carter?

It was bad enough to be taking leave of the Eldest Son of the House of Chou. He alone did not make any noise about his farewell, but there was an inexpressible gloom on his piglike face. "Of all foreigners," he said handsomely, "you are the best; but I am afraid your talk is only the 'good talk' of all who travel. When you have gone beyond us you will forget us, and I shall never see you again."

I shall take great pleasure in disappointing him, and one of these days I shall come round by the other side of the world and call at his home in Kuei-hua with a present of photographs and an extra special gift of sweets — tinned fruit of a syrupy kind, it may be — such as are a boon to the opium smoker's lacquered palate.

Moses had gone forward that same day with most of our stuff, in a heavy, two-wheeled cart. I was expecting to reach Urumchi at least a day before him, traveling by the fast cart service that carries mails under contract with the Chinese Post Office. These carts, an imitation of the Russian *telega,* are four-wheeled, have no springs, and are drawn by three ponies abreast, at a jogging trot, one in shafts and the other two running in traces. The narrow cart is open at the front, but has an awning of mats and is closed with a curtain of sacking at the back. Travelers may use the service, either as many as can crowd in, or one who has contracted for the whole cart for himself and his luggage. The journey of a hundred and fifty miles is by stages of about thirty miles, with no halt except for changing cart, ponies, and driver at each posthouse.

My most unpleasant prospect was the changing of my luggage, of which I had a couple of boxes and a couple of sacks, at every stage. Now carters, along with muleteers, caravan men, boatmen, — all those who handle transport, throughout China and its fringes, — have a repute of villainy. On this road, as on most others, the carter's business was only to drive from stage to stage. He had no concern with my comfort or the disposal of my effects.

Hope of relief came as we set off and the bells on the three ponies jangled cheerfully down the long main street of Ku Ch'engtze. The Turki driver turned and said to me cheerfully, in adequate Chinese, " These men of Shan-hsi — defile their mothers! — have no good talk. One opening of their mouths, and it makes my belly swell " — using in Chinese the Turki idiom for a damaged temper. " Oross are different. We two shall be all right; your trouble will come further on." I told him I was not an Oross, but an Amerikanski, — thinking that in a Russianized version I might come nearer his mark, — but it was a clean miss. " Well then, an Inglis," I ventured. At this he glowed with joy, going by an estimate which I afterward found common among the races — except the more sophisticated Chinese — of this part of Central Asia, that the Oross are brute-mad and child-foolish, while the Inglis are devil-mad, and as for their foolishness, who knows? — it is of a piece with their madness.

Thus my driver quite dropped his pretended ignorance of Chinese, and began to show himself half a friend and half a retainer. I in turn played this good lead, and found that he suffered from an itching eruption on the skin. More and better! I promised him a salve, of the most foreign and wonderful (mercury ointment), buried deep in a certain box; and while arranging to forward it to him from Urumchi through a relay of his fellows, we discussed freely all the drivers on the road. He told me that these were a hard crew, the offscourings of the province. Good men drove their own carts; the men in the post service were either those who had destroyed their own business out of recklessness and folly, or those who had touched worse things and were taking a spell off in the shelter of a quasi-official employ — an inversion of procedure indicating that the old Asia was, in this province, in full working order; and, in its way, quite cheering. These fellows, my man warned me, would do nothing for my help; no, not for money thrown before them. They took a pride in being undomesticated. He himself would help me shift my load at the first change. The man I should go on with was a T'ung-kan, and a surly devil. "After that," he said, "there is another T'ung-kan, and a couple of Tientsin men, and the Tientsin men are the worst of all. Yes, you are going to have a bad time." "

Only on this first stage did I suffer acutely from the cold; for the next few days I was just lethargically miserable. In spite of Russian felt boots, of the kind called *valinki* or *katinki,* and of breeches lined with raccoon-skin, and vest and greatcoat of sheepskin, the cold got at me. The covering of the cart was no protection at all, nor was there any way of keeping up a circulation of the chill blood, seemingly oppressed by the weight of bundled clothes. I have no idea what the temperature was; but on these open stretches, where the mountains merge to the desert, forty degrees (Fahrenheit) below zero about midnight of a still January night is no temperature at all. I lost all feeling in my feet and when this anæsthesia had got up to my knees I spoke to the driver. He yelled, and laid into his ponies with the whip. In twenty minutes we dipped into the bed of a small stream and found the hut of a T'ung-kan farmer. My man, storming at the door, woke the unwilling people; we found them strewn all over the k'ang, and a tiny fire of glowing red coals on a sort of mud pedestal projecting from the sleeping platform.

" Frozen, but not spoilt," said the interested people, crowding over my shoulder as I drew off the felt boots; they meant there was no frostbite. They made tea, as I thawed out slowly, at a cautious distance from the fire. The glow of the coals and the flicker of a twist of cotton in a bowl of oil threw a fluttering light up to black rafters and down to sleepy, peering faces. We thanked them and went on. As we started up, the frozen lather of sweat on the ponies tinkled, breaking.

When we finished the stage and had to shift my things to the next cart, I saw what I was in for. The knots in the heavy lash-

MOSES

THE AUTHOR IN WINTER COSTUME

ings that held all in place, to keep the boxes from knocking the crude wooden cart to bits, had all frozen. Nothing could be done with gloved hands, and to work bare-handed in a cold so cruel that any metal seared the flesh like a branding iron meant fifteen or twenty minutes of torture. Sure enough, the T'ung-kan, my next driver, would do nothing at all. He handed me over at the third stage to another T'ung-kan, who was equally surly. It was impossible to brace and lash my boxes unaided. I went into the room where the carters waited their turn of driving. It was lit only by the glow of the usual small fire on the usual base of mud at the front of the sleeping platform, as on an altar. Vague bundles of men lay beyond, one or two of them turning a little in their sleep. When I came in I heard a Tientsin voice that said, in effect, "Another damned Oross! Wonder what in hell *he* wants?" Then, as I began speaking: "Why, it can talk!" Chinese, of the ignorant classes, are apt to regard foreign languages, not as human speech, but as collections of animal noises. Only men who can speak Chinese deserve consideration as human men.

I spoke directly toward the corner from which the voice came. "Yes," I said, "I can talk; and what is more, I have come a long way, from Tientsin, and my talk is Tientsin talk. You are a Tientsin man, for I have heard your talk. Now, I am being *ch'i-fu* — harassed — by these people of these parts," — and I threw in a word about their younger sisters, for all to hear, to show that I had the Tientsin swearing, — " and if the good fame of all Tientsin men is not to be eternally ruptured, you 've got to lend a hand."

"Why, of course," he said, sitting up; "what's to do?" He shuffled on his sheepskins and came out into the cold. When the job was over and we came back for a moment to the fire before I started, he refused money. "We Tientsin men are not like this Western scum and these Mohammedan sons of thieves," he said in front of all the sullen Kan-su men, T'ung-kan, and locally bred riffraff. "They are animals, not men. *We* stand by our fellows. If this driver gives you any trouble, both beat him and swear at him. There will be Tientsin men at the next posthouse to help you. A man with your Tientsin speech has nothing to fear in this province."

I am not really sure what manner of country lies between Ku
Ch'eng-tze and Urumchi. The summary of it is that I was traveling along the northern foot of the Bogdo Ola, a part of the
easterly extension of the great T'ien Shan system. Ku Ch'eng-tze
had set a period to the caravan journey; this now was the road,
not only of trade, but of administration. The carts that jogged
along it, the rime-laden telegraph line that drooped beside it, the
startling fact that I was now traveling with the mails, in a province where the passing up and down of mails brought no astonishment, all proclaimed an emergence from the desert and an approach
to a capital of some sort. These thoughts I set straight and
squared with each other at a later time, when I had the books of
others and my own papers before me. For the time of my passage, I did not know how many miles, how many stages, how many
days, how many nights, I traveled. We went day and night,
through snow fresh-fallen on top of the old, trodden snow; it became too heavy for the ponies to trot, and we, in spite of the prestige of the post, did not come to Urumchi until between eighteen
and twenty-four hours after the official mail-time. At each halt
I had barely time to unload and load again; nor was I ever warm
but once. Huddled in my sheepskins, I watched the starlight
glimmering or the sunlight glittering on long desert levels buried
a yard deep under snow; unless of a sudden the desert broke for
a little and we passed down sunken lanes hedged with frosted
white willows.

The alchemy of speech wrought wondrously with the Tientsin
rascals against whom the friendly Turki had warned me as the
worst of all, and I had no more troubles. The cart wheeled
jangling in the night into the court of the last stage before Urumchi; whereas we should have left this place before noon in order
to reach the city before the gates closed. The post inn was kept
by T'ung-kan, who would neither prepare food for travelers nor
lend their own cooking pots, for fear they might be defiled by in-
fidels. Travelers, they said sourly, could get food at the cookshop
over the way, when it was daylight and the cookshop open. All
the world knew that inns were of two kinds: inns of rooms and
inns of eating. This was an inn of rooms, as we might see.

A mail-carrier on this road, and not to know yet that in this inn food was not sold? Ha! These Tientsin men, how vexatious, to force themselves thus importunately on honest people!

That was the T'ung-kan of it; and I had not eaten since leaving Ku Ch'eng-tze, fifty-odd hours before — all the food I had brought with me having been stonily frozen, and there being never time at the halts for more than a gulp of tea. Therefore I took counsel with the Tientsin man who brought me, and another of the same who had been roused out to take me on. We could not enter Urumchi until full daylight, when the gates were unbarred. Let us then take our leisure. I had cold pork and bread and good strong waters that had been given me in Ku Ch'eng-tze; let us find a room clear of Moslems, thaw out my provisions, eat a full Tientsin meal, in despite of all the Sons of Pigs, and sleep for a little like gentlemen, before starting in time to reach the city by dawn.

Nothing could have pleased them better. We found fuel in plenty, in an outhouse, and a room in which there was no one but a broken-down Kan-su opium smoker, and made merry through the midnight. The aluminum bottle in which I carried my shao-chiu was far too cold to put to one's lips without blistering them, and we had no cups, nor would the inn-folk lend us any; but gradually we warmed it up, and the bread and pork too, and ate and drank like princes of the road, while the poor opium smoker shivered and muttered because he had reached his last pipeful and could get no more till morning and had no money to buy it then. Full-gorged at last, I rolled up in my coat, with my legs stretched out as far as I could stretch them, — which, after being curled up in a cart for a couple of days and nights, was Heaven attained, — and sank into several hours of connected sleep.

The cold did not seem so deadly when we started again; one could bear it, as one bears a little misery to which there is a known period. In the unreal sameness of a land blanketed with snow we missed a bridge and trundled into a ditch; but with lashing at the ponies and heaving at the wheels we got out only the warmer. It delayed us, and it was not till the sun had risen that we came in sight of the wireless masts, three in a row on a small hill over

Urumchi. The tired ponies were beaten into a dragging trot for the last mile. We came in past a strange round tower, a memorable landmark. It is called *I p'ao ch'eng kung* — "One shot turns the trick." The story goes that in the final putting down of the Mohammedan rebellion which had driven the Chinese from Turkestan for many years, when at last the Chinese army of reconquest reached the capital they built this tower and mounted a gun. At the first discharge, the gates were thrown open and the bloody insurrection was closed. Others have it that when the Mohammedans first made a head in their rebellion they fired the unique shot, and the Chinese in Urumchi surrendered. Who knows? The Chinese rule there now, and they can have the story as they like.

There was a little delay at the jealously guarded gates, and then we drove in. The driver helped me to move everything to the best Tientsin inn, and soon cheery Tientsin apprentices were bringing tea and lighting a fire, and Tientsin merchants of serious port and prosperous attire were making me welcome with volleys of questions — which is the way of Tientsin men.

III

THE CAPITAL OF HIGH TARTARY

THE first thing I did in Urumchi — there being no question of changing my clothes, for I had none with me to change — was to waddle off to the Post Office, all bundled in sheepskins and felt boots as I was. Thus I fell into the grandeurs of a Central Asian capital all of a splash, for the place was replete with no less than two Postal Commissioners, of the Chinese Government service. One was an Italian, shortly going on leave, the other an Irishman, recently arrived to take over the postal administration of the province. They took me up to the Commissioner's House, a strange achievement in brick, built to plans drawn up in some far-away office. It stood on high ground, overlooking all the town within the wall. There Mrs. McLorn, the wife of the new Commissioner, presided with charming tolerance, and admitted me to her carpets and deep chairs; there I took in a whiskey-soda, made a start on the impressive mail which had been piling up for me at the Post Office, and ended with an inenarrable meal — Chianti, salami, meats and vegetables all in different dishes, and such wonders as accompany knives, forks, linen, and glassware.

It must have been nearly ten o'clock that night before they sent me back to my inn — a servant going before me with a lantern, because that is the rule, after the city gates have been closed, and both of us provided with sticks, to fend off the packs of curs which patrol the empty streets. When I got back, I found how strictly Urumchi was ruled. A message had already been sent to those in authority, telling of my arrival, and saying that I would call in the morning to show my papers and my person; but the chief of police in the precinct where my inn lay had become alarmed, and demanded instant knowledge of who I might be.

So I started off again, with the manager of the inn, to quiet him. He was most concerned to know what arms I carried, but showed himself friendly and jolly. The inn manager explained afterwards that it was not enough for me to declare myself; the chief of the precinct must also be prepared to send in a report of me, in good time, or fall under suspicion of insufficient zeal.

The next day I moved from the friendly Tientsin inn and its mess meals of travelers, traders, and staff, which would have been great fun had I only been able to disregard the social pressures of this weltering little capital city, and settled into equally hospitable quarters at the China Inland Mission. There I was the fortunate guest of two men who have been the hosts or friendly counselors during a generation of all the chief travelers in Western Mongolia, Chinese Turkestan, and Tibet, from Rockhill to Huntington and Carruthers — Mr. Hunter, stationed for more than thirty years in Urumchi, and a traveler throughout the province, and Mr. Ridley, who for almost as many years had been at Hsi-ning and Lan Chou, before moving still further to the west, to this ultimate station. In this quiet haven I could read, write, and as it were review and reform my forces.

The first thing to do was to get into touch with my wife, from whom I had letters, addressed to Urumchi while I was yet in Mongolia, but who had no idea where I might be. We had hoped, when I started on the caravan journey from Kuei-hua to Ku Ch'eng-tze, that I should be able to report my arrival at Urumchi within three months at the most. It was now four and a half months after my start, and though she had received two letters which I had sent back from Mongolia by friendly caravans, her last word of me was that I was camping and tramping in a desert, with more deserts ahead.

The hinge on which turned all the plans we had made to meet in Central Asia was the wireless at Urumchi. On receiving word that I had reached Urumchi, that I had been favorably accepted, and that the prospects of further travel in the province were good, my wife was to start from Peking, take the Trans-Siberian Railway from the border of Manchuria to Novo-Sibirsk (which under the Tsars had been Novo-Nikolaievsk), then a branch railway south to Semipalatinsk, and the Russian motor service from Semipalatinsk to Chuguchak, on the western border of Hsinchiang, the New Dominion, the united provinces of Chinese Turkestan and Zungaria.

All the really fashionable things in China of our generation are electric, and Urumchi is gloriously crowned with a wireless plant, not to mention being girdled with an electric light system; both of them tending to be intermittent, but both undeniably electric. The powerful wireless at Urumchi and a sister station at Kashgar had been furnished to the Chinese government a few years before by the Marconi company, and set up by Major Stephen Dockray; not without negotiation, because at Urumchi the old Governor, a man of powerful mind, but slow to give up the good things of the solid past, had first to be convinced that he was not boring for oil, and then that the transmission of messages through empty air was a reputable marvel and not an absurdity covering some sinister design. Later, at Kashgar, on the reasonable speculation that human voices must be necessary for the working of this magic, a yarn was put about that children were being slain and buried under the wireless masts. Dockray, who came from my old school of St. Bees, was in my time acting as the Marconi company's representative at Peking, and sped my own enterprise with a wild Irishman's accounts of the doings of Central Asia.

The wireless had been designed in the first place as a chain; the station at Kashgar to be in touch with Rawalpindi, in India, and with Urumchi, while Urumchi was to communicate with Urga, in Mongolia, where Dockray, the worker of wonders, had succeeded in installing another station. At present, because the Mongols have broken away from China and will have no more to do with their old rulers, the station at Urga is heedless and uncommunicative. Thus Urumchi is forced to transmit all the way to Mukden, in Manchuria. The resulting overload on the plant, together with a chronic lack of spare parts, makes it difficult almost always to send, and sometimes to receive.

These are not the only troubles of the wireless. The Governor, having succeeded ever since the Revolution in keeping the province under his undisputed control and in keeping it free from the civil wars of China proper, is none the less fearful that someone some day may get at him. He therefore censors personally every message that comes or goes, and keeps the whole staff under the strictest control. The director of the station at Urumchi, an attractive youth from Shanghai, trained in Peking and technically competent to do everything that could be done for his plant, had been sent up to take charge of the station at Kashgar as well as that at Urumchi. On his first arrival he had been detained under scrutiny for months, until the Governor was assured of his being free of political affiliations. He had never been allowed to go to Kashgar, for fear he might arrange some kind of illicit code with his colleagues there; and because all other communication between the stations was discouraged on principle and hampered by a grudging censorship, technical coördination was usually at a loss.

While I was at Urumchi sweating on the top line to get a message through Mukden to my wife at Peking, the Governor had first to be satisfied that I was neither the agent of a foreign government nor an adventurer in the pay of a Chinese general who might be plotting to invade his province, and so censored my innocent messages. Then a transmission belt of the plant snapped, had to be repaired with roughly cured local cowhide, and thereafter gingerly run. Then the message had to go to Mukden, the headquarters of Chang Tso-lin, rife with things political, and there pass another censorship, entailing an indefinite second delay. Finally, the Governor's private messages took precedence of all others. The Governor had a son in Peking, who about that time was sick of an influenza, or some such thing; and he had also by him in Urumchi a brother, a soothsayer in the old tradition, in whose counsels he put the strictest faith. With an old soothsayer and a new wireless in conjunction, there was no end of the Governor's activity. He kept the soothsayer busy at the stars and the forces of nature, and made the wireless hum, until the weak belting gave again and again, with interminable prescriptions and advice for his son. What with all these impediments, it was not so very surprising that I was in Urumchi a month before

I could get a wireless message to my wife and receive a reply that she was going to start through Siberia to join me.

In the meantime, I began to learn my Urumchi; and the first lesson was sudden. When, as I was chatting with the Most Important Servant of the Most Important Foreigner, I offered him a cigarette, all friendly like, using the manners of the road, he coolly refused it; thus putting me in my place as a "master." It began to be borne in on me that something different must be apprehended in the atmosphere and circumstances of Urumchi. Here was neither China nor Mongolia, but Central Asia, with a little cosmopolis of Central Asia governed by the most involved social standards of which I had ever run foul. Alas and alas, that the good caravan life should be over and done with! I don't suppose I shall ever again think and dream in a language not my own, as I did during those full months: not the Chinese of phrase-book and cultivated teacher, but the inimitable vernacular of the merry, vagabond, rascally classes. Now and then, with a carter or a pedlar, one can slip back again into the old run of talk; but the spell never holds for long. Suddenly the man notices your wrong clothes, or you trip over a wrong phrase, or a third person addresses you in the wrong way; and you come to, as the fellow changes the very words in his mouth. There is no remedy.

In Central Asia, almost all conversation between Chinese and European is carried on through Russian-speaking Chinese or Russian-speaking Asiatic subjects of Russia, the Russians themselves being bunglers at languages. In Urumchi they have not the phenomenon of the "China born," who have learned the language from "amah," "boy," and "coolie." More than that, any foreigner other than a Russian is a *lusus naturæ*, to be handled delicately by half a dozen interpreters. If the Russians know any language but their own, it is a Turki or Tatar dialect. Even the Chinese hardly hold one real until one has re-sorted one's too glib patter into the more opulently formal phrases of *kuan-hua*. There is an added psychological perplexity. There is a hybrid standard of manners for the entertainment of foreigners and stray travelers; a lower plane, to which the Chinese condescend. The possession of the right Chinese demands the abandonment of this plane; a difficult matter in mixed company, though easy enough when one is alone. I found myself forever shuttling back and forth between the two planes, with one ear taking in the " patter " and one cocked for the words that pass between men who more truly understand each other; while the answers had also to be shuffled and properly dealt out. It was acrobatic, but a wonderful game.

Then cropped up the difficulty of clothes. " Central Asia," I had thought in my innocence, " will be grand. I shall wear all kinds of play-acting clothes, and no one will know the difference." Did n't they! I could not wear the yellow elkhide Mongol-style boots I had bought with rapture in Ku Ch'eng-tze, because I might have been taken for a Russian fallen from the pride of Imperial days. Then, all through Mongolia I had girt myself with a sash of purple cotton, thinking it good enough for the desert, and saved my sash of scarlet silk for Urumchi, where it ought to have been appreciated, but was not. Were I to have worn a red sash, I should have looked too much in sympathy with the Soviets. Although there is a Soviet Consul-General in Urumchi, with a delightful staff, — indeed, quite the most civilized group in the city, with the exception of the Chinese, — it would have been scandalously unofficial for anyone else to have sported the most remotely Bolshevik touch in dress or manners.

It is a sad thing. Central Asia may be a little bit woolly about the edges, but it is not wild. Nor, so far as I can see, has it been wild within the last thirty years, or maybe fifty, except for a few irregular episodes, like the irruption of the White armies ejected from Russia, and their subsequent collapse. When I became a vagabond, I lost a last illusion, of the Adventurousness of Travel — the Great Traveler's Bluff. I weep for this loss, but, to put the matter severely on its right footing, mountains are only mountains, whether you find people living in them or not, and a desert is only a place where you have to be reasonably prudent about your water supply. A horse or a camel, if only you make an effort of the imagination of which nobody in this generation seems to be capable except Mr. Chesterton, is really a more natural object than a motor car. The trouble is that we have come to treat scenery and weather with a difference and a deference, if they occur beyond a minimum distance from the railway. We have taught people to demand a separate scale in writings which deal with, say, Tibet or Mongolia. When the road ascends above a certain height over sea-level, or the thermometer drops below a certain mark under freezing, the scale of your writing must adjust itself conformably. To cover up the scandal of not sleeping soft and eating delicately the traveler must insidiously call the life of caravan and cart inn " wild " and adventurous. I wonder how nine travelers out of ten who have proclaimed their prowess, supported only by assiduous retainers and alleviated only by supplies from home, would stand six months of the life, diet, and exercise of an English farm laborer.

I will only touch on the restaurants and bathhouses of Urumchi, because as a foreigner it was not credible in me to admit with conviction that I thought them good. The restaurants in truth are not so good as those of Ku Ch'eng-tze, but the baths are far better. It was there that I got rid at last of that quasi-intangible and hauntingly elusive feeling on my skin best described in Rupert Brooke's line about the

Feet that ran, but where he cannot tell.

In Ku Ch'eng-tze you can have a bath only in a common pool, where everybody brings his own soap, if he has any, and the dirt is averaged out so that you may go away not so clean as you came in. I had shied off from the baths of Ku Ch'eng-tze, after sending Moses in as a test case. In Urumchi I washed my body for the first time in five months. You can get there a private bath in an earthenware tub, in a cubicle. You have a drying-room where they serve you sweets, tea, and cigarettes, before and after, on a bench covered with snowy clean towels. An intelligent barber comes in who understands that you want your hair cut neither like a Chinese nor like a Russian, and though he has never trimmed a beard can see what you want done, and do it. The whole show is dispatched with Tientsin cleanliness, and costs less than a Tientsin dollar, including tips to three attendants who have been keeping your bath at the right temperature and changing steam-wilted cigarettes for dry.

Clean, police-registered, and recognizably dressed as a 'foreigner in good standing, I went forth to call at several *yamen*, putting first the office of the Commissioner of Foreign Affairs; at the Postal Commissioner's, — the unique social centre of an unique society, — at the so-called Bank, and at the Russian Consulate General. I had also a semiofficial audience of His Excellency the Governor, who talked with apparent freedom and with what seemed to me to be excellent observation and straightforward intelligence; though he may not have believed everything he said.

Gradually I emerged from the atmosphere of sheepskins, felts, and squatting conversations across a fire of camel dung or tamarisk, becoming less the boon companion of camel pullers and more the enterprising young trader on furlough; at the same time keying myself to the Chinese I found about me, as I lost touch with those who had been my familiars. In all the time I spent in Chinese Turkestan, foreign society hardly lost its weirdness, afflicted in my eyes with a borrowed unreality. Foreigners in Asia, and travelers too, are apt to consider it an affliction to have to eat the food of the country, which, whatever the country, is usually excellent on the spot. In Urumchi, the difficulty of getting anything either from Russia or the coast of China puts a pathetic value on tinned delicacies and three-star brandy. The Russians especially manage to do themselves well, though with a queer Russian attitude of self-depreciation, on wonderful fresh butter and milk, first-class homemade jams, pickles and sausages, and palatable homemade wines and spirits.

After all, it is the Chinese who retain the most rational standard of civilization, believing it to rest more on immemorial usages like education and the conduct of a family than on mechanical gadgets, or even clothes and food. Fortunes, it is true, are made by traders who bring up from the coast all the novelties that have their brief, intense fashions: straw hats in Homburg shapes, imitation-amber cigarette holders, hollow steel canes, luminous wrist-watches, and the Lord knows what not. One day, however, the truth was revealed to me. A Chinese caught up my electric torch. "What's that?" he asked. "Oh, only a lightning lamp! We all had those last year." To him it was not an essential, or even an imperatively useful article, but something fashionable, to be used until too definitely dropped on a brick floor, or until the battery gave out. Civilization would not topple if he went about the streets with a paper lantern borne before him, red bats flitting across one side of it for a good auspice, and red characters descending the other.

Once, at the Russian Consulate General, I saw a full muster of the forces of Western civilization, with something in it of spontaneous gayety, something of a wistful memory of life in Europe, and something of a shuffling parade of the asserted superior elegancies of the West. It was a " Club Night," or social gathering of all the registered Russian citizens, — thus excluding the pitiful remnant of irreconcilable anti-Revolutionaries, — with their guests. First we had good singing, good playing, a one-act play by Chekhov, and some comic singing in the kind that the Russians do better than anybody else, with dash, drollery, and a basic tone of invincible pessimism; supported and carried by a scratch company of musicians as adroit and inspired as themselves. There was also a tavern piece, presented with a superbly light touch, in which the " guest " mournfully played merry tunes by tapping a row of bottles with a knife, and the tavern staff accompanied him with brooms, chairs, forks, and plates. It only needed a suicide to complete the Russian scene.

Later, when supper had been served, the main room was cleared for dancing, while Russians, Russian Asiatics, and Russian-speaking Chinese still thronged the buffet-room. Benches were laid along the walls, where sat incredible dowagers and men who looked like Cruikshank drawings. Between dances the nubile girls walked up and down the floor in arm-linked groups, dressed in all kinds of long shots and wild guesses at what Russians call "the mode," believing it to be something quite apart from taste; with hair dragooned into tight curls over the ears and forehead and finished apathetically at the back in a skimpy knot. The two couples who could fox-trot — the orchestra knew one jazz tune — were passionately observed as they hopped the cracks in the flooring, but the free-for-all dancing was Russian waltzes, of a kind that I could not catch on to at all, and disgraced myself by trying. They thought I was drunk, because I crept so slowly; and I wished I were, because it seemed a kind of dancing done more easily when dizzy. The ladies — I am sure that, though Soviet citizenesses, they would consider it less than the mode to be called women, or even girls — hastily ranged themselves on benches every time the music began, whence the dominant males made their choice with wooden-jointed bows. Then they whirled up and down the floor, their breath hissing, sweating gallantly to revolve as fast, smoothly, and continuously as possible until, the lady beginning to wilt (for in Urumchi they abide by the mode of the weaker sex), she was deposited on a bench again and her partner, not lingering for anything so suggestive as conversation, withdrew to lean and pant against a wall.

Behind the benches and in every corner stood or sat the massed Russian Asiatics, Turki and Tatar and every mixed Turki-Tatar breed that lives in tent or house from Russian Turkestan all the way through the provinces of Semirechensk (the Seven Rivers) and Semipalatinsk (the Seven Tents). With beards cut in curious angles and shaved in sudden patches, lustrous eyes, suave lips, and velvet skullcaps embroidered in green and red and yellow, they watched all night in expressionless politeness. They might adhere in these mad latter years to the Soviets, and they had very kindly been invited to the show in parade of equality, but they left their own women at home and regarded those on view as if they were slaves exposed for sale in a market, and they did n't feel tempted to buy. I looked at those mobile lips, now composed in such serenity, and wondered what thoughts, if any, were going on behind those bland, dark eyes. For generations the importunate Oross heathen have harried them, now with troops and now with proclamations and now with incomprehensible licenses and liberties. No matter. Rulers must be soothed and cajoled, the while a man gets on as best he can with his business. At some hour on the edge of dawn, when they were released from this freedom, they would go back to the expansive comforts of home, with felts on the floor and women who only came in when bid. There they would meditate on the morrow's deal in lambskins with Ali Khan — that thief! but the skins were tempting — and perhaps on the possibility of one day amassing enough money to be able to go to Mecca on pilgrimage, if incomprehensible passports of the right power could be wheedled and bought out of all the endless, uncomprehending officials.

IV

THE ROAD NORTH OF THE HEAVENLY MOUNTAINS

THE province of Hsin-chiang, the New Dominion, commonly known as Chinese Turkestan, is more particularly divided by geographers into Zungaria and Chinese Turkestan. This corresponds generally with the Chinese division into T'ien Shan Pei Lu and T'ien Shan Nan Lu — the Road North and the Road South of the Heavenly Mountains. Urumchi,[1] or Ti-hua, the capital, is at the easiest point of traverse between these road divisions.

In ages of which our record is incomplete a great trade route led overland from China to Constantinople; one of the master-roads of history. The part of this road of which the Chinese had direct knowledge, and which they strove through centuries to control, emerged from modern Kan-su province by the Jade Gate, the westernmost portal of true China, near which were the Caves of the Thousand Buddhas at Tun-huang (a name which means the Flaring Beacon) which marked the verge of Central Asia. Then, through an appalling desert, it passed to the south of Lop Nor and so to Khotan, Yarkand, and Kashgar, whence there was a direct approach to the regions that are now Russian Central Asia, in which are the still almost fabulous cities of Bokhara and Samarqand. When Marco Polo traveled this route in the thirteenth century it had long been in decay and almost in desuetude. The main line of it had already twice been altered. First it was made to pass north of Lop Nor, striking more fertile regions at Aqsu and going thence to Kashgar. Then, at about the end of the fifth century, it had suffered a more pronounced

[1] From a Mongol word meaning, as I was told, Place of Good Hunting.

change, becoming practically what the Nan Lu is now. This variation of the route still crosses a great desert, part of the enormous Gobi, on the way from Ngan-hsi Chou, the last large town of Kan-su, to Hami, the first oasis of Chinese Turkestan.

The direct line of the Nan Lu or South Road goes now, as it did in the fifth century, from Hami to Turfan, but owing to the barrenness of the country and its heat in summer almost all the traffic except in winter crosses over the Bogdo Ola range, part of the easterly prolongation of the T'ien Shan, to Ku Ch'eng-tze and Urumchi. Thence it again crosses the Bogdo Ola to get back to the main line, which runs through Toqsun to Qara Shahr, Korla, Kucha, Aqsu, and Kashgar. West of Kashgar Chinese and Russian Turkestan are divided by a pass of no great difficulty, the Terek Dawan. From Kashgar the traveler can turn back toward the East by part of the original trunk road, through the great oases of Yarkand and Khotan. If the water supply were sufficient, trade could go back by the ancient Lop Nor route all the way to Kan-su, thus completing a circuit of the great central Taklamakan Desert. Indeed, this most ancient route has never quite been lost; in winter, with ice for water supply, a caravan now and then still hazards the journey.

There is far less historical record of the North Road, the Pei Lu, divided from the Nan Lu by the T'ien Shan, which makes a lengthwise division of the province. It runs the length of what was once politically and still is geographically called Zungaria. Our lack of historical knowledge is undoubtedly due to the fact that Zungaria, which is like a great trough lying east and west between the T'ien Shan on the south and the Altai on the north, was the most important avenue of the nomadic barbarians who poured in successive invasions from Asia into Russia and Europe, destroying as they passed every settled community and every written record.

On the southern edge of the Zungarian trough, along the foot of the T'ien Shan, where the Pei Lu passes, is a series of oases. The depth of the trough is the central Zungarian desert, while the northern edge, along the foot of the Altai, offers a continuous grassland. For the lack of any such continuous grazing country by which their mounted hosts could pass along the South Road, the Uighur-Tatar-Mongol hordes, one after another, turned through Zungaria to the West. This one corridor, by giving them access to the steppes of Semipalatinsk and Semirechensk, laid open before them all Russia and all the Near East. The Mongols were only free to dominate the South Road and to undertake the more organized conquests which bore them to Kashgar, to Samarqand and Persia, and to India, when at the height of their power they already commanded the Russian side of the T'ien Shan, which they had reached through Zungaria, with the resulting mobility and scope. At a later period the short-lived Zungarian or Eleuth Mongol Empire, barred by hostile powers from Russia, Central Mongolia, and Western China, turned in desperation to the conquest of the South Road for their necessary expansion, but were unable to maintain the conquest, evidently for this very reason of the difficulty of passage for mounted armies.

It is hard to realize, until one has traveled by desert and mountain pass from town to town, how truly the term " road " defines the social and economic structure of both Chinese Turkestan and Zungaria. Khotan and Yarkand draw their water from the K'un Lun, the trans-Himalayan range, but the rest of the province, along the North Road as well as the South, depends for life on the inexhaustible snow and ice of the T'ien Shan, the Heavenly Mountains. Under the snows are great crags and forests of spruce, under these are the upland summer pastures of the nomads, and under these again in some places are superb lower grazing grounds, while in other places there is an abrupt descent to desert conditions. The inner mountain heights, with a heavy precipitation of snow and rain, are almost everywhere barred off from the plains by a lower outer range, a sterile girdle of barren rock.

In the plains, rainfall varies from little to less. The only water is from snow-fed rivers, which, breaking through the intervening foothill ranges, run on across the plains until they perish in great swamps of reeds, beyond which are the encompassing deserts that divide the province from Mongolia and China. In between the streams are the minor deserts dividing town from town. These towns are at the points where the streams break down through the desert ranges and their water, expanded by irrigation canals and ditches, can be most easily made to support an oasis. Over the intervals of desert the two great Roads, threading town to town like beads on a string, provide the only lateral communication.

Because of this peculiar geographical construction, the ruling principle in the civilization of the province is as it were perpendicular, from marsh to snow. The marshes are too hot and mosquito-plagued to be habitable, during the summer, but along the edges of them, where shelter and coarse feeding can be found for flocks, many nomads make their winter quarters. Between the formless marshes and the desert mountains, at each point where a river issues, lies the irrigated land, in patches, with a town at the centre of each patch, where traders exchange the produce of nomad shepherd and settled farmer, bringing timber, coal, gold, and iron from the mountains and exporting the surplus of the whole community against their imports of cloth, tea, and manufactured articles from China or Russia. In the upper mountains are the true strongholds of the nomads, in some places Mongols, in others different clans of the Qazaqs, who barter wool and skins for the products of a civilization they stubbornly refuse to adopt, suspicious even of traders unless they speak their own language, and avoiding as far as possible the seasonal invaders, lumbermen or miners, who enter their mountains.

The intervention of a desert barrier-range between the oases and the productive inner mountains provides a strong check on communication between the two types of civilization, mountain nomad and lowland farmer and artisan, preventing the one from swamping the other and enabling them to remain distinct. The gorges by which the streams issue through the barrier are universally difficult of passage and usually closed to wheeled traffic; while snows in winter and flood-water at the height of summer reduce communication from the perpetual to the seasonal. At the same time each town, drawing as it does on the resources of mines, forests, flocks, and farms,[1] is able to maintain itself as

---

[1] This is not equally true of *every* town. I am trying only to give the general picture.

the centre of a self-sufficient polity, with no imperative need of trade with its neighbor. Thus the main traffic along the two lateral roads is either of surplus goods going, not from town to town, but beyond the province, or of imported goods, luxuries, or improvements on the strictly necessary, coming from outer countries. Urumchi, at the best gate of easy passage between the two roads, is the natural capital of all these towns isolated from each other by the minor deserts and minor mountains; while the whole province, sundered from the rest of the world by major deserts and major mountains, has remained for centuries inward-looking, changing more slowly, because less easily penetrable by influences from without, than almost any region in the world.

Moses and I were a little bit awed at our own splendor when we started out to travel the length of Zungaria, from Urumchi to Chuguchak, after a wireless had tumbled out of the sky to say that my wife was making the attempt at a winter journey through Siberia to meet me. The splendor was borrowed, for we were no longer vagabonds of imponderable "face," content with what we might find in the way of sleeping and what we could grab in the way of eating, but part of a convoy or procession. The Great Man who was the nucleus of the procession had come to China in the year in which I was born, and was proceeding on home leave for the first time. Moses and I put our hands before our faces in order to grin the less conspicuously when we saw his folding camp stools and chairs; air mattress to go on the camp bed, lamp to give light by which to read himself to sleep, and above all the number and plenitude of the courses laid before him at meals by his two servants, who rode in a second cart with some of the luggage. I need only add that he wore special clothes for going to bed and that from before the time he took them off in the morning until after the time he put them on at night he smoked chopped Sze-ch'uan leaf tobacco in a large briar pipe. I had become used to the *tung-sheng* tobacco, powdered and greenish, favored by Shan-hsi men and Mongols, the best to smoke when there is about a foot of stem between the jade mouthpiece of your pipe and the bowl of white brass, holding enough tobacco for less than half a dozen puffs. Being out of this tobacco for a while and moreover a little shy of brandishing such a pipe in such splendid company, I dug a briar out of one of my boxes and had at the chopped leaf. It threw me into a cold sweat. Only after a couple of months of gradual inoculation could I smoke it with pleasure. I was convinced that the Great Man was a very great man, morally even more than materially.

Moses and my luggage traveled in a cart, which they shared with a Chinese fatter than and quite as cheerful as Moses himself, a member of a Chinese firm in Urumchi to which I had introductions. I rode a pony which I had purchased in Urumchi. He broke down on the tenth day of the journey. Considering that until then he had averaged forty miles a day, there must have been good stuff in him, but as ponies go in Chinese Turkestan he was held to be a hollow sham, and I to have been cheated in the purchase of him.

From the saddle I got such an idea of the country as I had been quite unable to seize during the cart journey from Ku Ch'eng-tze; but even so the view was restricted. Not only was all the world buried under snow, so that size and distance were confounded, but of the dozen days of the journey only two were fine. All the rest of the time the road was a hard-trampled ribbon of snow between borders of deep, soft-surfaced snow, curtained about with gently, steadily falling snow. It was February, and a winter of unprecedented snowfall and rigorous cold was culminating in style; but the snowy weather at least reprieved us from the dreaded Zungarian winds.

Free as we were from winds, the traveling was almost ideal, for there was enough traffic on the road to keep it hard, and over the packed snow, free of ruts and free of bumps, the three-pony teams trotted doggedly, almost never slackening to a walk, for from six to twelve hours a day. The carts were of the same four-wheeled, narrow-gauge type that carry fast traffic between Urumchi and Ku Ch'eng-tze; but we were traveling not with post-carts but with privately hired men, who were to take us the whole way. When we had made the stage or double-stage the ponies were turned, without even a walk to cool them or a blanket to warm them, into roughly-roofed stables open all along the side. Within half an hour they had begun the feeding that would keep them busy until dawn.

In spite of all I had been able to read about what one may call the interior or domestic deserts of the province, I had not fully grasped what the nature of the Road North of the Heavenly Mountains would prove to be. Within a couple of hours after leaving the streets and shops of Urumchi — a city, as I suppose, of from fifty to sixty thousand people — we had traversed all the cultivated land about the capital of a province that is more than twice the size of the state of Texas, which is larger than all France, and were entering such a desert as I had vaguely taken for granted I should see no more after reaching Ku Ch'eng-tze, on the frontier of the province. A tiny hamlet marked the halfway stage, but for the rest, as through hour after cold hour I trotted away the miles, there was neither bush nor hedge nor tree nor house. Under the snow I remembered the feel of it; the ancient, irredeemable Gobi, of solid clay overlaid thinly with gravel.

Then, as abruptly as we had left it, we entered farmland again, and before long had sight of city walls and were putting up at an inn. The size and prosperity of this town of Ts'ang-chi, as of many others, appeared incongruous with the limited agricultural area around it, until I had sorted out my ideas of the geographical structure of the country. The sight of farms meant that we had reached the zone irrigated from a river that came down from the T'ien Shan, which lay off on our left, to the south. The size of the town meant that it did not depend entirely on the trade of the farmers about it, but that in the spring and autumn its merchants were in touch, by following up the river through the desert barrier range to the productive inner ranges, with coal, iron, gold, and forests, with the nomads and their herds of cattle, camels, and ponies, their flocks of sheep, and the fox pelts, ibex skins, and elk-antlers secured by their hunters. On the desert between stream and stream, as I saw for myself when traveling over the same ground later in the year, the melting snow leaves in places a crop of grass and shrubs, which make a grazing common during a few weeks for the farmers and for the camels of the caravans that camp

A Caravan Master

Qazaq Shepherds: Lao Feng K'ou

there annually to recruit, before the grazing is burned up by the summer heat.

This is the nature of the whole North Road and of Zungaria. On our right as we went — to the north, that is — lay the central depression of the trough of Zungaria, a desert, and still further to the north, where the lip of the trough rises again to the foothills of the Altai, were once more downland, mountain pasture, and forest. Northern Zungaria is not in easy touch with the North Road, however, because of this axial desert cleavage, and though governed from Urumchi and inhabited by the Kirei clan of the Qazaqs, it belongs more naturally to Mongolia. Indeed, the Altai region, under the Manchu Empire, was administered by the Amban of Kobdo, on the Mongolian slope of the Altai. Since the Revolution the Governor of Hsin-chiang has taken it into his quiet but tenacious grasp. It is a strategic frontier of his province, and his immediate problem has been to make good that frontier, and establish a definite separation between the Mongols within his province and the independent Mongols of Outer Mongolia, lest disaffection be communicated from the independent to the subject tribes. This he has accomplished by allowing the Kirei-Qazaq to take arms and to make raids and forays at their will into Western Mongolia, thus forming a hostile racial barrier between his own province and the quasi-Soviet, quasi-Nationalist, anyhow disorderly influences of Mongolian politics.

A secondary reason inspiring the Chinese to fix their frontier on the Altai rather than in the trough of Zungaria is the valuable gold-workings in the mountains, which are farmed out under provincial monopoly. The name Altai is from a Mongol word meaning "gold," — the Golden Mountains. There is a seasonal migration of laborers from the towns on the North Road, and even from as far as Turfan on the South Road, who spend the summer washing gold in the streams of the Altai; though this work is confined to a few valleys where the danger of conflict with either Qazaqs or Mongols can best be avoided. The laborers cross the Zungarian trough in the spring, after the worst cold and before the summer heat has brought out the pest of flies and mosquitoes that make a crossing of the marsh country practically impossible in summer. In the autumn the laborers return and later the Qazaqs move down from their summer pastures in the high Altai to camp on the fringe of the marshes, where their flocks can be sheltered and where fuel is plentiful. Their presence in winter prevents free communication between the Mongol tribes on either side, while in the summer the bolder spirits among them set out to raid the Mongols, thus keeping the frontier desirably dangerous.

V

T'UNG-KAN

On the third day, at a distance of about a hundred and fifty miles from Urumchi, we reached Manass, the biggest city (after Urumchi) in the biggest oasis on the biggest river of the North Road, and the chief centre of the T'ung-kan population.

The T'ung-kan have inevitably been miscalled Dungans by the Russians, whom other Western travelers have followed. The name is evidently not Chinese, yet it does not appear to be one which these people have chosen for themselves, but rather one which they tolerate, and the theory that it has been developed out of some word in one of the early Turkish languages meaning "to turn"—that is, "to be converted" (to Islam)—may possibly be correct. The history of the present T'ung-kan communities in Zungaria can be traced back definitely as far as the reign of the Manchu Emperor Ch'ien Lung, who in securing the borders of his Chinese empire in the middle of the eighteenth century undertook a war of extermination against the Zungars, a clan-group of Mongol tribes who had established a later Western Mongol empire, a predatory power still commemorated in the name of Zungaria. Six hundred thousand Mongols are said to have been killed in these campaigns, and to replace them Ch'ien Lung imported from Western China the forbears of the present T'ung-kan.

These Mohammedan settlers were not of pure Chinese stock, but were themselves descended in all probability from Mohammedan mercenaries from this very part of Central Asia who had been summoned within the Great Wall in the eighth century to assist in pacifying and settling the marches of Western China. These mercenaries had afterwards settled in China, taking wives of the people and becoming assimilated in varying degrees to the civilization of China, except that they retained the religion of Islam. Thus the colonies planted by Ch'ien Lung were, in effect, rooted anew in their original soil. It may be, therefore, that if the name T'ung-kan really derives from a word *tunmek,* "to turn," it was first applied to these colonists because they had returned to their own country; an exegesis which would appeal to me much more than that which gives a religious explanation of the "turning" idea.

The Chinese term "Hui-hui" for Mohammedans may also throw some light on the origins of the non-Chinese Moslems of Western China and Zungaria (as distinguished from the Turki). The term has never been clear of doubt. The characters with which it is written mean "return-return," a curious comparison with the "turning" theory that has been attached to "T'ung-kan." Because of the literal meaning of the characters, it has been argued that the name was first applied to Mohammedan mercenaries "returning to their homes" from China, who settled down by the way instead of completing the return. This explanation might appear to be exactly on a footing with the possible origin of the name T'ung-kan which I have already suggested above; but here I think it is factitious. I had already,[1] both from the form of the name Hui-hui and the distaste which Chinese Mohammedans have for it, been led to think that it must have been first used by non-Mohammedan Chinese for some barbarian tribe beyond their borders. After further reading[2] I find that "Hui-hui" was one of the forms under which the name Uighur was anciently current in China, and on reflection I am convinced that the name of this people must have been transferred to the previously non-Mohammedan people or peoples among whom Islam was later established in Western China. The Uighur stock, which at yet another and earlier period in the rich history of Chinese Central Asia had

---

[1] *The Desert Road to Turkestan,* page 226.
[2] See Rockhill's *William of Rubruck,* page 141, note 3. On a more careful rereading of Carruthers's *Unknown Mongolia* I found that he also mentions the identity of "Hui-hui" with "Uighur" on the authority of Bretschneider's readings of Chinese records. None of the authorities, however, appears to have resolved the old "returning" theory by the application of this test; nor to have used it to explain the dislike of Chinese Mohammedans for their colloquial Chinese name.

settled in Southern Zungaria on the North Road and at Turfan on the South Road, and had there established one of the most flourishing civilizations in pre-Mohammedan days, must have been strongly represented among the Moslems who entered China in the eighth century. As their tribe had long been known to the Chinese, it was natural that their name should have been transferred to all the Moslems. It would also be natural for the Uighurs, as a people of at least respectable civilization, to resent the Chinese form of their name, which undoubtedly was used by the Chinese as synonymous with " barbarian."

It would follow, from this reasoning, that the literal meaning "return-return" of the characters for " Hui-hui " is merely accidental; the repeated character must have been used as nothing more than a convenient phonetic transcription of an approximate Chinese pronunciation of the word Uighur. Colloquially, the general term Hui-hui is used much more frequently by the Chinese than the particular term T'ung-kan; the latter not usually being employed except when it is necessary to distinguish between the T'ung-kan and their fellow Moslems, the Ch'an-t'ou or Turki. The T'ung-kan are therefore in the ironic position of having brought back a form of the Uighur name to ancient seats of the Uighur power both unwillingly and, in so far at least as their modern understanding is concerned, unwittingly.[1]

After being inducted to Zungaria the T'ung-kan increased steadily in numbers, wealth, and power; but, though established to maintain the Chinese front in Central Asia, they retained by force of their religion a sense of quasi-racial difference from the true Chinese. At the time of the general revolt of the Moslems in China and Chinese Turkestan, which began in the sixties of last century, they also rose. They took Urumchi, the military capital, where they are reported to have slain 130,000 Chinese, and for a number of years maintained a turbulent independence. Yakub Beg, the adventurer from Russian Turkestan, had at the same time established himself as ruler in Kashgar and overlord

---

[1] It is curious that Chinese Mohammedans, though as a general rule they object to being addressed as Hui-hui, use the two characters of this name on shop signs; especially inns or food stalls that provide " clean " food for Moslems.

of most of the South Road. These two divisions of the triumphant Mohammedans fought against each other, with the result that the Chinese in the end were able to conquer the whole province again, though the whole geography of the Moslem strongholds was in favor of the rebels. In 1881, a year or two after the reconquest, the reunited province was formally constituted Sinkiang or Hsin-chiang, the New Dominion. In the war of recovery the Chinese made sure of the strategic split between Turki and T'ung-kan by showing a surprising clemency to the Turki, whom they regarded (and rightly) as misguided, half-unwilling rebels led by an alien adventurer, while they took full measure of revenge against the T'ung-kan, dealing with them as outright traitors, because of their strong tinge of Chinese blood and civilization. They broke the power of the T'ung-kan with fire and sword, laying waste their lands to such effect that the scars of empty towns and ploughland gone back to desert remain bold and significant to this day.

In physical type the T'ung-kan are predominantly Chinese, but they are distinguished by a much more pronounced growth of hair on the face. The children are very Chinese in appearance; the un-Chinese characteristics in their inheritance become more evident as they mature. They have in particular an assertiveness of carriage which even foreigners often recognize as un-Chinese, and the Chinese themselves consider barbarous. The Chinese have their own assertiveness, but they carry it with a difference. All writers agree on the commercial ability and energy of the T'ung-kan, as well as on the surliness, ill manners, and hostile suspicion of strangers, which increase the difficulty of studying them. As traders and carriers they are found at the hither end of the South Road (and even as far toward Kashgar as the important cities of Qara Shahr and Aqsu), but their most important distribution is along the North Road, where they form the bulk not only of the trading community but of the farmers. They speak, in addition to Chinese, a Turki dialect practically the same as that of the South Road Turki. This is an additional link between them and such strongly Turkish communities as the Salars on the Chinese side of the Great Wall, and distinguishes them from the Moslems of North China, who except for their religion have been almost totally assimilated to the Chinese. Their women have a peculiar style of black, turbaned headdress, and have never, like the women of some Mohammedan communities in China proper, bound their feet. The men can be told by their skullcaps, which are white, sometimes embroidered with a faint design in colored thread; whereas the usual cap of Turki or Qazaq is in colors, with much richer, heavier embroidery.

The T'ung-kan, in spite of their humbling of two generations ago, are still among the rowdiest of the provincial populace. Many travelers have written of them that they are "much more courageous" than the Chinese. This judgment, which does less than justice to the Chinese, arises from the fact that few of the competent observers traveling in this province have known much about China proper. The Chinese whose fathers have been in this outland for several generations are usually docile, and have the timidity of people who know nothing of the world beyond their immediate bounds. Then the lower strata of Chinese immigrants, the casual laborers and drifting men-of-all-work, are most of them from Kan-su; and your average Kan-su man (I speak not of the Mohammedans) is the most timid, ignorant, and easily put-upon of the sturdy North China stock, having been raided, invaded, harried, and ruled by men from Mongolia and Central Asia, more bold and bad than themselves for a tale of centuries. The bold, self-reliant fellow from Tientsin, or the provinces of Chih-li and Shan-tung, arriving in the New Dominion without a cent, will begin as a farm laborer and end as a landed proprietor, or start as a shop-sweeper and finish as the head of the firm, for the Kan-su man never has ambition and the Northerner is never without it. The great increase of Tientsin men particularly has been within recent years, and has not been noticed by travelers. At present, the rowdiest classes in any town are the Tientsin men and the T'ung-kan, and when it comes to a street fight the Tientsin guilds can usually carry it over the Mohammedan rabble.

At Manass we were the guests of the Catholic missionary, a

man built and bearded like one of Barbarossa's crusaders, his
mission house ordered like a monastery and his mission station
conducted with Teutonic precision. After seeing war service
as an officer of artillery, he had put on the habit of a priest and
volunteered for China. When he had been only a few months
in the country, and made only the barest start in the language,
he had been offered this lonely post. He traveled up through the
interior with one servant, learning as he went. His predecessor
had to leave the station some months before he could arrive, so
that he took over without instruction. Within five years he had
so mastered the language that he conducted even his own cor-
respondence, had made a position for himself with officials and
gentry, and had a prosperous mission well in hand. He was a
seigneur directing the farm and pasture owned by the mission,
and could sell the surplus of his produce at a profit in open market, competing with local farmers. He managed an orphanage
and a school, traveled among outlying Catholics, and still had
time to press wine from the grapes of his own vineyard, cure the
tobacco of his own growing, and cure venison and wild-boar hams
of his own shooting. He had a library of several hundred books,
not all of them theological. Among the languages I noticed
Greek, Latin, German, French, English, and Chinese. This library and that of the Reverend G. W. Hunter at Urumchi were
things to make a traveler give thanks.

The Reverend Father was now about to undertake the study
of Turki.

This was the first Catholic mission I had visited for several
years, and something in me responded to the atmosphere of it.
Much as I admire many Protestant missionaries, courageous and
undaunted souls, I find myself short of understanding their work.
Now it is the multitude of smug converts, ready to tell in what
sounds like suspiciously glib patter about the "change of heart"
that led them to "see their redemption." This one used to find
especially in regions that had been under the hand of the "Christian" General, Feng Yü-hsiang, and his armies. Again there
are stations of complete contrast, with only a few shifty characters about who look to the layman very much as though they

were imposing on the eagerness of the missionaries, in the hope of getting something out of it.

Here one saw radically different principles and practice. The Catholics begin with the land, which is at the heart of the Chinese people, and aim less at the soul of the individual than at the life of the community. The principle seems to be that if you build up a Catholic community, family by family, grounded on the Church, instead of gathering a lot of stray sheep, here a son and there a brother and there a grandmother, then the individual in the community will have the same chances of Heaven, Hell, or Purgatory as the individual in a Catholic community in Europe or America. There can be few competent lay observers who believe that Protestant Christianity in China, if deprived of foreign funds, would not become degenerate and distorted within a very few years. As for the Chinese, their testimony is eloquent. Those among them who resent Christianity and distrust all foreign standards hate the Protestant with contempt but the Catholic with fear. The vulgar prejudice against the Catholics is that they " add land to land " — and land, as I have said, is at the heart of the Chinese people.

Here, beginning from the land, were farm and pasture and live stock. An orphanage, supported by the land, raised up boys and girls to be good Catholics, without any chatter about " second birth." A church, decorated in the Chinese style, to which the Catholic Church accommodates itself, provided for the devotions of the community. The bell on its roof, rung by the firm hand or unalterable order of the Father, regulated the hours of work, of rest, and of prayer. When the children grew up they were paired off, married, and planted out to be a support to the community. In the grounds were a dispensary and surgery : the Father had taught himself out of books more than the elements of medicine, and even undertook operations under anæsthetics.

Like most Catholic missions, this was financed only in the minimum from outside. The expansion of the community, once begun, depended largely on its own wealth and worth. I am disposed to believe that this kind of work, if all the foreign missionaries and what foreign funds there are were abruptly withdrawn, would last much longer and in better integrity than the Protestant type, if for no other reason than that it is more free from the idea of "teaching Chinese to be foreigners" which the Chinese associate with all Protestant work. The jealousy that Chinese have for Catholic communities is directed at something different — at their solidarity and self-sufficiency. This very jealousy would, in the absence of foreign support, tend to hold Catholic communities together by the strength of outside pressure, confirming the strength of family ties and property interests into which the religious principle has been interwoven. Certainly communities of this type are less open to the aberrations of a T'ai P'ing rebellion[1] or the political manipulations of a "Christian" army than are the converts raked up by the more erratic, irresponsible, individualistic Protestant methods.

In one respect it seems to me that Protestants are apt to spoil both bait and hook. They try to live humbly, by Western standards; but these very standards are so much above those of the depressed classes among which they work that the Chinese, at once hearing the professions of humility and seeing what he considers a munificent way of living, is likely to set the missionaries down as hypocrites, working for ulterior motives. Stories current among the vulgar of the wealth taken out of China by missionaries are born anew every time that missionaries go on furlough or retire to spend their old age in the country of their birth. The Catholics almost never go on leave, and, as for retiring, they usually die at their posts; in a little garden at Manass lay the founder of that mission, and it was known to all that the prosperity he had created remained in the community. Moreover, the Catholics, by way of contrast, frankly set a standard of living calculated to impress not only the artisan and the peasant but the educated and the gentry of the people among whom they work. They make it plain that their profession of religion does not "lose them any face" in the world. With the scholars, they have a far better average of education and civilization to show than the

---

[1] This great rebellion, it may be remembered, which with the Mohammedan rebellion shook the Manchu Empire in China, was tinged with a debased Christianity.

average Protestant, who has often no credentials but his "call"; with the rich they are people who do not have to beg, while with the poor they are people who work for their own living.

The Father, having set before us good white wine and strong tobacco, enjoined us to drink and smoke "like good Christians," until we could be served with such German cooking as I had forgotten for years. Then, for several hours, we laid our ears open to the talk of a man who had moved in many circles of the world, a man at once administrator, scholar, soldier, doctor, farmer, and sportsman.

He told us — what we heard also at many places on the road — that in winter the roe deer, driven by hunger and cold from the snow-smothered mountains, come right in among the farms of the oases to browse on hedges and steal from hayricks, so that he shot within a few hundred yards of the mission all he needed for his larder. He said also that he believed the Central Asian tiger to be extinct. This tiger has not, I believe, ever been shot by a foreign sportsman. It lives in reedy jungles like the Manass marshes, and not so long ago was found also in the swamps on the lower Ili River, in Russian territory. Its food is probably the swamp elk and the wild boar. The swamps are difficult to penetrate in winter because of the intense cold and storm-tangled weeds, and impassable in summer because of the deadly mosquitoes and stinging flies. A few tattered skins are to be seen in bazars, taken from tigers that have ventured to the edge of the marsh country to raid flocks, and been poisoned. The recent introduction by foreign traders of an easy and convenient poison like strychnine has probably reduced their numbers, because the tiger is very valuable to the Chinese, every part of him being in demand as "medicine." Nevertheless, I incline to the idea that a few may survive. One hears of them everywhere, though no one claims to have seen them and a fresh pelt is never seen on the market; but then, the deepest reaches of many a great marsh have never been penetrated.

The thickets of the Manass and many other oases throng with pheasant, which are snared and sold at amazingly low prices during the autumn and winter. Every autumn and spring, at the edge of the marshes, wonderful sport can be had with geese and ducks. Wild boar are also plentiful; they retire in winter and summer to the remotest fastnesses of the swamps, but in autumn they come up in whole sounders to raid the harvest fields.

At last the Great Man and I, well filled with meat and drink and comforted with discourse, must depart to reach our inn within the city of Manass before the gates closed. The Father tucked us, with a large earthenware jug of his wine, into a minuscular Russian carriage, and we dashed off on the hard snow of the road. We had one pony in the shafts and a half-broken creature in a trace at the side. This wildling one cut such capers in and out among the moon-cast shadows on the snow that whenever we were not on one wheel we were thankful to be on two. At last the Chinese driver pulled up in the still shadow of a great willow and unharnessed the terrified one. Turning its head toward home, he gave it a masterly kick in the hams and a catholic but most unchristian valediction. "Go home," he said, "thou egg of bastardy!" — and the pony went, snorting like a dragon and rattling from side to side of the road. With one pony we drove on, the wine safe and ourselves rumbling with an inenarrable laughter, and squeezed through the gates of Manass just before they closed.

VI

WINTERING GROUNDS OF THE NOMADS

A LITTLE beyond the city of Manass we had to cross the Manass River, the largest of those that flow northward from the T'ien Shan into Zungaria. In June, when the snow water is at its highest, the river is difficult and dangerous to cross. The more cautious kind of traveler will wait sometimes for days until the waters abate, while the bolder kind are sometimes drowned in attempting the ford. Owing to the flatness of its banks, mere wastes of stone over which the river expands exuberantly in the time of its strength, the task of building a bridge is too much for the engineering talent of the province.

Instead of continuing to the north, the river in its lower course takes a cast toward the west, ending like all the streams of Zungaria in an enclosed inland basin, the marsh-edged lake of Telli Nor. Mr. Douglas Carruthers has suggested that it offers the best natural line for a trade route to Chuguchak and Siberia, one that will come into use when the lower course of the river is more developed by settlers. I imagine, however, that there is too much swampy country, which would make roads even worse in spring than on the present route, which runs through somewhat higher country, more to the west. Moreover, the potential low-country route would not have the advantages of coinciding, as far as Hsi Hu, with the Ili road, as does the present route.

After two or three stages through oasis country and a long double stage which took us up on the edge of the desert hills, the barren flanking range of the T'ien Shan, we reached Hsi Hu. The name of the town means, approximately, "western oasis," there being almost no cultivation beyond it until one approaches the Siberian border, either in the valley of Chuguchak or the Ili

valley. Here the Chuguchak road turns northerly, while the Ili
road continues more to the west, along the foot of the T'ien Shan.
The oasis, merging into huge marshes, is a famous rice-growing
district, and commands, moreover, both a Mongol and a Qazaq
trade, the Mongols being an important sub-tribe of the Torgut, a
stage or two away on the Ili road, while the Qazaqs are winter
visitors in the Jair highlands, on the Chuguchak road. The population of Hsi Hu, like that of Manass, is an amazing welter of
indigenous T'ung-kan, locally born Chinese, Kan-su and Tientsin
Chinese, and Turki immigrants from the South Road, both traders
and farmers.

Just beyond Hsi Hu is Old Hsi Hu, which must have been the
site of the town before the Mohammedan rebellion. For thirty
miles or so we went along the edge of great marshes, and past the
marshes to Ch'e P'ai-tze, or Cart Ticket. The name, showing
that the place was by origin no more than a tax-collectorate, a station for examining the licenses of carts, declares its unimportance.
We were now out of the true oasis country; high barrens thrust in
between us and the Heavenly Mountains debarred the flow of
rivers, and the road followed the line at which springs appear on
the slope of the desert, releasing a seepage of water from distant
sources. Above the springs is a rising desert of soft, clayey soil,
where the tamarisk grows head-high; below them the percolating
water spreads out in mournful reed-beds. Most of the water,
in its long imprisonment under the desert, becomes saline, but
at Ch'e P'ai-tze it is not quite so saline, nor is the land quite so
marshy. The shabby village of one street draws on a little cultivation, and on a half-hearted trade with the Qazaqs; though most
of the tribesmen prefer to ride in to Hsi Hu, where they can have
more choice of excitement for their bartering. This region, too
open and vulnerable for nomads if tribal warfare were unchecked,
appears to have come into favor as winter quarters during the
modern years of peace. Some of the Qazaqs live in mud hovels
during the winter; others build themselves an enclosing wall of
stamped clay, in the shelter of which they pitch their yurts. A
few of them, apparently, scratch the earth for a catch-crop of
some grain; and there is a tendency for Chinese to take Qazaq

wives and beget the beginnings of a mixed race, like the Erh Hun-
tze of Barköl and Ku Ch'eng-tze, conditions favoring a compro-
mise between the nomad and the settled life.

On the next day we made a spanking double stage, first crossing
a stretch of marsh on ice that rocked and sank a little, sickeningly,
under the cart wheels, letting a flow of slow water spread over
it from depths of black mire.   Then, disengaging ourselves from
the marsh and its ranked walls of tall yellow reeds, we went up
on the camber of the desert and dragged at a slower pace through
the soft soil of tamarisk jungle and occasional copses of writhen
wild poplars, under which their yellow leaves of last year lay
thick.   Snow does not lie enduringly on loose dirt, and here we
had only streaks and windrows of snow, leaving big patches of
powdery dust, heavily rimed with soda efflorescence.   When
we first saw wild poplars, I remember, I turned in the saddle, as
well as I could for my huge greatcoat of ibex-skins, faced with
an old army blanket, — a triumph of warmth which I had had
composed in Urumchi, — and shouted to Moses, who was in a
following cart.

"Look now," I said.   "Phœnix trees!   By the soda in this
dust I knew we should see them!"   I was riding then by one
of the Great Man's carts.   "The hell!" said the carter, admiringly (but I give only a pale rendering of his oath).   "He knows
his deserts!"

Then we went down, into a depression, where the tamarisks
were thinner and more stunted and we could see more widely
over them.   Crossing the depression, we climbed very gradually,
but long, until we were on the upper levels of a highland, and
wheeled aside to the dreary yards of a dreary inn.   This was at
Ulan Bulaq (Red Spring), a stage of the kind that the Chinese
call k'u, or bitter.   The mud sleeping platforms of the inn were
not heated, nor was there a stove in the place.   Travelers must
warm themselves and cook their food by a fire of tamarisk (even
the fuel is brought from the depression below) on a little mud
pedestal at the edge of the k'ang.   The Great Man, however, was
prepared.   He had with him a stove, an oblong affair of sheet-
iron with a jointed chimney that could be persuaded to draw most

of the smoke out of the window, and stoking this up we made a snug nest in no time.

Ulan Bulaq is on the edge of the Jair Mountains, themselves really an offshoot of the Ala Tau, and in reality a highland, partially blocking the Zungarian trough between the T'ien Shan and the Altai, like the incomplete bar of an irregular H. The hills, as the road turns among them, are not high — their extreme altitude is probably not much more than five thousand feet. They are a maze of approximate cones, grown on the sides with that " white grass " found in tufts among gravel-covered, clayey hills and beloved of wild animals. Springs are rare in these almost desert hills, but they are the winter quarters of a large number of western Kirei Qazaqs, and of part of the Kobuk division of the Torgut Mongols. There is no great precipitation of snow in the Jair Mountains, nor does the snow lie long when fallen, perhaps because the gravel coating of the hills catches the maximum of heat from the sun. Thus the flocks of the nomads can always get at the grass, while enough snow lies in gullies and clefts for the stock to eat and men to melt, so that a yurt can be pitched almost anywhere for the winter.

A stage of about forty miles brought us to the centre of this highland, at a point called Miao'rh Kou, or the Valley of the Shrine. A telegraph station is maintained here, not because Qazaqs and Mongols are fond of sending telegrams, but to keep a check on breaks in the line. A mud shrine, the inevitable first monument of Chinese occupation, gives the station its name. The telegraph official has one spare room, built apart from his own tiny house, to do service as an inn for travelers who do not prefer to sleep in their carts, while the inn servants and executors of all odd jobs are two or three soldiers of the road patrol. These men are posted at every stage to serve as escorts at need to official travelers. Soldiering in the New Dominion is what it used to be in all China in the proud days of the Empire, the profession of those without enough address to beg or energy to work; but the rifle carried by the soldier is a sign that it is against the rules to rob the cart under his escort, and that the traveler is entitled to less than the usual rudeness at inns.

We did not stop here, except to breathe the sweating ponies, before going on another few miles to a Qazaq military post, where we placed our camp beds in the midst of a host of snorers and did very well. When the nomads are in winter quarters among these hills, the road is safe. They themselves could not make trouble without their head men being apprehended, and marauding Russian Qazaqs could not reach the road without being observed. In the summer, when they have moved into the Tarbagatai range, Qazaqs from Russia make a long ride through the empty hills and lie in wait along the road, to plunder travelers, freight, and the mails. In the last two years the trouble had become so bad that special measures had to be taken, among which was this establishment of a post of Chinese Kirei in the worst area, and since the tribesmen have thus been made responsible for the peace of tribal lands, the road has become much safer.

The Torgut Mongols who share the wintering grounds are of a very degenerate class. Nominally, they have the ground to the south of the road, while the Kirei range to the north; but so far as I could see, they mingle promiscuously. While the robberies, both on this and the Ili road, are always blamed on raiding Qazaqs from over the Siberian border, I do not doubt that Chinese Kirei, from the vague, safe distance of their summer encampments, three or four long rides away, have also at times taken a hand in the game. I once asked a Chinese if he knew anything about tribal distinctions among the Qazaqs. "What odds does it make," he replied, "Kirei Ha-sa or anything else Ha-sa? They are all *tsei*-Ha-sa, thieving Qazaqs."

The Qazaqs at the post where we stopped were something of this order — and, indeed, it was said that their commander had been appointed for his knowledge of thieving. The maintenance of the post was a good example of the way in which the Chinese administration of tribal affairs works, the service being required by the Chinese authorities, but the men being appointed for duty in rotation by their own tribal chiefs. They were a cheery lot of rogues and loud in praise of the greatness of the Great Man when he desired to purchase a sheep, that all might eat of his bounty. Unfortunately, no sheep were available, all the flocks being at a distance; but this difficulty was resolved in truly Tientsin fashion by the Tientsin merchant who was traveling with us. His firm had provisioned him liberally at starting with good pork sausages, a thing hard to find except in the larger towns, because almost everywhere the butchers are Mohammedans and will have nothing to do with pig. Owing to the long stages we had been making, our friend had contented himself every evening with dry bread and tea, before stretching out to sleep, so that he had not diminished the sausages at all. He now made an offering of the whole supply to the delighted Qazaqs. None of them could speak more than a word or two of Chinese, and in our own party only one of the servants of the Great Man could speak a little town-Turki, with which he made shift among the Qazaqs. Our hosts paused only to ask if the sausages were of " clean " meat — a question easily understood. " Sheep, sheep," the interpreter assured them, vigorously; and " Eat, eat hearty," said the Tientsin merchant, heaping sausages into the great cauldron. He nodded and grinned among the Mohammedan barbarians, chatting, for all they could tell, in the friendliest possible way; but in fact he was making a kind of farewell address to the whole province and all its aborigines. " How many years have I been in this wild land Beyond the Western Gates? How much have I suffered of evil in leaving my doors! But at last now I return to Tientsin; and here by the road I cause you to break your faith, defile your younger sisters. Eat, eat well; eat well of pig, bastards! Break your faith, eat pig-meat! "

All the next day the Tientsin men rejoiced severally and in concert over this joke. Of our carters, one was a true Tientsin rascal, a big, swaggering, foul-mouthed bully, but the best driver and the most cheery, willing worker of the lot. Another was a Shantung man from just over the Chih-li border; his home and the village where Moses was born were within a long day's walk of each other, and they were sworn brothers from the moment of meeting. The Great Man's driver was a Siberian Tatar of some kind; a good fellow, but he knew enough Chinese only to feed his ponies and himself, and was put upon and bullyragged by the others along the whole road.   The pork joke they thought the best of the lot, and were at pains to make it clear to him.

At the post, however, all was well.   The men showed us a great hunting eagle belonging to their chief; a magnificent bird mewed all by itself in a yurt specially pitched in the enclosure of the post.   Then two of the men danced for us, and at last, when we had eaten and sat over our pipes in the long, dark common room where all slept, an old man played on a rough three-stringed guitar and sang Qazaq ballads.   My heart rose to this journeying and turned from the Tientsin man and his honest tradesman's desire for a well-stocked shop, a prosperous home from which he need travel no more, and children growing up to inherit his goods laid by; I wished that I might go on in this noble progress, without count of time, seeing all Asia unroll before me.

VII

OLD WINDY GAP

ANOTHER long double stage took us out of the Jair Mountains.
At the end of the first stage we rattled through Yamatu, a place
prominent on maps, with no more justification than a tumble-down
fort where half a dozen soldiers contemplate their chickens while
waiting for tips from escorted travelers, and an inn of one room
whose landlord is also telegraph linesman, expected to keep the
wire up over fifty or sixty miles of road. Between the Qazaq
post and Yamatu, while still on the upper level of the Jair, we
passed a stone which the carters call the *yu-shen* or grease-god.
Whenever they pass, they smear on it a daub of axle grease from
the can that swings under the cart. Not to observe this rite is to
put the cart in peril of a smash; but to observe it protects only the
cart, not the ponies, the driver, or the passengers. The stone
is honored, so far as I could hear, by carters only; but possibly in
earlier time it was a holy stone of the nomads, honored by them for
different reasons. In shape it is a natural phallus, about two
feet high, round and smooth. I could form no idea of how deeply
it was embedded in the ground, nor whether it had accidentally been
up-ended in a position to attract attention, or deliberately placed
by men. All the carters can say is that it is a "magic" (here a
better translation of the word *shen* than "holy") stone.

Passing the grease-god, we dropped into a sandstone gorge, a
sudden and surprising descent from the highland, a deep rift with
unassailable sides. This gorge is called Shih Men-tze, the Gate
of Stone, and issuing from it we made Yamatu, traveling on
through rounded hills and descending from plane to plane of the
northerly side of the Jair range. At last the hills opened out to
gently tilted plains, with far sights of mountains to right and

left; then, dropping down from a low shelf, we were in a wide depression, and in the depression we came to T'o-li, or T'o-lai, where one street runs through a cluster of mud hovels of little attraction. The change from the dry highlands of the Jair was abrupt, for now we were neck-deep in snow, being once more within the influence of higher mountains, which concentrate the fall of rain and snow, and in one of the regions where the snow piles deep and lies long. This place is evilly renowned for cold and wind, for the next day we had to face the Lao Feng K'ou, Old Windy Gap. The passage (for it is more a passage than a pass) is a wide gap between the spurs of the Ala Tau-Barliq-Jair system on the south and the Tarbagatai-Sair system and its buttress the Urkashar on the north. The altitude is given by Carruthers as 5945 feet.[1]

At T'o-lai we were met by a light-hearted young Russian Tatar who had been sent to conduct the Very Great Man into Chuguchak with a Russian sleigh, a comfortable, open, town-going affair having a real seat to it with a back against which one could lean. My pony, dismayed at the plunge into renewed snow, had lamentably and irrevocably broken down on reaching T'o-lai, and had to be led the rest of the way, so that I alone usurped the sleigh of honor, because the Very Great Man could not be persuaded to leave the nested furs in his cart. It was a most uncordial winter dawn, with blue shadows on the white snow and an illusion of smoke across the pale saffron of the eastern sky behind us, when we departed from that little village of bone-aching cold. My sleigh soon had the distance of all the carts, though they had been lightened of their luggage, which had been loaded on three Qazaq sleds.

[1] In his *Unknown Mongolia*, the most excellent and authoritative book on the region, Mr. Carruthers, I think, stretches a point in pitching on the Zungarian Gate, a deep trench cutting through the mountains between Ebi Nor and Ala Köl, as the key passage of the great nomadic migrations between Zungaria and Siberia. Notice has been directed to the Zungarian Gate for centuries because of the phenomenal winds that rush through it, and the legends associated with them. But the Zungarian Gate, by Mr. Carruthers's own account, is in desert country not suited to the migrations of great hordes with numerous cattle and flocks, while the Lao Feng K'ou route is still used at the present day by the nomads on spring and autumn migration. Moreover, the Lao Feng K'ou is at the natural convergence of the routes from the foot of the T'ien Shan and the foot of the Altai. For the position of Chuguchak as the natural outlet for barbarian hordes issuing from the Zungarian channel, see below, Chapter XIX, and for further reference to the Zungarian Gate, see below, page 204.

Although Lao Feng K'ou is, by a comparison of accounts, a better pass than the Zungarian Gate, it is dreaded by caravan men, carters and nomads alike. In spite of the relatively low altitude, it is one of those places of peculiarly Central Asian horror where the winter begins to be oppressive about the middle of summer, and does not end until the next summer. It is exposed to sudden, violent winds, which by Qazaq and Torgut tradition are born in a peak of the Urkashar spurs that fail to close the gap. As the winds converge on the gap and are funneled through it, blowing usually from southeast to northwest, they are hard enough for brute beasts to make head against, even when no snow is lying; but when they lift the snow before them they reach their full deadliness, for sight is then impossible and a traveler once off the track is not likely to find it again. On the northerly slope of the pass, at intervals, are the ruins of round mud huts, rather like yurts in structure, each with an opening on the downwind side. The people of the country refer them to a mighty emperor of time past, saying that once they were strong towers, whose eaves were hung with bells, by the sound of which a traveler struggling against the wind could find his way from one to the next. Were these towers kept up, they would still be of as much use as ever, for shelter if not as guides; for the winds of the pass are the true Zungarian winds, that start without warning in clear weather and within ten minutes are at their full strength, scouring the land with an impenetrable barrage of dust or snow, it may be ten or twenty or forty feet high, under a calm blue sky. The bad repute of Old Windy Pass was just then fresh in talk. Not so long before, the sleds of the new Postal Commissioner, then on his way to Urumchi, had been caught in one of these winds. Some of his party went off the line of march, and being dazed by the cold had nearly died. One of them lost all but two of his fingers from frostbite. As the story was told over for us, people seemed to argue that Old Windy Pass, being capable of such discourtesy toward a foreigner and such insolence to a man in high official position, must be a pass governed by devils of active malevolence.

Once more the road was of packed snow, bordered by snow so deep and soft that when I got out to take photographs I went in up to the waist. We climbed very gradually, and it could be seen that this was no true pass, of a climb, a ridge, and a drop, but a gap between groups of hills. We were rounding the lower spurs of one range, with a great slow sweep of hills rising on our left, and off on the right front was a knot of hills, the outwork of the opposing range. Suddenly the road dipped for fifty yards, toward a scattering of wind-writhen *toghraq,* or wild poplars, and the sleigh ran up to the eaves of a group of Qazaq huts, ensconced in the snow, to which one might descend by the area dug out at the side of each door, like that from which the London skivvy appreciates the feet of the London Bobby. We were now in the centre of Lao Feng K'ou, as I learned when I burrowed into a hut, to sit on a dirty felt and drink tea with the Qazaqs, all among their kids and lambs and suckling babies, mewed hawks and hunting eagles, lean hunting dogs and fat hunting lice. The Great Man could not be drawn from the furs that guarded all but his face, before which there burned the fearsome Sze-ch'uan leaf in the much-enduring pipe; for which reason he passed through Lao Feng K'ou innocent and unaware, without knowing it though he saw it all plain — a thing he was still lamenting the next time I saw him; and that was in Rome.

Thereafter we went downward, into the wide lands drained by the Emil River, the most westerly basin of Zungaria; but so imperceptibly that only by looking up could it be told that we were going down. At last we were on a great floor, a white floor of snow ringed about with mountains, the snowy Tarbagatai being on our front. The steaming ponies plugged away across the levels until we came to a place where the floor sagged somewhat, and we could detect watercourses under ice and snow. We were at the nadir, where the drainage flows together from all the hills, but chiefly from the Tarbagatai. A line of small villages proceeded down the valley, the valley of the Emil; but we bore away right-handed, upstream, until at last, much nearer the first rise of the Tarbagatai, we crossed the stream by a noble bridge of wood and entered Ho-shang, whose Mongol name is Dorbujing, having achieved two full stages and a little one, a handsome journey of at least sixty miles, between dawn and sunset.

This being a town of some size, a fitting reception had been prepared for the Great Man, and we suffered in consequence. Instead of being allowed to creep into the kennels of an inn, where we could prepare our own food and eat it and roll up and sleep and be done with it, we were taken to the chief Turki trading house. Two great rooms were opened before us, heated with Russian stoves and furnished with Russian tables, chairs, and couches. Burly Turki merchants, black-bearded, turbaned and gowned in colors, came to offer courtesy to our weariness. One of them could speak a little Russian, and attached himself to the Great Man, while another who spoke Chinese was attentive to me. They were men of Kashgar stock, who had settled thus far from home to do a good trade with the Mongols coming in from the hills, and to exchange the produce of the country for trade goods which they brought in from Russia. One of them had visited the great fair at Nijni-Novgorod, which to the Mohammedan peoples of Central Asia is London, Paris, and New York rolled into one, with a foretaste of Paradise to heighten the seasoning. Both of them planned to go to Mecca on Haj, and asked us eagerly if we knew whether the peace of Russia were truly stable, enough to be trusted while they journeyed by rail to the Black Sea and took shipping for Jidda. Above all, they desired to know if it were safe to buy enough of the paper currency of the Soviets to pay their way. It was true they had gold, — they took Russian gold pieces of Imperial coinage from their waistbands, — but they were men of Central Asia, though princely in their wealth, and it went hard to think of laying out good gold, even for the Haj.

After hours of waiting, when we were staggering with sleep, lordly platters of *pilau* — mutton, rice, and chopped carrots, hot to the point of agony and drenched in fat — were laid before us with suitable gestures. We stowed as much of it as we could, but even so were not free for bed. After us came the lesser folk, with greater hunger, and after them the lowliest. Nor even then were we left alone. It was a great house, but greatness in these parts is measured by having more than enough relations, retainers, and scroungers to swamp the state of the most lavish provider. When the last grain of rice had been chased off the platters, the company went off to get its bedding. Each man unrolled his quilts where he hoped he might be least stepped on; and in a short time — behold, our apartments of honor were sardined with men, lying under the table, alongside our camp beds, and on top of the table also. There was not a window that opened, the stove had been stoked as was meet for our honor, and in short order a thick fog of inert air stuffed the room. Through it all night hummed and drummed the simple, happy snoring of contented men, beautifully replete with fat food, poked down their throats to celebrate the Presence of the Great.

One last stage, through snow above which appeared only the pale yellow spikes of a little *chih-chi* grass, delivered us to our goal of Chuguchak. We bore off at an angle from our course of the previous day, traveling now in the same direction as the Emil River, but above it, on the swelling slope that rose to the Tarbagatai. Down in the valley-bottom were scant settlements, the slovenly agricultural holdings of Qazaqs that have relaxed from the nomadic life. Neighboring them were the winter lodgments of the nomadic Kirei Qazaq, many of whom house themselves in winter in huts, mostly dug out of the earth but roofed with logs and brushwood. The two sides of a triangle along which we traveled from Lao Feng K'ou to Ho-shang and so to Chuguchak represented the winter road; in summer a more direct way cuts along the shallow valley, but in winter traffic is turned away from this because of the strip of Qazaq land. This is by order of the Governor, because a heavy traffic through the midst of so many winter-idle Qazaqs would over-tempt them to thieving.

One long caravan strung out on the snow — a Barköl caravan by the look of the men, camels, and loads — was all the life on the road. When we had distanced them, we seemed sunk flat on the waste of white that swept out on every side. Minor hollows and folds of the land were obliterated under the snow; to all appearance, the tall Tarbagatai stood up straight from a dead-level plain. At last we saw a smudge low down before us. The Great Man and I (now together in the sleigh of honor) watched it thicken. Then we saw a darkness under the smudge, then tall naked poplars and bare rounded willows, and at last a city wall with battlements, with the pagoda-top of a drum-tower uplifted over the centre. As we drew near the city several sleighs came out, full of Russian and Chinese friends who had come out to welcome the Very Great Man. They bore him off to stay in a real house, with carpets on the floor, tablecloths, and all the things which are perfectly useless in Central Asia. I had recommendations to a Chinese firm, which made an additional business of putting up traveling merchants. There Moses and I stayed, together with the Chinese trader who had come with us from Urumchi, who was bound for the Trans-Siberian Railway and Tientsin. We were not disappointed in our hopes of being able to get garlic.

Chuguchak is the capital of the Tarbagatai district, which is, geographically, a nest of mountains and wide valleys, spliced in between the uttermost ends of Siberia, Mongolia, and Zungaria, and centring in the Tarbagatai range. The town of Chuguchak had in 1910 an estimated population of 9000; in 1927 I should say that it had probably increased slightly. Most of the land belongs nominally to a sub-tribe of the Torgut Mongols, but a share of the land suitable for nomad life is allotted to the Western Kirei Qazaq, who pay grazing fees to the Torgut. A number of the Kirei have taken to farming. They are the most rascally of their tribe. The reason, probably, is that among nomads the most enterprising and capable attain to the nomadic type of wealth — a plenitude of live stock. The weaker poor families are paid or compelled by their chiefs to raise a few scratch-crops whenever the country, as in the open Emil valley, permits. When the different tribes come under a firm overlordship, as has happened in this part of Chinese Central Asia and in many parts of the Russian provinces of Semirechensk and Semipalatinsk, these poorer nomads tend to abandon their ancient traditions, and, turning their summer drudgery into a permanent occupation, they settle on the land.

The Tarbagatai region was formerly administered, like the Altai, by a special viceroy appointed from Peking, but since the Chinese Revolution it has been controlled from Urumchi by the Governor of Hsin-chiang, who appoints a deputy at Chuguchak to control the important Mongolian and Siberian frontiers and to

supervise the relations of the nomads and the settled populations. Mr. Douglas Carruthers, in 1910, saw reason to believe
that the paramount chief of the Western Kirei was as ready to be
friendly with potential Russian invaders as with his Chinese
rulers. The same is probably true now; but here, as in all the
diverse and many-peopled regions under the rule of the wise old
Governor at Urumchi, mere disorder and riotousness are capably
dealt with, while discontent, the prime incentive to serious rebellion, is wholly absent, prosperity being made so easy for all. Only
the death of the old Governor and a scramble for power among his
successors, or the invasion of Hsin-chiang from China proper in
civil war, is likely to rend the province. Once the artificial cohesion of the province were destroyed, however, it could hardly
be restored again except by Russian occupation of dominating
positions along the frontier and an extension of Russian influence
almost up to the borders of China proper.

The settled population of this frontier territory is based
on towns like Chuguchak and Ho-shang, where the traders
are reënforced by neighboring communities of farmers. In recent
years both Chinese and Turki immigrants have taken up land,
but it is curious and noteworthy that the nucleus of these communities is a non-Chinese tribe, the Solons, whose occupation
dates from the eighteenth century. After the conquest of China
by the Manchus, the new Empire was dragooned into shape by
two of the early emperors, K'ang Hsi and Ch'ien Lung. When
his war against the Zungars had determined this remote western boundary, Ch'ien Lung secured it by planting colonies of
Solons in the key positions near Chuguchak, guarding the Emil
valley. The Solons were a Tungusic tribe, akin to the Manchus,
and from their ancient home in Northern Manchuria had accompanied the Manchus as vassal-allies in the invasion of China. Together with the Sibos, a tribe of the same race and character, they
seem to have played a great part in the wars of the western
frontiers. At one time they were stationed in the Koko Nor region, under the edge of the heights of Tibet, during the reduction
of the Mongol and Tangut tribes on that frontier. Then they
were carried to the ultimate West, where the Sibos were cantoned

as military colonists in the Ili valley and the Solons in the valley of the Emil. Solon troops also played an important part in the reconquest of the West, after the Mohammedan rebellion, and later provided an accretion of strength to the Solon colonies.

During the centuries that have passed over them since their astounding wars and migrations, they have retained their Manchu "banner" organization and their Tungusic speech, which is very nearly identical with the Manchu speech that has now vanished. This is undoubtedly due to the fact that they were settled on the land. With the intention of preserving the military character of the true Manchu tribes, the early emperors ordained that they were neither to hold land nor engage in trade. In the result, they became merely idle aristocracies, losing not only their warlike tradition, but even their speech, and almost every individuality, becoming gentlemen of leisure, indeed, but gentlemen of a Chinese and not of a Manchu character. Thus, after the Revolution, when deprived of their wealth, privileges, and Imperial subsidies, they found themselves merely a new class of indigent Chinese; while their poor Tungusic cousins retain not only the ancient speech, but racial integrity and economic solidarity. In the initial disorders of the Revolution, in the New Dominion, the small communities of aristocratic Manchus in the towns, who had represented the governing caste and existed virtually as parasites, were wiped out by massacre. The landed colonists, Sibos and Solons, were too strong to be meddled with. They not only survived, but still remain a strength to the province. The military character of the colonies had never been forgotten. Generation by generation they had provided contingents for garrisoning the frontier, and in spite of poor equipment and training they are at present the most soldierly material in the province. The contrast in history is worth notice, because it shows by experiment the value of two different methods of fortifying a governing caste, that of subsidizing the conquerers and that of founding a yeomanry. The subsidized Manchus have been obliterated as a force in modern Chinese affairs, while the Sibo and Solon yeomanry survive, to prove the rule that the man with land at his back to defend will die more stoutly, if he must die, and short of death will put a better face on bad affairs.

VIII

A FRONTIER OF INNER ASIA

THE traditional Chinese policy in the administration of Chinese Turkestan and Zungaria, since the decisive conquests under the Manchu Empire, now nearly three hundred years ago, has been straightforward. After establishing practicable frontiers, based on the mountain ranges dividing these far outer territories from the sphere of Russian power and influence, every effort was made, so far as the physical difficulties of great distance and intervening deserts would allow, to identify the province with China. The alien Ta Ch'ing dynasty created by the conquering Manchus ruled both China and the outer dominions, but the Manchus merged their interests in those of China, and directed their policies toward fortifying an integral Chinese civilization, which should be rooted in the heart of China and overshadow all the frontiers.

To this end, the westward frontiers of what is now Hsin-chiang were closed, but from the side of China trade was encouraged and the development of wealth and civilization was fostered as far as was commensurate with keeping the subject races militarily impotent. The North Road and the South Road were, in still more momentous epochs, channels leading on to the still remoter West; but from this time the flow of wealth in these channels was controlled in a new sense. The province was no longer an intermediate region, but a terminal area into which flowed exports of men and manufactures, and those more imponderable exports, arts and civilization. From it, as if in tribute, returned the produce of the less civilized subject races, raw materials of all kinds and jade and precious metals. Yet, until the end of the nineteenth century, China derived no substantial revenue from this remote dominion. Motives of policy demanded that the Chinese, both in

Mongolia and Chinese Turkestan, should concern themselves above all with the maintenance of buffer territories between themselves and the countries of the West, and with preventing any undue increase of strength among the subject races of those territories. True commercial exploitation depended on the later appearance of new commercial interests.

By the beginning of our century, traffic became more important. The development of foreign trade on the coast of China stimulated the demand for raw materials. Though the foreigners could not trade in the interior, away from the Treaty Ports, the Chinese traders who dealt with the foreigners were encouraged to go farther and farther into the hinterland, in search of cheap raw materials. The trade of Mongolia and Hsin-chiang, especially, woke to a new importance. The demand for wool and camel hair became one of the standards of commerce, and in return for the wool sold to the foreigners the Chinese merchants were able to buy and transport increased quantities of cloth, tea, and manufactured articles for sale among their distant fellow-subjects.

This increased prosperity demanded supplementary routes. The classical cart-road up through China to the Jade Gate of Kan-su and to Hami and the divergence of the North Road and the South Road along the Heavenly Mountains was hampered by the *likin* system, the collection of local taxes on goods in transit; and this led to the growth in importance of the caravan roads through Mongolia, along which travel and trade had been almost negligible·since the great days of the nomadic wars and migrations. After the Chinese Revolution, yet another emphasis was laid on these routes. The Governor of Hsin-chiang, whose life and policies are at the core of contemporary Chinese power and influence in Central Asia, gave his first consideration to the prosperity of trade. He relied on the material contentment of his subject races to check any tendency toward independence, reckoning shrewdly that people with money to lose would not be eager for the risks of rebellion. At the same time, Chinese economic domination, if only it could be kept free of political interference from the home country, was the best means to his hand for checking Russian penetration across borders which, he well knew, he could not defend in serious warfare.

This sound policy was hard hit, first by the increase of civil war in the provinces of China proper traversed by the classical road, and then by the collapse of Chinese rule in Outer Mongolia. The civil wars were, in the first place, damaging to trade, and in the second place they warned him that he must not develop communications on the approach from Kan-su to his own province, for fear they might lay him open to an invasion headed by some ambitious general from China. The establishment of Mongol independence under Soviet influence in Outer Mongolia at the same time smothered the most important of the caravan routes. One caravan route remained, that through Inner Mongolia, south of the main Mongolian deserts which make a natural division between Outer Mongolia, open to Russian penetration, and Inner Mongolia, to which the Chinese have free approaches. This route, however, lay through much more desert country, with a consequent loss in camels that put up the price of transport and checked the development of trade. Moreover, communications between the end of the Mongolian routes at railhead and the port of Tientsin, the distant source of the foreign trade which kept up the demand for raw produce from his province, were constantly hampered by civil wars.

In these circumstances, to prevent a collapse of prosperity leading to discontent, he was forced to open up a new trade with Russia. At the furthest extreme of the province, at Kashgar, the Russians had in the past generation exercised an influence great enough to alarm the Chinese. The construction of the Orenburg railway had at once consolidated Russian Turkestan and given the Russians an economic advantage over the Chinese in competing for the trade of Kashgar, Yarkand, and Khotan. During the most aggressive period of the Russian advance in Central Asia, there had been grave danger that they might occupy Kashgar or at least declare a political " sphere of influence." When the Chinese power was weakest in Central Asia, during the Mohammedan rebellion, the Russians, on the classical justification of " preserving order," occupied a part of the Ili valley. Later, on receipt of an indemnity on account of the expenses of the occupation, they returned most of this territory, but some of it they retained. Finally, at the time of the Chinese Revolution, the Mongols made a bid for autonomy which was supported by Russia, and which led to the recognition of special Russian interests and privileges in Mongolia. The Chinese in Hsin-chiang had for more than a genera‑ tion been in constant apprehension of Russian encroachment. They may well have felt, at the time of the Revolution, that it was only the prompt establishment of order, the assertion of auto‑ cratic power by the present Governor at the very beginning of his tenure, that saved them from a similar forward movement on the part of Russia.

Viewing Russia as a power of unknown force and incalculable policies, the Chinese naturally hailed the Russian Revolution and the civil wars and Terrors, Red and White, that followed it, as a deliverance. They had worked to the best of their ability to keep the trade of Hsin-chiang out of Russian hands and under Chinese control, and at the same time to keep the development of wealth within the province below the point at which it might be over‑ tempting to Russian ambition. The time seemed at last to have arrived, with the collapse of civil order in Russia, to close the borders completely. Trade was cut short, passports refused, and all communication discouraged. For several years the only con‑ tact with Russia was the incursion of bands of defeated anti- Revolutionary troops. These men, armed and officered, were a serious menace, but with skillful handling they were gradually eliminated. They might have seized wide lands which the Chi‑ nese could not adequately defend, lands which were "white man's country," but one band after another, escaping into the quiet of Chinese Turkestan from the incessant confusion of war, desertion, and "betrayal" in Russia, lost its morale and what cohesion it might have had. In the end the Chinese were able to seize some of the more dangerous leaders, and to deliver others in one way or another to hostile agents over the border. As for the men, some of them were disarmed, interned, broken up into small par‑ ties, and gradually cleared out of the province, to be added to the Russian wreckage that accumulated in China, while others were diverted toward Mongolia, where, after a brief career of the vio‑ lence born of terror and despair, most of them were either massa‑ cred, or died of privation, or were rounded up by bands of Red

"Partisans," as they were called, who thrust into Mongolia from Siberia.

Thus no part of the wars of revolution and counter-revolution was fought out in Chinese Turkestan. The Chinese governing caste in the province, with its nucleus of able officials directed by the ruthless old autocrat at Urumchi, were left in a commanding position. Year by year, however, the old Governor and his picked following, having triumphed as men, were forced to give ground against the urgent tide of circumstance. The material prosperity and contentment of the subject races, especially the Mohammedan elements, remained the key to safe rule of the province. Prosperity was increasingly threatened by the choking off of trade with China and through Mongolia. In Russia, in the meantime, the Soviets had captured destiny. Out of the ruins of one social order they founded and shored up another. Their control had expanded from Moscow over the country, and at last, along all her borders, Russia began to marshal her new strength.

The Chinese in Hsin-chiang, severed from China and denied Chinese aid except at the price of being involved in Chinese civil wars, were forced in the end to come to terms with Russia. The Soviet treaty with China in 1923 had not, in practice, affected Russian relations with Chinese Turkestan. The old Governor would not yield his position to the words and gestures of Peking; his ideas of negotiations with Russia were pragmatic. In this the Russians were not only at one with him, but prepared and in waiting. Within a year, however, he made a regional agreement with the Russians, affecting his own territories. The Russians abandoned all claim, on paper, to a favored position in Hsin-chiang, in return for a trade agreement. Consuls were appointed at Kashgar, Kulja, and Chuguchak, and a Consul-General at Urumchi. Trade opened across the borders into Russian Turkestan and Siberia.

This development, on the face of it no more than a temporary regional accord, has all the makings of a turning point in the history of Central Asia, if not in the relations between Europe and Asia. The Chinese control of Chinese Turkestan, though maintained with admirable ability, is only maintained as it were from month to month. To judge it on its immediate merits, it hangs by the life of the Governor, who is over sixty. A struggle for the succession to power at his death would precipitate Russian control, if not formal Russian rule. To judge it from a view of longer perspective, Chinese power in Central Asia is, in effect, in recession, not only from Chinese Turkestan, but from Mongolia, and perhaps Manchuria. In China itself, the welter and turmoil of the political and economic adjustment to new standards has drawn all the blood of the country to its heart, leaving no strength to animate control in what were once its outer dominions, the buffer territories between Asiatic and European. For more than two thousand years the power of China in Central Asia has waxed and waned, countering or retrenching before the strength of different alien races — Huns, Tanguts, Uighurs, Tatars, Mongols. In our time it is waning, as Russia grows to a new stature. Russia controls Outer Mongolia, a Russian shadow falls across Manchuria, and the potential wealth of Chinese Turkestan, for which outlets were dug and laid toward China three hundred years ago, is now laid open to Russia.

The immediate result has been a quickening of trade at the three gates between Siberia and the New Dominion — Kashgar, Kulja, and Chuguchak. Less than ten years ago Tientsin, two thousand miles or so away on the coast, was the port of Chinese Turkestan. All the trade routes, those through Mongolia, those following the valley of the Yellow River, and the classical road, the old Imperial Highway, abutted on railways which directed their traffic to Tientsin and the sea. Ku Ch'eng-tze, with its command of Mongolian routes and an easy traverse to Hami and the Imperial Highway, was the capital of the caravan trade; and because of its proximity to Urumchi the economic pulse of the province was as it were under the hand of the Governor. Even the products of the furthest oases, Khotan, Yarkand, and Kashgar, were drawn toward the East, and passing through Urumchi were dispatched from Ku Ch'eng-tze. The Governor, in the interest of trade, showed that he was not disposed to press too hard the treaty regulations which restrict foreigners from direct trade in the interior. As a result, some of the soundest foreign firms in Tientsin established agencies in Urum-chi. A number of these were no more than the old-fashioned Chinese agencies, but others were branch offices of the Tientsin firms, managed by Russians who, having lost their treaty rights, were considered good representatives for this kind of semi-legitimate business.

As a matter of fact, the selection of Russians was a serious error. The type of man required was the old " factor " breed, a man of tact, sagacity, and confidence, fitted to run an old-fashioned, remote trading post on the strength of his own personality and capability. Men of this kind were far to seek among the Russians, whose whole history of action in Central Asia was based on strong military support and diplomatic backing. The most cursory reading establishes the remarkable contrast in, for instance, Russian and British method and temperament : Colonel Bell, V. C., or Captain Younghusband (as he then was) traversing the whole of China, Mongolia, and Chinese Turkestan with only one or two chance-picked followers, Chinese or Turki, while the Russian explorers, like Prjevalsky, never moved without a squad of armed Cossacks; or the famous Russian consul at Kashgar, Petrovsky, with his detachment of Cossacks, his parade of force, and his domineering methods, as against Macartney, the equally famous and more reputable British representative, who alone and unsupported gradually won the confidence and accord of the Chinese officials by his integrity and invariable " soundness."

Some of the Russians who had been selected to establish British trade in Hsin-chiang were supposed to have a knowledge of Central Asia; several of them had a smattering of Turki. They were chosen presumably with an eye to the immediate chances of profitable trade; but not one of them was chosen as the right kind of man to understand the Chinese rulers of the province and work in with them to give their firms a permanent and secure grounding. At the first pinch, when disorganization along the trade routes began to make trade a little more difficult, they went to pieces. They were men without confidence, psychologically unfit for original action because they had been bred in the Russian " steam-roller " tradition of Central Asian advance — not in development, that is, but in occupation. They had been taken on by their employers because they had abandoned Russia after the Revolution, and were thought more trustworthy than the bugaboo Reds. As a matter of fact, the moment that the Soviets began to gain ground once more in Chinese Central Asia, they let go all holds, and began to drift. They felt themselves men without a country, and, so far from being able to work in accord with the Chinese to strengthen the Chinese position, they went in terror that the Chinese, whom they did not understand, might deliver them over bound and trussed to the Soviets, as a sacrifice to sweeten the Soviet-Chinese trade negotiations. Foreign trade (British trade being in the forefront of it), instead of commending itself as a link binding Chinese Turkestan to China, simply died out. Most of the foreign firms lost money and withdrew.

At the present time foreign trade in the province, apart from the Soviet firms, is represented by a German firm and several catch-penny firms registered as American, enterprises of New York Russian Jew fur buyers. The success of the German firm is dependent on a postal agreement with Russia. It receives by " sample post " a steady supply of the cheapest kind of trash, which is used to stock stores in several towns. From the sale of this trash, funds are acquired with which raw produce is bought and shipped out to Siberia. The firm was originally established from Tientsin, but, adapting itself to new conditions, now works almost entirely through Russian toleration. It is represented by a German, an old Englishman Russianized these fifty years or so, and a number of Russians.

More interesting are the enterprises of two remarkable men, one a Siberian Russian peasant and the other a Siberian Tatar. Both of these men, who speak Chinese fluently, are in fact trade and business agents of the Governor and the clique of Chinese officials indirectly interested in trade. By becoming naturalized Chinese, they have given a sure pledge to the Governor, making themselves subject, without chance of protest, to the action of the Chinese police and the Chinese law. Neither of them is affiliated with the Bolsheviks, but their Chinese registration makes it possible for them to come and go freely between the Soviet officials and the

Soviet trade agencies, developing the possibilities of trade. These men are interested in every sort of activity, not only the straight-forward export trade, but gold mining, transport, and projects for cotton-spinning and oil-refining.

The Soviet trade agencies, at the time I was in the country, could hardly be said to have reached their full working efficiency. Their potentialities were being studied by Chinese and Russians with equal interest. As is well enough known, the foreign trade of Soviet Russia is confided to regional monopolies. Most of the Russian products which they market in Hsin-chiang are de-livered to them by other monopolies within Russia, for which they act as foreign agents. About three of these foreign trade monop-olies operate in Hsin-chiang, each in an allotted territory. This means that they are able to quote flat rates in each territory, both for buying and selling, without fear of Russian competition. The decrease of trade with China, for the reasons I have quoted, means that the Chinese traders who formerly ruled the markets are handi-capped in competition with the Russians.

The total of trade under the new conditions may well increase, but it is doubtful whether the Chinese merchants can retain their old share of the profits, and quite evident already that the first-cost prices of all raw products are being depressed by Russian manipulation.

Briskness of trade in the bazars of Chuguchak is therefore com-patible with discontent on the part of the Chinese. Chinese mer-chants formerly bought a good many furs, the best of the province, in this market, sending them all the way to Ku Ch'eng-tze, to be dispatched by caravan through Mongolia. Now they see these furs bought away from them by the Russians and taken into Si-beria, at prices against which they cannot bid, because of the lack of buying power at Ku Ch'eng-tze consequent on the decline of the caravan trade. The main stream of traffic is no longer out of Chuguchak toward Urumchi and Ku Ch'eng-tze, but through Chuguchak into Siberia. Cotton from Turfan and wool from Qara Shahr are brought all this way by cart train and camel cara-van, consigned to the Siberian and Russian Tatar agencies; and though the internal carrying trade of the province suffers no loss by this change of direction, the Chinese merchants of Chuguchak itself complain of their small share in what is doing.

The change in the direction of trade has also had an important effect in its tendency to decentralize the political control of the province. During the period when trade was drawn toward the East, Urumchi, by virtue of its unique position controlling both North Road and South Road, was like a great valve, through which passed the circulating wealth of the province before being discharged, or after being received, at Ku Ch'eng-tze. With the reopening of the Siberian frontier, minor controlling centres of wealth have developed at Kashgar, Kulja, and Chuguchak. It is fortunate for the Governor at Urumchi that his lieutenant-governors in these regions are men who prefer to face outward toward Russia, having the Governor at their backs for support, rather than use the newly negotiable economic resources at their disposal to assert their personal political importance.

There is no doubt that the Chinese fully appreciate the position, but, as I have already said, they are yielding perforce to circumstance. The degeneration (or, if you will, the reformation) of China is bleeding them. A political collapse might necessitate the open assertion of Russian control. In the meantime the economic keys of the province, to which the Chinese in modern practice have trusted to lock their political rule, are passing into Russian hands. I do not think that villainous designs can be imputed to the Russians in their forward policy. It is true that the Soviets are developing, almost unaltered, the old forward policy, the *Drang nach Osten,* of Imperial Russia, and that a lot of what they practise does not fit very well with what they preach. It may also be true, as some of us believe who think ourselves farsighted, that the Chinese failure to dominate Mongolia and Chinese Turkestan, the buffer territories for twenty centuries between Europe and Asia, may lead to a direct opposition between East and West along such a frontier as history has never seen for length and provocation of hostility. Yet it must be borne in mind that the Russians are just as truly impelled by historic forces, in securing their hold on these intermediate territories, as are the Chinese in relaxing theirs.

IX

MEETING

CHUGUCHAK disputes with Barköl the horrible fame of being the
most uncomfortably cold place in the world. It is not so much a
question of temperature as of the quality of the cold, the fiendish
malevolence of it, pursuing one from bed to breakfast and then to
bed again. There is coal at some distance in the hills, but either
the supply or the method of working or the transport is inadequate, for the price is in startling comparison with the price in
places like Urumchi or Manass, where the poorest can warm
themselves handsomely for a penny. In Chuguchak the better-
class houses are heated by stoves of the Russian design; furnaces,
that is, built into the walls. They can be stoked with anything you
please, they burn a slow, smouldering fire that has to be renewed
only once in twenty-four hours, and they warm the whole house
with devious flues which go along the walls. In Chuguchak they
are usually fed with either cow-dung or a kind of brushwood,
both of which are brought in to town by Mongols and Qazaqs.
Many of the Chinese have adopted this Russian method, but some
of them also use *ti-k'ang,* which are brick floors heated by flues.
Some of the Russians, moreover, try the old remedy of getting
warmth out of bottles; but all in vain. There is no word for the
cold of Chuguchak but an old provincialism; it is a perishing cold.
I have a friendly regard for cow-dung, when burned in a circular
heap in an iron grate in a well-felted tent; but I think it must be
better in cows than in stoves, for cows are warmer.

In two or three days my friend the Very Great Man left for Russia, on his way to lands where they think they have better things
to talk about than the relative merits of cow-dung and coal. He
went away nested in his trusty felts, but this time in a sleigh, not

a cart, for the snow along the onward journey was beyond all wheels, and was escorted out of town by deputations of the high and concourses of the low; in fact, by everyone but me, for I had " seen him off " the night before. Be it known that the name of Chuguchak is said to derive from the Mongol, and to mean "the wooden bowl," which argues a tradition of serious drinking.[1] The tradition holds, for they drink almost as much in Chuguchak as they do in Ku Ch'eng-tze. Now Chinese wines (or, more truly, spirits) are what one calls, technically, honest. That is, they vary in strength, but from the first drink one knows the course to be covered and the pace to be set; and the next morning is the next morning, not a hangover of the night before. In Chuguchak, however, they have plenty of wines and spirits manufactured by one of the Soviet monopolies, which are full of quips and cranks and wanton wiles. I believe the alcoholic content is controlled, but there must be something weird in the processes of making them. The more highly colored and heavily sweet concoctions, which the Russians like so much, can easily be detected and shunned, the vodkas usually are the soundest drinks they distill, but the brandy is a deadfall.

The first time I drank that brandy, my stomach was more prudent than my head. I awoke the next morning as calm and free as one of Wordsworth's evenings, while everyone else, who had drunk less and kept it down, complained of the feeling that comes of eating bad crab. I have a great respect for the Bolsheviks, on account of many of the things they have accomplished against odds; but their brandy is not one of their successes. The next time I was matched against it, the night before the Great Man made his departure from Central Asia, I drank too little, thinking that I ought not to drink too much (for both Chinese and Russian hospitality is hard to evade), and, having gone to bed sober, awoke

---

[1] I was told that the town takes its name from being set in the valley as in a bowl. It is more likely that it is an old trading post name, from the sale of birchwood bowls, such as the Mongols carry with them in the bosom of the gown, from Siberia. Compare Kukuirghen, "Blue Cloth," near Kuei-hua. The commonest Chinese name for Chuguchak is T'a Ch'eng, more colloquially T'a'rh Ch'eng, City of Tarbagatai. Like almost every town in the province it has also other names. Tarbagatai is more properly Tarbagantai — Marmot Mountains.

half paralyzed. Thus I never saw the Very Great Man any more; at least, not on that arc of the globe. We did indeed foregather again, both of us being born lucky, and our next communion was when we knelt together on the floor of the Vatican and were blessed by our Holy Father the Pope, no less; but what has that to do with this narrative?

But it was a superb night — a Central Asian night. It began at a full-length Chinese dinner and ended at a Russian birthday party, where two or three score people were massed in two tiny rooms and four couples at a time danced in the midst, where was not room enough for one. The music was copious and excellent, the work of three Tatar fiddlers, all of them fiddler-drunk. It was the first time I had seen such a thing; and, believe me, it was an impressive condition of beatitude. The general plan was that one fiddler should fiddle while two lay handy, snoring under a protective table in the corner. When the fiddling fiddler sagged off his chair, one of the others would be roused out, and after tilting a bottle to his mouth he would tuck his fiddle under his chin and play all the music of All the Russias. Up to that time I had not taken much stock in the famous Russian melancholy, of which I had seen displays in dance halls and different low places of the China Coast; but this was something else again. It was the Russian melancholy, beyond all doubt, turbulent and surging, and it turned you inside out and did you good. These three fellows, as a man very carefully explained to me, were not of the ordinary kind that deal in tiddly polkas and folk dances; they were the Three Fiddlers of Chuguchak, three dissolute Tatar brothers. When you were giving a party, you went out and sought them in a ditch. You took them to your house and supplied them with drink for the ten or twelve or fourteen hours of a Russian party. Then you pushed them out of your door, and when the next man gave a party he found them in some other ditch.

Besides the music, we had Russian things to eat, which are so much better than Russian things to drink; sausages innumerable, salt fish, raw fish, and pickled fish miraculous, and red caviar, which is as cheap as you please throughout Siberia. We had also Russian dances, which are better still. Every imaginable dance was danced that night; singly, in couples, and in pairs of couples. Best of all is the dance which needs long Cossack boots; one youth takes the floor, whirling and stamping and sinking until he ought to be squatted on his heels, from which position he shoots out one booted leg and then the other, until at last he seems to be seated in the air a few inches off the ground, with his heels alternately drumming the floor out in front of him. Then a girl comes into the circle to dance a variation of the same dance opposite him. They play each other up, coquetting in unimaginable gyrations, until in the end they fly off at opposite tangents into the outer circle, exhausted. The tension breaks, and the drinks go round again.

A number of the people there were Little Russians, and over and over again they sang the heart-compelling song of Little Russia — "Volga, Volga, Mother Volga." I sang it too; it is a music of lament, and one of the very finest in that kind, but, not being able to get the hang of the Russian words, I sang it with the words of "She Was Poor, But She Was Honest." A shame, perhaps, but what would you? One has emotions, and in Central Asia one must do one's best. I found it very soulful.

Of the host's family, every one, including the youngest child of about nine, could play the fiddle, the balalaika, and two or three kinds of guitar or mandoline. Most of the guests also could play, and had brought the things they played, and did play. Plenty of children were about; indeed, as I remember, the birthday we were celebrating was the eleventh birthday of a daughter of the host. The children were big-eyed with joy, but no more pleased than the rest of us. Everyone was so pleased with himself and everybody else, with the salt fish and the vodka, the dancing and the brandy, the music and the talk (but all I could do was grin), that it seemed a shame to have to run away for fear of the headache that visited me in the morning after all. Every good fellow came up in turn and said, perfectly plain to see if not to hear, "I cannot understand your talk, nor you mine, but at least we can have a drink together," and thereafter, more often than not, leaned on my shoulder and told me all the sorrows of his life and exile.

One saying on which they relied as on a talisman of good-fellowship pressed sorely on my determination of sobriety. This was the lethal word *barmasu*. At first I thought it an urgent Russian exhortation to get drunk with the least possible delay; but no, it was not that. It was an appeal they made in the confidence that I would recognize it. I went to a Russian-speaking Chinese for enlightenment. Was it the Russian idea of some provincial Chinese word? No, he said, but together with me he hunted it down. *"Barmasu, barmasu!"* entreated the Russians, hanging over our shoulders and pouring drinks down their gullets, as if in demonstration, then exhibiting the empty glasses, bottom up. *"Amerikanski barmasu!"* and they did it again. "Aha, yes! Indeed!" cried the Chinese. "I remember! Undoubtedly it is the American *barmasu.*" Then he explained that in 1925 two American scholars had passed that way. They had come from the Caves of the Thousand Buddhas, at Tun-huang in Kan-su, and they had followed the North Road from Urumchi to Siberia, heading for the Siberian railway and Peking. It was most true; they had halted at Chuguchak while their Russian visés were devolving from higher quarters, and they had taught all Chuguchak to drink in the American way, *barmasu.* Then I had it, with a great shout; *barmasu* was "bottoms up!"

I was amazed at the amount that I could understand, what with bits of French and German flung about. All of these people belonged to the exile class. They were outcasts of the Russian Revolution, who had been flung across the border. Some of the men had served in anti-Revolutionary armies. One had seen the horrors of the winter campaign in Mongolia, when a broken force fought its way past Kobdo and Uliassutai, to join the forces with which Baron Ungern-Sternberg established a White Terror at Urga, but after appalling months of which he had no connected memory had drifted back to Hsin-chiang. He had survived this although he had been rejected for service in the war as physically unfit. Most of the exiles had caught up scraps of existence in Chinese territory, where they had waited to see what would happen in Russia. A few of them in good time had registered as citizens of the Union of Soviet Socialist Republics; others had waited overlong, intending to make sure that the Soviets had indeed made good their rule. These people were now trying to secure amnesty and citizenship through the Soviet Consulate; but they were being made to crawl for it. It was inevitable in such a broken society that spying and tale-bearing should have grown to be a minor terror. Only a very few were irreconcilable Whites, and most of these were men whose record in the anti-Revolutionary wars debarred them from amnesty. Most of those who were scrambling to make their peace at the Soviet Consulate, however, were trying to ingratiate themselves by spying on their fellows. It must have been easy. At a party like this, the moment that men were well gone in drink they harked back to the old days. They sang the old songs, — many of them forbidden, — and one after another, unable to deny himself the sentimental hope of momentary sympathy from me, a foreigner, would come up to me and boast that he had been an officer, that he was no Bolshevik, and say all manner of foolish things.

The next morning, I knew, the first out of bed would be the first at the Consulate to tell on the others. I perceived that it would be well for me to talk much — and innocently. My position in regard to the Russian consular authorities was difficult enough. I counted more than a little on their goodwill. Yet I knew perfectly well that they were bound to report all the doings of any traveler in these regions, regarded by Moscow as highly political. Even if the people on the spot were convinced of my honesty, could see that I had no "mission" (word of awe to all Russians), they must take care to report to Moscow, for the sake of discipline, anything that might cast the suspicion of "secret service" on my travels. Were the superiors not to do so, and a scarehead report be passed on without their knowledge by some subordinate eager for promotion, it would be a stab in the back for them. Even good men — and some of the Russian officials in Chinese Turkestan were first-class men for their jobs — are hampered by a system that values espionage so highly. It was a difficult situation. Had I seemed to keep a watch on myself, it would have been told at the Consulate the next day that I had been prying into the affairs of the Russian community. Therefore I showed myself talking freely and having a riotously good time, with little (but not too little) interest in politics and plenty of interest in people and dances. Yet even so, I wonder whether they counted it unto me for righteousness.

Then at last, the party showing no signs of coming to an end, I fled into the frosty starlight. The Great Man lent me the sleigh which had been lent to him, and I was driven over the creaking snow in the streets down from the "bazar"—the Russian Concession of Imperial days, now only the Russian quarter — to the Chinese trading quarter where I lodged. No one was astir except an occasional late returner, holding a bobbing paper lantern in his hand, or a knot of patroling Qazaq police — useful fellows who speak no language but their own, whose duty is to beat up any night wanderer who is not in a respectable sleigh or provided with a lantern; a duty they can perform all the better for not being able to listen to excuses.

The next morning Moses and I regarded each other in the loneliness of Chuguchak. Before his going, the Great Man had helped me no little at the Russian Consulate, as indeed he had already helped me at the Consulate-General at Urumchi. The situation stood thus: my wife had been able to get a Russian visé to travel through Siberia, but I was not sure of a visé to enter Siberia to meet her at railhead. For one thing, the sort of human nature from which not even officials are exempt makes it seem somehow easier to grant permits for a woman to travel through "political" territories to join her husband than to grant the husband permission to cross cherished boundaries to fetch his wife. The Consul-General at Urumchi, again, though I think he was reasonably assured that I was not a bundle of "secrets" rolling through Central Asia acquiring more "secrets," might well fail to persuade Moscow of the accuracy of his observation. In such an affair the most revolutionary Commissar would be inclined to look up the dossiers of the old régime, to see what used to be the attitude toward stray travelers in Imperial days. I knew that for myself, both from reading and from my slight acquaintance with Russians of the old régime: in the Russia of the Tsars, if the reports on a traveler in Central Asia read innocently, the conclusion drawn was that either the officials on the spot were stupid or they had been bribed.

The Consul-General at Urumchi, within the two years that he had been there, had been more than kind in assisting two parties of Americans in their travels, but both of these parties had had other introductions, cross-references which could be compared at Moscow. I suppose I was a more difficult object of political charity; it was true that my wife's credentials had been satisfactorily passed upon, and that she was being allowed to use the well-guarded Russian entries of Chinese Turkestan to meet me, but as for me myself, I had popped out of Mongolia into Hsin-chiang, and, for all anyone could prove, I suppose I might have been " spying " on Russian activities. It was the official attitude toward Central Asia that was at fault, not the personal attitude toward me of the Russian consular representatives in Chinese territory. The Consul-General had telegraphed from Urumchi to Moscow, asking for permission for me to go as far into Russian territory as Semipalatinsk; but when I reached Chuguchak, I found that a denial had been returned from Moscow. The Consul at Chuguchak, however, showed himself kind and friendly. He spoke German fluently, as did one of the minor officers of the Consulate, a man from the old Baltic provinces. He had no particular knowledge of the Mongol and Qazaq tribes in the territory to which he was appointed; but indeed, I was disappointed throughout the province in my hope of finding a Russian who had special knowledge of that kind. Our conversation was too limited to be very interesting, — at Urumchi I had been able to speak through interpreters in French, English, or Chinese, — which was a pity, because the people at the Consulate, as usual, seemed much more " alive " and more interested in what their own brains could do for them than the other Russians.

The Consul, though unable to permit me to enter Russian territory officially, did me the great personal kindness of promising that when my wife's arrival was reported I might go as far as the Russian frontier post at Bakhti, over the border, to meet her and bring her back through the Chinese post. He also dispatched telegrams for me to Semipalatinsk, and through him I received one of the telegrams my wife sent from Semipalatinsk to say that she would start alone. Unfortunately, most of the telegrams were smothered by the heavy snow, which had drifted over the single telegraph line in many places, breaking down the wire and shutting off communication for days at a time. After the one word that my wife was going to start by herself, there was a silence of more than two weeks.

Before learning that the Russians would not let me go to Semipalatinsk, I negotiated with the Chinese for a permit to leave Chinese territory and reënter it. The lieutenant-governor of the Tarbagatai region being away, my business was all done at the regional Bureau of Foreign Affairs. The office of Secretary for Foreign Affairs was held by a strange old man. He had been a great Viceroy under the Manchu Empire and in the past generation had several times traveled from this remote frontier of the Empire and seen the face of the Emperor himself. When I was told that he was a " Bannerman " I naturally expected to meet a Manchu of the old tradition, and to hear the speech of Peking in its courtly perfection. On the way to the yamen in which, after exercising powers almost as arbitrary as the direct mandates of the Son of Heaven, he now spends his business hours in issuing licenses to carters and sleigh drivers to cross the frontier, I scrambled in my brain to assemble a parade of my most lordly-humble phrases. It was a shock to be received by a hale old barbarian who knew only a few words of the corrupt local patois, not being able even to read the Chinese of my passport. The room was littered with more swords and rifles than seemed becoming in a civil yamen, and there was a throng of blunt-featured, burly men, most of them armed. Their language, I could tell, was neither Mongol nor Turki, and, though their dress was Chinese of a kind, they did not look precisely like Chinese or Manchus. I found out later that I had been misled by the term *ch'i-jen,* " bannerman," and that they and their old chieftain were Solons, of that people of which I have spoken, wardens as by right of these marches.

When I was not at the office of one official or another, I called on the charming Chinese postmaster, a Northern Chinese who had forgotten most of his English in favor of Russian. I played chess also once or twice with the Russian Consul, who skelped me for fair, and I even raked up three books to read: a school edition of the

Chesterfield letters (of the best use as a stay and comfort to one dealing much with officials), a French survey of Germany (also a school book), and a horrible French novel, *Le vice de Lydie*. Lydia's vice was that she was shy of marriage, and most of the book was a description of what she was missing.

Almost every day I went also to see a Russian couple, of whom one spoke a little French and the other less German. The one who spoke less German took me out duck shooting. We drove in a sleigh out of the town into the encompassing snow until we reached a watercourse and a pond,[1] beside which there stood a mill. The miller was a Russian, a most curious and peaceful survivor of days of violence. In the period of civil wars just after the Russian Revolution he had commanded a freebooting force of about two thousand peasants, who made a stronghold for themselves in the frontier ranges. These men seem to have had no political object; they were peasants of the Siberian frontier type, hot against Tsarist and Bolshevik alike because the civil wars had made their farms untenable. They withdrew to the mountains under this illiterate leader and turned their savagery against all the world. The Chinese fostered them, privily, because they were of use in keeping the conflicting armies out of Chinese territory. When the Bolsheviks had stabilized Siberia, most of these outlaws, having had enough of the swingeing ferocity of their mountain life to last them for a good many years, faltered and broke away from their leader, entering Siberia again to take up farms. This man, their captain, however, was badly " wanted " on the Russian side, but the Chinese allowed him asylum and he was now settled at this mill, in the employ of a Chinese firm. He and his family had made themselves a peasant farmyard and a log house with a Russian platform-stove to sleep on, like an exaggerated Chinese k'ang. The man was a bearded giant, of slow action and little speech. The violence of his days of fight and flight and leadership had passed from him; there was no notion of command in him; he had become a peasant again. We went out and dug holes for ourselves in the snow, where, powdered for concealment with

[1] The pond must have been fed by warm springs, as it showed no signs of freezing.

QAZAQ CARAVAN: SPRING MIGRATION

MRS. LATTIMORE AND HER SLED NEAR CHUGUCHAK

snow, we waited for the duck in the rasping cold of a bitter evening. A rusty sunset flared over the white wastes until a soft blue light came in edgewise and soothed its harshness. The ducks began to flight.

Thus the days turned past me, assembled in idleness and dropping away one by one in nervous tension. It ought to have taken ten days by sleigh between Semipalatinsk and Chuguchak; sixteen were told over, and there was no word of my wife.

She traveled alone from Peking to Manchuli; from Manchuli by the main Siberian railway to Novo-Sibersk, and thence to the South by a branch line ending at Semipalatinsk. Although diverging so far from the International Sleeping Car Route along which a few travelers are transported as it were in sealed compartments (and usually, by their own predisposition, with sealed minds) through Bugaboo-land, she was treated always with the greatest consideration by every class of official. She was granted the courtesy of special permits which ensured the minimum of trouble at the dreaded Russian Customs. By reason of unavoidable delays the time limit of her visé had expired before she could leave Russia, but even this bit of red tape was cut without question. Every Russian official she encountered did everything in his power, not only to set her on her way, but to ensure her comfort and safety. By Russian travelers on the railways and Russians at Semipalatinsk she was treated with a kindness without which it would have been impossible for one knowing so little Russian to make the journey.

As her journey had been planned for the late summer, we had counted on the Russian motor service to bring her from Semipalatinsk to Chuguchak in between a day and a half and three days. That service, however, was in abeyance because of the snow. The one available interpreter in Semipalatinsk arranged for her to travel on, not by a regular passenger sleigh, but with a sled train carrying matches. The chief reason for this was that a courier from the Chinese Consulate at Semipalatinsk was going with the same convoy, and as he spoke both Russian and Turki, and she could talk with him in Chinese, she had in him an interpreter and guide. The Steppes of the Great Horde, across a part of which she had to travel, are reputed to be a "pole of cold," with a lower average winter temperature than the North Pole. The snow throughout Siberia, as in Mongolia and Zungaria and clear away to the Himalayas, was heavy that winter beyond usual record. The freight sleds did not travel the accustomed passenger stages, but as a rule kept on the road for eight hours and spent the next eight hours in feeding and resting the ponies — though often the eight hours on the road were stretched to twelve and more. Instead of staying at the posthouses at the regular stages, she slept in Qazaq winter huts, buried under the snow, among the Russian sleigh drivers and the Qazaqs and their lambs and babies and calves and hunting dogs and international love affairs. The convoy had fewer drivers than sleds, and once, during a snowstorm, she had to drive her own sled. Even when the road was better the convoy never went beyond a walking pace. Every day she had no food but frozen bread thawed in tea, with occasionally a stew of mutton or horse-flesh.

Because the telegrams sent for me by courtesy of the Consul at Chuguchak (who even refused payment for the service) had not reached Semipalatinsk before she left, being delayed along the snow-encumbered line, she did not even know whether I should be at Chuguchak to meet her. The arrangement made by the Consul that I should go "privately" across the frontier to meet her on her arrival at Bakhti, twelve or fifteen miles away, also broke down; because, I suppose, of the weather, or because she reached the frontier at last under the escort of a Chinese of official character.

Thus it was on the seventeenth day without news, when I was at the house of the French-German-speaking couple, disguising my dejection somewhat, but unable not to reckon over to myself the things that might have happened to her on that road, among those people, in that snow, that a strange Chinese in many furs burst in. He had tried me several times in Russian and Turki before I tried him in Chinese, then he tugged me into the street, boasting in a rush of words his prowess and chivalry in bringing my wife to me. She stood, almost unrecognizable to me in her furs, beside a small heaped sleigh in the wintry street. She had brought off the incredible, and we were together, and in Central Asia.

X

ON BECOMING AN EXPEDITION

THUS we had vindicated our folly, having concerted in all success our meeting in a hole in a corner of Central Asia with such an un-Cook-like name as Chuguchak. We had each of us accomplished, alone, the hardest and most uncertain part of our traveling. This we had done simply, as travelers. From now on we were, by ample modern precedent, no longer travelers, but an expedition. We could lounge and stare together as expeditions do, along roads not perfectly understood, perhaps, but at least known, with no more noble duty than the invention of counter-spellings to set up against the spellings on the maps of others, hopefully confounding, in the cause of knowledge, things already well and earnestly confused.

This matter of becoming an expedition had unfortunately slipped our attention in Peking, so that we had not provided ourselves with the distinctive expeditionary insignia of stamped letterheads and personal titles. My wife had even submitted, in filling out her Consular papers, to the description of " housewife." I had fallen into a loose way of regarding myself as a person interested in people, rather than as a person interesting to people, as a true expeditionary should be.

If only we had thought about the expedition in time, we should undoubtedly have enjoyed the superior advantage of being received with smirks as well as mere courtesy during our travels, for travelers by my observation are apt to be treated as people and expeditionaries as personages.

That letterhead would have looked extremely well too; as thus : —

The First

Lattimore-Moses Independent Expedition

OWEN LATTIMORE, Leader (*Sometimes*)
ELEANOR LATTIMORE, Leader (*Usually*)
MOSES, Assistant

This requires, perhaps, a little elaboration (publicity is the regular expeditionary phrase). "First" means that you intend to do it again if the bluff holds. "Independent" means that you print in the newspapers the name of your tooth-paste makers, but do not state on your income-tax returns that you have been paid for it. We have not revealed the brand of tooth paste used by us, because we ran out of it too soon.

But beware of second thoughts; an expedition deferred maketh the press sick. In Chinese Turkestan we were too late. There is no printing press in the province except the one reserved by the Governor for printing paper money.

Whether expedition or no, we did not move from Chuguchak for about a fortnight. As I have said before, the commercial importance of Chuguchak is in goods in transit to and from Siberia, a traffic of long hauls and a traffic less and less in Chinese hands. The effect is that most of the carts on the road are the heavy two-wheeled carts used for hauling cargo, while the four-wheeled *t'ai-ch'e,* or "stage carts," on the model of the Russian telega, preferred by the Chinese merchants in their journeys because of their better speed, are in irregular supply. The Shantung carter who had brought Moses and our sausage-supplied companion lingered for several days in Chuguchak, but at the first offer of a fare felt bound to return to Urumchi. Pony feed, he said to us mournfully, was much higher in Chuguchak. The sorrow was his, but he must attend to business; but first he urged a plan on us. He would sell his light cart, buy a heavy two-wheeled cart and good ponies, put a wooden house on the cart, and carry me, my belongings, my *t'ai-t'ai* (lady), and my Moses all through the province, and all for nothing. Only, when we reached India, we in return would ship him from India to China at our charge. "Look you," he said, "this is from the Lao T'ien-yeh, from Old Man God. Moses and I are earth-brothers, being born in neighboring villages; and you — never was such a man, to speak the Tientsin speech and accord with Our People in heart. Also, by the word of Moses, the t'ai-t'ai is excellent among t'ai-t'ai, knowing the road, without excess of talk, making not a great many businesses when she goes out of doors" — that is, when she travels. "Thus we travel as one family. I have been on the South Road in my time, and I know many words of the turban-talk (Turki). When we come to India, Moses has enough of the foreign talk to bring me back to China There we await the return of the Young Master, and lean on his destiny to become rich. My fortune in this country is but half-good. Two wives have I had, and no sons; yet I have laid money by. I would return to China and breed sons; but passports are hard to get, for us common people. In the train of the Young Master I could pass the mountains to India. It is a good *pan-fa,* way of management." I must say, I leaned to his persuasion, for he was a hardy, villainous man, of an excellent kind for travel, who for the sake of his own profit would save us from being cheated by others. I could not take him on, because we planned to travel in the mountains with pack trains, which did not fit with his carting skill. Yet he gave me an earnest of what could be done in this province by following the Tientsin lead.

No other carter showed up for a number of days, but we set up happy house in Chuguchak, my wife needing the rest after her Siberian travel. The owner of the caravanserai was a fat, genial fellow, the leader of the Chinese trading community, a notable robber in the past. He had come to this border in earlier, wilder days and made a name for himself plundering the trade roads and the nomads. When he had made his name great enough, he had set up as a trader, being by then well able to secure the safety of his own dealings. He was a true Tientsin man, thoroughly capable, and a man of his word in business as in thieving. He had failed, however, to get himself a son; an evil fate which the Chinese are always ready to blame on a sinful past. In the end he bought a Qazaq baby, a little imp of twelve or so at the time. talking Chinese with a proper Tientsin twang. Relatives from

Tientsin had several times come to Chuguchak, it was said, looking for fortune and favor from the old man; but he had put them
all out of the way.   Either they had died in the mountains or some
upset had put them in prison.   Not long after we left Chuguchak
he came to his own end; a man whom he had broken shot him with
a revolver, and his chief partner also, and gravely wounded the
postmaster.   The affair made a stir as far away as Urumchi.

The old man had private grounds at the back of the inn, and a
summerhouse in the best Chinese style, walled apart, with a garden
before it hidden under snow, and an avenue of gracile, leafless
poplars.   In a corner of our room was a great built-up brick bed,
heated like an oven and enclosed by carved woodwork that made
it like a pavilion within a pavilion.   The rest of the room was
warmed by a Russian stove, and, though our feet were cold
if we trusted them too long to the brick floor, we were well
pleased with our quarters.   Moses popped in and out to see
that we wanted nothing, and twice a day our food, rich, Chinese,
and hot, was brought to us from the inn kitchens, while we could
make coffee and cocoa for ourselves on our alcohol stove.

Before we left, the lieutenant-governor of the Tarbagatai returned, a man I was well pleased to see because of his fame and his
unusual character as a Chinese empire-builder.   He was known
throughout the province as Li Pai-k'a'rh.[1]   Li the Native.   The
name showed that he was born in the province of Chinese stock
settled there for more than a generation.   He was a man of a
courage and vigor rare among the provincially bred, a man of the
stoutest frontier mettle.   He spoke more than one native language, and Russian as well, could ride and live like a Mongol or
Qazaq, and handle the tribes at his will.   Nor had he relapsed, on
achieving success, into the sloth which the Chinese too generally

---

[1] The term *pai-k'a'rh* is one of the most curious in the province. It comes
into the Chinese, through the Turki, from a Persian word meaning "not
working," "no good." The Chinese use it for anything cheap, inferior, spuri-
ous, unserviceable, impracticable. The slang name for a Chinese born in the
province is lao pai-k'a'rh. Like most slang names, it is pejorative, and the
people to whom it is applied do not use it of themselves. It implies that a Turke-
stan-born Chinese is inferior to a China-born Chinese — "nearly as bad as a
native," as one might say, using the term "native" in its lowest sense. As so
often happens, the name applied to the lieutenant-governor was one of derision
used in back-handed admiration, according to the racy humor of the people.

think decorous. As a step up in his career he had married a well-bred Tientsin wife. She rebelled at the idea of nothing but milk for breakfast, — the true Chinese hold milk, butter, and cheese unclean; only those who have taken to Mongol " barbarities " will touch them, — but he disciplined her in the best Chinese manner. " My mother drinks milk," he said; " are you better than my mother?" — for a Chinese woman at her own peril sets herself above her mother-in-law. He had just returned from a visit to his home in the Ili valley. So far from traveling in the carted dignity of official precedent, he had taken the shorter, little-used byroad through the mountains, by way of Ebi Nor and the Borotala, and this in winter snow, riding all the way and sleeping in the open. Moreover, — an unprecedented, not to say unthinkable, thing among Chinese of gentle breeding, — his girl-daughter rode all the way at his side.

Li the Native's most prominent service to the old Governor had been his masterly handling of Annenkoff, a White Hope of the anti-Bolshevik forces during the evil years of 1920–21. He commanded a detachment of Cossacks, driven out of Siberia but still holding well together, and capable of founding an independent Russian power in either Mongolia or Hsin-chiang, in conjunction with the nomad tribes, against both Russians and Chinese. When, after bickerings among their leaders, the amorphous armies of anti-Soviet exiles about Chuguchak began to break up, some of the men under minor leaders moving off into Mongolia, Annenkoff with his formidable little following began a direct march along the North Road, aiming apparently for Kan-su province. The Chinese, though afraid of him, showed him no hostility, being unable to cope with his troops. They induced him, however, not to bring his main body into Urumchi. Then, according to the most usual relation of the story, they provisioned him as if for the difficult journey to Kan-su (there are eighteen desert marches between Hami and Ngan-hsi Chou, in Kan-su) and started him off again. It appears that Li understood a danger in this disposal of the Russians; were they to prove that troops in fair numbers could move across the Gobi barrier of the province, they might hire themselves to some general in Kan-su and return at the head of a hostile Chinese army to overthrow the established order in the New Dominion. Therefore, while the Cossacks were on the road between Urumchi and Hami, a message was sent to Annenkoff, inviting him to return for a formal reception and celebration of farewell with the Governor, allowing his troops to proceed slowly. In his innocence he returned with only a very small guard, and was thrown into prison. Li the Native counted shrewdly on his knowledge of Russian character. The Cossacks, instead of facing about and bluffing their leader out of the hold of the Chinese, lost their last grip on themselves. The officers quarreled for leadership and the men, unled, were without purpose. The Chinese disarmed them. Some they dispatched in small parties with caravans bound through Mongolia to Kuei-hua; others were moved on out of the province to the borders of Kan-su, where they were interned in the Tun-huang oasis. Scribbled epigraphs of these lonely prisoners on the frescoes of the Caves of the Thousand Buddhas attest their forlorn captivity.

The further story of Annenkoff is remarkable. As it is commonly related in the lands Beyond the Great Wall, he was placed under the guard of opium smokers, from whom in his idleness he learned the vice. The Governor (this again is the popular relation) decreed that when he could smoke two Chinese *liang,* or about two and two-thirds ounces, a day (an enormous quantity, enough to poison several men) he might be released. In the end he was released, for the Governor said that he need fear nothing from a man so far gone in opium.

This is a story of the kind that may be called popular history, there being nothing to show that the Governor or Li his lieutenant deliberately planned to make an opium smoker of their captive. I fancy that most prison guards in the province are opium smokers, and Annenkoff was a dissipated man who might readily take up the handiest vice to pass away the time.[1] The latter end

[1] The story of Annenkoff, the Governor, and the opium, if not a factual record, is good popular history in its appreciation of the characters of the people concerned. Popular history can rapidly become true legend in Central Asia, among thinly scattered peoples differing widely in language, habit, and religion. Thus I heard a charming legendary version of the story, from a caravan man in Mongolia, in which it was told that Annenkoff was confined in a hollow tree and told that he must learn to smoke opium as the price of release.

of him was that after his release he went to Kan-su, where he settled, probably in the Nan Shan highlands, to breed an improved strain of ponies for the Chinese market, using Russian stallions which he bought from among the Russian refugees. In 1925 Kan-su province was taken over by Feng Yü-hsiang, the " Christian " General, who began about that time to receive at Kalgan munitions of war brought from Russia across Mongolia by motor transport, along the Kiakhta-Urga-Kalgan route. In 1926 he seized Annenkoff and presented him to the Soviets. The former Cossack commander, to save his life, then entered the Soviet service. His " conversion " made an excellent newspaper announcement throughout Russia, but especially in the Cossack communities. He seems to have been returned by the Russians to the service of Feng, to train and lead light horse; and to have died, it is reported, in a skirmish in Inner Mongolia, against cavalry of Chang Tso-lin, who were scouting toward the Kalgan position of Feng, being hit by a stray bullet.

Li the Native, after engineering the removal of Annenkoff, was marked for promotion. After being employed on special missions he was appointed to the Tarbagatai, a post for which he was well fitted by his knowledge of nomad tribes and his understanding of Russians. He was a great burly man, a "man of the people," without the manners of the old-fashioned "cultured" official. We were hardly seated in his reception room when, after a friendly greeting, he ordered brandy. It was a three-star brandy, brought from Tientsin, having traveled through Mongolia by camel caravan, a better draught than the Russian brand. Three sherry glasses of this we put down, as fast as they could be filled, dispatching them barmasu, in what I had learned to respect as the right Chuguchak manner. Li the Native was widely known for his prowess at a drinking bout. I wondered if this were a diplomatic approach he had perfected for Russian use. When the brandy was down, he set to business. " Let me point out," he said in a friendly but blunt way, " that in this province you ought to follow the provincial regulations by registering wherever you go. The Governor's orders are very strict." I bowed, guessing what had happened. " I have been too long in your noble coun-

try," I answered, "not to learn manners. You will find that my
card is in the gatehouse of your yamen, and my passport in the
Bureau of Foreign Affairs. Others have been slow in referring
so small a matter to you on your return from Ili." Forthwith,
men were set running. I could guess by the yells heard faintly
from outer courts that orderlies were being hauled away from their
opium pipes on the k'ang to rout my passport (a provincial passport from the Governor himself at Urumchi) out of the Bureau
of Foreign Affairs. After I had given the lieutenant-governor news of mutual friends at Urumchi, I took my leave, and
he came all the way out to see me mount and ride away, a mark
of extreme courtesy.

Two or three hours later, as we were setting out for a walk, we
heard a tumult approaching through the inn yards. Moses burst
in. " The Great Man Li," he announced, and cleared the room in
a whirl. I went to the door. There came the Great Man, accompanied by a compact escort of handy-looking cavalrymen, real
soldiers in a smart uniform of good khaki, very different fellows
from the scarecrows in coarse gray cotton cloth, wadded with raw
cotton, who fill the "regiments of the line." Li the Native ranged
his barrel-bellied ambling pony alongside the rail at the top of the
steps, put out a foot, and came tumbling down over the rail; being
loath to soil himself in the thawed ooze at the foot of the steps. He
had brought back my passport himself, endorsed and made out
for the return, and after talking in a jolly way for half an hour,
looking over my armory and field glasses and professing disappointment that I had no telescopic sights, rolled out to the doorway,
clambered to the rail, bumped down on his pony, and went bucket-
ing off in a distracted blare of inharmonious trumpets.

We spent several more days waiting for a cart and going for
muddy walks in the three towns of Chuguchak, Han, Man, and
Huei, the Chinese, Manchu, and Mohammedan towns of before
the Revolution. Off at one side is the bazar, the old Russian concession, and, as if trade had been attracted toward it, the Chinese
trading population is mostly concentrated in a vague suburb, outside of the city walls but leaning against them. The suburb
throughout the province is a convenience to the trader and espe-

cially the traveler, because the city gates are closed at night. Thus the traveler puts up at an inn near the gates but outside of them, and the trader also comes out of the gates to lie in wait for the traveler and supply the inns. The earliest city of Chuguchak was Emil (or Imil or Omyl), founded in the neighborhood, but probably not on the actual site of the present town. It was a city of the Khara-Khitai, who in the twelfth century, after being driven first from Northern and then from Western China, passed through Zungaria to settle in the Emil and Ili valleys,[1] with their pleasant bays opening into what are now the provinces of Semipalatinsk and Semirechensk. There may have been a still earlier city on the Emil; if so, it perished without record. From the twelfth century, however, in spite of recurrent wars among the Central Asian peoples, and tides of conquest turning out of Mongolia through Zungaria to the West, each conquest in succession strove to lay a permanent hold on these pleasant territories, leaving in default of written chronicles the buried bases of a few towns and the burial mounds of a few kings and chieftains. By the town of Emil passed Pian de Carpine in 1246 and William of Rubruck in 1253,[2] on their different embassies to the Khans of the Mongols, the successors of Jenghis.

The three towns of our time are almost empty, the population huddling outside of the walls in the bazar quarters. Within the walls we saw signs of open fields under the snow, and rabbit tracks crossed the snow in bold patterns. In the Manchu city we saw a Taoist[3] temple, small, but built with dignity in terraces rising up against the city wall. In it we found an old priest, a simple, witless peasant who had drifted there in the old days when

---

[1] This Emil was built about 1125. The dynasty of the Khara-Khitai was founded by a prince known to the Chinese as Yeh-lü Ta-shih, who himself derived from the Khitan or Liao dynasty in Northern China, which was destroyed by the Nü-chen Tatars. The Khara-Khitai kingdom was called by the Chinese the Western (Hsi) Liao.

[2] Not to mention Friar Andrew of Longjumeau, and possibly Friar Ascelin, about the year 1250.

[3] Taoism, in a degraded form, appears to have been the only religion imported by the Chinese or their Manchu rulers into Central Asia, in their modern occupation. I do not remember to have seen a single Buddhist temple. Nor did I see any Taoist priests who were not Kan-su men, or of Kan-su stock. The only official recognition of the temples is that the priests are feed on occasional festivals, or for special services, such as prayer for rain, by the local magistrates.

the Manchus ruled and the temples were subsidized; a sad man, who mewed himself in a tiny room on a faintly warmed k'ang and remembered better days.   Besides this temple and the drum tower, the navel of the city, few Manchu monuments remain, and it is doubtful if there be any monuments older than the Manchu dynasty.

Life was brisker in the suburbs, with a grain market, and markets for skins, and bazars for Russian goods and Turki cloth and leather boots displayed by merchants from the South Road. Qazaqs and a few Mongols entered the streets during the day, and many sleds laden with brushwood or cow-dung for fuel.   Before we left the sleds were dragging dirtily through a slush of snow and swill in the streets.   The coming thaw had made little advance in the outer country, but in the warmer town it was already at work.   Gangs of men, many of them soldiers working for a few extra pence, pottered about the edges of the mess, clearing some of it away, but when they had spread the swill out thinner by sweeping it with brooms, and shoveled off the upper layer of decayed snow, there remained still a good two feet of snow packed and trampled and frozen almost as hard as ice.   On the skirts of the town the crows were beginning to take an interest in old nests, lodged at a great height in disreputable colonies in tall poplars. Each glowing evening they debated more loudly in ragged parliaments, and as they talked over their first recurrent ideas of home, the true presage of spring, we for our part grew more eager and restless for the road.

XI

NOMADS OF THE WESTERN MARCHES

"You might as well move," said the carter in a friendly tone to his off-side trace pony, which had fallen in the mud again, its breath rattling like a decayed engine, "because I am going to beat you so that if you were a wooden bench you would have to go, never say a horse." That was about the tenor of our return to Urumchi. We had hired the first "stage-cart" to be had in Chuguchak, only to find after we started that the carter was far known for having the worst ponies on the road. He was also known for his humor and wit, and it was a standing joke, well suited to the humor current in those countries, that he always got the pick of the travelers, men paying a premium for speed, always brought them days overdue to the end of their road, yet never had them dissatisfied. It was his weakness that he had an uncommon skill in the Central Asian and Chinese ways of horse doctoring, as well with knives and needles as with the more rarely used decoctions poured down the throat. As inn by inn we picked up gossip along the road, we heard that it was his practice to buy the cast ponies of others, trusting to his horse-fair faking skill to keep them alive, but often running it too fine. On the way to Chuguchak he had lost one pony, and out of the advance installment we had paid over to him he had bought another "lantern," as they call them in the New Dominion, a pony through whose ribs a light would glow. He was both honest and a rascal, a "lewd fellow of the baser sort," and in all a right Tientsin vagabond. He was in debt so heavily along the road that he declared he must make his next journey in a different direction; but, as he said cheerfully one day when a wheel came off, "You may be traveling for pleasure, but I travel for fun."

On the whole he suited us well enough. We had by long use become callous to the sight of ponies covered with raw sores, kept open by daily flicking of the lash to make them trot. We were in no hurry to reach Urumchi, the slow pace of the cart on the heavy roads of the spring thaw gave us time for long walks, and halts at several towns gave us time to see more of the country. I had planned to buy a pony for my wife at Chuguchak, so that we could both ride, but the market there proved not so good as at Urumchi, and more expensive, owing to the demand for cart ponies on the Siberian haul. My own pony had been carefully handled during his long rest, but was never truly fit, and broke down again before we reached Urumchi, where I cast him. Thus for a large part of the time both of us, and Moses too, rode in the cart.

In Chuguchak the thaw was well on, the streets running with slush which froze again at night. In the open country the snow held better, but it too was wasting and long tufts of sere chih-chi grass began to spread a thin yellow gleam over it. We took a sled for the long double-stage to Dorbujing, where the cart had been left. Our first check was at a small stream, where the bridging snow had collapsed and the way was blocked with heavy carts laden with wool, mired hub deep in mud and snow. Teams of fourteen and sixteen mules and ponies had been tallied on to each of them, laboring and weltering, but when we had heaved our own way over, in half an hour of sweat and flurry, they were still there. The road had then an easy downward trend and we made gay time over good snow. First a noble sunset out of Mongolia, and then that true twilight of the gods, the first veils of night dropping gently over great snows, steadied us to the essential loneliness of Central Asia and the sustained impulses of the road and travel. In that miraculous light we passed first a pony newly dead, with carrion birds of a more than ordinary size already lurching unsteadily beside it, gorged to the crop; a savagery not unfitting to that raw country. Then we saw a riderless pony, trotting in no hurry, but purposefully. It wheeled into the snow to let us by, watching us with a falsely uninterested eye, then took the road again. A quarter of a mile on we met a Mongol, a Mongol unhorsed, a woeful sight. He was breathless with running on unwonted legs, but could still curse us with certitude for not stopping his pony. I glowed. So, so! Even unto Mongols were such things dealt? The Lord hath an even hand.

At Dorbujing we housed in the worst inn of all Central Asia, a thing to be remembered, and a contrast with the reception the Very Great Man and I had had in the same town. A general rule of the country is that the larger the town, the worse the inn. We stayed there the whole next day, while the carter tinkered with wheels and axles and shored up his ponies with props lest they fall down incontinent and die. A light fell, however, into our sty: in the afternoon an orderly rode into the inn yard, and close after him lurched a tiny Russian cart, with Li the Native seated enormous on it, like Juggernaut. He squeezed into our cell and sat for a while in good talk. He had made a dash to Dorbujing to inspect the big wooden bridge there, a thing in which he took pride, having himself paid Russian artisans to put it up the year before. The ice was going out in the stream and the swelling water was hungry at the bridgeheads. He was much concerned. A bridge is a Good Work, the kind of monument that a governor likes to leave behind him, but not to pay for more than once. As he went out he brushed by a squatted carter who was sifting pony feed. He stooped over and took a handful, rattling it like a man who knew grain. "What are you sifting?" he asked the carter, being a Man of the People. "Feed," said the man sourly; "defile the ancestors of it! What should I be sifting, and I a carter?" One who stood by and had recognized Greatness put out his foot and hoisted the fellow. "Defile your mother!" he said in a shouting whisper. "Have you no understanding yet? The Great Man!" But the lieutenant-governor had laughed and gone already. "Defile his grandmother and to the point of death!" returned the carter, sullenly. "How should I know him for a Great Man? Talking to us, like, with no more governor about him than a sable hat!"

The next day we felt the power of the thaw, which is worse than winter. We took the direction of the Dorbujing tributary of the Emil down to the lap of the valley, where we crossed the combined rivers by what is known as the Triple Bridge. The lowland was clogged with watery marshes and full of duck, of which I killed one handsomely at more than a hundred yards with my Savage .22 rifle, causing a huge astonishment, especially to myself. Then we had a maze of tracks in rapidly loosening snow, leading off to Qazaq camps as well as to the pass, Lao Feng K'ou. We took one in a promising direction, but it led us into quags. Before long we were three wheels deep. The carter got down. "We've got there!" he announced admiringly. He and Moses and I put our shoulders to it, but got nothing out of the bog except a sucking noise. Two soldiers had been detailed to us by order of Li the Native, a courtesy I had not been able to evade. They were to be relayed at every stage, which meant tips at every stage. The better soldiers we drew turned out handy as servants, but these two were dazed with opium and merely gaped at our plight.

Then from behind a Qazaq came riding; a pock-marked, rascally-looking fellow with a raffish beard. He leaped off his piebald pony, grinning from chin to eyebrow, greeted us all, to our astonishment, like old friends, in very incomplete Chinese, and, with a surprising reversal of the usual attitude between "native" and Chinese, ordered our dumbfounded soldiers into the mud. With a heave all together, the cart came out. Hardly was this done when two Qazaqs came riding from the other direction. With a whoop, the active stranger rushed over to them, pulled one out of the saddle, flung off the saddle, and led back the pony, whooping still more. Moses hitched up his trousers. "A meeter-by-the-road," — a robber, — he said, resignedly. "Unpack the revolver, Young Master." The Qazaq who had lost his pony lay down on his belly in the wet snow and howled, a long, dismal, retching, Asiatic howl. His companion danced up and down by the edge of a pool of slush, waving his hands and screeching. Our doubtful friend only grinned the more cheerfully. He dug into the bosom of his sheepskin greatcoat for documents in Chinese and Turki, with which, and with much garbled chatter, he made it clear at last that he was a courier from the civil yamen in Dorbujing, sent out as a supplement to the military escort. He would accompany us all the way to Hsi Hu, the next District Magistracy, before being relieved. He proved himself an excellent sort, and did us much service.

He was concerned at this moment to explain that as a Qazaq he was empowered to levy ponies from any Qazaq to enable him to keep up with us. His pony was a starveling. Better take the other man's. No trouble at all. Business of State. We persuaded him that for the day he did not need a good pony to keep up with us, and at last we went on, heavily. He proved his worth that night. It was plain that we could never make the stage at Lao Feng K'ou, but he led us aside to a blotch on the snow, and there we found a Qazaq winter encampment.

My wife had stayed at places like this most of the way between Semipalatinsk and Chuguchak, but it was my first trial. An easy ramp led down to a warren tunneled and built in the earth. It was a sort of communal farmyard, roofed over with brush, bundles of grass, and sod, at a height only a little above the ground level. Stables, cow pens, and sheepfolds were all marked off separately, some by earthen walls and some by hurdles and some simply by poles lashed to the roof-poles. Little granaries, where women worked with hand querns, held the winter store of grain and meal. One or two living rooms were entered by tunnels. We took up our stance on a parallelogram of territory in one room, marking it off with our camp beds. Moses cooked for us, using our own supplies and one of the cooking places in the warren, buying a handful of fuel from the people. Bits of several families — hags and graybeards, matrons, young men, youths, maidens, and children ranging down to the most minute cradle dwellers — filled up the rest of the room. Their company was rounded out by a black ewe tethered in a corner and a greyhound bitch hunting for fleas and scraps of food.

The greyhound was of a dun color, with a show of feather on ears and tail, a good type of the Kirei long-dog.[1] These hounds,

---

[1] The Qazaq long-dog must be of the stock, somewhat deteriorated, of the Persian gazelle hound. A Chinese breed, with almost no feather on ears and tail, appears on very ancient monuments, but may also be of Persian origin. It survives in Shan-tung province, where the peasants course hares in the stubble after harvest. The Manchus of Peking and North China took up coursing with some enthusiasm. Their dogs were probably a mixture of the Shan-tung and Western strains, with perhaps an infusion of English blood from greyhounds brought as presents by the East India Company. The Manchu breed has been almost extinct since the Manchus were overthrown and lost their wealth. They are very rare in Peking.

which are on the small side compared with an English greyhound, are almost invariably dun-colored, but show some range of variance in feather. They appear to be bred exclusively by the Kirei Qazaq, and more by the Western Kirei than by those about Ku Ch'eng-tze. The Qazaq tribes on the Ili side of the Heavenly Mountains do not seem to breed them at all; probably because they have not nearly so much open country suited to hounds. The Kirei greatly value a good running hound, of which an excellent one is worth more than a good pony and second only in price to an eagle. The nomads take pains to keep the breed pure, but in the towns mongrel specimens can be seen. A noteworthy thing about the Kirei hound is that it runs by both gaze and scent, a good hound being one that will not run a stale scent, nor, when once laid on to a fox, turn aside when the trail is crossed. Their chief use is for taking foxes, but they will sometimes run a hare on their own account.

Like the hound the *berkut*,[1] the great hunting eagle of the Qazaqs, is used above all for taking foxes. The eagles are captured from the nest, in itself something of an exploit for bold young men, the nest-robber being most often swung out on a rope over bad crags and sometimes attacked by the parent eagles. The eaglet is kept hooded almost from the beginning, and fed choice meat from the hand. It is usually so well in hand by the beginning of its first season that it will return readily to a lure. It is first flown in the autumn of the year after its capture, being then more than a year old. The female, larger than the male, is always the better.

Both hawks and eagles are fasted before being cast at a quarry, hawks for seven or eight days and eagles for as much as twenty days. When well fasted, they will strike at the first quarry sighted; otherwise they are likely to tower, waiting for a quarry of their own choice. A good eagle, when striking at a fox,

---

[1] Eagles are also used by the Turki of the South; Skrine calls them black eagles. I think that the eagle of the North Road and the T'ien Shan (*berkut* in Qazaq-Turki) may be a true golden eagle, and the eagle of the South Road (*qara-qush* in Kashgar-Turki) a darker variety of the same species. The *qara-qush*, however, seems also to come from the T'ien Shan; but perhaps from the southern slopes.

CARTS IN MELTING ICE

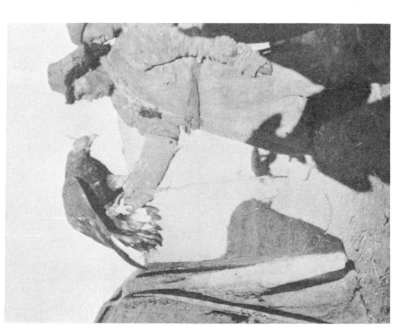

QAZAQ WITH HUNTING EAGLE

will fix its talons at the back of the neck, the talons penetrating through the soft base of the skull into the brain and killing it instantly, without a flurry or damage to the pelt.

Hounds and eagles are sometimes worked together,[1] to make sure of the quarry, which in doubling back to escape the strike of the bird falls to the hounds. The Qazaqs, however, everywhere maintain that the best of eagles will take even a wolf unaided. All of them assert also that in the eagles' eyries are found the bones and horns of full-grown roe deer (which can weigh forty pounds) and the bones of full-grown wolves. The eagles pass their prime at about seven years. After that they are still good to be flown at hares, but no longer at foxes. It is only natural to assume, however, that eagles in the wild state retain their vigor much longer. Among the Qazaqs a good eagle is a possession of much honor; it has a nominal price of two or three good horses, but in fact is rarely bought and sold. It is reserved as a present of more than usual splendor to tribal chieftains, or exchanged between close friends.

The hounds also can run a hare when they can no longer overtake a fox, which argues that most of their courses are not a straightaway dash, but a trial of endurance even more than of speed. Hares are of little value to the Qazaqs except for the skins, which are sold. Everywhere in Central Asia the hare, though sometimes eaten by the nomads, is not considered good clean food, but a wild relation of the cat. This distaste is to some extent shared by the Chinese.[2] That winter, because of the snow which had fallen to an exceptional depth and lasted very long, the hares were weak with starvation, having been unable to get at the grass roots. Hare-skins were selling in Chuguchak for five cents of the Urumchi paper tael, or say a halfpenny each.

The next day we made much better going to the crotch of the pass at Lao Feng K'ou. We traveled over a sweep of rising land, from which most of the snow had been blown away, but the line of the road was marked by remains of a sort of causeway, where

---

[1] Long-dogs and large hawks are also worked together in the chase of hares, in the Manchu or North China school of falconry.

[2] The commonest Chinese colloquial name for the hare is *yeh-mao,* wild cat.

the snow, packed down by winter traffic, had become almost as hard as ice and still endured. Our carter told me all over again about the line of posts which in the great days of the vague past had marked the direction of the pass; but in his version they had been Mongol yurts hung with bells — a version that must have originated in the round shape of the present mud shelters. The thaw at the pass had brought to the surface a military post which I had not before seen, inhabited by a few surly men all busy with opium. We slept in the cart.

The pass itself was deep still in snow, but on this side the snow was a great activity of Mongols and Qazaqs, halting for a night while on migration from their winter quarters in the Jair highland to their spring and summer ranges in the Tarbagatai and Urkashar, along the headwaters of the Kobuk. Torgut Mongols and Kirei Qazaqs were camped all in and among each other in amity, though later, when scattered among their roomier summer grazing grounds, the truce of the winter and the road would be in abeyance, and they would rob and raid among each other's flocks and pony herds. In this temporary camp the full yurts were not set up. The felts and trellises which go to make the side walls were left in their bundles, while the people of the tribes huddled for the night under the yurt tops. These are the curved birch rods, like the ribs of an umbrella, which are the frame of the domed top of a yurt. Instead of meeting at an apex, as the ribs of an umbrella meet, they are socketed in a wooden ring, which provides a round opening at the top of the yurt. In the full yurt, the lower ends of the ribs are lashed to the top of the vertical trellis-wall which makes the round sides of the shelter, but in the order of travel they are rested directly on the ground, making a low coop, which is covered over with felts.

These Torguts are an important section of the tribe, numbering three *hoshun* and best described as Kobuk Torguts, after their summer grounds. Like the rest of the Torguts, they are the remnants of a tribe whose fortunes are an important illustration of the history of Central Asia. With all the Mongols and the kindred races which first come within the scope of history in Mongolia, their ultimate origin and earlier chronicles must remain vague if not doubtful. They came to the fore in a comparatively modern period, the late seventeenth century, following on the Manchu conquest of China. The time was one of the recurrent cycles of unrest in Central Asian history; indeed, the Manchu conquest is better understood if it is regarded, not as a catastrophic event, but as an incident proceeding from a general stirring through the whole belt of Central Asia, from Turkestan through Zungaria and Mongolia up to Manchuria and the Pacific.

Like the Mongols, the Manchus had once before been rulers of China, first as the Khitan Tatars of the Liao dynasty, then as the Chin Tatars, whose dynasty, also known as the Chin, was overthrown by Jenghis Khan early in the thirteenth century. The remnants of the Chin withdrew to what is now Manchuria, emerging several centuries afterward to their latter conquest of China and the founding of the Ta Ch'ing dynasty. The forbears of the Manchus, when as the Chin Tatars they had been dislodged from China, had undoubtedly taken back with them into Manchuria enough of Chinese civilization to tinge their barbarity during the succeeding centuries. Moreover, during that time they had undoubtedly kept up a certain communication with China, so that even the language was not by any means unknown to them. The Northern Chinese had by that time been so much influenced by successive barbarian conquests that they had a good idea of the various tribes, and indeed there was a strong tendency among them to affiliate themselves with their Northern neighbors rather than with the more Chinese Chinese to the south of them. Thus, when the purely Chinese Ming dynasty was falling into ruin and the empire was being disrupted by a serious revolt, the Northerners were ready to align themselves with the Manchus rather than submit to the capture of Peking by rebels from what is now Shen-hsi province; there being by then no power about Nanking, where the Ming Empire had been founded, to reassert the rule of the dynasty. This led to an understanding between the Chinese armies on the Manchurian border and the Manchus on the outer side of the Great Wall, and a united march of Chinese and Manchus on Peking. With Peking once taken, the Manchus were primed to take over the rule of Northern China and later by con-

quest to extend that rule over the rest of the vast country. This
coming of the Manchus and the way in which the Northerners had
concurred in it established a cleavage that has become permanent
between the Chinese of the North and South, the Southerners having never forgotten what they regard as the betrayal of their
country by the Northerners, while in the North, from association
with the conquerors, there persists a feeling that the Southerners
are unfit for rule and doubly unfit to rule the North. This an-
tagonism, not yet sufficiently understood, works potently to the
present day in the conflicting policies of modern China.

I have spoken thus fully of China and the Manchus only in
order to throw up some sort of background for the later history of
the Mongols in Central Asia, which otherwise might appear nothing but a barbaric senselessness of violence. As I have said, when
the Manchus entered China they were not alone in moving toward
conquest. All Mongolia, the breeding ground of warlike migrations, was then restless, whether by pressure of a natural increase
of population or because some fluctuation of climate had tended
to dry up pastures and forced the nomads to look for fresh grounds.
Both in Central and in Western Mongolia a succession of fighting
leaders were trying to weld the scattered tribes once more into
conquering hordes. Had they succeeded and made head against
China, the new Manchu dominions would have been gravely threatened. Thus a first requirement of the Manchus was the consolida-
tion of their northern and western frontiers and the assertion,
in so doing, of their influence and authority among the Mongol
tribes.

In Central Mongolia, the threat was pointed by the conquests of
Likdan Khan of the Chahars, under pressure of which the tribes
of Inner Mongolia were actually alienated from their own kin,
turning to the Manchus and acknowledging an overlordship in
return for protection. In the West, the new Mongol ascendancy
was headed by a federation of Western tribes, known (apparently
from the name of an early chieftain) as the Ölöt or Eleuths.
These Mongols, under a leader called Galdan Khan, had achieved
such power that they had in 1690 conquered Samarqand, Bokhara,
and Yarkand. The successor of Galdan Khan was his nephew

Rabdan,[1] whose own tribe, one of the Eleuth federation, were the Zungars. Under his rule the name Zungar supplanted that of Eleuth, and the central nomadic ranges of this latter Mongol Empire are for that reason still known geographically as Zungaria. The last Zungar emperor was an adventurer called Amursana;[2] then the Zungars and their federated Eleuth tribes came into direct conflict with the Manchu power in China and were obliterated.

Luckily for the Manchus, two of their earlier emperors were men of great force, both as conquerors and as rulers. First K'ang Hsi established the Mongolian frontier, consolidating the tribes south of the Gobi, as vassal-allies of the Manchus and then initiating the wars against the Chahars. From the circumstance that the tribes south of the Gobi were associated more or less voluntarily with the Manchus, while those north of the desert barrier had to be convinced by conquest of the Manchu superiority, springs the division of Inner (Southern) and Outer (Northern) Mongolia, a division which continues to remain effective in our own time. After K'ang Hsi, the rectification of the Empire was completed by Ch'ien Lung. Going further to the west, he overthrew the Zungars, conquering all of what is now Zungaria and Chinese Turkestan. Of the Zungars he is said to have wiped out six hundred thousand people. Then, with both Central and Western Mongolia at his disposal, he began to set matters in order, causing migrations of peoples and tribes as imposing as anything in the history of nomadic races.

The last remnants of the federated Eleuths were removed from what had been the seat of their power, some of them being transported to the Koko Nor and Tsaidam regions of Tibet, and one small group being lifted from beyond the western to beyond the eastern borders of Mongolia proper, and settled in the Hei-lung Chiang division of Manchuria, west of Tsitsihar, where they remain to this day, to the number of one hoshun, known as the Mannai-Ölöt. For the repopulation of Zungaria, Mohammedan

---

[1] Or Tsevan Rapadu. See *The Desert Road to Turkestan* for an account of the Torguts of the Edsin Gol and the dissension between the Torguts and the rest of the Eleuths.

[2] For a good account of wars, migrations, and the succession of races in Zungaria, see Carruthers's *Unknown Mongolia*.

immigration from Northwestern China was encouraged, founding the T'ung-kan population now established in the oasis division of the Great North Road. This was supplemented by the removal of part of the Chahar tribe from Central Mongolia (since their power had also to be broken) from their original ranges north of Kalgan to the Borotala valley of Zungaria,[1] and the recall of the Torguts.

Thus, against a background of the wars which established the Manchu supremacy in China, Mongolia, and Chinese Turkestan, and suppressed the last emergence of the ancient Mongol lust of conquest, we approach the spectacular history of the Torguts, who rank before even the dispossessed Chahars and Zungar-Eleuths in the last and one of the most impressive periods of the migration of whole peoples in huge numbers up and down the blood-marked highways of Central Asia.

At the time when the Eleuth tribes were first being welded together in a series of tribal wars to form one powerful federation, the Torguts, although Eleuths themselves, stood out against the leaguing of the tribes, preferring a free life under their own chiefs. When the amalgamation had so far succeeded that they could no longer stand against their united kinsmen, they gathered their flocks and herds, took down and packed their yurts, and departed, a whole people in retreat, from their ancient pastures centring about the Tarbagatai ranges on the western verge of the Eleuth countries. Heading across the steppes that lie between Southern Siberia and Russian Turkestan, they carried their migration to the astounding distance of three thousand miles, until they came into conflict with the Russians. In the end, accepting Russian overlordship, they took up a grant of lands on the lower Volga. That was about the year 1690, when Galdan Khan, the triumphant leader of the majority of the Eleuth tribes, began to overrun what is now Russian and Chinese Turkestan. Evidently the position of the Torguts, astride the approach to Siberia and Russian Turkestan, had a great deal to do with the pressure of the other Eleuth tribes in a search for outlets of expansion. The Zungars were unable to move freely along the South Road, because the deserts

[1] For the Chahars of the Borotala, see below, pp. 188, 203, 207.

between oasis and oasis were a bar to the passage of mounted hordes. They were forced to go by the ancient way of the nomads, through Northern Zungaria, following the pastures at the foot of the Altai, not the T'ien Shan, until they came to the Tarbagatai. Then, crossing into Siberia (the Torguts being out of their way), they could turn along the Northern edge of the T'ien Shan, following the rich pastures of the Issiq Köl region, until they reached a position near the point where Andijan now stands. Thenceforward not only Russian Turkestan lay before them, but they could turn aside easily over the T'ien Shan and descend on the open oases of Kashgaria.

The Torguts had not found on the Volga a land which fully accorded with their desire, but seem to have been at odds both with the Russians and with other nomad tribes. No other lands being open to them, however, there they stayed for eighty years. About 1750 Ch'ien Lung set in motion his campaigns against the Zungars. About twenty years later, having laid Zungaria finally under his hand in the quiet of destruction, he invited the Torguts to return, and in 1770 they undertook the reverse migration, back to their original lands. It is impossible to estimate their numbers accurately, but Russian accounts put the number of families that turned back to the East at forty thousand families, while the Chinese claim that fifty thousand reached Zungaria.[1] About fifteen thousand families remained on the Volga, their descendants being known in our time as the Russian Kalmuks.

The returning Torguts accomplished their journey in the face of appalling difficulties, which must have severely reduced their numbers. It took them eight months, including a winter on the open steppes, to retrace the three thousand miles, and they were harried all the way by hostile tribes of Qazaqs and Naiman Tatars. When at last they came within the frontiers of the now established Manchu Empire, a part of them were assigned the tribal lands about the Tarbagatai which had once belonged to their fathers; others were established along the Altai, and others were given the ranges once held by Eleuths akin to them in the Yulduz region overlooking Qara Shahr. To these regions they have been confined

[1] Carruthers's *Unknown Mongolia*.

ever since, except for minor redistributions during the troubles of the Mohammedan Rebellion two generations ago. Their migrations are restricted to their summer wanderings, when they travel frequently for short distances, moving their flocks in search of the best pastures, and to two longer journeys every year, back and forth between their summer and winter ranges. Owing to the distances between the Altai, the Tarbagatai, and the Qara Shahr-Yulduz region, their tribal affairs are not administered by one paramount chief, but are controlled regionally by local princes. They have, I understand, six princely families of different ranks, which were confirmed under the Manchu rule. The senior line seems to be that of the Prince (Han Wang) of Qara Shahr, whose people number four hoshun. Of the other princely families, I know that there are two over the Kur-khara-usu Torguts, near Hsi Hu, who number two hoshun; one over the one hoshun of Ching Ho Torguts, and one over the one hoshun of Edsin Gol Torguts, having the rank of Pei-le. The other princely family must belong to the Altai and Kobuk Torguts. All of these families are linked by marriage.[1]

These, then, were the people we saw in camp on the western side of Lao Feng K'ou, and on the next day in the deep snow of the pass, engaged in the ancient struggle of the nomad, which is as bleak and yet stirring as a saga; staking their children and their fortunes in the primal quest for grass, that their flocks might have plenty and increase. The world beyond their vision might change from the age of the nomad to the age of ploughed lands and walled cities, and then to the age of commerce and the railway and the conquest of sea and air; but for them the same pitiless wind blew over the same unforgiving snow, and they turned with the turn of the year between highland and lowland, as their fathers in the savage past had turned between Tarbagatai and Volga, the whole force of their desire still bound on one object — open pastures and free ranges. The sight of their caravans in the snow, cattle weakened by the winter and men and cattle equally suffering in the cold,

---

[1] For the Torguts of the Qunguz and Tekes (without princes) see below, pp. 270–272; for the Torguts of Kur-khara-usu or Ssu-ko Shu, p. 185; for the Torguts of Ching Ho, p. 185.

struggling but keeping inexorably on the move, tents packed up and children swaddled — all that, and the immensity of their hidden world, lost in the unconfined plains and locked in the uncatalogued mountains of Central Asia, was of a kind to pluck the spirit of man back into the dark, rich, violent past, where death gives vigor to the roots of the future; a most noble and a healthy thing.

XII

SPRING MIGRATION

THE first time that I had come to T'o-lai, riding from the East, I had halted on a ledge, a low outer ledge of the hills, and seen the hamlet as a small irregular stain in an immense and hollow world of snow. This time, coming back to it from the West, the snow had thinned away to a ragged ugliness, uncovering the bare, cold earth. That was in the hollow plain; but where the plain narrowed and lifted toward the Windy Pass the snow held still, in vast rotting drifts. From T'o-lai to Lao Feng K'ou we had trotted between dawn and mid-morning, in a cold so deep and frosty that the arrested air seemed resonant; but this time, between Lao Feng K'ou and T'o-lai, we plunged and heaved from early morning until after dark; and out of the obstinate snow, wasting slowly at the end of winter, rose a wet, malignant cold more vexing than the hardest dry cold of winter.

Finding poor quarters at Lao Feng K'ou, we had backed the cart up to a dyke next the barracks and slept in it. Our escorting soldier the next morning, seeing the promise of a turn of business, hitched his mount to a small sleigh and offered it to lighten the cart. Then we went at the drifts; but even so, had it not been for a Chinese official traveling in a big two-wheeled cart, built up with mats like a summerhouse on wheels and drawn by five ponies, we should have been hard put to it. We were on the wide, easy slope that crowds in at one side of the vague-seeming pass. Above us was the winter road, now rotted and pitted, with wallows in it where ponies had fallen through. The little sled, drawn by one gaunt, wise pony, bumped and tumbled along it, but passage was denied to our wheels; it was better for us to take the untouched snow. The ponies of the big cart bucketed into it; all in a moment they were up to their breast bands. The carter's long whip swung out over them, and with tossing heads and quivering haunches straining low in the traces they flung themselves ahead and heaved the cart for thirty yards. Then they stopped. The carter jumped into the snow, cursing prophetically, and looked to wheels, traces, and harness. Then he got up again; he could only control his ponies well from his perch behind the shafts; he had four trace-ponies ahead and the one in the shafts, and not a rein in the lot. He drove by whip and voice alone, and were he to get down from his usual place the team would veer to one side. The cart went on, jerkily, for another thirty yards. After it followed another big cart, then came our little four-wheeled cart, with a much narrower gauge. The big teams broke down the worst resistance of the snow, but it held heavily against our smaller wheels. The breath began to roar and rattle from one of our ponies which was broken-winded. It was going to be a bad business.

The sun was high and we had not yet struggled to the middle of the snow when we began to meet Torguts and Qazaqs, more companies of the same migrants that we had seen already in camp the night before. They were strung out in irregular caravans, grouped in units of camps, reaching further back into the snow than we could see; miles and miles of tribesmen measuring their skilled knowledge of wilderness travel in the ordeal of the Great Spring Migration. First came pony herds, driven ahead to trample down the going, herded by the most hardy and skillful of the young men, armed with long poles with a running noose of rope at the end, — a crude anticipation of the lasso, — the herding pole of the Qazaqs and Mongols. After them came oxen and cows, loaded with tents, babies in their cradles, new-born lambs; or bestridden by women with babies in front of them and puppies or cooking pots tied on behind. Behind them again were the camels, more heavily laden still, sprawling frequently on the slippery footing that camels hate most and having to be rescued with digging, beating, and pulling of the tail. Many of the cow camels carried their January-born calves lashed on top of their own loads, bulging with yurt-felts and the tent-chests in which the nomad carries his more

precious things. The calves nodded and bobbed unconcernedly in
their high nests; but the mothers could not see them, and, thinking them lost, howled and moaned bubblingly, one of the worst of
noises. Last of all came the sheep, in bumping, humping, struggling flocks; slowest and most unhandy of all the stock, but precious, being the basis of wealth in the nomadic life; thousands
of sheep and a few hundred goats. They were in the charge of
half-grown boys and girls, riding half-grown ponies and bul-
locks and cows, who leaned frequently from their crude saddles
to pick up exhausted lambs until cantle and pommel were all hung
about with little bleating bundles of wool and snow. The lambs
ranged all the way from the autumn-born, already able to fend
for themselves, through the winter-born to the spring-born; nor
was the season over, for at least one ewe cast her lamb on the
march, as I saw. The great camp dogs ran where they liked, quiet
on the march as a good dog should be, but the shivering greyhounds
were dragged in leash. Most valuable of all, the hooded berkut,
the magnificent hunting eagles, were in the charge of graybeards
not fit for active work up and down the line of the caravan, whose
burdened wrists were supported on crutches, socketed in the stirrup. Then there would be a long gap in the trampled snow, before we had toiled toward the next caravan and they had toiled
toward us.

When the faint upward trend of the pass had turned to the
slow downward trend, we came to a few hovels grouped about a
miry yard; another barracks. We stayed only long enough to
breathe and to find that it would be too filthy and uncomfortable
to do more than boil and drink a pot of tea. Then we went on
for T'o-lai. The snow diminished and the wheels began to slew in
a thin mud, broken here and there by dirty patches and ridges of
snow; but the ponies were done for. My own riding pony was
pretty well foundered, but he could just keep up a faster walk than
the cart ponies, and I drew ahead until I sighted the village as the
dark began to hover. I rode through it till I reached the inn where
the Great Man and I had harbored, but the one halfway decent room
was taken. After a search at worse hovels, I found a Turki
inn, with a big room, fairly new; it was a common room, but I

Torgut Caravan: Spring Migration

secured the whole use of it and had it cleared, while I stabled my pony in the least exposed of the open sheds. Then I walked out into the one street, to meet the cart; but the dark was on us. I could see no further than the edge of the village, and no cart. I went on, and met my wife, on foot and alone. She said that the carter had deserted her and Moses, and that Moses had tried to drive the ponies, poor flagging brutes, used only to a known voice and a skilled whip, and they had stalled and at last — it is the best phrase — died on him entirely. I took her to the inn, ordered that tea be made, and paddled off into the slush and the thickening dark. In twenty minutes I found the cart, out of which crawled Moses with a grieved voice. I asked him why he had let the carter run away, — that was a little funny, I swear it was, even with the only wife I had and my only Moses dumped in that way in the middle of Central Asia, — and he said the fellow had got down to walk, and, thinking his feet were numb, he had said nothing; but of a sudden he had gone off ahead, that son of a turtle, and that was all that Moses knew. I sent Moses off to the inn, — he was even more tired and hungry and miserable than my wife, — and then sat on the front of the cart and mused, being by gross error without tobacco. The swingle-bar of the near-side trace-pony had come adrift (that was by Moses' idea of driving), and the cold was too much for any mending with my bare hands; so that was that.

After a time that seemed long I heard a shout, not by any means the shout of a civilized man. I responded, not by any means with the shout of a contented man. In a moment a shape came out of the dark; a leggy Qazaq youth riding one wild-eyed pony and leading another. We gibbered at each other meaninglessly, he having no Chinese; then with a whoop he rode off. It was a little puzzling. He might be a straggler from a caravan, and if there were more of him about they might think the cart easy pickings for a little rapid work; but there was no cause for worry. We were too near the village for a serious attack, and I had my rifle in the cart. Before long I heard more shouting, and out of the darkness the leggy youth came back, not heading an attack, but bringing my carter astride yet another pony.

That was a relief. Off the back of my tongue I scraped a unique accumulation of phrases, the store of my experience among the Mongolia-going caravans, and gave him the pick, rounding off with some plain filth of old Tientsin — he was a Tientsin carter. He was hurt. He said that he had been walking to warm his feet, when the idea came to him that he had better get relief ponies; so he had gone ahead to the village, to get them; but the people of these parts! What thieves! All his debts were as nothing to the hire of these ponies. The debate ended in the air; we reshuffled harness and ponies, and drew lamely into the village. Moses had quite blown up; that night my wife made supper for him and for us — and she too had had quite enough. The next day we remained in those choice surroundings, none of us, on two feet or four, hankering for the road.

Mounting from T'o-lai to the Jair hills on the day after that, the last day of March, we had no more drifts to deter us, but a great cold and a light fall of fresh snow. Out of the hills, as we went, we could see caravans converging on the track, both Torgut and Kirei-Qazaq. They traveled alike and on the same migration, but review-ing them thus as they went by in numbers one could pick out signifi-cant differences. Every Qazaq group had its long-dogs and hunt-ing eagles, which are so rarely used by the Mongols as not to be typical of them at all. The Qazaq, in all his hunting, is very hit-and-miss; he likes the dash and scurry of riding to hawk and hound. He has not the patience and not nearly the skill of a Mon-gol as a stalker. The Mongols, on the other hand, had far more camels in their caravans than had the Qazaqs. They are much the better camel masters, and for that reason they breed larger herds. Among the Gobi-going caravans, where you find the keenest judg-ment of camels, Qazaq-bred camels (which can be recognized by a grayer coat, a more awkward gait and above all a different and less workmanlike piercing of the nostril) are ill-considered.

Still traveling in short stages, by necessity of our inferior ponies, we halted that day at Yamatu. It was yet early, and we walked down one of the shallow valleys among the conical hills. There was not much promise of life, for the smooth slopes, littered with flat fragmentary stone and grown only sparsely with small coarse plants and tufts of "white grass," were of the kind that fills so much of Mongolia; almost as poor as an utter desert. Yet the nomad and all his cattle are of the type of the camel; they can nurse their pinched bellies over the winter in very lean countries, enduring until the snow recedes, uncovering better pastures. At a turn we came on a Qazaq encampment, the felt yurts weathered to a gray inconspicuous against the drab hills. Flocks of sheep, working homeward, were scattered thinly over the hills; tethered lambs of the encampment bleated for their return, dogs rushed out toward us, children began to caper, idle men to come out of the yurts, and women straightened up from their tasks to stare.

Returning to the inn with the spoil of one chukor partridge, flushed by the way, we found ourselves once more in company with the official whose heavy carts had preceded us through the snow of Old Windy Pass. He had been Member of Parliament in Peking for the province of Chinese Turkestan — meaning no more than that he was an appointee of the Governor, residing in Peking and acting as a political agent. He was now returning to Urumchi, to take up a new post as Chief of Police; but so strict is the control that the old Governor lays on all subordinates that he had been delayed for days at Chuguchak, while his application to reënter the province and proceed to the capital was being considered; in other words, while other equally confidential agents of the Governor were ascertaining that he had not returned from Peking tainted with unsuitable ideas, or contaminated by extraprovincial affiliations. He was convoying a consignment of machinery for a new cotton mill that had been under construction for about two years near Urumchi, a venture of the Governor's business representatives. Part of the machinery had been sent by the desert route through Mongolia, divided into weights suitable for camel loads. This machinery was of English make, but the purchase of it had been made through a Japanese firm in Tientsin, British traders not liking to carry the deal on credit terms and the cotton-mill promoters of Central Asia liking still less to pay cash, partly because the not-yet-wholly-respectable wheels of still-slightly-incredible modernity might after all refuse to go round, partly because there was no use in paying cash when you could get credit on the Western scale of interest and keep your own money earning interest on the far more lavish Oriental scale. We remained companions of the road with the official and his convoy for a number of days, until, with the ingenuity that distinguishes Asiatics in affairs of machinery, they dropped off one of the carts the box containing all the screws that were to hold things together. Thereupon the official was fain to halt and recover them, a task in which luckily his new distinction as Chief of Police enabled him to dispense with detectives, thus ensuring success.

The official, the innkeeper, and the carters crowded together on the k'ang of the inn's one room to chat, with the true and delightful democracy of China. Now the innkeeper was the brother (whether by blood or courtesy, I am not sure, but I think only because the two men came from the same village) of the carter who had driven Moses and the sausage-dispensing merchant to Chuguchak. Therefore Moses accosted him with joy, sure of a welcome. "I was in your village in the Boxer year," said Moses, "but never since. Where were you then?" "Pieh t'i!" cried the innkeeper. "Mention it not!" — and all Moses' assurances that he had been himself a Boxer would not draw him on to talk of his old home or his past: for which reasons Moses assured me that he must have been one of those Boxers proscribed after the failure of the rising.

The Boxer, in addition to keeping the inn, was charged by Government with the duty of keeping the telegraph line in repair. Throughout that stage, the wire held up the poles at least as much as the poles held up the wire, though in many places neither did either. The official asked (not at all as a high official to an underling, but as one man chatting with another) how this should be, when a large number of new poles lay by the Boxer's door. "In the first place," replied the Boxer, in the tone of a man who knows that he carries conviction, "the ground is yet frozen, so that the work of putting in new poles would be more than what I get paid for. Then again, those new poles brought by the contractor are so rotten that if I were to put them in it would only make more trouble for me, keeping them standing." The conversation then turned gracefully to the merciful functioning of a decent postal service in a province where all hope of the telegraph has been so long abandoned that it is universally known as the "camel lightning."

Talk came back for a moment to the telegraph when the official tried to remember how many years it had been established, and could not. At this there was a general scratching of heads, and profoundly reflective spitting, for the matter was felt to be important, touching as it did on regions highly official — national as well as provincial. It was an embarrassment, as all perceived, that none should be able to inform so worthy a lieutenant of the Governor on a point of such importance. Then spoke up my carter, as one who comforts children: "Let us not waste many words. As many years as it has been, so many years let it be counted." And this master-stroke of coolie humor kept everyone chuckling until the tea boiled.

Electricity led us to earthquakes, and earthquakes to Japan (for, let me repeat it: easy manners apart, we were in distinguished company, and parading our knowledge decorously) and Kan-su, and then to a famous pass in that province, the Liu P'an Shan or Six Loop Mountain, over which lifts and coils the Great Imperial Highway, the arterial road from the depths of China to the farthest West. I had just been reading the *Golden Bough,* of which we had the boiled-down version with us, and was primed to understand from the tales of the carters that a sacred mountain cult, with sex taboos, lingers about the pass. It is said that the presence of a woman on the pass must be kept as quiet as possible. If she should get down from her cart, setting foot on the sacred ground, heavy rain will surely fall to wash away all traces of her. Nor must carters preparing to cross the pass flirt with women, or talk licentiously about them — a restriction undoubtedly irksome to the generality of carters.

We slept in the cart that night, and the ponies were all over the inn yard. They kicked each other in the ribs and squealed, and they fought with each other to thrust their heads in at the front of our cart and nibble at our sleeping-bag toes.

The next morning we went up through the Shih Men-tze, the Gates of Stone, to the central Jair plateau. The pass was busy

with migrating tribesmen; the Jair hills were draining through all
their valleys toward the Tarbagatai. At a spectacular height
above us, far away and small, but wild and proud, I saw a wild
sheep looking down on us all, the people of the shifting tribes
and the two itinerant aliens with Moses their henchman. This
led to talk of shooting, and toward evening, as we neared the end
of the stage, shooting we had. A low-running shape went across
our front and the carter in great excitement drew up: a wolf, he
proclaimed. I said it was not, but a *hsi-kou*, a "thin dog," for it
looked to me like a cross-bred Qazaq hound. However, the carter
swore it was a wolf, and our Qazaq outrider backed him, and as
they ought to have known, and I had heard tales of the wolves to
be seen in broad day at this end of the North Road, I drew my
Savage out of the sheath in which it lay in the cart. The animal,
trotting on a wide circle, had obligingly halted. I stretched out
on my belly, for the range was well over three hundred yards,
and the mark not large. I fired, and the beast went down limply,
with never a kick. Would that I might shoot like that some day
at a worthy mark; for going over we found no wolf, but a half-
bred hound. Moreover, from where the dog lay we could see
Miao'rh Kou, the night's halt; but, luckily, the shot had not been
heard, and, luckily again, the dog did not belong at the tiny post
of Miao'rh Kou, but must have strayed from a Qazaq caravan;
had it been otherwise, then by all I know of China that murdered
brute might have been held up as the best running-hound within
a three days' ride, with a remarkable worth in silver.

We stayed at the telegraph station at the Valley of the Shrine,
and noted an effect of the civilizing telegraph line. Hens had appeared, to signify the settled life, and a couple of Qazaq families
had brought themselves to a standstill to look after the hens and
the sheep and cows which the telegraph master was buying up as
his savings permitted. They had built mud walls in squares about
their yurts, the first step of the settling Qazaq. Not until the
yurts were quite worn out would they roof over corners of the
mud square, thus easing themselves by degrees out of their nomadic
traditions. In the middle of the next day's stage, of which we
covered the first half in a scanty fall of snow and a searching wind,

Stevens ?

M AD hill

luw EC

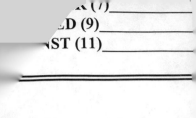

X (7)_____

D (9)_____

ST (11)_____

ok Identification Number, in
catalog item number is avai
titution, society, agency, corp
ample: The History of Wisco
If not sure, leave blank.
fficient for well-known comp
one numbers for unlisted pub
ublishing country. Do not co

we found another example of Chinese frontier occupation: a yurt where a sergeant of the road patrol had quartered himself with a Qazaq wife and was raising a half-breed family. This part of this stage was one of the loneliest lengths of road, most open to raids from Russian Qazaqs during the summer. Therefore the one soldier in permanent occupation was advanced to an under-officer's rank. That is, he commanded the road, if not a force to patrol it. As for the following appropriate to a sergeant, patience, patience! That might come in time. He himself escorted us for the rest of the stage to Ulan Bulaq, or IIan chan T'ai, the Waterless Mountain Stage, as the Chinese call it, the name referring not so much to the halt at Ulan Bulaq as to the country between it and the Valley of the Shrine. Thereafter we were officially in safe country.

XIII

THE LAND OF PIONEERS

On the first day of April our cart drew out of the sordid inn at Ulan Bulaq and began to rattle down the long dry slope declining eastward from the Jair highlands. We were headed away from the strongholds of late-lying snow. The cold of early morning was no longer so insistent, and the air had a kindlier touch; it was the mild rathe air of spring, invading the earth and bringing a reprieve to men and beasts. Wherever the wind left us alone and we passed into the glow of still sunlight, the instinct of the spring loitered near-hand, urging us to idle and relax. Yet for people of the road there was little license. We might take our ease when halted, and be sluggards before the start, but while on the road, between halt and halt, we had still to contend with the worst thing of all, the sloughs and mire left by the vanished snow.

Far away on our right front we saw the lifted snow-peaks of the Heavenly Mountains; on our left the desert, immense and vague, tilted imperceptibly to a bare sky line. Antelope were on the move; they had not been there to see when I was westward bound in the company of the Great Man, but now they were trooping with the season from unknown winter quarters in the foothills, returning to the desert. Though we saw them deployed like skirmishers all about us, and crossing the road ahead, they kept a distance of several hundred yards, appearing elusively among the tamarisks that masked the desert. A faint mirage, wavering low on the ground under the dusty gray tamarisks, made shooting impossible.

Down in the trough of the desert we halted to eat at a tiny place, bare and starveling but clean, called Hsiao-ts'ao Hu, the Little Grass oasis, where a couple of Chinese families had newly taken holdings and were to attempt farming by the aid of natural springs. As we went on, heavier sand in the desert clay checked our pace and we entered a growth of stouter, more vigorous tamarisks. We were approaching the same marshes that I had before crossed on ice, but it was now necessary to veer well out into the desert to skirt them.

My wife and I were walking ahead, I leading my pony and she having got down from the cart to give the scarecrow team a lighter haul, when we came to a place where the road forked. We took the fork to the right, after I had shouted back to the carter and he had shouted assurance to me. A few minutes later we saw the cart bear to the left. Our Qazaq courier had kept with us, and I asked him what this meant. He said that the two roads were one road; the standard phrase in this country, as on the caravan trails of Mongolia, when a route divides and the two branches, making an ellipse, later come together again. We went on, but before long, seeing the cart diminish in the distance and realizing that the ellipse would prove a long one, I sent the courier after the cart, with orders either to bring it back to us or to halt it and come back for us. We went on at our own pace, until my wife began to tire, and we found ourselves astray among high tamarisks, with only a lame pony between us, and no guide. After that, for about four hours we had no comfort but the passing sight of a sleek antelope buck. He stepped out of the tamarisks, not fifty yards ahead, paused a moment at gaze, and slipped away again, a hesitant, gleaming dun shape, fearful but not terrified.

There was nothing to do but keep on keeping on. Luckily I had the hang of the road well enough to know that we must work left-handed round any bad going, and thus edge our way into Ch'ep'ai-tze, the halting place. Heavy jungle growth proved the nearness of the great marshes, tamarisks giving way largely to *toghraq* poplar, unrecognizable mossy trees of small stature, thick bushes, and tangled briars. Now and again we skirted huge reed-beds, the edges of which were like ten-foot yellow palisades, with inlets through them giving sudden ranges of sight over black water and the sullen darkness of impassable morasses. Cart tracks crossed all about us in confusion; not true roads, but marks of passage where men had come to cut out building timber or gather fuel. Then we found portions of rotting embankments, the relics of abandoned human occupation, long relapsed into jungle and marsh, and a little farther we began to see clearings, distant farms huddled on raised ground, and bare sloughs with the gleam of stubble showing; these were rice paddies, reclaimed by labor from the marsh. At last a by-pass brought us out toward the steading of a half-nomadic Qazaq. I gathered a long pole to repel dogs, and we approached. It was no more than a mud-walled enclosure, with lean-to sheds against the walls and yurts pitched in squalor in the centre.

We halted at the entrance of wooden bars, behind which dogs raged at us. A black-a-vised and villainous-appearing Qazaq came unwillingly forward. He had, or pretended to have, no knowledge of Chinese, and would do nothing but wave us off. It was a demonstration of the value of appearances when traveling in such countries. Had we arrived with the jangling bells of many cart-ponies, and couriers and escorts who would demand food, tea, and lodging, and all without thanks, much less payment, the man would have shown himself diligent. It is becoming, all the world over, to accommodate the rich, and the poor when they wander are sure in Central Asia of the humbler sort of charity; but the beggar on horseback is apprehended for a rogue as well as a vagabond. That we had the speech of strangers counted for nothing with the scowling Qazaq; we were a harassed-looking couple with one lame pony between us; better let us continue to be harassed.

Then I changed my tone of politeness for a tone of command, ordering him repeatedly in Chinese to show us the road to Ch'e-p'ai-tze, of which he must recognize at least the name. At the same time, as if unregardedly, I let my coat fall open to show the cartridges and revolver in my belt; not by any means threateningly, but because, in this closely ruled province, the carriage of any modern-seeming arms is in itself a badge of consequence. The fellow at once discovered better manners, and showed us how to find the main road, which was at no great distance.

We had not followed it far when we came on our Qazaq courier at a place where a cluster of trails came together out of different quarters of the marsh. He was well soiled with mire and much dejected. He had ridden a wide circuit and lamed his pony, and failed altogether to come up with the cart — a poor enough performance for a nomad. We took his pony and pushed ahead the few remaining miles, each of us on a lame mount, entering Ch'e-p'ai-tze totally without triumph. The cart did not come in for a long time, the carter having first taken the road to Old Ch'e-p'ai-tze, the former centre of the district, and then mired his cart so deep that he had been forced to look for a farm and hire ponies to drag it out.

Worst of all, at the moment we entered the inn yard, while I was helping my wife to find a room, — for she was very tired, — someone out of the crowd that had followed us pilfered my field glasses from their place on my saddle. There was a petty military official at the place who could easily have issued such orders as would have caused the glasses to be astonishingly found on the roof of a house or in the middle of the road; but this man had been insolent to the Great Man when we halted there before, and as the Great Man had put him in his place he was only too glad now to disoblige me. He gave orders that a search be made, but at the same time grumbled aloud that it was no business of his and that I ought to look out for myself. That was hint enough to the villagers that they need not bear over-hard on the communal conscience, and of course the search became hopeless. I do not doubt that we had hardly left the village when the officer issued fresh orders which secured the glasses for his own use, and that he still sports them — unless, indeed, they have been levied from him by some superior. He was a nasty fellow; the kind of understrapper swelling with unmerited importance who is a pestilence to all travelers; but one reason that I mention him is that he was the only official in the whole province who showed us anything but the most whole-hearted courtesy.

As we were late in starting the next morning, all the horseflesh in our convoy being little better than animated carrion, I levied a pony from the village headman and rode back on the trail of the day before. The headman had been able to identify from my description every person we had met, and with an escort of the more sober and substantial people of the village I rode off to visit and question them all. It brought no result, but it gave me an interesting survey of the fringe of settlement in this wilderness.

The headman was a delightful old Turki, speaking little Chinese, and the better class of traders were all Turki. The Chinese in the village were mostly innkeepers and petty traders, dealing in spirits, opium, and "pickings"; they were of the rascally breed that is to be found in any remote pioneer community, always on the lookout for questionable business and scandalous profits, and relying on the bribery of petty officials to confirm their transactions, dragoon their victims, and assist in the collection of compound interest indefinitely re-compounded.

Many of the settlers were of better stuff; but even so, it is, I am convinced, a fallacy to suppose that the pioneer type is a superior type; that only the boldest and most vigorous men break away from civilization to found new communities in the wilderness. On the contrary, the men who stay behind in the old well-populated districts are those who by their ability are able to maintain themselves, while pioneers are recruited in the main from those that are inferior to the competition and drift out to the frontiers, always hoping for something new to turn up, for a lucky rise in land values or big profit from half-hearted labor. Most of the Chinese farmers had migrated from the Manass and Hsi Hu regions. Some were of the stock that has been long enough in the province to lose all affiliations with Old China; others were Chih-li people who had been there at most two or three generations. The T'ung-kan farmers also were from the Manass country, and traces of old cultivation indicated that probably a small T'ung-kan community had existed before the Mohammedan Rebellion. The Turki farmers were the farthest-fetched, coming from such places on the South Road as Kucha and Qara Shahr. Scattered among these people were Qazaqs in more or less advanced stages of breaking away from the nomadic life; for the region is of old a Qazaq wintering ground. Among these were Chinese who had taken Qazaq women and were raising half-breed families.

Many of the holdings were no more than sties; others, with neat little Chinese shrines near their gates, had the clean, substantial air of prosperity, with fields hedged and ditched and houses built on embankments to keep them drained and dry. These belonged to the more active men who are the stiffening of such a community; and most of these men were of the Chih-li stock. They received me with a certain timidity, showing that they lived withdrawn, meeting few strangers; women and children all scampered away, to return in a faint-hearted backwash and peer and chatter from gateways and around corners. Nor were the people grouped in villages after the Chinese custom, but two or three related families at the most would be housed together, a mile or two from neighbors. As we rode through the empty lanes from one place to the next, hares lolloped out of covert, and from the bushes covering unreclaimed patches of bog pheasants rocketed astoundingly into the air. It was a peaceful, thinly held, easy enough country.

Among such outlying people, prosperity is well bounded. There is no great difficulty in reclaiming land and establishing cultivation. A man need not strain too hard for food and clothing. Trade is the difficulty; it is hard to realize on surplus wealth, unless by establishing grown sons on the land and increasing the population of well-fed people. Some of the grain can be sold to the cart caravans that lumber past on their way to or from Siberia; but the merchandise on these carts is not for local distribution. The main trade is a through trade, not affecting such borrel folk as make clearings on the edge of swamps. They have not enough variety in their produce to stimulate a trade of their own, and city markets are too distant and too well supplied for them to dispose of their produce at advantage. As near as can be found anywhere on earth, they are a self-supporting community, and the only traders who can find much to do are the inconsiderable hucksterers who are established in the short single street of Ch'e-p'ai-tze, the regional centre.

We started away from Ch'e-p'ai-tze through brushwood alive with pheasants. We saw them every few yards ahead of us on the road, but they would not rise, preferring to scuttle off into the underbrush, and, as they were most hardy and skillful runners, I failed to bag one. Then the road grew quaggy, leading through swamps and past reed-fringed pools, the haunt of waterfowl. We drew up for the night, after about thirty miles of this progress, at a lonely place with a Mongol-sounding name; a solitary inn, kept by a Chinese with a Mongol wife. The place was mournful, and we were dirtily housed; but it is in such chances that above all the commanding attraction of travel is asserted — I do not know why. A fire glows in the dusk, and as it flares up you see wrinkled, leathery faces in a red glow, and the crooked posts and sagging brushwood roof of a shed stand out for a moment. A laugh comes out of a shadow and you hear wayfaring men chatter in a medley of the languages of the country.

In the afterglow of sunset we went down to the marsh and threaded our way as far as we could among the harshly whispering reeds until we stood at the edge of darkling water. The raw colors of such a sunset as is not granted to mortal sight in countries where froward men have tamed the earth were softening a little as they trembled on the verge of dissolution in darkness. Even as we ended our progress and looked out into the heart of the marshes, darkness hovered low on the face of earth and water; light survived only in the west, flaring as if from a casement in heaven. Vast companies of geese and ducks were flighting homeward and planing down on strident wings to the still water; out of reedy recesses the contented clacking and gabbling of incredible multitudes of them palpitated on the air. The stars came out and we went in.

As we came near Old Hsi Hu the next day, the mud got heavier. It is rice-paddy country and in the spring thaw the road, as it approaches the village, breaks down in despair and departs in various directions in the form of shallow trenches brimmed with swill. We abandoned them, in favor of a stretch of waste, from which most of the moisture had drained into the roads. Leaving the ponies, yawing and slithering, to struggle for an hour over a quarter of a mile of this, we walked ahead to the village, the mud sucking at our ankles.

Old Hsi Hu, before the Mohammedan Rebellion, was the centre of the great Western Oasis, but the city was destroyed in those wars and afterwards removed and built anew on higher, drier land, in a better position to command the trade of the road branching toward the Ili valley, as well as that of the Chuguchak road by which we had come. The site of the old town is now occupied by a large agricultural village.

Most of the people were busy, ditching and digging to get in order the elaborate drainage of rice cultivation. Little attention was paid to us, so, leaving my wife by the earthen outdoor table of a tea-house, I picked up a couple of eager guides and went into the paddies to shoot duck, which congregated fearlessly within a few yards of houses and working men, eagerly feeding on grains of rice shaken into the mud during last year's harvest.

When I heard the shouts and cracking whips which meant that the carts were out of the mud I went back to the road. Then I found that my wife had been annoyed by an infantile persecution. A few village children had gathered and thrown bits of mud at her, at the same time calling her Oross, — a Russian, — their behavior showing a reflection of the contempt into which Russians had come during the tragedy of the Revolution and the civil wars, when refugees had drifted this way. Older people looking on had paid little attention; none of them had taken part, but on the other hand none of them had rebuked the children. I was angry, and reproached the two men who had been with me concerning the manners of their village. They were abject in apology, but protested that "it was only child's play." Bad manners in Chinese children are no bad manners; children, especially boys, are given a license that by our standards is monstrous. Indeed, there is hardly a crime graver than to make a small child cry, or to thwart it in any way. There is even a proverb, *ch'u men pu je san tze:* when traveling, do not annoy the three *tze;* these three tze being bearded men (old men), children (boys), and the blind. "Bearded men" does not in the least refer to foreigners, for the hairiness of foreigners is matter of reproach; but the scantiest beard of a mature Chinese (formerly a man was not even allowed to maintain a beard until he was past forty) is a mark of reverend dignity. Of the heinousness of annoying children I have already spoken; as for the blind, they are everywhere in China entitled to courtesy, and are commonly addressed as *hsien-sheng;* a term which, as it is ordinarily used for one's teacher, is even more respectful than our " sir." Thus, for an affair of children, however unmannerly, too much stir could not well be made. Nevertheless, the villagers were publicly shamed when I reproved them; it was not at all because the children had thrown mud, but because I had mentioned it. An insult in China is not an insult unless you take it up.

The road began to rise a little in the six or seven miles from Old Hsi Hu to Hsi Hu, so that, as it was much drier, we had no more difficulty. We entered the town when it was in a great bustle, for this was the eve of some important Mohammedan festival. I think it was the end of Ramadan, but I am not sure. The Chinese called it Mohammedan New Year, but then the Chinese in this province call any Mohammedan festival a New Year; it is all barbarian doings to them, and they do not inquire into it. Our carter was loath to proceed the next day, as were all the carters in town. A holiday was a holiday; if it was someone else's holiday, that was no bar to their enjoying it. Our man spent the morning taking the wheels off his cart and putting them on again, after an examination of the bearings. The axles on these carts, unlike those on some Chinese carts, which are fast to the wheels and turn with them, are fixed, and the wheels turn round the axle. The hub of the wheel is fortified with two metal rings, and the bearings on which they turn are slips of iron slotted into the ends of the axle. "My cart," said our buffoon with his usual cheerfulness, " is not much better than my ponies; but I cannot afford to repair it. Now let us go and see the fun."

All morning our inn and the streets were thronged with Moslems, Turki and T'ung-kan, spotlessly dressed, with white turbans of ceremony bound round their skullcaps, paying formal calls. In the afternoon came the great public spectacle, a game of *baiga*. This game of baiga, throughout Turkestan, celebrates the height of jollification and good-will. Town dwellers and nomads alike play at it, though properly it is a nomad's game, and it is frequently staged in honor of an important visitor, who is expected to defray the cost of a sheep and a gift to the winner. Prowess at baiga is a high proof of manly performance.

The game should really be played with a freshly slaughtered

sheep or goat; but a skin stuffed with straw costs less, and being lighter in weight is favored by townsmen, who cannot equal a nomad for strength in the saddle. At the start, a man gallops off with the carcass or stuffed skin on the pommel of his saddle, followed closely by all the competitors. When the whole troop is going headlong, he casts it away from him, and a free fight starts for the recovery. The nearest men lean from the saddle to pick it up, others crowd in on them, trying to push them out of the saddle, trying to force them away by the weight of horse and rider, trying to beat them about the head to make them let go. Fists and whips are freely used, and the excited ponies join in the fun with biting and kicking. If a man secures possession, either of the whole, or — if, as frequently happens, it has been torn to pieces — the largest fragment, he sets himself to break away and ride clear. The others keep after him, wrestling in the saddle, lashing with whips, tugging as they ride at the man's legs or clothes or the pony's bridle, mane, and tail. If the holder can escape, or if, preferably, he can ride back and cast the trophy in front of the judge or the man in whose honor the game is played, he is the winner.

The town was full of rumors, the usual fast-flying rumors of Central Asia, where the telephone is a traveler's tale, where only one man in two or three hundred can even read an official notice in simple language, where all news is carried by word of mouth, and where, on such an occasion, thousands of people, speaking several languages, have thronged together, all wrought up to excitement. The game had been held in the very early morning; the game would be held the next day; the game was about to begin; the game would be held on one side of the town; no, on the other side; the game was held up until someone could be found to present a sheep; the game had been officially forbidden, as inducing too much excitement. I should not have been surprised if it had been forbidden, for the Chinese authorities discourage too much high spirits; and in fact many extra troops had been called into town, from outlying posts, nominally as escorts to officers paying formal calls.

We had procured ponies once in the morning and ridden out with our jolly carter on a vain search for the game. Then, late in the afternoon, strolling out of the town on foot, we found the game itself in progress. It was held on a flat but most deceptive terrain, all the edges of which were steep gullies. The sheep had already been torn apart, but men with fragments of it were galloping about, fighting savagely as they rode. A pony would come down, neck under croup, and the pursuer would hurdle the spinning pony and rider, or cannon into them. A girth would part and a recklessly riding young blood, brilliantly gowned in his holiday best, would be thrown, rolling helplessly under the hoofs of half a dozen madly excited ponies. Two men, neither of them with even a portion of the sheep, but both with their blood up, would thunder past, riding knee to knee and hitting out savagely with fist or whip; or wrestling and heaving in the effort to throw each other. No one was hurt.

The sight of my camera made us the centre of the whole mob of several thousand people, who had seen the best of the original spectacle. The usual request to clear a lane through the crowd so that I could take a picture went unheard or unheeded; everyone in the crowd was carried away with excitement and eager to express it in physical exuberance. I saw that we had been foolish to come out unmounted, and tried to get away quietly. The best thing to do in an excited Chinese mob is to pick out the oldest and therefore most respected man in sight, and ask his escort in getting back to your inn. We could not manage it this time; old men had kept out of the rabble. A few rowdies saw that we did not like the treatment we were getting, and set out to torment us. Then a Chinese voice called out: " They don't like to be crowded! Let's push them, jostle them, hound them!" A wholly Chinese crowd would have been fired by the suggestion, and might have surged recklessly over us; but in this crowd a few Turki and Qazaq lads, not wanting to get into trouble, began to back out, pushing away from us and easing the pressure. We edged out, keeping as unconcerned as possible, — for to show that we were being galled would have precipitated trouble, — and slowly worked free, followed only by the taunts of one Chinese lout. We kept strolling aimlessly on the far side of the crowd, away from the town; to halt would have collected a fresh crowd, and anything like flight would have brought pursuit. When the main body of the concourse flooded back into the town, we started to walk in. Only a few young ruffians, most of them T'ung-kan, harried us, keeping at our heels or running up beside us to stare and guffaw. Even they fell off as we got near the centre of the town, where they might be reproved by more responsible people.

The excitement of a big baiga game keeps up several days; and as we journeyed on from Hsi Hu, we would suddenly meet a party galloping headlong down a road, several miles from a village, fighting lustily.

Hsi Hu — I was there three times altogether — was the roughest of all the towns we visited, though some of the Ili towns with big Chinese populations are pretty undisciplined. The lack of decorum is explained by the mixture of races; each race losing its own polish and picking up only the least desirable habits of the others. Hsi Hu is not only the centre of a rich agricultural district, but stands at the junction of three great roads — that from Urumchi, that from Chuguchak, and that from the Ili valley. Thus it has a large floating population. Moreover, it is the trading centre both of a Mongol tribe not far distant on the Ili road and of Qazaq tribesmen coming from the Chuguchak road. Places where the nomads trade are the worst of all centres of knavery. First the nomad must be cheated when he comes to market, and then, if he has any money to spare, he must be led to spend it in dissipation, or made drunk and robbed outright. In such places yarns are always told of people knocked down in dark lanes. The numbers of carters, pedlars, cheap-Jacks, cattle-dealers, horse-copers, occasional caravan men, touts, thieves, bullies, and plain vagabonds are swelled by tribesmen, both Mongol and Qazaq, of the kind lured to such a town; the spendthrifts and drunkards. These fellows acquire a smattering of all the current languages and thenceforth rely for their dubious living on acting as decoys for the " untamed " tribesmen from far-away camps, conducting them to the more villainous inns and delivering them into the hands of fly-by-night traders. The general atmosphere is one of bullying, swaggering, sly tripping, and outrageous imposture. Many of the younger

Chinese like to lord it as members of the ruling race, domineering over the barbarian natives; but this is Asia, where contradiction riots. Caste, creed, and tradition are firm and unshaken at the core; yet on the fringes of each race and social group expedient shifts and compromises prevail. Thus among the " natives " who have acquired what passes for a town smartness you find old scally-wags and young hellions matching swagger for swagger with the dominant Chinese. Survival in such a town requires a ready tongue, a front of brass, and, preferably, a pair of eyes in the back of one's head.

The game of baiga topped the peak of excitement in the day's diversions, but other things led up to it and lingered after. One of the best was the egg-knocking game, apparently sanctioned from of old by Mohammedan custom for celebration at this festival. All true sportsmen, having furnished themselves with hard-boiled eggs, issue into the streets to challenge other egg fanciers. The egg is grasped in the hand so as to expose only a minimum of the more pointed and harder end. Thus guarded, it is knocked against the point of a rival egg. The man whose egg is cracked loses it to the other man; and, as often as not, some money with it. This led Moses to inform us that the Chinese have a custom at their New Year of presenting eggs to people who have had a son during the year. The flattered parents boil the eggs, dye them, and return them — this being, I can only suppose, an acknowledgment of the compliment, meaning " We hope you'll have a son yourselves."

" T'ien-hsia i li," expounded Moses; " all under heaven is ruled by one law. About the time of the Chinese Ch'ing-ming, the Clear Brightness or Festival of Spring, there occurs the Christian Easter; and in Tientsin we call this the Wai-kuo chi-tan chieh, the Egg Festival of Outer Countries."

On arrival at Hsi Hu we had parted in all friendliness from our Qazaq courier, giving him a good tip. At Ulan Bulaq we had passed out of the "circuit" or lieutenant-governorship of Chuguchak, but he had been bound to see us as far as Hsi Hu, there to recommend us and his documents to the officials of the next circuit. On the evening of the festival he reappeared, his knowledge of the Chinese language much fuddled and his Plimsoll mark for

Chinese spirits well submerged, bringing a large present of cracked hard-boiled eggs, to judge from which he must have been a preëminent egg-knocker. Probably his original calculation had been that they would be good for another tip. Our cordial reception, however, so much elated him that he patted us both in the most fatherly way, beamed for a space with a vague devotion, and started to rock out of the door to tell his friends what noble folk we were, forgetting his ulterior motives. Moses detained him while we dug out a present. "How's that for a barbarian?" said Moses, the canny Chinese in him overcoming for a moment the single-minded retainer. "A couple of drinks, and he has no more sense. He goes and gets generous."

XIV

BEYOND THE BOGDO OLA

EASTWARD bound from Hsi Hu, we had a much fairer view of the country than I had been able to get when riding for the west through whirling snowflakes. On the south loomed up occasionally above the Zungarian dust the snow-peaks of the Heavenly Mountains; but ranged between them and our road, and growing more pronounced as we progressed to the east, was the minor, barren chain of foothills. On our north were the marshes, merging downward, somewhere in the haze of dust, to the melancholy trough of Zungaria. Coming down through the foothills and discharging into the marshes were turgid torrents, their rufous color showing that they were carrying off the spring melting of the lower snows, not the great summer dissolution of the snow-beds among the high peaks. The largest of these rivers is the Manass, which after entering the marshes bears on to the west and north, dying at last far out in the trough, in the marshes of Telli Nor. We found this river roaring briskly over the shale between its indeterminate banks. Shelves of ice along its banks yet withstood the spring warmth. At a convenient place, blocks of this ice had been heaped into buttresses, logs thrown across the stream, brushwood laid crosswise on the logs, and earth heaped over all, forming a bridge that would do for the season.

At Manass we had done with the greatest marshes. We found beyond, on level plains, the brief spring crop of grass appearing. Caravan tents were pitched here and there. No merchandise was parked before the tents; only provisions, felts, and pack-saddles, for the caravans were *tso ch'ang,* "sitting on the fields," putting the camels out to pasture for a respite after the winter's voyaging. The pasture on these low plains would parch as the heat increased, and the caravans would then remove eastward to the hill pastures of Ku Ch'eng-tze, and later perhaps Bar Köl, to give the camels the good lush feeding that would condition them after the season when they shed their hair, and fit them for the greatest journey of all, the hundred marches and more back through the deserts of Mongolia to Kuei-hua — Kuku-khoto, the Blue City — and the rim of China.

Our last *impression de voyage,* in the phrase of the Abbé Huc, was at a place in a hollow, locally called Hu-t'ou-pi, which according to the etymology of Moses is nothing other than Hu-t'ieh'rh Pei, " Butterfly Cup." We came to a ditch athwart the road, and the carter essayed to take it obliquely, to save the bump and drag out. He slung us right over, and the ponies went down in a whirl of hoofs. Luckily the hoops of the top held, so that we were no more than stood on our heads for a moment, in the soft gloom of bedding rolls and felts, with a touch of excitement added by the angles and corners of boxes. We crawled out to sit down on a bank, weak with laughter.

The carter looked at the wreckage. " Good," he said bitterly; " *tao-lo mei-liao!* " — a phrase meaning " finished," " annihilated," or " gone to hell," according to the intensity of utterance. " Cart upside down, horses flat on the ground, and all they do is to laugh! "

On the edge of Urumchi town the spring thaw was over and done with, and a tinge of green refreshed the land. In the town itself all was not yet well. We had to dismount at the outermost suburb and walk to our lodging. Throughout the winter the snow is trodden deep and hard in the streets. As it melts, the streets become channels filled with black liquid mire of an amazing viscosity; it may be two feet or a yard deep. For more than a month this must be laboriously scooped, swept, pushed, and carted out of the way, leaving sunken passages that show the foundations of houses and walls. During this period one must go abroad either in a small city cart or capering with the best agility one can summon along little raised footways at the side, where the drier mud has been heaped. In the summer the sunken streets become carpeted with soft dust, several inches thick, a chief ingredient of the next year's mire. It took three "Peking" carts to haul our luggage to us from the edge of town.

We did not stay this time at the friendly China Inland Mission, but in the guest quarters of a trading firm in which an interest had formerly been held by my friend Pan Tsilu, and which had formerly dispatched cargoes of Turkestan produce by caravan to the firm for which I had worked on the China Coast. It was more than two years before, in Tientsin and Peking, that I had come to know young Mr. Pan. He was then looking after business and family affairs, and perfecting his knowledge of English. It was with him that I had made the first journey to Kuei-hua, on the edge of Mongolia where the caravans gather and depart, that originally fired my ambition to travel in Central Asia. I learned then something of his talent in handling men and affairs. When I told him of my determination to travel by caravan, he had assured me of his interest and aid. I knew already his qualities as a charming companion, with a delightful sense of humor, and I knew that in spite of his youth he was already a traveler of distinction, having made the journey between Peking and Central Asia by three different routes. His modesty had not led me to divine how high a position he held in his native province. His father, who had died not long before, had been the stately, wise, and scholarly official who had held high rank as Governor at different times of Khotan and Aqsu, and finally as Provincial Treasurer, and had done a great deal to further the explorations of Sir Aurel Stein. He had been known throughout Chinese Central Asia as Pan the Good. His son had rapidly been promoted in the civil service, his knowledge of the world and his capacities as a linguist making him an ideal man in the handling of foreign relations. In his youth in Chinese Turkestan not only had he learned Russian, but a Catholic missionary had taught him French, and the Protestant missionaries had laid the foundations of his fluent command of English. He had also a knowledge of Turki, which is exceedingly rare among high officials.

When I reached the border of the province and was imprisoned,[1] it was his influence more than any other that had obtained

[1] See *The Desert Road to Turkestan*, p. 293.

permission for me to proceed to Urumchi. Later, his assurances
to the old Governor secured the commendatory passports that enabled us to travel so widely and freely. Wherever we went in
the province, the knowledge that we were " the friends of Mr.
Pan " secured us the most cordial treatment. When I first reached
Urumchi, he had been absent, holding the post of Civil Magistrate
in Aqsu; but he had returned since my departure for Chuguchak.
His agents at the trading establishment entertained us in a manner
to make us feel that we had at our disposal the whole province
and all that therein was. We had even to make our purchases
almost secretly. If we asked where a thing might be bought, the
answer was, " We will send an apprentice to get it." Nor could
we find out the price, nor pay for it when bought. Take money
from a guest? Not likely! We had even the greatest difficulty
in making a present to be dispensed among the apprentices at
our departure. In addition to being complimented with all the
entertainment that could have been offered a distinguished foreigner, we were advanced — which was far more flattering — to
the status of being of their own people. This even led to a few
evanescent embarrassments, especially for my wife. A household
servant, among the Chinese, is indeed *res domestica;* it is a part
of the charmingly unaffected relationship between master and
man, and in keeping with the tradition of the closed courtyard.
Servants pass in and out of the most private rooms without a shadow
of restraint. All the rooms open on inner courtyards; the outer
wall excludes the general world, while all within the courts are of
the household. That is why the stranger is not lightly admitted
to familiar standing. Once we had been so admitted, the apprentices saw no reason why they should not enter our room simply
by lifting the door curtain, without announcement, as they came
in soft-footed to bring a plate of cakes and dainties, or make sure
that the tea in the pot had not all been drunk, or grown stale.

Naturally, in such a traders' household as this, women are not
ordinarily found. Chinese traders going to reside in such a remote province as Chinese Turkestan, even if it be for a period
of years, almost never bring their families; though a man who can
afford it may very well set up a supplementary family if it suits

his convenience.   For officials to be accompanied by their wives is not nearly so uncommon.

With Mr. Pan we rode on excursions into the countryside, paid visits, and even attended a Russian wedding in the " bazar," formerly the Russian Concession, now a quarter of Rusian exiles and Russian Asiatic traders, provided by the Chinese authorities with special police and having special regulations as to the opening and closing of gates and other municipal matters.   In the midst of it the Soviet Consulate-General occupies the old consular quarters, but does not have the old jurisdiction over the concession area.

I think the best fun of all was our picnics at Shui-mo Kou, the Valley of Water-mills, not far from Urumchi.   You ride over bare downs, with a splendid vision, in clear weather, of the snowy Bogdo Ola, to find an easy valley with old willows and many flour mills.   A brick chimney gives the only modern touch; it stands over the arsenal, which also uses the water power of the stream.   The mill pools are full of variegated ducks, which are bred from wild ducks.   In glens off the valley are shrines and summerhouses and pavilions with a quaintly sophisticated air faintly reminiscent of the far-off Western Hills of Peking, which is explained by the fact that this was the place of exile of a Manchu prince of the blood who had been too much to the fore in fomenting the Boxer Rising and the attacks on foreigners in 1900.   The foreign powers demanded his exile from the court; but one version of the story current locally is that this quiet retreat was only a blind.   These princely quarters were kept up, but the prince himself, they say, evaded the ultimate bitterness of passing beyond the Great Wall, and spent his last years in the sufficiently remote province of Kan-su.

These picnics were cosmopolitan enough: McLorn, the Irishman, and his wife; a Russian friend of ours, formerly in charge of the Russo-Asiatic Bank, until its collapse, which left him stranded in Central Asia; Mr. A Hsing-a (the Chinese form of his name), a Sibo from the Ili valley who was in the postal service and spoke Chinese and Russian perfectly; and so on.   The presence of Mrs. McLorn and my wife allowed the wives of some of the Chinese to accompany them — mixed company being still a stiff hedge for the Chinese to jump except when following a foreign lead. Mrs. McLorn spoke no Chinese, but perfect Russian, having been born in Petrograd, whither her parents had gone from England. Thus with Russian, English, and Chinese no one was baulked of conversation. It was only at parties where many Russians were present that French and German were sometimes called in as auxiliary tongues. The strangest case, however, was that of the wife of a young Chinese in the postal service. She had come to this uttermost province straight from Swatow, in the far South. She did not speak a word of Mandarin, the official language of the North; nor did anyone in Urumchi speak a word of the dialect of Swatow, which is so distinct to those who speak it, and indistinct to those who do not, as to constitute a language apart. Thus she could not even talk with the wives of other Chinese officials except through her husband; which, as ladies in official life usually call on each other without the presence of men, was a minor social marvel of Urumchi.

Once we rode out to an isolated temple on a small hill. The red walls of this temple account for its popular name of Hung Miao-tze, the Red Temple. This name is frequently extended to Urumchi, so that the town is known as Hung Miao-tze, as Urumchi (a term of Mongol origin, used currently by Mongols and Turki-speaking people), and as Ti-hua — the official Chinese name, and that least in use. Perhaps the most generally used Chinese name is Hsin-chiang Sheng — Sinkiang Province, that is, which is used far more commonly of the provincial capital than of the province. There is also a highly colloquial expression, Sheng-shang, meaning, literally, " At the Provincial (Capital) " — that is, Urumchi. Between Hung Miao-tze (the temple) and Urumchi can be seen the fragmentary walls of a ruined city. At a casual glance they appear to be of no great age. They may well date no farther back than the Mohammedan Rebellion; but on the other hand it may be that their foundations rest on the unguessed-at ruins of a far more ancient city.

Thus passed a most pleasant interlude, while we were contemplating a short journey to Turfan. I was anxious to make this

excursion, both to get some knowledge of the trade-route communication between the two great divisions, the northern and the
southern, of Chinese Turkestan, and in particular to visit the area
of inland drainage known as the Turfan Depression. The eastern
end of Zungaria, at Urumchi, is divided from the South Road,
or Chinese Turkestan proper, by the Bogdo Ola. This range, the
name of which means Holy Mountains, is an extension of the T'ien
Shan system of ranges. From out in the desert it appears to rise
in majesty as a solitary peak, but it has in fact three peaks of an
altitude of more than 20,000 feet. According to Carruthers, the
Bogdo Ola was first reported as a volcano, by misapprehension.
In fact, to the present day caravan men scores of marches away in
Mongolia talk of it by their tent fires as a mountain that gathers
clouds about it "as it were like smoke"; but they have no de-
lusion whatever that the smoke is real, much less that the mountain is a volcano.

There is a gap between the Bogdo Ola and the main T'ien Shan
through which, at a height of no more than 5000 feet or so, goes
the pass that connects North Road and South Road. Not only is
this the point where North Road and South Road are closest together, but it is the only point where communication between the
two is comparatively easy and — above all — open all the year
round. It is the key to the government, trade, and strategy of the
whole province. Practically, the South Road terminates at Turfan.
In winter, it is true, there is fair communication with Hami
(Qomul) without crossing the pass to Urumchi; but this route
for a great part of the year is too hot and droughty for the slow,
heavy traffic of trade. In general, trade crosses over to Urumchi;
thence it can be directed either to Ku Ch'eng-tze for dispatch by
caravan, or along the North Road toward Chuguchak or the Ili
valley toward Siberia; or traversing by the gap between the Bogdo
Ola and Qarliq mountain masses it can be taken to Hami and
thence by the Great Imperial Highway toward Kan-su and China
Within the Wall.

Chinese Turkestan proper, south of the Heavenly Mountains,
comprises two enclosed areas, the Lop (or Tarim or Taklamakan)
and the Turfan. In both the water supply, flowing from the high

partially enclosing mountains, comes down in gorges through the desert barrier-ranges, and, after being tapped for the irrigation of oases lying in a line parallel with the mountains, sinks or evaporates in the ultimate deserts, salt marshes, and salt lakes. The difference between the two basins is best described by Professor Ellsworth Huntington, whose book, *The Pulse of Asia*, though hardly the Whole Testament, Old and New, of the geography of Central Asia, may perhaps be rated as its Book of Revelation.

" Turfan," he says,[1] " is small enough to be comprehended at a glance. It possesses the qualities of the life-sized representation, as opposed to the colossal. The basin floor extends scarcely one hundred miles east and west by fifty north and south; the area is only about two per cent of that of its gigantic neighbor [the Lop or Tarim basin]. From the west shore of the evanescent terminal salt lake of Böjanti, in the bottom of the basin three hundred feet below sea level, one can see at a glance all the features which, in the Lop basin, can become familiar only after months of travel; the ring of encircling mountains; the concentric zones; the dwindling, withering rivers, flowing from terraced valleys out upon the plain towards the inconstant lake which most of them strive in vain to reach; the zone of piedmont gravel; the gently sloping plain of the basin floor covered in part with dry brown reeds and pale green camel thorn also dry, and in part a mere waste of naked clay or hard, white salt; the aggregation of huge, sombre sand dunes five or six hundred feet high . . . the villages set in dark patches of irrigated land; and the ruined towns and dead vegetation giving evidence of a former more abundant water supply."

Moreover, the Bogdo Ola, from which Turfan derives its water supply, do not hold so much snow (at least on their southern versant) as do the main T'ien Shan. For this reason the water is at its highest in the spring, and there is not the increasing supply all through the summer that makes life easy in other oases along the South Road. For this reason also the oases of Turfan depend entirely on oasis products; there is not the " perpendicular " structure that I have described, which elsewhere provides trade be-

---

[1] *The Pulse of Asia,* pp. 295-96.

tween the people of the oases and the people of mountains rich
in pasture lands, or forests and wild animals, or gold-bearing
streams, or coal and iron.

From Urumchi we ascended through bare foothills, and on the
second day were in the great valley between the Bogdo Ola and the
main T'ien Shan. On the northerly side the Bogdo Ola appeared
as one commanding peak, with a band of rising desert between
it and our road. At an altitude of over 6000 feet, under its
final summits and at the foot of its magnificent glaciers, is a sacred
lake. On an island in the lake and in temples beside it are Chinese (Taoist) monks, who undoubtedly inherit from a long tradition of holy men of other races; for throughout history the peaks
of the Bogdo Ola appear to have been sacred to the peoples of this
part of Central Asia. About the lake is a forest sanctuary, where
trees may not be felled or game hunted; it conserves, as it were,
the "life principle" and nourishes the sources of life of the whole
region.

On our southerly side was a lake, which has no visible affluents
or outlet; but undoubtedly it derives its water from under the piedmont gravel of the enclosing mountains, and is drained, through
subterranean connections, by the stream that flows down the pass
toward the South Road. On the far side of the long, narrow
lake were barren mountains covered to a great extent along their
sides with "skirts" of broken scree. The savage winds of Zungaria and Chinese Turkestan are commonly said by the people
of the country, whether nomads or settled folk, to issue from a
hole in the bottom of some lake, which is protected with an iron
gate or lid. If this lid could be properly fitted, the winds would
stop. The winds of Turfan are said to come from this lake.[1]
At the end of the lake, towards Turfan, are three monoliths, one
of them fallen, and five large tumuli arranged in a line, surrounded
by curious broken circles of small boulders on the bare ground.
The disposition of the whole site is a little confused by the mounds
about the shafts giving access to an abandoned *karez,* or underground irrigation canal. Professor Huntington seems to have
missed the fallen monolith and the human face faintly carved on

[1] *The Pulse of Asia,* p. 300.

it, which resembles the " Uighur " standing stones found in parts of Eastern Siberia and Northern Mongolia, sometimes with complete heads and sometimes, like this stone, only carved with a face in shallow relief.[1] " The whole aspect of these relics of an unknown race," says Huntington,[2] " is almost identical with that of certain mounds and stones which I saw . . . at Son Kol and Issiq Kol, six hundred miles to the west." The Reverend G. W. Hunter told me that there were a number in the Ili district; of which we ourselves later saw not a few.

Beyond the lake the road runs for a long stage through dried-out swamps to a town with the hybrid name of Dawan Ch'eng, "the City of the Pass." Leaving the city one comes immediately to the Dawan, the pass leading down to the South Road. Here a river, originating in the swamps, cuts through an almost flat-bottomed gorge toward the south. Along the edge of the water is an ancient Chinese road, marked by stone tablets, which in recent times has been so undercut by floods that it has been abandoned. When the water is low, carts bump along through the boulders of the stream-bed, but during high water they climb out to the pass itself, which crosses two very steep cols, where sliding surfaces of scree and gravel make haulage appallingly difficult; and not only is the ascent laborious, but the descent is dangerous, for a cart is likely to get away, and overrun the team.

Beyond the walled-in part of the gorge, filled at the water's edge with willow thickets and poplar, the road climbs out on to the gravel desert of the sloping piedmont zone. Here, at a lonely Chanto inn under bluffs of clay by a tiny spring, the road divides, the minor branch leading to Turfan and the major one to Toqsun, on the direct route to Kashgar. At this place a few curious domes of clay appear, like anomalous bubbles forced up through the shale and gravel. We " holed up " at the inn during the heat and glare of the noonday, going on by night to a group of inns at a place called Three Springs. When we started once more with the first streaks of dawn, we saw that we were in a scene of strange, unreal,

---

[1] Carruthers, *Unknown Mongolia,* Chap. II, " Ancient Siberia "; illustrations at pp. 54, 60, 66.

[2] *The Pulse of Asia,* p. 300.

harsh beauty, in the middle of a desert of naked stone. Near the drab gray inns, all squatting close to the ground and all windowless without, opening on interior courtyards, was one of the Three Springs; a trickle of water among the stones — water which, starting among the snows of summits now invisible to us, being hidden by the convexity of the lower mountain slopes, and sinking untimely into the masses of shattered rock that bury the foot of the range, here came to light for a few scanty yards. The water had miraculously afforded an irregular patch of green among the stones, where tufts of iris were blooming. Away to the left, up the incline of the piedmont slope, were the other two springs, each marked by a spot of green, showing that some fault in the underlying rock-strata here lifted the water to the surface. For the rest, as far as we could see, was nothing but the slow undulations of the desert of broken stone, which had slid from the tops of the mountains through the ages and lay piled to unknown depths about their bases. We could see that this wan desert pitched downward to the unseen South Road, and that we were to travel across it at a crablike angle; but that was all.

XV

THE LAND OF LOST CITIES

WE were now traveling in a new style. My wife and I had saddle ponies, while Moses traveled more slowly in a two-wheeled Turki cart, with our kitchen battery and a few effects. My wife rode a splendid black which we had just purchased in Urumchi, while I rode a raking bay lent to me by Mr. Pan; a friendly attention which can only be fully appreciated by owners of horses, and those who have traveled in Central Asia. Pan Tsilu is a traveler of contemporary fame in Chinese Turkestan. The Chinese official, proceeding from one post to another, travels usually with all the dignity and leisure possible, even if comfort is hard to achieve. With Mr. Pan, however, every journey is a succession of forced marches. Before returning from Aqsu to Urumchi, he had bought a choice company of ponies. Putting his light baggage on pack ponies, and accompanied only by three or four attendants, he had ridden the journey in double and treble stages. They were ponies of fine quality, for not one of them had been abandoned on the way.

The pony lent to me, although bred in the famous Qara Shahr district (or rather the Yulduz plateau above it), had an unmistakable Russian strain. It was not Mr. Pan's own mount, not having the *ta-tsou* or " great amble," the most fashionable gait. It had a racking trot, but for long marches was trained to the *hsiao-tsou* or " small amble," than which nothing can be more comfortable. It was characteristic of Mr. Pan that he did not tell me what a valuable pony he had lent me. Months later, at Aqsu, I heard this pony described, and was asked if I knew anything of it; for it had, apparently, won an all-comers' two-mile race. That the pony should have been lent to me for a ride to Turfan was enough to enhance my dignity. That is one of the jolliest things about Central Asia—the way you will hear the points of a pony discussed when he is hundreds of miles away; and the way that your having seen or ridden him establishes you as a friend among strangers. The stranger, to be sure, is rarely more of a personage than a private soldier dressed in rags, with an undischargeable rifle; but he can do a lot for you on the road.

The dawn was chilly and fresh at the Three Springs, but with a dryness in the air giving no promise that the freshness would last. No sooner had the sun come up than the hot light struck us like a blow, and the blow became a steady, increasing pressure that crushed one to the hot, sullen stones. Beyond the verge of the springs there was no more sign of any life at all, not even the meagre growth of stunted tamarisk that you find in the Black Gobi. It was worse than any desert I had seen in all Mongolia. Our ponies were as crushed by the heat as we, and jogged dispiritedly over the stones, every drop of sweat dried off them by the heat pulsating above and all about, and reflected from below. At sunrise a sudden wind had torn off my hat and sent it racing away at an incredible speed, until, even as we watched, it was torn apart on the stones. I had nothing to put on my head but a thin handkerchief; but, though the dry heat wilted us both, body and marrow, I had no signs of a sunstroke. The road took us a full thirty miles over this waste. Insane mirages jerked and jumped all about us. At times the horizon broke into bays and inlets of unreal water; at other times illusory hills, trees, and travelers hovered in the air. The real world you did not see. Once the mirage parted a bare fifty yards or so before us, and we met a few jaded Turki travelers on woebegone donkeys; all of them having been invisible as they approached across the open, stone-littered desert, because of the shrouding heat-waves. At last, in the afternoon, we saw the road sink before us, and the flash of real though dusty green. Either the ponies also saw the treetops, or else the scent of water reached them, for they cantered willingly, carrying us down to the first water, the first oasis, and the first inn of desert-girdled Turfan.

We were now at the edge of the piedmont zone, where water, breaking out from under the gravel, had cleft a ravine through cliffs of loess. Despite the heat, a few men were at work on an aqueduct, built of halved and hollowed poplar logs, carried across the ravine on trestles. We found a rill of water in a ditch under young poplars. There my wife hung her feet in the water and her tongue on her chin, while I, going farther up, found a place where I could strip and lie down in the ditch, with the shallow water sluicing over me.

The heat, in that boxed-in place, did not abate even when the dusk came, and after it the night. After Moses and the cart had overhauled us, we ate sweltering at the inn, the single candle that lit up our grimy, mud-walled room seeming to heat the place intolerably. We lay down for a few hours of fretful rest, and at midnight rose again to begin a last march that should bring us to Turfan Town itself. The air seemed still to cling about us in stifling folds, and even in the darkness one could taste dust. In a little while an old and haggard moon came up and threw a sickly light on steep-sided bluffs of clay, among which we burrowed on a dark, sunken road. It was only our ponies, who shied at vague shapes and snorted at what they could not see, that kept us from falling asleep. Then the stars began to pale, dimmed by something more than the struggling light of the moon, and all at once the sultry end of night cooled in the breathing space before dawn. As the gray light spread we came scrambling down the clay sides of a gully to cool, sweet water, and looked back and up to a wilderness of riven clay like the fragments of huge fortifications. On the other side we climbed again to more flat-topped bluffs, where we met the full dawn and saw scattered groups of trees and houses, ditches of water, and green fields, broken by stretches of flat clay desert. The early morning was already hot when we reached the sanctuary of the walled city.

"You are going to Turfan?" an old Turki yamen-runner and interpreter on the North Road had asked me. "Ah, Turfan! It is a good place. Clean, clean! I left it when I was a boy and have never saved the money to go back. But it is clean, clean. The streets of the bazar are cleaner than the k'ang of the Chinese. There not even the horse of a traveler can leave anything in the street without someone rushing up to tidy it." He had no higher praise. As usual, however, we found that the inn of the big town was more filthy, more smelly, and in the hands of people more impudent, lazy, and thievish than the inns of tiny halting places by the road; but even while we were lamenting the evil prospect, there sought us out a Russian Tatar. He was a merchant I had met in Urumchi, and having seen us pass through the streets he had come to rescue us and install us in a cool Turki room, with thick clay walls and arched windows opening on a private court. Then, our lodging settled, we went to " open our eyes," which is the admirable Chinese phrase for staring, in the bazar or trading quarter.

The walled city, in vivid contrast with the open country, is cool and green. Over the central streets, which are at once passageways and market-places, are trellises, covered with mats, gourd-vines, and the branches of willows and poplars. In the chequered shade the people step softly, loose-robed and barefooted or slipper-shod; and as they chatter in Turki, guttural but soft, the eyes of women flash under stenciled eyebrows and the teeth of men flash from black beards. From wells and ditches at the city gates of battlemented mud little boys drive innumerable donkeys carrying water pannier-wise in wooden butts, to be splashed over the streets. From the time that the struggle against the heat begins in the morning until it slackens at dusk, the whole population flings water on the walls and floors of houses, on the streets, and on the vegetables for sale in little booths or spread out on the clean streets. Although we splashed water copiously on the walls of our room, it dried in a few minutes. The streets, thus constantly moistened and patted with bare feet and slapped with slippers, do indeed become beautifully smooth and clean.

The shopping hour is over by nine in the morning. After that, riding along the empty streets, one may see only in the recesses of the shops figures seated cross-legged, magnificently set off by the muted glow of carpets and bright wares in dark corners; poised in that most commanding sloth which goes by the name of Oriental dignity. Through deserted gateways one gets a glimpse here of the carved wooden galleries and plaster domes of mosques and

COVERED STREET IN TURFAN

OLD TURKI SHAVING CHILD'S HEAD

TURFAN ROAD

there of caravanserais, with courtyards walled about with bales of cotton and populated by somnolent donkeys.

To break the spell of this daylight trance one has only to produce a camera. At once appears one of those small boys who are the forerunners of crowds all the world over. Then another small boy abandons his donkey-load of street-assuaging water and with whooping and capering musters the full citizenry — Hajis who have seen Mecca, but not a camera in action, traders who would not walk ten yards to close a deal but will run fifty to be in at the taking of a picture, bold maidens, jaunty youths to elbow the maidens, and ecstatic matrons whose bliss would be complete if somebody would elbow them. The Turkis of Turfan Town, by reason of their nearness to Urumchi and the coming and going of Chinese traders, have many of them a knowledge of Chinese. With the power of speech with the ruling race they have lost much of the deferential timidity of the main Turki population toward Kashgar. Their excitement, however, does not tend to get out of hand and turn, as that of a street crowd on the North Road sometimes will, into furtive mobbing. The front ranks readily understood when we wanted a clear space for the cameras, and tried to give it to us; but nothing could be done with a crowd fifty yards deep and steadily agglomerating, who could not hear our words. We had in fact to go out usually on horseback, and to take most of our photographs from the saddle; an exciting recreation in which it is always touch and go whether one gets the picture taken first, or whether the unfailing small boy, diving under the belly of one's pony at the last moment in hope of a better view, sends him panicking for forty yards through cabbages, cook-shops, and babies.

My wife was a centre of the most fervid interest. We were several times told that she was the first white woman ever seen in Turfan; she never went through the streets except at the head of a procession. For all that, the natural manners of the people were delightful. When we tried to buy a saddlebag of soft Lop Nor wool, picked out with bright colors in bands of angular designs, — such a saddlebag as is brought occasionally from the most

remote corner of Chinese Turkestan, by trade routes only inter-
mittently in use, — a reverend Haji was elected with astonishing
rapidity to preside over a committee of purchase. The committee
settled a fair price without further reference to us or the shop-
keeper, took the money from us and the bag from him, and exchanged them with deliberate gravity. Fee to the Haji, one photograph; the multitude holding back with arrested breath while it
was taken.

Turfan Town is the head of all the towns and villages of the
Turfan Depression. It stands just south of the Fire Mountains,
a line of red hills which mark a geological " fault " at the foot of
the piedmont slope from the main Bogdo Ola range. At this
fault the water of the high mountains reappears from its burial
under the slopes of gravel, and flowing through gorges in the red
hills emerges into the Turfan Depression. The water of each
stream is dispersed over the plain through ditches, while between
the streams and beyond the limit to which their water can be carried the farmers depend on *karez,* a Persian irrigation device imported to Turfan only at the end of the eighteenth century. Karez
are wells, dug in series to tap an underground flow of water. Each
well is sunk until it strikes water, and by tunneling from the bottom of each well to the next, a distance of only twenty or thirty
feet, an underground canal, or rather sewer, is constructed. The
mouths of the wells serve as approaches from which the sewer can
be cleaned. The wells decrease in depth from the direction of the
mountains out into the plain, until at last the water is brought
to the surface and runs into a ditch.

Huntington,[1] twenty years ago, estimated the population of the
entire Turfan basin at about 50,000, of whom about 20,000 depended wholly on karez water. Beyond the area of karez irrigation, the bottom of the Turfan Depression becomes too saline
and swampy for human habitation. Turfan Town stands at
about sea-level; the lowest level of the hollow goes down some
three hundred feet below sea-level, at the evanescent lake of Böjanti,
which holds a measure of water in winter, but only mud in summer.
An ascent to the far rim of the hollow then begins, with a belt of

[1] *The Pulse of Asia.*

piedmont gravel rising to a desert range and the unexplored deserts that reach all the way to Kan-su.

In ancient times, though the use of karez was unknown, the climate of Turfan must have been much more favorable: according, at least, to the cogent arguments of Huntington, the protagonist of the theory that climatic variation must be used as the key to understanding the cyclical waxing and waning of civilization in this inner region of Central Asia. He points out that even now, with the added resort of the karez, which supports about 40 per cent of the population, the limits of agriculture are more restricted than they were in the remote past, and the total population cannot by any reckoning be as great as it then was. The water supply must have been greater then, and it must have been possible to carry the water farther than it is now carried by karez, as is proved by the numerous ruins beyond the zone in which cultivation is now possible by the aid of karez. About the beginning of the Christian Era there existed in the Turfan basin, as in the greater Lop or Tarim basin, a much denser population, of a high civilization. Then came several centuries of drought; ice caps in the far mountains receded, rivers withered away, and the population dwindled. The steady relapse from the high point of culture in the period just antecedent to the birth of Christ was varied by intervals of partial recovery. At the end of the first millennium A.D. Islam was implanted in Central Asia,[1] and thereafter the arts and letters, and all but the thinnest shadow of the memory of the old opulent Buddhist culture, were utterly forgotten.

In Turfan, a period of climatic amelioration, at a comparatively late period, flowered in a second civilization of the highest significance; for it was a point of fusion of the cultures of many lands and peoples of varying traditions. To this period belongs a secondary series of ruins. "Qara-Khoja, the largest of the ruined towns, was founded between 874 and 913 A.D., and existed until 1644 A.D. or later. In its days, Turfan was renowned for its library, its art, and its craft, as well as its might in war. . . . An examination of the languages [from manuscripts on paper, leather, and

---

[1] That is, it first became permanently established at that time, though known long before.

wood, recovered from the ruins] shows how, when favorable climatic conditions caused Turfan to become capable of supporting a dense population, people poured in from every quarter. Speakers of Nagari and of two dialects of Brahmi came from India on the southwest; Tibetans and Tanguts brought their language from the southeast; Chinese from the east; Uighurs and Turks from the northeast, north, and northwest; while from the west came people who were probably Nestorian Christians, and who brought the Syriac and Manichæan tongues and an unknown language allied to Syriac. The presence of Tibetan manuscripts in Turfan is especially interesting because at the end of the eighth century there was a great incursion of Tibetans into Chinese Turkestan. The underlying cause of this is not known with certainty; but apparently, during the preceding dry, warm epoch, Tibet had become relatively habitable, while now, when the climate became colder [that is, when the ice-caps on the high mountains advanced again, resulting in a renewed flow of water during the summer, and the enclosed basins of Chinese Turkestan could once more support increased populations], the Tibetans found difficulty in raising crops or in maintaining flocks upon their high plateau, and so sought new homes." [1]

Islam entered Chinese Turkestan, beginning at Kashgar, about the year 1000, in the train of conquerors from the West; but though thereafter the climate revived to some extent, culture never again reached the height attained in the Buddhist era; probably because, though life became easier and the population increased, the ancient trade routes were never restored to the free use they had enjoyed during what we may call the two Great Periods — that of the Chinese Han dynasty in the second and first centuries B.C., and that of the T'ang dynasty, whose apogee was in the seventh century A.D. To my mind, the stimulus of a great through traffic along the line of oases, kept up by the great dynasties between China and the thither West, must have played a major part in developing wealth, providing an occupation for large town communities, and encouraging the growth of a superior culture. Without the stimulus of a through traffic the natural tendency of these enclosed regions of Inner Asia, as can well be seen at the present time, is to fall into

---

[1] Huntington, *The Pulse of Asia,* based in part on Grum-Grschimailo and von Lecoq.

a sort of timeless, enchanted stagnation, neither decaying nor progressing.[1]

Islam deletes most of what has gone before it, but two series of links continue to bind Inner Asia to the high days of its past: one, a reliquary chain of monuments; the other, an umbilical connection of living tradition, obscure though that tradition be. Search in the vicinity of what are now Mohammedan shrines or places of pilgrimage has never failed to show traces of older holy places and an older religion. Some of these are associated with legends of the struggles between the Mohammedan invaders and the supporters of Buddhism. The legends of some of the shrines are obscure; people worship there simply by the force of inherited veneration, because the place has been holy since time out of mind. A holy place of great fame may lie far out in a desert totally beyond redemption; the pilgrims who resort there may be ignorant of the fact that not far away are the ruins of a city once flourishing; or if they know of the ruins, they do not realize that the shrine of our time occupies the site or the neighborhood of a shrine of that obliterated city. The way in which traces of many different religions may adhere, with the passage of time, to one holy place could not be better shown than by the picture I took of a cemetery near Turfan. The domes of the graves are Mohammedan. The short, straight wall built across the entrance way as an apparently needless obstruction is nothing but the Chinese *pi-hsieh ch'iang,* or "avoidance-of-uncanny-influences wall." The Chinese believe that ghosts and evil spirits can move only in straight lines. By putting such a wall in front of the gate of a city, private house, or cemetery, they force whoever enters to go around before getting at the gate, and evil influences are thus circumvented. The wall, in this instance, is surmounted by the skulls of wild sheep, which, everywhere in this part of Inner Asia, are relics of the most primitive religious instincts of the people, a witness of the shamanism or "witch-doctoring" which is older than even Buddhism, and still survives among the nomad tribes, and can be traced among the lowland Mohammedans as well.

The monuments — ruined cities, forts, and temples — occupy

[1] See also my article, "Caravan Routes of Inner Asia," *Geographical Journal,* December 1928.

almost exclusively sites out in the desert, on the dry courses of what were once living streams. I have described how the oases of the present day are near the end of a stream that flows down from the glaciers and high snows of the great mountains, out through a desert barrier-range, and into the desert, there at the end either to die in a marsh or saline lake, or wither in the sand. The dead cities were once the centres of similar oases, which were abandoned because the decreasing water supply from the distant mountains failed to continue flowing so far out into the plains. Owing to the fact that the tendency to an increasingly dry climate has been on the whole progressive, the cities are found in zones, or roughly parallel lines; the line farthest out being that of the cities of the Golden Age of Central Asian Buddhism, and the lines between it and the modern oases representing periods of recuperation, when the streams revived and people pushed out again into the desert. Apparently none of these periods of recuperation quite equaled its predecessor; so that, although sites are found where new cities were built on the foundations of cities that once had been abandoned, it is more usual to find that each dead city represented a period of its own.

Once the supply of river water had ceased, the dry climate, almost as rainless as that of Egypt, allowed the fabric of silk and paper, and the colors of paintings and stuccoes, to be preserved almost inviolate; dry sand invaded the abandoned cities and shrouded them in a clean, mummifying sepulchre. In the places where cities were built successively, one above the other, the different strata allow the determination of dates and periods. Other cities, the nearest to the present water supply, may never have been abandoned for lack of water, but have been wiped out in war. The increase of agriculture, the extension of irrigation, and the growth of population in the last two generations of peaceful Chinese rule have brought a few of these places once more within the range of cultivation, so that fields reach right up to and within their crumbling walls, and digging peasants have brought to light and destroyed many of their treasures.

We had planned to visit Qara-Khoja and perhaps other ruins that could be reached by riding out a day or two from Turfan; but we had not reckoned with the weather. We knew that Turfan at the end of April would be hot,[1] but we had not reckoned on being there in the worst season of dust storms. Every day, as the sun grew hot, a strong wind rose, bringing sand from the desert and lifting the loose dry soil of the fields. Air and sky turned yellow, and to venture out of doors, even in the city, was highly unpleasant. Sometimes the wind fell at evening, but sometimes it continued into the night. As nothing can be seen in the ruined cities except mud walls crumbling above the surface, unless one digs, and we had not come to dig (to the disappointment of a large number of guides who offered themselves), we stayed only three days. Near the city we did see the ruins of one large town, which may have dated from the mediæval Mohammedan period, but was more probably destroyed in the wars of the Mohammedan Rebellion fifty or sixty years ago. The scars of its abandonment are being wiped out by tilth and harvest. The chief monument near it is a great brick tower, built apparently by a local ruler, Suliman, at the end of the eighteenth century. Like many a monument of Chinese Turkestan, it harbors " holy " pigeons; but we found some small boys catching pigeons in the cavernous and vault-like spaces of an abandoned mosque near the tower. They simply kept the birds fluttering through the building until, dazed by the dim light and the pillars, they cowered on the ground. A stew of holy pigeons probably tastes as good as any.

When we said to our friendly host the Tatar that we were going away from Turfan, after such a short stay and without having " done " the more genteel sights, he was horrified. People would know he had entertained us at Turfan; they would think he had done it poorly. We must at least picnic with him at Grape Valley. In spite of the weather, we decided to risk another day, and he started with zest on the assemblage of a picnic.

[1] Skrine (*Chinese Central Asia*), writing of Kashgar, points out that, owing to the extreme "continentality" of these regions, April is warmer than October, which in other parts of the world is the warmer month. Even so, we were surprised at the heat. It was quite as oppressive as Peking ever is in July and August; the thermometer must have stood steadily at over 90° in the shade, after morning. The fact that only a month before we were struggling through the snow of "Old Windy Pass" is as good an example as I can recall of the extraordinary range of temperature and sudden contrasts of climate in Chinese Central Asia.

XVI

VINEYARD AND DESERT

IN several gorges of the red sandstone hills called the Fire Mountains — a name which once gave rise, like the "smoke" of the Bogdo Ola, to reports of a Central Asian volcano — almost nothing is grown but grapes. The most famous of these valleys is that of Tuyoq, where stands the shrine of the Seven Sleepers.[1] The grapes from this valley were formerly dispatched exclusively to Peking, as Imperial tribute. The gorge nearest Turfan, however, is that called by the Chinese P'u-t'ao Kou, Grape Valley, a famous beauty spot and picnic resort. In these valleys of vine culture almost nothing else is grown, the villagers drawing even their food supply in large part from the plain. Many varieties of grapes are grown, including one which makes a tolerable brandy, which has lately become popular; though grape wines are not characteristic of either the Chinese or the Turkis. The most famous grape is that from which tiny seedless raisins are made; this is the old Imperial variety. The raisins are still dispatched in hundreds of camel loads every year from Ku Ch'eng-tze. They make a favorite Chinese New Year gift, but above all they are prized both in rich Mongol lamaseries and in Chinese Buddhist monasteries. A tray of delicacies is always offered to distinguished visitors and the guests of abbots, together with the tea of formal welcome, and on the tray should always appear a few raisins of Turfan; only a tithe of a handful, but still raisins of Turfan. These are the grapes of the Chinese proverb, which enumerates the Three Marvels of Chinese Turkestan: —

---

[1] A. von Lecoq, *Auf Hellas Spuren in Ost-Turkistan.* Leipzig, J. C. Hinrichs'sche Buchhandlung, 1926.

T'u-erh-fan-ti p'u-t'ao
Ha-mi-ti kua;
K'u-ch'e-ti ku-niang
I-chih hua.

(Turfan for grapes, and Hami — Qomul — for melons;
  The girls of Kucha are all like flowers.)

In Turfan also we ate melons, kept in cellars from the last summer's crop, that anyone would call the best in the world who had not heard of the melons of Hami.   Melon preserve is also made by cutting ripe melons into strips, which after being dried in the sun are braided into flat round cakes.   The melons of Hami are the best for drying, because they retain the most flavor: these braided melons are rich, sticky, and sweet, and reminiscent of figs.   The intense dry heat makes it possible to dry the melons before they rot.

Our host came for us in the morning; in fact, so anxious was he to borrow the manners of the Chinese and show us honor by coming early that he arrived before the day was fully light.   He took us out to the hills in a cart of the kind which foreigners call a "Peking" cart and the Chinese a sedan-cart: a two-wheeled, springless affair with a little blue kennel or sedan for the passengers.   The best of these carts used to come all the way from Peking, hauled for two thousand miles or so across Mongolia by camels; but most of them are made now in the province itself.   A drive of six or seven miles took us across a skirting plain, mostly desert, to the mouth of the red gorge.   Then, entering it, we found terrace above terrace grown with vines, and in the depth of the gorge brushwood and jungly trees.

We found the picnic prepared for us under a huge trellised vine, the pride of its owner, who declared it was at least a hundred and fifty years old.   It enclosed a room or bower, a place about forty feet square.   The owner, the host of our host as it were, was a tall, white-bearded man of eighty-eight, not in the least enfeebled by age.   In spite of the dust and the summer heat, the climate of Turfan is so dry and regular, and the life led by peasant cultivators so easy and untroubled, that they say men frequently reach the age of a hundred.   This patriarch had been a rebel, and evidently a man of consequence, in the days of Yakub Beg, for after the suppression of the rebellion he had been held as a prisoner or hostage in China for fifteen years.

Besides our host, the Russian Tatar, and his younger brother, the party included a young Turfanlik who had received in Urumchi the Chinese education offered to Turkis who wish to enter the lower official ranks. After a few years in the government service he had returned to Turfan to become a merchant. With him was another Turfanlik, who spoke Russian and had twice been to Nijni-Novgorod, to the great fair which gives a Russian focus to all the traders of Central Asia, and which indeed ranks so high in their affairs that Nijni-Novgorod, Mecca, and Roum, or Constantinople, are the only points beyond their own periphery by which the people of Central Asia orient themselves; as for Bajin, or Peking, it is so remote as to belong more to legend than to sober voyaging. His having resorted twice to Nijni-Novgorod, whence he had brought back shiny yellow boots and the theory of evolution, made the young merchant the leading sophisticate of our party.

The rule of China is in general laid very lightly on the shoulders of her subject races in Central Asia; but the strong hold of her culture appeared in one remarkable thing. There was no Chinese present in the party, there was not one of us who spoke Chinese as his native tongue, and yet the only language common to us all was Chinese. Moreover the language that we spoke hovered like a quaintly distorted shadow over our proceedings, obtruding at moments odd formalities and the stiff, set phrases of Chinese etiquette into what otherwise would have been the pure joviality and hearty fun of a Central Asian good time. Our manners, indeed, were a mixed parade. The Tatars, from their Russian associations, brought something of the comfortable fussiness that is considered good form among the Russian middle classes and petty traders. Most of the time, the prodigality of the Turki was in the ascendant; and as for us, we shed as freely as we could, seeing that it was expected of us to display a little superior Western worldliness, the awkward deportment of the alien, and the callousness of the tourist.

Our host, except for the skullcap of the Moslem, was dressed in Russian " store clothes," while his younger brother wore the Russian peasant blouse. The two Turkis wore their own costume,

THE AUTHOR AND THE LUSCIOUS TURKI
GRAPE VALLEY, TURFAN

modified in cut to show a hint of Europe, as seen through Russian eyes. He of Nijni-Novgorod, with his oval, olive face, his full, languid eyes, his petulant but dainty mouth with the demurely precious, heart-captivating little oiled moustache, suggested the French idea of a really delectable young man all dressed up to receive in his Oriental apartments a woman married to somebody else and old enough to be his aunt; but at the same time a suggestion of the fat that in a few years would obliterate his lithe waist and cushion his ravishing hips, hinted at the Turkish bath attendant.

He, however, was nothing but a sketch of the full-blown beauties of the sometime official, whose charm lingered more in his luscious nature and engaging soul than in his figure, for he was built in ovoid curves, and signally large, perspiring, and soft withal. The smaller end of this fleshly ellipse was decorated, very much at one side, with an embroidered skullcap of mulberry plush, while the lower outlines were veiled more with hangings than with clothes. Under a white jacket he wore a frilled white shirt, and below the shirt his flesh heaved tumidly in a pair of purple trousers, which, to be really devilish, had been cut European-fashion, to button in front. They must have been executed in his more frolicsome youth, for none of the buttons would contain him, and his shirt hung out like a wilted sporran. He spoke fluent — nay, copious — Chinese, of a high-flown sort, in a saccharine voice like a nightingale choked with Turkish delight. His mind, besides being above trouser buttons, was out of sight of them.

He had not been educated for nothing, and surprised me by being conversant with the civilization of the Uighurs; for most Turki people are not interested in the pre-Mohammedan past. The people of Turfan, he said, really represent the ancient Uighurs, but have totally forgotten their own origin and written language since the Mohammedan conversion nearly a millennium ago. As a matter of fact the people of Turfan can hardly be Uighurs, if Huntington is correct, for he says [1] that in the middle of the seventeenth century Turfan was practically depopulated, owing to Mongol raids, which made the oases untenable for cultivators. It is a little surprising that Huntington, who is much concerned to show

[1] *The Pulse of Asia.*

the effect of climatic variation on the movement of peoples, should speak so casually of "raids"; for the period in question was that of the great upheaval among the Zungar or Ölöt Mongols, north of the T'ien Shan, who extended their conquests to Samarqand and were at one time like to challenge the Manchu conquest of China. After they had been overthrown by K'ang Hsi, Turfan was peopled again by Turki stock coming in from the oases to the west, along the Kashgar road.

Our Nijni-Novgorod-haunting friend was not much concerned with the doings of the dead past. He proclaimed himself an intellectual, a freethinker, but concerned primarily with the world we live in now; and prepared, moreover, to think as freely about new creeds as about the old. Evolution, he informed us, is the new religion of Russia, where people are mad after theories; but, according to the canons of his free thought, to say that man and monkey are the children of the same father is as idle a superstition as to say that three gods combined in having one son by a virgin, or that Mohammed really had arguments with a mountain about whose move it was next. As for our host, he was a plain, practical man. He believed that getting together and good-fellowship were conducive to the prosperity of business. He dealt mainly in the celebrated Turfan cotton, which is derived from an American long-staple stock. The cultivation of it in Central Asia began after the American Civil War, which had cut off supplies from Russian spinners, causing great hardships. Consequently when the Russians, at about the same time, began their sweeping march into the Central Asian Khanates, they were much interested in the possibilities of cotton cultivation, to give Russia supplies of her own. They introduced American cotton in Bokhara and Samarqand, and above all in the province of Ferghana; and the high prices brought by the new crop led to its introduction in Chinese Central Asia. This cotton was marketed exclusively in Russia until the war, when the shutting down of trade led to an attempt to introduce it on the China market. The cotton-spinners of Shanghai then found that Central Asian American cotton could be brought all the way by camel caravan across Mongolia, a journey of from three to four months, sent by rail from Kuei-hua to Tientsin, and by sea from Tientsin to Shanghai, and still compete with the American product. Since then, however, the revolt of Mongolia and the civil disorders in China, leading to prolonged stoppages of railway traffic in China, have thrown the trade back toward Russia. The Chinese merchants can no longer compete, and the Russian monopoly of the cotton market in Chinese Turkestan is one of their major economic holds on the province. Although the long-staple cotton is always known on the China market as Turfan cotton, the best grade is in fact grown about Kucha, farther to the west.

Having discoursed on these matters, the Russian Tatar went on to expound the commercial benefits and personal pleasures of motor traffic. Central Asia, he said, deprecating the fatigues of our journey to Turfan, would not be such a bad place if you could scoot about it in a car. We suppressed our exclamations of horror, for it is much more an article of faith with all the nations of Asia than it is even in America that the faster you can travel through a place the nicer it must be. That is one reason why they all think America must be such a wonderful place.

On the whole, our questions did not begin to come so thick and fast as those of our companions; but at last Purple Trousers threw a monkey-wrench into our high intellectual debates. He approached as it were sidling, with the monkey-wrench concealed behind his back.

"Why do the foreigners want to buy all our wool? They have many sheep in Russia; surely there must be sheep in America also."

I assured him that we had a great many.

"Well, if American sheep grow wool, just like our sheep, I suppose they make bleating noises, just like our sheep."

"Oh, yes; sheep are much the same, all the world over."

"Well, then, why, if sheep in Turfan and sheep in America make the same noise, do not men in America and men in Turfan speak the same language?"

It took a great deal of eating to get round questions like this. We began with walnuts and raisins; enough, we thought remorsefully, to spoil our appetites: but they revived at the appearance of kabobs, bits of mutton, fat and lean alternately, roasted on wooden skewers over a fire and eaten off the skewer, sprinkled with that peculiarly aromatic pepper which reaches Turkestan by caravan from China. It comes from I know not where, and the peculiar fragrance is probably due to shrewd commercial adulteration. Our hosts, though they had brought a whole camp-following of cooks, fire-tenders, and the peculiar functionaries common to these parts of the world who can only be described as gapers-about-the-edge-of the-proceedings, took turns in supervising themselves the cooking, which was done at a mud fireplace built for just such picnics at the edge of the arbor.

We ourselves did not get an intermission until a walk was proposed. We went up the side of the gorge to look at the cages of perforated brickwork, in which raisins are dried by warm air blowing through the structure, so that their superior pale color is not darkened by direct sunlight. Standing beside them we looked out over a fair sight, the rich, well-tended green of the trees in the gorge and the red grape-terraces on the sides of the gorge, all bounded by just such cliffs as that on which we stood, and by the far hazy plain into which the stream vanished. The structure of the land could not be more evident; abundance and ease wherever water could be carried to the terraces, by ditches taking off from the stream, high up in the valley, and an unforgiving desolation crowding jealously up to the edge of that narrow strip redeemed by the art and labor of man. On the lip of the gorge, right at our feet, verdure ceased as abruptly as if searing irons had been passed along it.

We then went back to eat more mutton, this time boiled, but still sprinkled with the delicious pepper; and when it was evident that we must walk again or not have room for the next course, we went up the gorge to look at relics of Buddhist cave-chapels in which a few tiny fragments of fresco still adhered to the walls. " We are sorry we can show you no images or paintings," they told us politely, " but they have all been taken away by foreigners who came before you. If you want anything in these days, you have to dig." That was not strictly true; they were only working on our eagerness, in case we should reveal ourselves as serious antique-buyers, in which event they hoped to appoint themselves our agents. The comparatively few archæological findings that have been taken by Russian, German, French, and British expeditions have been rescued not only from oblivion but from destruction. The Chinese overlords have never been excited over the archæological wealth of Chinese Turkestan, because they have had no enthusiasm for Manichæans, Uighurs, Nestorians, or other incomprehensible barbarians, and the dead cities are comparatively poor in Chinese manuscripts, which alone would interest them. The Turki cultivators have the hearty Mohammedan contempt for all the works of the infidel, and destroy every evidence of pre-Mohammedan culture that crops up. Frescoes that the dry climate would have left unharmed for another thousand years have been hacked to bits by the pious and the idle, "just to learn them." As for manuscripts, they most unfortunately make, with the addition of moisture, a handy rotting composition, which is spread on the fields for manure. An instance of what is perhaps the most tragic destruction is given by von Lecoq;[1] a peasant described to him how, five years before the arrival of the first German expedition, he had turned up no less than five large cartloads of manuscript, most of it said to be "the small writing" — probably the Manichæan script, the most valued of all. The finder was afraid in the first place of evil influences that might lurk in the "heathen" script, and afraid in the second place that the Chinese might inquire into so large a find, suspecting treasure-trove. Therefore he incontinently tipped the whole lot into a stream.

Late-comers, and ignorant to boot, our sole homage to the past was to stroll up the valley, under the blind eyes of the oblivious caves; I scrambled on a crumbling path along the face of a loess cliff to enter what had once been a cave-chapel or the cell of an anchorite, from which, crouching, I looked out over the tops of the frondage of rank poplar and willow groves. The darkness of the interior cave struck into me like a reproach. I scrambled down again and went back to the friendly chatter of our companions. We returned

---

[1] *Auf Hellas Spuren in Ost-Turkistan.* Leipzig, J. C. Hinrichs'sche Buchhandlung, 1926.

to our arbor and one more distending feed, this time assisted by the serene old patriarch, son of the soil and lord of the unbelievably huge and old vine under which our feast was spread.

At the last and largest eating we devoted ourselves to a monumental pilau of rice, mutton-fat, and chopped carrots. The trained eater of pilau juggles and squeezes it in the hollow of his hand into a little ball, which he then spins with a flick of the thumb into his mouth. All Turki eating should be done with one hand only; no chopsticks or other adventitious aids are employed. It is indelicate to use more than one hand, except when dealing with more-than-mouthful sizes of mutton. It is then permissible to hold the chunk of mutton in the mouth and the left hand, while with the right hand one produces a knife and hacks off the mutton close to the lips. We lost a good deal of rice in our endeavors to eat according to etiquette, and greased ourselves from ear to ear; but of the others, the only one who dissipated more than a grain or two of rice was Purple Trousers, owing to the great distance his hand had to travel from below his stomach, and up around it, sight unseen, before attaining his face. Even his loss was not absolute, for most of the scattered rice went into his buttonless trousers.

Eating with the hand explains the Mohammedan custom of washing the hands before and after meals; the water is brought to the guests in a copper ewer, and poured over the hands. This manner of eating a pilau is regarded by the Chinese as one of the more barbarous habits of the Turki, and they call it *chua-fan* — grabbed, or clutched, rice.

By the time that no one could think of anything more to eat, or where to put it if he had it, the day was cooling toward the dusk. It was our only day of perfect weather. Even the haze over the plain was thinner. Bowing as we took our leave before the dignity of the old vine-cultivator, a worthy patriarch and a noble exemplar of the Turki people, who are surely the most kindly, simple, and lovable folk among the troubled nations of the earth, we drove off in three carts on our return. The Turki driving boys raced for the lead, to be free of dust. The first race caught me with a cigarette in my mouth. Before I had recovered it or my poise, I had burned the top-side-hangings and cushions of the cart. We won, owing to the masterly practice of our driver. He wasted no time in laying on the lash of the whip, but placed the butt of it on a raw spot of the pony's back and worked it steadily. . . . Nor could he understand our protests.

Thus, in a regular outbreak of amity, we ended our stay in Turfan. In returning to Urumchi, we went first to Toqsun, on the main line of the South Road, and then bore back right-handed into the same *dawan* or pass as that by which we had crossed on our outward way from Urumchi. The road to Toqsun lay for two stages through a desert of soft clay, partly covered with a dusty growth of low scrub, and with ancient beds of dead reeds, of which nothing was left but the roots. Owing to the smaller water supply, the Turfan Depression is not so rich in trees, and consequently in building material and fuel, as other oases. Thus we found parties of people out in the ancient reed-beds, digging up the roots for fuel.

On account of the heat we did not start from Turfan until late in the afternoon, intending to travel well into the night, rest a few hours, and make Toqsun on the next day before the full heat. We were riding ahead of the cart, and had not long lost sight of Turfan Town, when a little before sunset we fell in with an old man. It was near the mouth of a valley opening out of the red Fire Mountains, we having ridden aside to look at what seemed to be old cave-chapels almost lost to recognition in the soft cliffs. "Foreigners!" said the old man. "Have you come to dig up ruins? Many Oross [Russians; foreigners generally] have been to this valley; and all of them dig." We turned at once up the valley, leaving the old man sitting his pony askew on the sandy road, wagging his old gray beard. Twenty minutes brought us to a huge bluff of clay, wallowing in the centre of the valley, which parted in narrow gorges on each side of it, like a battleship in a dry-dock. A road like the ramp of a city wall took us up the side of it, and we emerged suddenly at the top in the midst of ruins. The sun was just setting, and for a few minutes only we sat in the saddle and looked through the flushed haze as it were through a window over a vista of lost centuries. The entire bluff was crowned with ruins — only the worn stumps and fragments of clay walls, monuments, and towers. Pits here and there witnessed the exploratory burrowings of Turki treasure-seekers or foreign archæologists. One shaft looked as though it might have been a well of great depth, sunk for the water supply of the ancient city. Only the coarsest structures were left above ground, for nothing else could have withstood so many generations the unremitting attack of wind-driven dust. Most undoubtedly this was Yar-khoto, the City of the Cliff, sought out by all archæologists.

On the brink of the ravine at one side was a terrace of old shrines and cave-temples. On the other side was a modern village, and all along the terraces of the valley the water was carried to its fields and its rows of willows just as it had been carried to the terraces of this dead city, centuries ago. The far-descended cultivators of our own time have changed little of their life and less of their methods of tilling the soil. Most of their architecture and the fashion of the things in their houses, we know, have hardly varied. Only their religion is different, and graybeards in the white turban of prayer resort to little, clean, bare mosques instead of cliff-chapels divinely peopled with serene Buddhas and mellow wall-paintings ever so faintly alive with a transmuted memory of the last inspiration of Greek art. The kindly, easy-going people, whose religion, the one inspiring influence of their lives, is now oriented toward Mecca, do not even know that in those ages, obscured from them by war, invasion, and the desert winds that in time erase everything, their oases were touched by the Light of Asia, and permeated by the Græco-Bhuddist Gandhara art which from Kashmir traversed Central Asia and left its mark, not only at the Tun-huang gate of the desert caravan roads, but at an even more commanding distance, in the towering rock-chapels near Ta-t'ung, in northern Shan-hsi. Even less are they aware of the obscure tenets and rites of Mani, or of the masses of the heretical, far-wandered Nestorians.

Or perhaps it is not so much oblivion as unconsciousness. After all, the name of Alexander yet survives in their common legends; and, most prodigious mark of all, they still perpetuate the name of Ephesus. Von Lecoq says [1] of the city of Qara-Khoja, " This city also bears, in the mouth of the people, the names of Apsus

---

[1] *Auf Hellas Spuren in Ost-Turkistan.*

(Ephesus), City of Dakianus [from the Roman Emperor Decius, the convert to Christianity], and Idikut Shahri. The old Chinese name was Kao-chang."[1] The name City of Dakianus is explained by the circumstance that "in the immediate neighborhood, in the valley of Tuyoq, is a sanctuary of the Seven Sleepers, which is still sought out at the present day by Mohammedan pilgrims, even from Arabia and India, and has a reputation for great holiness. The legend, however, was not first brought hither by the Mohammedans, — Islam first reached this region in the thirteenth or fourteenth century, — but goes back . . . to Buddhist times": for, as he later discovered, there is an ancient temple carved out in the rock behind the modern mosque.

As the sunset died and the dusk deepened, the dust-laden air, so harsh in daylight, turned soft and kindly. We were just wheeling our horses to go when the old man who had put us in the way of this discovery came up the ramp on a disgusted pony. He was afraid the mad impulse he had started in us to look at ruins might cause us to lose our way, and so had ridden all the way back to look after us. "It is too late for me now to go on my journey in the dark," he said simply; " but I will just put you on your road again."

We rode in quiet down the valley, whose waters hardly reached its mouth before vanishing in the importunate desert. I wondered restlessly what it is in dry mud ruins, the speech of alien people, the mixed drabness and gay colors of a caravanserai, the smell of camels in a camp in the desert, that makes a struggle in one between the richness of the present vision and the vague offer of the next horizon, that leads one to the noble aspiration and perpetual renunciation of travel. I think myself that the real ritual of travel is a sort of processional celebration of the mystery of life.

> Out of the red-brown earth, out of the grey-brown streams,
> Came this perilous body, cage of perilous dreams.

If the initiate traveler, taking his dreams in his hand, goes abroad to traffic with dreams of the past and wonders of the vanishing present, what is his profit? To touch the present at many points and

---

[1] The Turki *qara*, black, is commonly used of ruins. *Khoja,* " my lord," " of my lord," may possibly be derived by phonetic confusion from " Kao-chang."

to keep the past shining through it like a light is to remain secure in his revelation or mystery, which concerns not death and resurrection, but death and continuity. There is no future but the next horizon; but when "this perilous body" has reverted to earth and water, and the dreams are released from the cage, who comes next, to cage perhaps a few of those dreams again?

There is a passage by Sir Aurel Stein [1] that gives the true feeling of the past continuing into the present. It is from his description of the successful crossing of the worst part of the Lop desert in six days, by a route for which he had neither guide nor map.

" . . . one of the younger camel-men shouted that he could see a *p'ao-t'ai !* All eyes were directed eastwards where he pointed, and soon I verified with my glasses that the tiny knob rising far away above the horizon was really a ruined mound, manifestly of a Stupa. . . . The men from Charklik were all buoyed up with sudden animation. . . . But the most curious thing to me was to watch the triumphant figure and pose which Hassan Akhun, my quick-silvery camel factotum, presented. There he stood on the top of the Yardang, with his right arm stretched out and supported on a staff like that of a triumphator, while his left rested akimbo. He was addressing his audience of laborers, whom on the march he loved alternately to cheer and to bully, with a mien half that of the prophet proved true and half of the exultant demagogue. Had he not always tried to drum it into their thick heads that under the guidance of his Sahib, who could fathom all hidden places of the dreaded Taklamakan with his 'paper and Mecca-pointer,' *i.e.* map and compass, all things were bound to come right? Now by the appointed day he had brought them to the promised 'Kone-shahr.'. . . I always knew that my troublesome and mercurial myrmidon had his uses, especially for any tough bit of desert work. But never had it struck me so clearly that in him lived the spirit and manners of an old Greek adventurer. As he stood there, full of jubilant conceit and heroics, in his bright red cloak and high-peaked purple cap, his moods of dejection and petulance clean forgotten, he called up to my mind a vision of one of Xenophon's Greek mercenaries who shouted: *Thalatta! Thalatta!*

[1] *Ruins of Desert Cathay.*

More than once after this day in the Lop desert I felt haunted by the thought whether it were not from a drop of Levantine blood, bequeathed by some remote ancestor who had found his way to Seric regions like those agents of Maes, the Macedonian, that Hassan Akhun derived his strange jumble of versatile ingenuity and exuberant temper, fitful energy and classical impudence."

What are stupas for but to illustrate this sort of thing? This is the root of the matter.

XVII

WESTWARD FOR KULJA

ToQSUN we found to be much like Turfan, but more lively, with a bigger T'ung-kan population, more Chinese in its bazar, and its inns thronged with the traffic of the Great South Road. It is the first town on the South Road in touch with fertile mountains, in which there are Mongols, and its wool market is one of the best in the province, for the quality of the wool is fair and it is near the headquarters of trade in Urumchi. We harbored in a huge caravanserai: an alley led from the main bazar street into a vast sprawling enclosure, off which opened minor stabling corrals. In the main yard were whole convoys of carts, and only along two sides of it were ranged the mud kennels which are the sole accommodation for travelers, who must even go into the bazar to eat at cookshops, or buy food for their own cooking. Most of the carters, as a matter of fact, slept out on top of their loads, or under the carts, between the six-or-seven-foot-high wheels. Small boys went scrambling up on the roofs of sheds to pull down armfuls of fodder, and bearded carters waddled in from the bazar with sacks of golden maize over their shoulders. In the stabling yards, ponies fought and kicked and squealed. Once a stallion made extra diversion, going on the rampage and having to be beaten back to his manger with long poles. A dry, hot, yellow air trembled over all. It was a good, lusty town.

A Chinese boy of fifteen or sixteen picked us up in the bazar, into which we had ridden in advance of our cart. He had spindly legs, a shriveled body, and the face of a mature and crafty man. He reminded me in a strange way of Father Time, of *Jude the Obscure*. Like many boys of his age, in this province as in China proper, he was a soldier. He told us that he had been in Afghanistan, — meaning, I suppose, one of the Chinese outposts on the Pamirs, — that he was the sole support of an aged mother, and that he was a great friend of Americans. He had evidently fallen in with an American expedition which had passed that way a year before. He told us that, having eaten the food of Americans, he felt a spiritual tie with the whole nation, which he intended to renew when his mother died and he was free to travel. To cement this tie he had presented the other Americans with a melon; and he added swiftly that in return they had made him a money present of twenty times the value. If we would give him money to buy a melon, he would make us a present of it. In conclusion, he asserted that he knew all the ruins there were, and would be delighted to offer us his escort.

The ruins proved to be the old Mohammedan town, more than half demolished in the wars of the Mohammedan Rebellion; for the fighting had been heavy in this region, not only between the Chinese and the rebels, but between the local T'ung-kan forces and the armies of Yakub Beg of Kashgar, who had endeavored to assert his rule over them. In the middle of the demolished city, tenanted by a few Turkis who had patched up lean-tos against ruined walls, was a fine mosque, with a muezzin tower over against it that looked like Magdalen tower heavily imitated in mud. The sheikh of the mosque, an old man with the dignity of much white beard, graciously showed us into his room, which was cool and dark, and served us tea and women. The women were for the benefit of the foreign woman, not of the foreign man. Granted even the cordiality toward strangers, and the frank, interested manners of the Turki, a sheikh in charge of an important mosque would hardly have allowed his womenfolk to appear before a *parang* (*farang;* Frank) had not the Frank been accompanied by his own woman. Yet the fluttering, delighted women, though they subdued their chatter, were not timid in the presence of strangers; they did not even veil their faces, but showed in their behavior the tolerant way in which the easy-going Turki folk let slide the strict Mussulman standards in regard to women.

A half-stage the same evening took us to the edge of the piedmont desert, where we lodged at a Turki inn; a half subterranean place where the stabling was contained within the living quarters. We led our two snorting saddle ponies through our sleeping quarters into an alcove-stable, where they fed by the light of a smoky wick in a broken earthenware vessel. The quarters of man and beast were so thickly walled and roofed, as a protection even more against the summer heat than the winter cold, that we seemed to be immured in a series of caverns.

We rose again when the night was little more than half spent, to get as long a start as possible of the sun on the hottest stage of the journey. Until the dawn we jogged, half asleep and wholly chilled and unhappy, behind the cart; but within an hour after sunrise we were too hot. For nearly twenty miles we went slowly upward over a slope of gray shale and gravel. At one point, seeing a mound of earth and gravel, we rode over. We found a hole with no bottom. We were told later that it was an unsuccessful attempt to sink a well. The boring, or rather digging, had been carried, men said, to a depth of forty *chang* — which would be more than four hundred feet; somewhat more, I suspect, than local engineering could really achieve. No signs of water were reached, and, when the bottom of the shaft began to cave in dangerously, it was abandoned.

At the end of the twenty miles we came to a lonely inn set down in the gray waste, and dismounting we woke up a benevolent old Turki who, after rising with the dawn, had fallen asleep in a bare mud inglenook over a volume of the Quran, while his chickens hopped between his horny bare toes, looking for the crumbs of his breakfast. Bustling about to bring tea for us in cracked cups, he told us that the stage was known as Ta Kang-tze, Big Jar, because he kept all the water he had in a big stoneware jar. Travelers forced to halt there could make tea for themselves, but their beasts must go without water. The water he kept in his jar was brought to him, with his food, on donkeys from the next stage, his son making the journey every few days. Travelers never halted there if they could help it, and for thirty-five years he had kept the inn with little company but his Quran and his chickens. In that time ten men, besides uncounted animals, had died of summer heat or winter cold in the stony desert that stretched for twenty miles

A Cliff with Cave Chapels near Turfan

Ruins near Turfan

in either direction. He stood at the gate of his forlorn hostelry with the few coins we gave him cupped in his hand, peering after us as we rode away in the dazzling heat-waves. It was only seven in the morning.

We had yet a full stage to ride. Reaching a crest in the scree, we turned parallel with the long confused ranges of desert hills that flank the mountains. At this height they are all buried to their tops in scree wreckage, with here and there clay heads appearing through it. Our ponies were spent by the time we reached a little shelf of green that lay just above the river which comes down from the dawan or pass through which we had taken the Turfan road and which, though at this point it diverges from the trade route, flows on down and enters the Turfan Depression near Toqsun. The place is called Little Grass Oasis; a spring sends a tiny brook through it, and it supports enough grass for a very few sheep and the donkey caravans that come from the South Road with wool and cotton; and a flock of cranes, moreover, hovers about its edges. At this place we were detained a day by a violent storm of wind and dust, and met a party of Russians who had been two months in carts on the way from Khotan, where their business had failed. One of them was married to a pretty Armenian girl who could speak a few words of English, and told us that she had a brother in New York. They seemed stranger to us than the old man of Big Jar.

Two more days, over what seemed like easy going, brought us back through the pass and back to Urumchi, for our last stay, of which I write with a sort of sorrow. Indeed, it was hard to leave Urumchi for the last time, after having known it in the winter, when the nicest place in town was the steamy Chinese bathhouse with the understanding barber; in the spring, when along the liquescent streets the Chinese began to appear in gay colors and flowered silks and satins, and the Turkis, abandoning the reds and purples and greens of their long winter gowns, to put on the white cotton robes of warm weather; and in the beginning of summer, when the early leafage of the trees was not yet dulled with dust, and to walk on the city walls at sunset was the crowning charm of the day.

Because we spent most of our time with our Chinese hosts, we did not see a great deal of the small foreign community. Still, at the Russian Consulate-General we met numbers of charming people, who by virtue of the frequent transfers in their service had seen most of Central Asia, or in old days of political exile before the Revolution had been students in France or Germany. Very often, when among them, I wondered that some of these men — and women — did not show more deeply the scars of their past. There must have been a bundle of strange histories among them, for some of these were the very people who for years had dreamed and striven for the Revolution. They belonged to the class who had been despised as addled intellectuals, derided as dreamers of the impossible, harried as political mad dogs. Then came the war, the Revolution, and the bloody tide of the conflicting Terrors. After it had all died down they had emerged, and here were some of them representing the Russia for which they had staked everything, and in which they believed as the promoter and defender of the true creed of humanity, at the capital of what was more a Central Asian state than a Chinese province. It seemed to me that the Russians were wise and on the whole successful in the choice of their representatives, though I heard that at times all did not go well between them and the Chinese officials. They drew their personnel not only from the ranks of what one may call the Revolutionists by faith, but from that very sound class, the people who, without any very ardent political convictions, had accepted the new Russia as she was, and had thrown themselves into the rebuilding of the new nation for the sake of the nation.

We had a friendly reception among them, talking or essaying to talk in half a dozen languages, either directly or at second hand. Even if the first language that a man tried on you was a complete miss, and you grinned bashfully and waved your hands, he would be likely to call someone who could speak Yiddish.

At what was left of the former Russo-Asiatic Bank was served superlative food, with dill pickles that could not have been bettered at the old B. A. T. mess in Kalgan, — now closed, as I hear, through the vicissitudes of civil war, — while at the Postal Commissioner's, on occasions of high state or rejoicing, appeared cocktails of real gin and undeniable vermouth: the only gin and the only vermouth marked on the map between Kuei-hua and Kashgar.

But best of all were the riding parties to the Red Temple or the Valley of Water-mills; and it was by a party of riders, with Mr. and Mrs. McLorn in a Russian carriage, and our Chinese merchant friends in a train of blue-hooded " Peking " carts, that we were escorted out of town on our last departure. Mr. Pan was the last to whom we said farewell, and both my wife and I could hardly speak when at last we turned our ponies to ride away from the happy capital of Chinese Central Asia. At least our parting vision of Urumchi was perfect, with the snow-peak of Bogdo Ola, thinly outlined against a thin sky, rising in magnificence and yet delicately, behind the city.

We were now bound for Kulja and the Ili valley. Thence we should go up into high mountain country, and, having at last followed out the two major ramifications of the Road North of the Heavenly Mountains, climb up and over the range at its most lordly height and descend again to the Road South of the Heavenly Mountains. We should follow that great highway to Kashgar, and there make our preparations for the journey out of Central Asia and into India.

Carruthers[1] puts the total distance between Urumchi and Kulja at 430 miles. The journey is divided into eighteen regular stages, or an average of twenty-four miles to a day's travel; but several times we rode less than ten miles in a day, and once or twice we rode as much as forty miles. Moses once more traveled in a light four-wheeled cart, with three trotting ponies, which carried all our gear. We were accompanied the greater part of the way by a party of Tientsin traders traveling in the same fashion. Most of the heavy traffic goes in the winter, on roads of hard snow. In the summer the Ili trade is dominated by Russia, owing to its proximity to Siberia; but as the Ili valley is the greatest centre of the " Tientsin " population, the Tientsin traders can still raid into it, as it were. Parties of them go in these light, fast carts, each man with little more than a pedlar's pack of silk, satin, and other " lux-

[1] *Unknown Mongolia.*

ury goods," returning either with Siberian-grown opium or with other light and valuable cargo.

The first part of the journey lay over the well-known road to Hsi Hu. It was the middle of May, and the roads had dried off, while the streams were low, being at the period between the spring thaw of the lower snows and the full summer spate when the water from the high snows and glaciers comes down. The Manass River was a puny trickle in its wide shingle bed; so insignificant that after our ponies had splashed through it we rode for several miles looking for it. Our chief excitement during these stages was the portent of a motor car. The Russian Consul-General at Urumchi, borrowing the Governor's car, was driving to Hsi Hu, there to meet and consult with the Consul from Chuguchak, who was driving to the meeting in a car procured from Russia.

This meeting was intended to demonstrate the possibility of motor traffic between Urumchi and Siberia. The Russian interests had been pressing for a motor-truck company, to increase the volume and speed of trade. The Chinese had been hanging back. More trade was all very well, but they did not like the notion of throwing economic control in the direction of Siberia. Moreover the improvement of the road to bear motor traffic, and the existence of a fleet of trucks, would orient the province strategically, as well as economically, toward Siberia. The continued decline of trade with China, however, bore too heavily on them. At all costs the prosperity of the province must be kept up. The more prosperous all the different subject races, the more they all had at stake in the continued peaceful rule of the Chinese, and the less likelihood of any revolt under the spur of Mohammedanism, nationalism, or political faction.

Thus the motor service was already being planned: I believe that now it is at least in partial operation. A school of drivers and mechanics was already being recruited in Urumchi. It was an illustration of the complex and paradoxical conditions in the province that, although the Chinese ruling element leaned so heavily on the Chinese economic control, the regulations for the new motor company prohibited the employment of Chinese as either mechanics or drivers. The small body of men employed in the motor service would not only be a closely associated group, but would monopolize the technical skill of the province. If they were Chinese, they might too easily be approached, either by a political faction within the province, or by a political or military faction in China itself, and thus be used with deadly effect against the régime of the old Governor.

The existence of a car in Urumchi was due to the failure of a previous attempt at motor transport. The Governor already owned, it is true, a couple of other cars, but they were pre-war German antiques, neither of which would work. They had been brought in from Siberia. The other was a ramping great Packard twin-six, belonging originally to the Russo-Asiatic Bank. This bank had long survived the Russian Revolution. It had once been a semi-official organ of the Imperial government, and a powerful instrument in the extension of Russian interests. After the Russian Revolution, the branches of the Bank in Chinese territory set up more or less " on their own." The branches at Urumchi, Kashgar, and Kulja, having no way of remitting or otherwise employing their funds in the province, invested them in raw produce which they began to transport to Tientsin, on the coast, for sale. At first the business went so well that they were encouraged to attempt a motor service. Eventually they went bankrupt, and the only official employé during the time of our travels was the liquidator.

The motor service was attempted at the time when the Outer Mongolian route was still open to Chinese trade. There was no reason why it should not have prospered, except that the enterprise was in the hands of Russians of the " exile " class, who did not know how to conciliate and ally themselves with Chinese interests, with the result that they were regarded with more than suspicion by the old caravan traders. They had, perforce, to take as guides veteran caravan masters who knew the lines of travel on which wells were to be found, and who were supposed to seek out the firmest, most level going. But men bred to the caravan trade are not to be won from caravan notions except gently and step by step. The fear of sudden motor competition troubled them. " When the motors come, the camels will go," they argued; " and since we do not understand these foreign machines, how shall we live?" Therefore they led the innocent pioneers, with their fleet of thirteen or fourteen cars of different makes, out of rocks into sand and out of sand into rocks again. Two cars got as far as the edge of Chinese Turkestan. One was abandoned there, and the big Packard was the only one to reach Urumchi. When I was in Mongolia the caravan men dwelt often on this tale, applauding the wily men who had defeated the alien engines. I was most heartily in accord with them.

The Consul-General passed us when we were nearing Manass. He reached Hsi Hu easily on the second day, covering a distance that it took us six days to ride. We met the car again early in the morning of the day we reached Hsi Hu, the Consul-General having started betimes, in an effort to get back to Urumchi in one day. We were breakfasting at a tiny hamlet high on the great gravel slope that cants toward Hsi Hu, when someone spied the curl of rapidly approaching dust which marked the approach of the fantastic, incredible machine; for undoubtedly this was the first time that Chuguchak and Urumchi had been linked by car, unless the old German cars had come in under their own power. "The gas-cart, the gas-cart!" he yelled. The whole population rushed to doors and windows, or clambered to the flat mud roofs. The car went by, roaring and stinking.

"Nothing but a frog-cart, after all," said Moses, using the Tientsin slang, which refers to the raucous motor horn. But the people of that mud village, roused from the apathy of their dusty hole in the desert, chattered in subdued amazement. "How does a thing like that cross the Manass River?" asked a moon-faced man. A goat-bearded elder pulled himself together. As the one old man of the village, he was accustomed to the dignity of the court of last appeal, and of final pronouncement on all things of the outer world. He must not let his authority be overwhelmed. "Hai! These machines of the foreigner!" he said. "How would *you* know what sort of thing machinery is, bred as you are on the flat of the Gobi? It's the machinery that does it. Isn't the machinery of a gas-cart a vapor machinery?" (The *ch'i* of the word "gas-cart" means air, breath, vapor; whatever hyper-material "force" may be supposed by boorish minds to inform material things.) "When this vapor machinery approaches a river, the waters divide before it, and it rolls over on dry land."

At Hsi Hu, leaving the Chuguchak road on the north, we diverged on to the Ili road. Then for five days we rode through the winter camping ground of one of the major divisions of the Torgut Mongols. At the first stage we reached their headquarters, at Ssu-ko Shu or Ssu-k'o Shu, Four Trees, a little village of Chinese trading with the Mongols. It is on the line where water appears at the foot of the mountains, and reed-beds and marshes break away at the edge of thick scrub and wild-poplar jungle. Thus the Chinese name, though meaning Four Trees, is probably only a corruption of a Mongol name. The halting point is a little short street of dirty booths and inns and drinking shops. This jungle belt is a notorious haunt of rapacious gadflies and mosquitoes. Owing to the thickness of the ju gle, the mosquitoes are even worse by day than by night. We traveled through it at night, thereby avoiding the gadflies, and by fast riding keeping as few mosquitoes as possible about us. As the track was vague, we did not like to get too far ahead of the carts, so we would ride fast for a few miles, then halt and wait, covering ourselves with mosquito netting propped on twigs.

At Ssu-ko Shu there is a Mongol prince of the high rank of Chun Wang, and also a prince of Pei-le rank, while farther on, at Ching Ho, there is another Pei-le. This is the region commonly called Kur-khara-usu. The latter part of this name would mean Black Water. The river, starting near this point, bends round by Hsi Hu, and, running through some of the marshes we had passed by on the other arm of the North Road, falls into Ebi Nor from the east.

The Mongols total one *aimak* of two hoshun at Ssu-ko Shu and one aimak of one hoshun at Ching Ho. According to a remark made by Prjevalsky,[1] it would appear that all these Torguts migrated from the Yulduz plateau during the troubles of the Mohammedan Rebellion. One of the princes at Ssu-ko Shu is a son of

[1] *From Kulja Across the Tian Shan to Lob-Nor.*

the famous Prince Palta; but we did not know this (as will appear) until we reached Kulja.

From the end of the jungle belt we crossed, in a night's march, ten miles or so of sand dunes, that stretched from barren rubble hills on the south far away to a distant depression on our north, in which lay Ebi Nor, for this depression runs all the way across, from arm to arm of the North Road. It is the same depression as that we had crossed when descending from the Jair plateau at Ulan Bulaq and making for the line of salt marshes about Ch'e P'ai-tze. Though the dunes are nowhere more than twenty or thirty feet high, — nothing like the three days' wilderness of sand that the caravans cross in Alashan, — they are regarded with great dislike by carters. It is said that, when wind has covered up the track, men are frequently lost. No man must speak boastfully before entering the dunes, or loudly while among them, lest he draw the notice of evil spirits who will mislead him, talking with human voices, and leave him to die of thirst. There is a plain echo in all this of the demons which from the time of the earliest Chinese records have been associated with the deserts of Lop Nor, but which owe their greatest celebrity, among nations other than the Chinese, to the mention made of them by Marco Polo.[1]

We departed from the desolate " stage " where a crumbling mud fort and one inn occupy the edge of the sands, in company with a Turki trader who was driving nearly three thousand sheep from Manass to the Ili valley, there to put them on the Russian market. We rode ahead of the cloud of sand that the sheep scuffled up, suffused with the red and yellow glow of the sunset, until in the middle of the sands we found the advance party, who had pitched camp and were waiting for the great flock. The camp was at a well which was boarded inside to keep the sand from filling it, and which tapped at a depth of ten feet or more water with the bitter taste of tamarisk roots. The trader's men, as hearty a hedge-levy of ruffians as could have been recruited at the edge of any villainous bazar, mixed Turkis and Qazaqs, gave us a friendly reception. They were all swaggering fellows, of the kind that have but one shift of clothing for all the year round, and they wore their

---

[1] Yule, *The Book of Ser Marco Polo*, ed. Cordier.

fur caps awry and their heavy gowns open to show hairy chests, because of the sultry heat. They had lit three fires as points between which to fold the sheep, and we sat for a while in the glow of the fire nearest the well, drinking bitter tea which they offered us with guttural words, in the free manner of wandering men, which is different from the manner of the friendliest serai, and varies but little from Kuei-hua forth into the West, wherever camp fires mark a night's halt.

Then the moon rose and showed, like a vision, beyond the flickering fires, a pale golden wilderness of glimmering sand and black tamarisks, all enclosed by the sinuous ridges of the dunes, marked with a deceptive sharpness against the faint stars. At the other fires we could see the black shapes of men and hear their deep-toned speech, and at our own the light wavered on dark, bearded faces, and the fox-skin helmets of the Qazaqs and the round sheepskin caps of the Turkis, edged with black lamb's wool. The full magic of the road overwhelmed us. At last we began to hear the strepitant blather of the approaching host of sheep and goats, and dark scuttling waves of them flowed in around us over the dunes. In a few moments we heard also the hortatory bellowing of carters, the cruel crack of whips, and at last the desperate, roaring breath of the ponies as they lugged at the sand-encumbered wheels.

We rose to go, for a T'ung-kan trader who had at some point in the vague march ridden into our company, and said he knew the road, offered to go with us. The men at the camp fire stood up to speed us. " May there be a road," they said, and we rode away into the dunes, which in a few moments hid the firelight and shut off the sound of speech. Beyond the dunes we rode for several hours through lighter sand, passing in silence a guardhouse called in hybrid style Qum Ch'ia-tze, the Pass or Station of the Sands. Beyond it a spur of the rubbly hills on the south pushed out across our way.

The Mohammedan had been telling us once more, what we had heard ever since Hsi Hu, of the raids of the Russian Qazaqs. From this part of the road it is not more than two days' hard riding to the Russian frontier. The border ranges are high enough and deep enough in snow to keep raiders out during the winter;

but in the last two summers they had been coming over in parties of ten men or more, driving off thousands of Mongol sheep and hundreds of cattle and ponies, and had even beset the roads until peaceful men were afraid to travel. We were told that men would lurk in the poplar jungles through which we had been riding; they would hide in overhanging trees, and, as a horseman passed below them, slug him on the back of the head with a blackjack. Our own carter had met with raiders the year before. He was driving several Tientsin merchants, with a valuable cargo of opium, but the Qazaqs, not recognizing the opium, only robbed the travelers of their ready cash and the carter of his ponies, after beating them all for good measure. This year fresh Chinese military disposi-tions had been made, and it was hoped that the trouble would be checked. This raiding of Qazaqs from the Russian side is no new thing. Carruthers [1] mentions it in 1910, when both China and Russia were still empires. It has one most curious effect, in that the Chahars of the Borotala use their highest pastures in winter rather than in summer; being enabled to do this because the upper valleys are so scoured by wind that sheep can find grazing free of snow, while the actual passes remain choked with snow, keeping out the Qazaqs.

As we were crossing the low spur of hills, we saw a mounted man coming up the other side, his pony stepping silently through the moonlight. Our Mohammedan friend was asleep in the sad-dle, but when I said to him, "What's that?" he woke with a jump and had his pony fifty yards off the road in about two wild bounds. The stranger saw us at the same time, and gave us fifty yards' room on the other side. Even when both men had thus seen that each was afraid of the other, they kept warily apart and passed without greeting.

The moonlight was growing dim as we rode down from the hills into a stretch of bare gravel. Then a black bulk of trees rose out of the formless night; we splashed through running water, and by that token passed out of desert into oasis. We had ridden from before sunset until the dawn, for by the time we rode under the trees the birds were beginning to wake. On ahead, at one

[1] *Unknown Mongolia.*

side of the road, was a deep grove of old elms, under which in the uncertain light showed the wry walls and sagging eaves of a temple of battered splendor. As the light grew stronger, we rode under a noble *p'ai-lou* or ceremonial arch, and saw the decaying mud walls of a fortified city. In the bazar that straggled at one side of it, not even a dog howled at us. We hammered on the toppling gates of a serai until a wan opium smoker opened them and we, almost as uncertain on our feet with sleep as he, found ourselves a dark windowless cell in which to spread a blanket that I had brought rolled behind my saddle, and lay down to sleep, having attained Ching Ho, the town of the Pure River.

XVIII

PONIES

WE had already bought the black pony my wife had ridden to Turfan, and on the very morning that we left Urumchi we bought another, a bay stallion from Badakshan, which I rode thenceforward. He had just been ridden for more than two months from Khotan, by the Russian husband of the Armenian girl we had met at the Little Grass Oasis. The Russian had bought him from an Afghan opium smuggler who had ridden him so unmercifully through the Pamirs that on reaching Khotan both he and a companion horse had been sold for little better than carrion. The other horse had died, but the Russian had been able to bring this one back into condition again, as was proved by the fit state in which I took him over, when on the morrow of his arrival from Khotan I set out to ride him the four hundred and more miles to Kulja. He proved himself a gallant and willing pony all the time I had him, and, for all he was a stallion, was no more trouble to handle than a large dog.

I am sure he had been under fire. I know that a rifle shot used to throw cart ponies and suchlike into a wild panic, even when they were dead weary. But one morning when we were riding in the high T'ien Shan a roebuck sprang up a hundred yards ahead of us and ran downhill, leaping high through lush grass. I had my rifle on the pommel; slinging my left leg over Iskander's neck, I slipped down on the off side, knelt, and fired. I expected that he would bolt and give me a ten-minute chase. Instead, he only snorted, then stood stock-still and watched. I could easily have trained him to stand while I shot from the saddle. Even the way he did not shy when I slithered down all in a hurry on the off side was astonishing. All Central Asian ponies, especially those ridden by the nomads, being but half broken, can be approached only from the near side. If a man appears at the off side, they will shy violently, if they do not bite or kick. With my Badakshan stallion one could mount or dismount on either side. The universal practice of approaching a horse only from the near side is in itself a curious tradition. I believe it is a relic of the days of the sword. Because the sword must be scabbarded on the left, so that it can be easily drawn with the right hand, a man must mount on the left side, in order not to be impeded by it. I believe that the American Indians of the Great Plains, who never had the sword for weapon, were the only race of horsemen with whom it was a matter of course, and not a trick or display of skill, to mount and dismount indifferently from near side or off side.

We called the bay stallion Iskander, or Iskander Beg, — Lord Alexander, — because of the legend that the horses of Badakshan are of the strain of Bucephalus, the horse of Alexander. He was a true horse in his paces, whereas Mæander, as we called my wife's pony for no very good reason but that of euphony, though a tall pony, was a true pony in his paces. Iskander's traveling gait was a fast running-walk. Our cart ponies jog-trotted at a rate of from six to eight miles an hour, depending on the road, but Iskander's running-walk kept him ahead of them easily. Mæander traveled at a delectable trot, with no up-and-down in it at all. He was a curious pony, for he bore a Qara Shahr brand but had none of the points of the Qara Shahr pony. In fact, he looked an unmistakable Ili pony. He must have been stolen by Yulduz Torguts from an Ili herd. His one blemish was that he had very small, pig-like eyes; and true enough, he had the nervousness and " small gall " (timidity) which the Chinese predicate of horses with this blemish. Also he stumbled at times. Nevertheless, he was an unbeatable pony for a long journey. He would eat stolidly anything put in his manger: a matter of no small importance, for the standard feed changes in different regions, and very often a pony, when first offered, say, maize, will refuse to touch it, because he has never seen it; which is apt to be worrying when one has to ride him thirty miles the next day.

We paid high for our ponies, — about $150 (gold) for the two together, — which was a heavy outlay, considering that $40 will buy you, in that part of the world, an ordinary sound traveling pony, or what is called a one-stage pony, that is one which will do a stage every day, month in, month out. Still, we were making an important investment. We were getting ponies of proven quality, whose appearance would do us credit. They were not young, by local standards, which prefer four- and five-year-old ponies; but such ponies are rarely seasoned. Ours were full-grown, travel-seasoned ponies, the black of ten and the bay of twelve or thirteen years. Prices for good ponies, in this land of horseflesh, go up to startling figures. The reason is that no traveler walks, if he can ride. Even a Chinese official, traveling in a cart, strives to create an impression of splendor by mounting his outriders and retainers as showily as possible. Because even the greatest, when on the road, must put up with rough lodging and many inconveniences, no traveler is pretentious about his personal appearance on the road. He bundles himself up for comfort. Moreover there is the universal Asiatic caution which prompts a rich man to dress no better than the rest of the world when he goes abroad. The upshot is, that the social position of a traveler can be judged more readily from the pony he rides, or the ponies of his retainers, than by any other gauge. If you are more than ordinarily well mounted, you meet with courtesy on the road and deference at inns. The idle and the curious, who in other regions consider themselves entitled to a free look at travelers, and who closely inspect one's clothes and personal appearance, are here more likely to examine one's horses first. It was always a pleasure to me, at inns, when the hangers-on gathered around our ponies and exclaimed admiringly, " *K'o! Che lia' ma! Ni k'an k'uo pu k'uo!* " — " Ha! These two horses! Look you, are they swell! "

Our ponies were admired in spite of the fact that they did not have the final seal of magnificence, the *hsiao tsou* and the *ta tsou,* the small amble and the big amble. These gaits, though abnormal, are sought after by the Central Asian peoples, both settled and nomad, as well as by the Chinese. The only reasons are that they are absolutely smooth and level for the rider, allowing him to sit at ease on a saddle padded with huge cushions, while at the same time giving the pony an appearance of dash and impetuosity. In the big, or more showy amble, the two legs of the near side are put forward together, and then the two legs of the off side, each side thus moving independently in an alternating rhythm. It is really nothing more glorious than a kind of waddle, but great speed can be obtained. A pony can often be trained to it by linking the two legs of one side with a rope shackle, so that they must be moved at the same time or not at all. The acquired gait, however, is never so smooth as the natural trick. Its damning disadvantage is that the pony, when ridden hard, is apt to go shoulder-lame; and once he has gone shoulder-lame, you are never certain when the disability may not recur. A " big-ambling " pony should be reserved for town use.

The small amble is not in fact related to the other. I could never catch the rhythm for sure, but, as near as I could make out, the pony canters in single time, as one might say, on his forehand, while trotting behind in double time. It has a number of variations, each with a technical name. It is a very comfortable gait, rarely faster than a normal trot. The disadvantage is that the pony wastes a lot of motion, therefore tiring himself needlessly, so that it is not a sound gait for long-distance travel.

Ponies are bred in every oasis, as well as in every Qazaq, Mongol, and Qirghiz camp throughout Chinese Turkestan and Zungaria, but the three breeds of fame are those of Bar Köl, Qara Shahr, and the Ili valley. In spite of the way that tribes, nations, and peoples have been moving and shifting through these regions throughout history, their ponies have not merged into a common type any more than have the peoples themselves.

The Bar Köl ponies are named from the lake near which is the town of Barköl, whose official Chinese name for centuries has been Chen Hsi — Controlling the West. These ponies are bred on stony, mountain pastures on which the grass is sweet and nourishing, but never lush. Even their wintering grounds are comparatively exposed. They are small, wiry, and tough, able to fast, able to forage for themselves, able to face any weather, and without equals in hill country. The average height is not more than twelve hands; but they are valiant weight-carriers. They have no end of bottom. The desert-going and hill-ranging Chinese of these regions are as knowledgeable as any nomads about horseflesh. They say that a good mount and a good man are equally matched so far as endurance goes, but that the strongest rider is ready to drop out of the saddle before he has ridden a Bar Köl pony to a standstill.

This, of course, does not refer to a straightaway gallop, but to a long ride at a well-judged pace. I am quite prepared to believe the tales I have heard of these ponies being ridden more than a hundred miles in one day. When I was under arrest in San-t'ang Hu,[1] I hired a pony of this breed for my camel man to ride to Barköl. The distance was about eighty miles, through a snow-filled pass. The pony was very lean, being in starved winter condition, living on nothing but coarse, withered grass to be found in sun-warmed hollows. The man started late in the morning and rode through the short winter day and well into the night. When he got up to forest level, he built a fire and waited for dawn. The pony had nothing to eat. With the dawn, the man mounted again and reached the town early in the morning.

The Bar Köl ponies are big-hearted, in that they are hogs for work and distance; but, as the Chinese put it, " the holes in their hearts are crooked " — they are wily and vicious. As cart ponies especially they are hard to handle, being subject to wild stampeding panics. Now the Bar Köl mountains were once the stronghold of the Huns, who raided across the desert well into Kan-su province and gave the Chinese trouble for centuries. In fact it was only when the Chinese, under the T'ang dynasty in the seventh century, mastered the Bar Köl Huns that they gave the town they founded the name of Chen Hsi — Controlling the West — and were able to marshal their advance farther into the western regions on what are now the Great North and Great South Roads. Thus it is fair to call the Bar Köl breed the true Hun pony.

The breed owes its greatest fame, however, to the Imperial herds established under the Manchu dynasty. Several herds were kept up around Bar Köl and several at Ku Ch'eng-tze, each herd bearing a separate brand. Ponies were periodically sent all the way to

---

[1] See *The Desert Road to Turkestan.*

Peking for the Imperial stables. To harden them to the reception they would get, they were first put through a course of firecracker bombardments — a most necessary precaution, in view of their liability to panic. After the Revolution, the Governor of Hsin-chiang seized all these Imperial herds to form a reserve of cavalry mounts. He transferred them from the care of the Manchu families who for so long had made a good thing out of the privilege, and put them in charge of the sub-tribe of the Kirei-Qazaqs who are the only Qazaqs allowed in the pastures of the Bogdo Ola. A specified increase in the herds is yearly required from the Qazaqs, who are allowed to sell any extra increase for their own profit. Thus the old Bar Köl and Ku Ch'eng-tze herds are now merged; but the true Bar Köl breed survives in the herds belonging to the Khan of Qomul (Hami) pastured on the northern side of the Qarliq Tagh, and in the herds of the Qazaqs and Erh Hun-tze, or Bastards of the Bar Köl range. As for the Ku Ch'eng-tze pony, I do not know it well, but I think it runs larger than that of Bar Köl, and shows a strain of Qara Shahr blood.

In addition to the historic distinction of the Imperial herds, the Bar Köl pony has a certain legendary celebrity. The legend is known to every Chinese whose affairs have touched that part of the world. It is quite evidently one of the class which, attracting the national fancy, have been formally listed in the chronicles and at the same time have for centuries been popularly current. It was related to me by a vivacious old trader, a master-merchant and captain-traveler, who had *p'ao-liao,* " run over," all Chinese Inner Asia, from Manchuria to the country of the reindeer-riding Urian-ghai, thence to the oases of the South Road, thence to the rim of Tibet, and at last had died of the opium sickness a few marches north of Kuei-hua, the caravan city from which he had always traded. He said (and it was confirmed when I reached the West) that a certain dragon lives in the mountains over the lake of Bar Köl; or else he lives in the lake itself, or in a smaller lake up in the mountains. The dragon rouses himself at times from his lair, goes among the pony herds and covers the mares. The get of the dragon are the *ch'ien-li chü-tze,* the thousand-li colts. These heroic animals can be ridden a thousand li — three hundred and thirty miles, by and large — in one day. This is undoubtedly the origin of the colloquial phrase, " a thousand-li horse," for an animal of superlative quality. The dragon, most unfortunately, used to appear more frequently of old time than he does in our insipid age. I imagine, from what I have heard, that in the early summer, when some sort of horse festival is common among all the nomads of Central Asia, reminiscences of a sacrifice to the dragon could even at the present day be recovered in this region, in ceremonial observances of some sort.

Now Ma Tuan-lin,[1] a Chinese writer of the thirteenth century, records that, among the Tokhara of the Oxus region or Bactria, a stallion living in a cave on a mountain used to cover the mares pastured at the foot of the mountain; and the get of the stallion were none other than the blood-sweating ponies of Central Asia. Yule[2] notes this legend, but not the blood-sweating ponies. He merely suggests that Polo, telling of the descent of the horses of Badakshan from Bucephalus, the horse of Alexander, may have got hold of a version of the Chinese story. However that may be, I think the Tokhara story and the Bar Köl story are the same in origin. The Tokhara or Tur Qara were established once in Chinese Turkestan before moving to Bactria. They were known to the Chinese as T'u-hu-lu, a name that survives in at least three place names in Chinese Turkestan and Zungaria; of which the most easterly is Tu-hu-lu in a valley of the Qarliq Tagh, divided from Bar Köl only by Dead Mongol Pass.[3]

I never saw one of the " blood-sweating " horses, but they were at different times reported in China as a Central Asian marvel. Mr. Langdon Warner,[4] when traveling to Tun-huang, bought a team of Turkestan ponies, of which he writes, " I was worried at first to find them bleeding from various sores after the day's work, but I was told that all the western ponies did that, and it never for a moment slowed them down." He describes this as " a curious disease, probably the result of some parasitic insect." He was also referred to the old chronicles, and indeed it is evident that he had

[1] Rémusat, *Nouveaux Mélanges Asiatiques*, Paris, 1829.
[2] Yule, *The Book of Ser Marco Polo*, ed. Cordier, London, 1921.
[3] *The Desert Road to Turkestan.*
[4] *The Long Old Road in China.*

secured ponies of the kind which accounted for the original reports
of the " blood-sweating " marvel.

The ponies of Qara Shahr are as much worth mention as those
of Bar Köl. They get their name from being marketed at Qara
Shahr on the Road South of the Heavenly Mountains. They are
bred by the Torgut Mongols who winter in the lowlands of the
Qara Shahr oasis and spend their summers in the Yulduz plateau
and contiguous valleys of the high T'ien Shan. The most remarkable thing about them is the formation of head and neck and the
way that the ears, much longer than the stubby ears of the true
Mongol pony, are set on top and in front of the crown of the
head. The head, while heavy in proportion like that of the Mongol pony, is peculiar and striking in profile. The neck also is
like that of the Mongol pony, in its heaviness at the joining with the
shoulders; but the whole outline is astonishing in its resemblance
— which, though heavy, and as it were debased, is undeniable —
to the head and neck formation of the horses of Greek sculpture.
One might almost say that the Bucephalid or Macedonian strain
should be sought here, not in Badakshan. Certainly there would
be little hazard in pointing out these ponies as the type from which
were drawn the " T'ang horses," modeled in clay, which are found
in excavations in China, and which so little resemble the " China
pony " of our time, which is drawn almost entirely from the markets of Eastern Inner Mongolia.

The Qara Shahr pony, while much valued for swank in town,
is not so hardy a road-goer as the ponies of Bar Köl and the Ili.
He is liable to shoulder lameness. Many fine *tsou-ma* or amblers
are drawn from Qara Shahr, but the breed does not produce so
many natural amblers as the Bar Köl strain. These ponies are no-
ticeably bigger than those of the Bar Köl, running from thirteen to
fourteen hands. The present Prince of Qara Shahr (not, that is,
of the town of Qara Shahr, but of the Yulduz-Qara Shahr Torguts)
is a minor, so that the affairs of the tribe are in the hands of his
guardian, a lama. This man, who is full of energy and action, is
much interested in horse breeding. He has imported at great price
a number of stallions from Russia. Fine horses are to be had out
of Russia, because under the old Imperial government studs were

placed in different parts of the country, to improve the local breeds, and private owners also kept up good studs. English thoroughbreds were imported in no small numbers to these studs. In the Qara Shahr market at present one can buy many ponies with a strain of true or European horse; the pony I rode to Turfan was one of them. In Urumchi also I saw a fine Russian stallion, belonging to the Qara Shahr Lama, as the Regent is popularly called. Unfortunately, all the pony-breeding people of Central Asia have no other standard but size for a " foreign horse," as they call them, so that they are too often fobbed off with the raking great brutes that are the height of fashion in Russia as the centre horse of a troika team. They are all trotters, and the finest of these trotting breeds was the great Orloff strain. Unfortunately the introduction of such carriage-hauling blood produces high, gangling, narrow crossbreds, with a hard, high trotting action, most unpleasant under the saddle.

The " Ili horses," which used occasionally to reach China, brought back usually along the Imperial High Road in the train of an official, were almost always ungainly half-Russian crossbreds, high-actioned trotters. The Ili breed had the reputation in China of being the finest of all those within the Chinese dominions, wherefore it was thought that any example brought back must be something at least bye-ordinary in size. The true Ili pony is something quite different; a most noble, gallant pony. He is bred more in such highland valleys as that of the Tekes than in the plains of the lower Ili, and the best herds are those of the Qazaqs. This indicates that the original strain must have come farther from the west, for the Mongols on the Qunguz, near as they are to the Qazaqs of the Tekes, have a true Mongol pony, which they must have brought with them from Zungaria, or rather from the Altai. They are fine, mountainy ponies, but not the same thing as the " Ili " pony. Probably the distinguishing strain of the Ili pony comes from Russian Central Asia. He looks a relative of the very fine breed of which I saw one or two examples at Kulja, which Russians told me came from Pishpek; and these Pishpek ponies, I am pretty sure, must be related to those of the Turkomans.

The Ili pony, in short, has much the character of a small horse.

He has more of a pony head and neck, and is heavier in bone, than such a Badakshan horse as my noble bay stallion, but he can be seen at once to be more shapely than the true Mongol breeds. He is very sweetly gaited, has a nicer temper and finer spirit than the Mongol pony, is a tireless traveler, can forage under snow, and if handled constantly with understanding no better companion could be found. The breed undoubtedly has retained its excellence because, though not stall-fed, it ranges over such summer pastures as can hardly be equaled in Central Asia; and because it is easy to harvest enough wild hay to give him an extra ration in the winter. Thus he grows more freely, and escapes the stunting effect of winter cold and starvation during the first years of growth, which accounts for a great deal of the coarseness of the Mongol pony. In height there is not much to choose between the ponies of Qara Shahr and the Ili, unless the Ili ponies are a shade taller, averaging pretty nearly fourteen hands; but within that height the proportions of the Ili ponies are unmistakably sounder.

Although the three notable mountain breeds are kept distinct, the *hu'rh-chia ma,* or ponies bred by the oasis folk, are a mixture of all the different characteristics. They are not esteemed. They have the advantage of being largely stall-fed in the winter, but they are " softer," owing to the crushing summer heat of the lowlands. In such an oasis as Turfan, indeed, ponies cannot be bred at all. They come almost entirely from Qara Shahr, and for the first three summers, during which they are being acclimatized, they have to be watched with great care, being taken to bathe morning and evening, and tied in the shade during the heat of the day. By the time they have become acclimatized, they could no longer endure a mountain winter. All through the oases, fresh blood must constantly be imported from the mountains.

The chief characteristic in the horse mastery of the Turki people in the oases, becoming more pronounced as one goes west along the Road South of the Heavenly Mountains, is the predilection for stallions. Neither Chinese nor nomads like stallions. They say they cannot stand such hard usage, and age more quickly. Even the nomads, who breed ponies, let their stallions range with the herd; the man who wishes to display a good mount picks the best of his geldings.   As for mares, they are a most undignified mount, the Central Asian nomads being in this respect quite different from the Arabs.   Undoubtedly the prejudice against stallions is because, being kept only for breeding, they rapidly become soft.   The Turki oasis-bred stallions, which are constantly in work and rarely put to a mare, are sound and hardy.   My own stallion, belonging to a race accustomed to constant handling, had the manners of a gentleman.   When saddled, he was perfectly easy to control in the vicinity of a mare.   The only trouble I ever had with him was at a small inn, one day, when he scented a mare.   He nibbled loose the knot of his halter rope and went a-courting.   By the time the affair was discovered, he was in a frenzy.   He savaged every pony in the place, and it was dangerous for even me to approach. An agile carter at last secured him, creeping along a manger and with a long pole slipping a noose over his head.   Even then, when led back to his manger, he began eating heartily at once, quite forgetting that ten minutes before he had savaged his companion, my wife's pony, whose shoulder he had ripped open for six inches. The mare, poor dear thing, felt much abused and terribly shocked, for she was already carrying a colt.

It is plain that the reason the oasis Turki prefers a stallion, and will use a mare if he can get hold of one, is that if he can breed ponies he does n't have to buy them.   For the same reason the nomads in the mountains do everything in their power to keep mares and stallions out of the hands of the lowland people.   One fine strain is bred in the oasis of Manass.   This is the pony herd of the House of Shih, who are probably the richest family in the province.   They are great landowners in the Manass oasis, and are said to own half the city of Manass.   They pasture their noble ponies in meadows in the oasis, but they also have pastures in the mountains to which they drive them in the summer; and it is these mountain pastures which account for the excellence of their herd.   The ponies they breed are in appearance like a herd of the finest pick of the Ili pastures.

Perhaps it was because I no longer had with me the great caravan dog who had accompanied me through Mongolia that I turned so eagerly to horses.   Also, the people of the land had horses always in their minds. I sat idly in mangers, watching our ponies feed; I squatted on my heels in the dust of caravanserai yards; I sat cross-legged on felts in mountain yurts; I talked with men of every race and tribe in those closed-off lands of Inner Asia, and talk of horses was always running in and out of what we said. But above all there was the fact that I fed and watered and saddled our ponies every day, and groomed them too, such grooming as they got. When you are about your ponies as much as that, and when they are ponies who will take you willingly as much as forty miles a day, and when they are two such ponies as that patient, swift Ili black and that long-stepping, eager gentleman from Badakshan, then companionship enters in.

XIX

SAIRAM NOR AND THE TALKI PASS

CHING HO is a town of another order from the little villages of one street of wattle-and-daub hovels in which we had been halting since Hsi Hu. It must have been built under the Manchus to serve as the administrative centre of a large Mongol territory, and to impress the tribesmen in the way that the Manchus understood so superbly with the splendor of the Ta Ch'ing Empire. Yet there is one mark common to all such Manchu building. It was never kept up on a scale commensurate with its planning. The arches along the wide causeway of approach are now falling to pieces, the noble temples are choked with bat's dung, and officials quarter themselves in patched-up corners of what once were spacious yamens. Even so, the free, strong lines of many buildings, the amply executed wood-carving on the temples, and the dignity of the temple frescoes, prove that once artists and artisans were to be found in the province, far superior to the slack bunglers of today. Trade being now so much more important than it was under the Empire, all men of any talent become shopkeepers and merchants, the employments of the artisans being regarded as inferior, and left to the incapable, or to Turki workers who have neither the skill nor the tradition of the Chinese.

From Ching Ho to the Talki pass, the stages being open to Qazaq raids, we were provided with an escort. We were riding now through a spacious country of meadows and streams, stretching away toward mountain walls. On the south were Torgut lands, now being taken up, along the streams, by T'ung-kan and Turki farmers. On the north and northwest we looked toward the Borotala, still reserved to the Chahars. Carruthers, who visited them in 1910,[1] speaks of them as far less degenerate and more prosper-

[1] *Unknown Mongolia.*

ous than the other Mongols of the province. At that time a few farmers were settling among them, " renting land at an exorbitant price from the chiefs, who were said to extort from them 50 per cent of their produce." The Chahars having lost since the Chinese Revolution the privileged position which they held under the Empire, colonization appears now to be making more rapid headway among them. Their chief trading centre is Ta Ho-yen-tze, but the old garrison post or fort from which they are still administered lies in the Borotala valley itself. It is commonly known as Ta Ying-p'an, the Big Barracks.

The Chahars were among the most stubborn opponents whom the Manchus had to subdue when, immediately following on their conquest of China, they proceeded to assert their sovereignty over Mongolia. In order to break the power of the Chahars after their defeat, the Manchus transported a large part of the tribe from its ancestral territories north of Kalgan and quartered them in the remotest west, along the Borotala, from which they were forbidden to wander, but where they were assured of the freedom from contact with other tribes and races which Mongols cherish more than almost any other condition of their nomad life. It was by such drastic removals of whole peoples that the Manchus demonstrated their power among the outer barbarians who ringed their empire, cantoning these Chahars in the west, and at the same time lifting some of the remnants of the Zungar tribes and setting them down as far east as Manchuria.

I understand that the Chahars of the Borotala, like several other tribes which had held out against the Manchus with especial determination, were deprived of their own tribal organization and divided afresh into Banners, on the Manchu plan. Thus they became Imperial military reservists, liable to regular service in contingents whenever required. Other Mongols were not called on directly for military service, but when extra levies were required each tribal chief or prince mustered such following as he could summon, and presented himself before his Manchu overlords, each prince with his " tail," like a Highland chief. By a paradox of the true Asia, the drafting of the Chahars as Bannermen, designed originally to curtail their power, came in the end to give them the privilege of a special position; for they thus became the Emperor's "own people." They were free from all Chinese interference, and from the jurisdiction of local civil authorities, being amenable only to direct commands of the Chen-shuai, or high military authority of the Ili valley. Since the Chinese Revolution in 1911 they have lost this privileged position, and are now liable to the same taxation and conscription as other subject races in the province.

Our first stage was Ta Ho-yen-tze, which is marked on maps as Takianzy. Either this is a local name conveniently corrupted by the Chinese into this form, which means Great River Bank, or, as I think is more likely, Takianzy is a Turki corruption of the Chinese name, owing its place on the map to the employment of Qazaq guides by the early Russian explorers. The stream here, after draining a marshy bottom-land, falls into the Borotala, which empties into Ebi Nor. There is a gradual slope to Ebi Nor, from which a wide lower valley opens into that part of the North Road on which we had traveled between the Jair highlands and Ch'e P'ai-tze. Then again there is a desert sweep toward the main Zungarian gulf. The depression of Ebi Nor opens on the north into a savage defile between the Ala Tau and Barliq-Maili highlands; the great Zungarian Gate, the lowest depression in Central Asia, with the exception of the basin of Turfan. Carruthers [1] describes it as "a rift valley caused by the movement of the earth's crust, not by the action of water. This valley once formed the connecting link between the drainage of Zungaria and that of Southern Siberia. The chain of lakes at either end of the valley (Balkhash, Ala Köl, Ebi Nor, etc.) are the remains of the great Asiatic Mediterranean Sea; if their waters were to rise a few hundred feet they would break through the Gate, flooding the plains to the north and south." He describes the defile as about six miles wide at its narrowest point and forty-six miles long. From his description, both the defile itself and the mountain slopes immediately facing it are a fearsome desert.

It is true that the striking geographical configuration of the defile makes it an obvious "gate" between Zungaria and Siberia,

[1] *Unknown Mongolia.*

and for this reason Carruthers assumes that it must have been the line of passage of the major nomadic migrations of the past. I think, however, it is more likely, for reasons that I have already indicated,[1] that the migrations went by the way of Chuguchak and the Emil valley, which is connected with the Altai and Western Mongolia by routes of easier passage, with continuous grazing.

Bearing in mind the relative positions of the Zungarian Gate and Lao Feng K'ou, the Old Windy Pass, it may be possible to clear up to a certain extent the apparent confusion and wrong order in the accounts of this region given by both Pian de Carpine and William of Rubruck, in the thirteenth century. The former seems to reverse the order of his reaching Omyl or Imil (the city then standing in the Emil valley) and his passing the Zungarian Gate. The latter seems to reverse the order of his accounts of the Emil valley and the Tarbagatai. These contradictions made Rockhill[2] suppose that in both instances paragraphs had been transposed by copyists.

I think that in Pian de Carpine's narrative there is a "telescoped" account of *two* defiles celebrated for high winds; the Zungarian Gate southwest of the Emil, and Lao Feng K'ou to the southeast. Either he himself ran together the two accounts and then went on to speak of the Emil, or else an early copyist, thinking he had repeated himself, did the telescoping. As for Rubruck, he was traveling in December, whereas his predecessor had traveled in May. It is therefore more than likely that he did not go on across the snow-buried plains between Ala Köl and the Emil, but struck up into the Barliq-Maili-Jair highlands, which even now are winter quarters of the nomads because of their freedom from snow, came to what is now the trade highway, actually passed through Lao Feng K'ou, and so reached the Emil. In this case the high mountains and rock gorges which he describes would not be the Tarbagatai, as Rockhill supposed, but the region about Shih Men-tze, the Stone Gate, which I have described in the Jair plateau.

[1] See also "Caravan Routes of Inner Asia," *Geographical Journal*, December, 1928.

[2] Rockhill, *William of Rubruck* (with accounts of Pian de Carpine), Hakluyt Society.

From Ta Ho-yen-tze one goes by Fifth Stage (Wu T'ai) and Fourth Stage (Ssu T'ai) up a long, bare valley, half filled in by piedmont detritus. In gorges far away on both sides are spruce forests, high up, but these are said to depend on winter snow for life, as there are very few springs and the subsoil drainage is lost in the detritus filling the valley bed. At Ssu T'ai (Fourth Stage) water is brought from one of the rare springs in a line of wooden troughs laid for several miles. That evening some antelope came to drink from the trough. They were the tamest I have ever seen in the open country they frequent in summer, though they are notoriously easy to shoot when they resort in winter to the edge of lowland jungles. They came within three hundred yards of the barracks and the tiny travelers' quarters, and let me walk out in full view with a rifle in my hand, lie down on a knoll, and pick off two of them from a two-hundred-yard range.

Beyond Fourth Stage the road crosses over at the head of the valley to Third Stage (San T'ai) by Sairam Nor. Because this watershed is the very worst place on the road for banditry, a small wooden fort, surrounded by a palisade, has recently been built in the maze of knolls which make good lurking-places for raiders. When we passed, only three of the garrison of ten were in the fort; and two of them were sunk in an opium stupor. Of the others, two were out on escort duty, one had gone to fetch water, one was dying of an unknown sickness in a fort a stage away, and three had deserted. A well sunk at this fort had failed to find water at a depth of forty feet, so that it was necessary for a man to go several miles into the hills to fetch water from a spring.

Around the lake of Sairam Nor, we were told, a man can ride in a day; but he would have to have a good pony. For several simple, striking reasons, the lake has an immemorial repute of holiness. It has no visible inlet or outlet, yet the water is drinkable; but although the water is good, no fish are found in it. Near the lake we saw a large flock of bustard; the only ones I saw in the province, though both the greater and the smaller bustard are said to be common in many places. No shooting is allowed within sound of the lake, for it is believed that any violence, and especially the sound of firearms, would bring a change in the weather. Near the shore where we passed is an island, with several smaller islets, and on the island is a temple, showing how the Chinese in their turn respect and do honor to this lake.

Sairam Nor defines one end of the reserves of the Borotala Chahars, who camp near it in winter, and the boundary between their winter pastures and the pastures used by shepherds coming over from the Ili country is marked by a large *obo*. To the east lie the Borotala and the easy divide by which we had reached the lake; on the north and northwest, beyond a crest of mountains, is all Siberia, and to the west, over the Talki pass, is the Ili. Near the village and barracks of San T'ai (Third Stage) the road is pinched for a few hundred yards between the lake and steep hills which come down to the edge of the water. At the narrowest point is a short obstructing wall, battlemented, with a fortified gate. They say the fortification was touched up again to see its last fighting during the Revolution, when there was a brief struggle for power between the Chinese of the Ili country and Urumchi. The wall may have been built during the Mohammedan Rebellion, but it is probably much older. Near it are tumuli or grave-mounds which must be very old.

From the edge of the lake there is a climb of only a couple of hundred yards to the head of the Talki pass, where a Chinese shrine and an obo stand side by side. Then, in turning down the pass, one enters a new country, as through a gate. Instead of passing distant forests among dry hills, we rode under the shadow and through the fragrance of spruces, mixed with wild fruit trees, from which the Chinese call the pass the Valley of Fruits. The road, though carts can use it, was much more steep and stony, and every fold in the hills held its watercourse. A storm broke over us on the crest of the pass, but, after one strong burst of hail, held off for a while. We rode as fast as we could over the stones, down a valley that seemed to sing with water, looking up all the while to hanging copses and alps of pasture. In many places the spruces had been logged off, and a young second growth of birches was taking their place. Lower down we met gangs of motley laborers, all shifty, shiftless, ne'er-do-well Turkis and Qazaqs, with a few Chinese among them, on their way into the hills to dig *pai-t'u*, which was explained to me as the roots of a medicinal grass. We passed now and again the little caves, protected with brushwood shelters in front, in which they lived. All through the province, the seasonal labor of logging, gold-mining, and other hard work with poor shelter in the mountains, witnesses a great muster of bad-hats, who come out of the towns where they have spent the winter. Their camps are the most troublesome centres of gambling, fighting, and knifing.

Then we rode into Erh T'ai (Second Stage), a village of log huts and lumber mills, with a faintly Alpine air, populated by lounging Turkis in gay robes, Qazaq hangers-on, and a few Chinese traders. The hailstorm returned, with new vigor, so we sheltered about two hours in a wood-paneled room each half of which made a raised k'ang-platform, the two divided by a passage about two feet wide. When we left again the ground was covered an inch or two deep in the slush of melting hailstones, and each little stream was roaring with a turbid flood. As we went down the valley, it widened, the hills were not so steeply pitched, and the forests were broken by wide sweeps of mountain meadow, at the edge of which we passed many Qazaq yurts. The mouth of the valley closed in somewhat, giving the effect of another gate, and when we rode out of it we were in an open country of downs, where Qazaq camps could be seen widely scattered. We urged our ponies on, making one of the hardest and longest stages of the journey, and at last reached Lu-ts'ao Kou, Valley of Reeds,[1] where is one of the "cities" of Ili. A last shower caught us on the edge of the town, and we must have made a bedraggled pair, even our fine ponies being muddied and wearied. We were taken for wandering Russians, for our transport was miles behind and we had outridden our escorting soldier, who was far gone in opium and had been suffering for hours the peculiar agony an opium smoker feels when he gets wet and cold. A great hulking Chinese, a buffoon loitering in the crowd, caught at my bridle and offered us the foulest insults I have ever heard. I countered by asking if any Tientsin men

---

[1] The name of this place has been written by different travelers in different ways (I think mistakenly), one form being Lao-ts'ao Kou, which would be Old Grass Valley.

were in this town, who had better manners, and if there were a Tientsin inn. There was an instant change. The report went about that a new kind of foreigner had arrived, who spoke like a Tientsin man, and before long a Tientsin youth was making us as comfortable as he could at an inn smothered in mire, and Tientsin traders of the better class were calling on us, asking me eager questions of Tientsin and the world.

The next day we went on to Sui-ting, one of the greatest of the Cities of Ili, a place that relies largely on trade with the Mongols. We were lucky to find there a Catholic priest, a man from what used to be German Poland, who kindly went with us the next day to call on the Military Governor in Hsin Ch'eng, in whose yamen he had friends. We were also lucky to be able to leave Sui-ting so quickly, for it is an unprepossessing place, the great mixture of races there and the opportunities offered by the Mongol trade to rogues of all sorts conducing to ill-manners and rowdiness even more than in Hsi Hu. Sui-ting is in striking contrast with Hsin Ch'eng, the New City, only three or four miles away, with which it is connected by a brisk " omnibus " traffic of light, four-wheeled Russian-style carts, which rattle merrily along the hard mud road, picking up passengers as they go.

The difference is partly historical and partly, I fancy, a reflection of the dominating spirit in the New City, the Chen Shuai. Hsin Ch'eng appears to have been built afresh and complete, following the reoccupation of the Ili valley after the Mohammedan Rebellion, as a garrison town to hold down the mountain tribes, and to make a good international appearance on the Russian frontier. It is thus one of the last monuments of the Manchu Imperial tradition. The clean lines of the solid walls, the wide streets, the temples built not by chance in corners but planned with dignity in commanding sites, all show the mark that the Manchus were able to leave, here and there, in the very farthest of their dominions. Here were stationed, in Imperial days, the officers popularly called the Four Great Commanders, who under the authority of the supreme Military Governor administered the Manchus, the Qazaqs, the Mongols, and the Sibo-Solon bannermen.

The Chinese Revolution was more violent in the Ili country than elsewhere in the province, and witnessed a great massacre of the Manchu bannermen in the different cities. As is usual in the history of such uprisings, throughout the Chinese dominions, the townsfolk seem to have shut themselves within their walls and there awaited death, whether by starvation or by assault, according to fate. The Solons and Sibos, by contrast, being settled on the land, were able to survive; for they were not immobilized by walls, and yet had the solidity and coherence of a landed community prepared to put up a bitter resistance rather than be dispossessed of its lands. Under the Republic, the Manchus have lost their identity; of the few who survived, most have taken Chinese names and are not prone to admit their Manchu race. Yet the race does survive, and one may hear in the streets of Hsin Ch'eng a provincial echo of the noble speech of Peking.

There is almost no trade in the New City. Most of the men on the streets are in uniform, and their soldierly appearance must be remarked at once by anyone coming from the direction of Urumchi. In the rest of the province there is little need of an army, and into it are drafted all the beggars and broken-down opium smokers that can be caught. In Ili, the old tradition, and the need for it, still persists. The pick of the garrison are of Manchu and Sibo stock, men with a fighting tradition, supplemented by a few " tame " Qazaqs and Mongols, and stiffened with a sprinkling of adventurers of the stout Chih-li and Shan-tung breed. On the whole, they are the kind of material to delight an officer.

The Chen Shuai, or Military Governor, whom we reached after passing through wide yamen-courts of gray bricks, is concerned only with the tribes of the mountains. We wished to get from him a special permit to travel in the high mountains, and an interview was arranged after we had seen his chief A.D.C., a young man who turned out, to our delight, to be a son of our friend Governor Li of Chuguchak. This young man, dressed dashingly in silks and speaking in the most gracious accent of Peking, and with a charm and lightness of manner that were irresistible, showed not the faintest touch of any fashionable " Westernisms "; yet he had spent much of his boyhood in Russia, where he had gone for schooling, and spoke, as I was told, perfect Russian. After chatting a little, he took us on to our interview with the Governor; one of the most pleasant " official " interviews I have ever had, and a most unorthodox one, too, seeing that I was accompanied by my wife.

My wife, however, had a most exceptional measure of respect throughout her travels. It was true that conservative people might think her only a " traveling wife," since no respectable woman would abandon the dignity of her position as head of a household. On the other hand, the better-informed people admired her spirit and appreciated her interest in her travels. The common people were immensely impressed with the information, which Moses was never tired of putting about, that she had a university degree. I used frequently to overhear lively discussions at inns or by the wayside, something like this : " These people are Americans; they are of a country new, but very rich. They are not like the English, who are unbending, nor like the Russians, whose affairs no one can make out. The woman? *Ai-ya!* But a very special woman. She has a degree! Yes, a degree. What talent! Undoubtedly her people are officials [that is, because of belonging to the literary class]. Her husband has no degree; all his life he has never been more than a merchant. The truth of it is, that all decision is with her; he is only the executor."

The Governor was one of the finest types of Chinese administrator I met in the province; a Yun-nan man, like the Provincial Governor. He was then only thirty-seven, but had already held his high post for six years. In that time he had dealt with at least three outbreaks of bad trouble, of which the last was a great incursion of Russian Qazaqs, who drove off wholesale the cattle of the Chinese Qazaqs and Mongols. The Chen Shuai in person led a force into the very difficult hill country, and after a brilliant little campaign in that most embarrassing kind of warfare, guerilla fighting, cleared his frontiers. A great and much-needed prestige accrued to the Chinese administration. As I have said before, the Qazaqs on the Russian side of the frontier are able to purchase modern arms, a liberty not allowed by the Chinese. Moreover, that part of the old province of Semirechensk adjoining the Ili territory is now the Autonomous Soviet Socialist Republic of Qazaqistan. The Russian Qazaqs therefore have a dash and initiative to which their kinsmen who are subject to the Chinese cannot aspire. Consequently the triumph of the Russian Qazaqs in all encounters of border thieves and cattle lifters has a galling effect of attrition on the Chinese prestige.

The Governor was a pale, slight young man, with the delicate hands of a *literatus* and an air of reserved command. They say he is immensely respected by the litigious Qazaqs for the skill with which he awards justice in their innumerable lawsuits, to cope with which he extends his office hours from noon far into the night. Under the Han dynasty, in the earliest period of Chinese domination in what is now Chinese Turkestan, they seem to have had such able administrators, fit to handle subject races soundly; and the continued supply of them, in a period when the influence of far-away China is weakened by a cycle of social and political transition and confusion, is a sure sign of the unimpaired virility of the race.

The General not only furnished us with a pass, but with an escort of two men. They reported themselves that evening at the clean little Sibo inn where we were staying, and we were able to go on the next day to Kulja. Moses, in the meantime, had been accosted by a noncommissioned officer of the quarter-guard at the yamen entrance, who swore he knew his face, though Moses protested that he did not know him. " Were you never in South Africa? " the man asked. Moses admitted it. " I thought so," the man went on; " then who were you? " " My name is Li," said Moses, " and that may mean nothing to you; but I will tell you, I have also a foreign name. My name is Moses." " And then," said Moses, " the man called me ' sir.' For when I was in the gold-mines of South Africa, I picked up a little Kaffir and a little English. I used to interpret for the Boss, so they gave me a desk in an office. Yes, I who can neither read nor write, I used to have a desk in an office, and pen, ink, and paper in front of me, and thousands of men knew who I was."

The soldier, in fact, still knew who Moses was. He told him that there were more than twenty Shan-tung and Chih-li men, all officers or noncoms, who had drifted to the Far West after old South African gold-mining days, most of whom would know him,

and he was eagerly invited to a feast of reunion.   I told him to go,
but he said his clothes would not do; he could not foregather with
men to whom he had once been an important name, looking as if
he had come down in the world.   It was true; with his tattered
trousers, patched jacket, and face weathered to mahogany, he
looked a villain of the road.   He had not only steadily refused
the purchase of new clothes, but when I wanted to buy for him a
fine lambskin coat to take back as a present to his family, he would
not allow it.   " I know you are poor," he said stoutly, " and that
you are not getting any salary, but traveling on your own money
and hoping for a job in the future.   I did not come with you to
get rich, but to go adventuring, and because I worked for your
father.   When you come back to China, that will be different;
then I hope to get rich along with you."

Still, I did not want him to miss such a great occasion.   " You
can wear my riding breeches and tweed jacket," I said, " and I
have a pair of woolen stockings, and my biggest shirt will fit you.
We can get you up fit to kill."   But he still refused.

" It would only be one more drunk," said Moses.

XX

" ICH WEISS NICHT, WAS SOLL ES
BEDEUTEN "

"Ich weiss nicht, was sol es bedeuten," murmured a voice beside me, and added, in a warm, comfortable, chuckling tone, *"Dass ich so traurig bin."* I waved toward the open-air stage on which two or three Tientsin actors, assisted by " locals " trained to use a Tientsin accent, were prosecuting a riotous play. It was not the classical, but the colloquial drama; but the Tientsin accent made it the height of Ili fashion, and it was noisily splendid with stamping warriors and gymnastic clowning. *"Ein Märchen aus alten Zeiten,"* I assured my *traurig* friend. The play, racketing within ten yards of us, made connected speech impossible, but my heart warmed to him, because he led off with *Die Lorelei.* It took me back from the heat under the awning and the rich composite smell of a Kulja garden party, pervaded by seventeen kinds of tobacco smoke, the muttony aroma of the Turki peoples, and the tremendous scents used by Russian women of what used to be the mercantile and petty-official classes, who take baths only after the most considered premeditation, being brought up in the belief that getting wet means going in danger of a cold; back to the snowy cold of Chuguchak. When I came to Chuguchak all the German I could speak was *Die Lorelei;* but the Russian Consul, I found, could speak all the rest of the German language. He was a very good fellow. He did his best to help me find my wife, he strewed Siberia with telegrams to find out where she was and tell her where I was; and before I left Chuguchak he had showed me that I could not play chess, and I had picked up from him some other German, which came in very handy at Kulja.

But we were at an official garden party. A screen of trees in full June leafage intervened discreetly between us and the badly decayed magnificence of the huge yamen. In a wide space under the trees, in what had once been a viceregal garden, a succession of pools, groves, and fantastic rocks in the most painted Chinese style, was a vast *p'eng,* which is an awning of mats on a scaffold of bare poles. At one end of the long space was a raised stage, on whose elastic boards, which emitted dust at every bounce, postured and stamped the rustic actors with magnificent gusto. At the far end from the stage was a railed barrier, behind which in formal reserve sat the women and girls of the ruling race, the Chinese. Compared with their flowered silks and sleek, jetty, jeweled hair, their slight bodies and sweet faces, their studied grace of carriage breaking at times into fluttering animation, the undulating mob between looked wildly barbarian. At separate tables to one side, admitted more as lookers-on than guests, were groups of the " turbaned people," the subject races, minding their manners with a pathetic, indescribable, hairy sedateness, belied by the vivid colors of their long robes.

Around a central table a group of officials were playing a Chinese game of cards for high stakes, with so much paper money piled on the table that one could scarcely see the play. Over their shoulders hung eager friends. The older men were dressed in plain dark colors, but some of them had replaced the round black cap with bowler hats or wide-brimmed gray felts, brought tenderly from the coastal provinces by camel caravan. The younger men affected light greens and blues. A few smoked the old-fashioned long pipe, or the bubbling brass water-pipe; others waved fabulous cigarette-holders. None of them paid any attention to the play. Mobs of the vulgar — friends of the friends of the under-cook's wife's relations — hung about the fringes, gaping impartially at the play and the bidden guests. A list of scenes from plays, the repertory of the actors, was brought round to the guests of honor, who chose each a scene, which would be presented in due course, and inscribed, with their names, the sum which they would present to the actors. It is a high compliment to be offered this list. It is not that you are paying for your entertainment, but that you are being given an opportunity to display your

splendor as a patron of the arts.   The actor-manager comes round
next morning to collect.   Acting companies from the coast are
rare in this province starved of the amenities.   If an impresario can
procure girls really from Tientsin or Yang-liu-ch'ing — for these
companies are of the somewhat raffish kind in which girls as well
as men take the female parts — and hold on to them, he makes rapid
money.   Sentimental exiles are eager to refresh in such feminine
company the associations of home.

When luncheon was served, with the din of the theatre undimin-
ished at our shoulders, we found ourselves in a crowded company
at a round table.   We foreigners, after our barbarian custom, had
thrown our womenfolk among the men.   There were two or three
shy Russian girls, and a saturnine old matron who could not handle
chopsticks, and whose frizzed curls bobbed without respite at the
edge of the bowl from which she pushed food into her mouth with
a spoon.   A Russian woman, the wife of a Soviet official, whose
clothes and unmistakable manner distinguished her at once in our
concourse of opposites, was chatting in French with a Mongol
princess.   She spoke English and German with equal ease.   We
were told that she was the daughter of a distinguished Moscow
family, and had from the beginning been ardent in the cause of the
Revolution.   There are many such figures in the new Russia, whose
unwavering faith carries them in the service of their cause to the
farthest limits of the Union of Soviet Socialist Republics.

It is a tradition in these parts of the world that in such parties,
where lack of language is a clog on good feeling, there must be
plenty of drinks.   The old Russian consulates, by all accounts,
used to set a rattling pace.   The Soviet consulates, to point the
contrast, make a point of reserve in their own hospitality.   They
offer plenty, but force nothing.   They do not riot at the table.
At the same time, in all other points of outward show, they are
most particular about their dignity and prestige, and for this reason
Soviet officials serving abroad draw far more pay than in their own
country.   Our host, however, a high official, had studied hospitality for foreigners in the old school.   He believed that a foreigner drunk was a foreigner happy; an opinion probably confirmed by observation in the past.   A secretary or attaché was

therefore told off to keep each guest of note drinking even, and if possible even more. It happened, however, that the man who courteously ministered to me began by urging on me three successive bumpers of that Russian brandy of which I have already spoken. He set the example himself. The result was that by the time we were bowing our farewells and going out through a shrubbery avenue down which underlings ran before us, bawling out our names and summoning our carriages, he had been laid to rest in a quiet little arbor, next to the discreet pergola reserved for opium smokers.

The Mongol princess of whom I have spoken ranked to the fore in Kulja society. She was the daughter of a famous prince of the last generation, who had ended his days in Peking. During her childhood in Peking she had begun a foreign education, which in time she was sent to Paris to complete. On her way home, with a university degree and an armament of Paris clothes, she had been seized with a notion to visit the yurts of her ancestors and make acquaintance with her Central Asian relatives. She traveled to the end of the Orenburg-Turkestan railway and then by cart along the Pishpek road to Viernye, and so to the frontier at Kulja. The Chinese officials were at a complete loss. Here was a princess of the most notable Mongol family in the province, but she was less like a Mongol than they were. They did not want to offend her relations, but according to the strict rule of the old Governor at Urumchi she must be kept in a sort of quarantine until she had been officially reported on, before being allowed to proceed. In the meantime, Mongol emissaries from encampments in remote valleys were trooping into Kulja to receive her with proper honor; and what they made of a princess of their tribe in Paris clothes, with shingled hair, the Lord knows.

It was hard enough for the high official whose duty it was to entertain her. Among his peers, women were carried along in closed carts in the train of their masters. As for appearing in public . . . But here he had on his hands a young lady who looked like a foreigner, dressed like a foreigner, and had the most scandalous foreign ways. With no man of her family to give her countenance and keep her in decorous seclusion, she would go into the street, command a telega, and drive off to shop for herself and visit whom she pleased. And she went into mixed company with a nerve-destroying nonchalance. He was a courtly gentleman of the old school, and what he thought of all these goings-on I can imagine, but I cannot put it in words.

We met the Princess at a party at his house. Her shingled hair was beginning to assert itself since its last manipulation by a Paris barber, and her Paris clothes and shoes had been saddened by a fortnight's experience of a Russian telega on Russian roads, but she came forward with the gay assurance of a true princess. Our host asked me in Chinese, in a badly worried way, if I spoke French. I said that I did, wondering what was to come next, and he sighed in relief. The Princess bore down on me with a gleam in her twenty-year-old eye, assailing me with sprightly chatter in the most limpid French of Paris, and an ironic use of drawing-room platitudes about the length of our stay in the country, the weather, and a subtle implication, to forestall criticism of her turnout, that by the look of our own clothes we must have had hard traveling.

After letting me struggle for a while, wishing I knew *Die Lorelei* in French, the Princess said demurely to my wife, in English, " Your husband speaks French really rather well, for an American." " God's teeth ! " I said, but under my breath, because the only possible retort would have been that she spoke French altogether too damned well for a Mongol. However, we relapsed into English; for the Princess, besides her native Mongol, spoke English almost as well as French, passable Russian, and impeccable Peking Chinese. We had much news to exchange, all about people in Peking. The Princess, from time to time, roped in the old official with a quick translation of what we were saying.

The imagination of our host could almost be seen to boggle. It was only the day before that the Princess, the most un-Mongol Princess, had appeared at the frontier, announcing that she was on her way home from Paris to the yurt. The next day, who should drop in but a couple of Americans (people whom he had never yet encountered) who did not speak Russian and did speak Chinese; two things which, in foreigners, went against all the canons of his experience. And not only did the Americans and the Mongol fall to talking merrily in some mutually intelligible speech; but behold, they all knew who was going to have a baby in Peking. He could think of only one thing to say; and he said it like a man. He told the Princess that she ought to get her senior male relative to find her a husband, quickly.

Among other residents of the incredible town of Kulja, we found a German tanner. He had arrived many years before, to set up what he called a Stinkless Leather Factory, of which he was justly proud. He complained, however, that he suffered from being unable to export into Russia his beautifully supple horse-hide and ibex-hide leathers for making riding boots. He said that by their favorable trade agreement with Germany the big semi-official monopolies or trusts of Russia were able to import manufactured goods which they reëxported into all parts of Central Asia. This gave their trade an expanding or outward thrust which was carrying them forward against all competition. To prevent any counter-current, they had raised a prohibitive tariff against all manufactured goods coming into Russia from non-Soviet Central Asian countries, because what they required, in return for their export of manufactures, was an influx of raw materials.

There was also a padre, who appeared at several of the parties at which we were unceasingly entertained, and himself entertained us at the last party of all. We had a good time, but I am afraid that we wounded him, which was the greatest of pities, for he was a man of the most genuine friendliness. There was hardly room to eat, the table was so loaded with Russian relishes and German eatables : but that was not the hardest part. He had learned from Chinese and Russian entertainments to insist on a giddy circulation of the drinks. He started us off on *zakuski* and vodka, which was all very well, but when at last we sat down we were overawed by a regiment of bottles on a sideboard within arm's reach. Most of the bottles held an excellent white wine, his own vintage, while others held a flat, locally made Russian beer. An empty bottle he hailed as a conquest or victory: he ranged the " dead men " in full view, and applauded as their numbers grew. On the other hand, a glass not emptied he considered a reflection on his hospitality: he was set on breaking all known records. " It is

a good white wine," he said; "I made it myself.   Nowhere else
in the province is there such wine.   But it needs drinking.   Only
in large quantities is it good for the digestion."

When at last we broke away, after a "lunch" that had lasted
from before noon until four or five o'clock, he was plainly upset.
"You do not like my house," he said, opening another bottle in
desperation.   "You go away without enjoying yourselves.   Kulja
is a sad place, for we seldom see travelers.   I thought we were going to have a good time.   Twenty years I was in the province of
Kan-su, which is far better than dreary Kulja.   There I had many
travelers, not a few Americans, as my guests.   I know what a
good party is, and I know you have not enjoyed yourselves.   What
is wrong, what is wrong?   All Americans came to my house in
Kan-su, and were happy.   Never, never before have I had one go
away from my house without falling off his horse."

XXI

THE VALLEY OF THE ILI

KULJA, it may be seen, has an air of its own; but that air is rightly come by, for it is the capital of the Nine Cities of Ili. This is a frontier, and the most vulnerable and hazardous frontier for a journey of many hundred miles. All the contrasting peoples that congregate there are aware that the possibility of upheaval and terror underlies the prosperity and ease of life, and for that reason take on a spirit of recklessness and devil-may-care. The town populations especially are unruly and dissipated.

The valleys of the Ili River and its tributaries are the richest ground in Central Asia. As we talk of " white man's country " in Kenya or some other territory that lies outside of our natural heritage, so the Chinese talk of the Ili, as a fat, desirable land, but one in which, in that phrase which has no parent language, " the natives must be kept in order." Not only is there an abundant supply of water in the streams, but there is also an ample rainfall, so that almost no true desert is to be found between the streams or between the towns. Bread is cheaper here than anywhere else in a province of cheap food. In the mountains, iron is easily accessible, besides gold and other metals, while coal is even more readily obtained, and there is a great supply of timber. All the materials of necessary clothing, and even the more solid comforts, are also produced in the sub-province, so that imports of Chinese origin are restricted to tea, silks, and articles of luxury requiring skilled manufacture. This tendency to be at the same time claimed by a ruling Chinese population and divorced from economic dependence on China explains much of its bloody and revolutionary history; but indeed, its modern history is only a pendant to a long and savage past of invasion and war.

The Ili valley opens on to what must have been one of the most important of the intermediate regions on the cardinal route of migration between Mongolia and Southern Russia, the route used in the epoch-making migrations of the nomads. The forest shelters for winter and inviting pastures for summer seem to have tempted every tribe in temporary occupation to abandon the long trek and make a bid for permanent possession. Yet it was a trap, for the very fact that it was intermediary between the two great steppe regions, that of Southern Russia and that of Mongolia, laid it open to every horde in passage; and whatever tribe had occupied it, instead of having the freedom of movement of the open steppe, and the ability of evasion (so necessary in the warfare of mounted nomads), was bottled up by the T'ien Shan at its back. Thus there is at least enough evidence to suggest that the migrations of the Tur Qara, the Yueh-chih,[1] the Huns, and the proto-Turkish tribes were halted for longer or shorter periods on the lower Ili, and from the early Middle Ages we have an increasingly coherent record of the successive rise to power, decline, and migration into new regions, of the Uighurs, Qara-Khitai, Mongols, and Qazaqs, and their different sub-tribes. It is at least fair to hazard that a thorough examination of the tumuli of the Ili, ranging as they do from graves near the highest headwaters to dead cities on the Balkhash plain, may give us a more complete and accurate review than we yet have of the long and turbulent epoch of the movement of whole peoples. It may even do something to help us identify the Scythians, that race whose culture has been traced from the Black Sea to Mongolia and North China, and whose characteristics and historical function, especially their apparently inverse migration (from west to east, that is, as against the later trend from east to west), are one of the most speculative problems of the springs of history.

The present disposition of the richly confused peoples to be found in the Ili valley derives from the measures taken by the Manchus

---

[1] If indeed these two are not alternative or successive names of the same people, who may have been connected with the " Scythians " of earlier time, and who were probably a blond Indo-Germanic race. Von Lecoq (*Auf Hellas Spuren*), bringing to bear the knowledge gained from manuscripts and even portraits recovered in Turfan, suggests the possibility of new identifications of the very highest importance in respect of the shadowy but fascinating study of the earliest tidal folk-movements.

after their war against the Zungar Empire. When Ch'ien Lung, not content to rest on the conquest of the Zungars, had wiped them out by massacre, a new population flowed in from different sources. It was then that the Qazaqs took up their pastures, coming in on a backwash from the Siberian plains. With them or after them returned different groups of Mongols; all of them related to the Zungar federation, but some of them being clans hostile to the central Zungar federation, who had been wandering on the fringes of their old lands, and others being survivors of the defeat and massacre, who, after taking refuge in Russian territory, were in good time allowed to return as a subject people to the territory they had once ruled.

It was then also that the Manchu town garrisons were planted, together with the Sibo and Solon military agricultural colonies. To recruit further the settled inhabitants, since they made so much more valid a frontier population than the evasive nomads, the great Emperor Ch'ien Lung plucked six thousand Turki families out of the oases of the Great South Road, from Aqsu to Kashgar, trundled them over the T'ien Shan, and planted them in the Ili valley. They became the Taranchis, the grain growers, a name deriving from *taran,* the word for millet. Their descendants are still the bulk of the agrarian Turki population, and they were strong enough to fight on their own during the wars of the Mohammedan Rebellion, when each racial group in that mountain-walled kingdom turned against all the others. It is said that in the different village groups can be traced the dialects of the different oases on the South Road from which the settlers were drawn. In the towns, however, it is impossible for the casual visitor to distinguish Taranchis from Turkis who have more recently immigrated; for the towns, and even to a certain extent the farming communities, are continually being re-enforced by fresh arrivals from over the mountains. It appears that Kulja grew up as the central town of the Taranchis, and the most important town of trade (a position it still holds), in contrast with the other towns, which were in the first place fortified frontier garrisons.

The Manchus were also assiduous in introducing Chinese into the Ili country, along with T'ung-kan colonies which were planted here at the same time as the colonies on the Great North Road. The distance from China, the difficulty of the journey, and the reputation for savagery and warfare of this new frontier, made a forced transportation of Chinese at first necessary. Thus throughout the Manchu rule it became a place for quartering exiles and convicts and undesirables of all kinds, both political and criminal. It appears that not a few Boxers were also transported hither after 1900, it being considered that they were stout, hardy fellows who would make good frontiersmen. Although the Chinese now emigrate to the Ili without urging, it is easy to understand the persistence among them of the old tradition of recklessness, enhanced as it is by the memory of different bloody uprisings and the feeling of being quartered in minorities among groups of subject races who are as race-conscious as they, as compact, and much more independent than anywhere else in the province. It is no wonder that the Chinese, instead of soberly laying aside their gains, in the tradition of their people, get quickly and spend quickly. They live in an atmosphere of potential hostility, which is much harder on the nerves than expressed dislike for their rule would be. If another revolt ever comes, they will do as they have always done — shut themselves up in their walled cities and await brutal destiny, whether by assault or by famine and pestilence. It is small wonder that even the assertive confidence of the Tientsin men here becomes more febrile, more like vulgar pushfulness.

There is nothing stranger than the " Tientsin " associations of the Ili Chinese. Elsewhere they are small groups of prosperous traders; here they are a whole community, ranging from barbers and food-stall keepers to wealthy traders and landholders. In fact the name Tientsin is changed for that of Yang-liu-ch'ing, a village not far from Tientsin. They say that there are — or were in the days of prosperity before the civil wars — many snug homes in Yang-liu-ch'ing supported by fathers or sons far away on the Ili. You hear the saying constantly, *"Ili hsiao Yang-liu-ch'ing,* Ili is little Yang-liu-ch'ing." It is hard to explain how so many people should have been drawn from one country town. Some say that they came as pedlars and camp followers with the armies of Tso Tsung-t'ang, when he reconquered the province at the end of the Mohammedan Rebellion; although he was a Hu-pei man, and his troops, besides the Solon bannermen, were largely drawn from the good fighting material of the provinces of Hu-pei and Hu-nan, so that after the reconquest the civil and military administration was almost entirely staffed from those two provinces. Undoubtedly many Yang-liu-ch'ing men also arrived after the hard times of the Boxer year.

Although the Yang-liu-ch'ing men carry themselves with an air in the Ili country, one must be careful in one's use of the term. Pronounced too meaningly, it implies insult and an attribution of the lowest moral depravities. Yang-liu-ch'ing, it appears, is famous in North China for supplying the *ch'un-hua,* the Spring Pictures, or immodest and salacious paintings illustrating the technique of sexual intercourse. These books of pictures are, or used to be, entirely the work of unmarried girls; a fact which is enough to point to a very old origin for these pictures, as promoting fertility. T'ang-shan, a town not very far from the Shan-hai Kuan end of the Great Wall, has a repute for similar pictures.

The map discloses the vulnerability of the Ili valley as a frontier, further illustrating its history of unrest, and explaining also why the Qazaq tribes, persistently resenting the political frontier, from time to time make efforts to migrate back and forth between Russian and Chinese territory. The valley, in fact, like the basin of Issiq Köl, which is actually in Russian possession, is no more than a bay on the northern side of the T'ien Shan. It is a sound rule that frontiers which cross valleys or follow valleys are uneasy frontiers, because valleys, while they are conduits of trade and civilization, are also the channels in which move competition and war. The soundest frontiers are those which follow mountain chains, making a natural " divide " between climates, races, and cultures. Yet if the frontier between Russia and the Central Asian dominions of China were carried along the vertebral ranges of the T'ien Shan, it would form an ominous wedge, its apex resting on the Muzart or Ice Pass, and one face almost overlooking the Road South of the Heavenly Mountains, from Aqsu to Kashgar, the other strategically overhanging the Road North of the Heavenly Mountains, from Manass to the Talki Pass.

The Russians did move in and occupy this wedge, during the troubles of the Mohammedan Rebellion. The Chinese were naturally anxious to recover the territory, for reasons both of prestige and precedent, and in order to reëstablish their control of the mountain tribes subject to them; for the Ili problem is a double-edged problem. The valley is more accessible from Russian than from Chinese territory, yet it is vital to the Chinese control of trade and of the nomads. For these reasons " Manchu Kulja," as it has been called, or Sui-ting, was much more the capital of Chinese Turkestan and Zungaria than Urumchi, from the Manchu conquest until the outbreak of the Mohammedan wars in the eighteen-sixties. The Russians did not return the Ili country to China until 1881, and then only in exchange for an indemnity and for a measure of concession by China in the strategic control of the passes leading from Andijan to Kashgar. The Russian forward move into the Ili has usually been described as an act of thinly veiled aggression. It is, however, evident from the impartial account of Schuyler,[1] the competent American who was there at the time, that they did, and with justification, take the step only for the reason that they gave themselves — the necessity of preserving order, of putting a stop to the internecine quarrels of different factions, which were overflowing into Russian territory, and of protecting Russian interests. The local authorities did not proceed without hesitation. On the other hand the Petersburg authorities, once the thing was done, and when it came to negotiating with the Chinese for a return of the territory, played up the fact that they were in strong occupation. Diplomats run true to their own form.

Nothing is more evident than that the vast tract of Asia, from Manchuria to the Pamirs, is destined to be one of the most pregnant frontiers of the future. The region that is in question comprises something like half the nominal territory of China.[2] Out of it, in the past, came conquerors who subdued China more than once. Although the Chinese, for their part, have never held it with abso-

[1] Eugene Schuyler, *Turkistan.*
[2] Including Outer Mongolia in the territory nominally ascribed to China, although it is now a Soviet Republic, affiliated with Russia.

lute control, even since the turn of history which has witnessed the decline of the nomad as a fighting force, yet China, in spite of its present weakness along its land frontiers, is now within sight of the beginning of an era of formidable expansion. The first heave of that expansion has broken down all the old social standards and political forms in China. The next surge will be outward, bearing on all her frontiers; but it will have to meet the thrust of the expanding Russian people.

The mountains and deserts of Inner Asia have now lain for several centuries like a buffer between Russia and China one of the greatest nations of the West, and the greatest nation of the East. From both sides a flow has begun into these thinly held lands. Russian and Chinese must in time come face to face. There is no meeting in history to compare with it. The only open frontier of China has yet to be determined. Frontiers that are now, in effect, nothing but vague swaths of country will then have to be narrowly delimited. Already a thrust and counter-thrust is bearing on them (as in Manchuria and Mongolia). It is a play of primal forces, far more significant than superficial considerations of politics, which are only symptomatic, and will vary and be transformed, in the confounding way that symptoms have. The cardinal route of the ancient migrations, which passed from the borders of China through Mongolia into Southern Siberia, Central Asia, and Russia, and passed the valley of the Ili, and which in so many centuries has been put to so many uses, is not yet obsolete. Nor has the geography which has governed the history of the Ili valley changed, nor is there any reason why like causes should not continue to produce like results.

I have spoken already of the way that the Ili opens into Russian territory. One thing in its geography has been noticed, I think, by no one but Stephen Graham.[1] He points out that in order to get full value for irrigation out of the lower Ili, in Russian territory, the Russians would have to construct canals taking off from points upstream well within Chinese territory. Nor is the country affected by this potential improvement of water supply any mere parish and a half; for it should be recognized that the Ili is a stream of

[1] *Through Russian Central Asia.*

enough volume to allow river steamers to ascend from Russia all the way into Chinese territory (though not as far as Kulja).

One might think that legends current about Russians in the depths of China, and about Chinese in the depths of Russia, would be a little mitigated when the peoples approached each other along an open, easily traversed frontier. Not at all. People walk warily and with suspicion in border countries. Credit is grudged to the alien for any of his good motives. The strangeness of the stranger becomes more obvious, and his motives are always suspect. Thus on the Chinese side of the border, though high officials are able to distinguish the different personal characters and official policies of Russians in a position equal to their own, the popular conception of what an " Oross " is like remains unaltered. The Oross is a savage more uncouth than the barbarians under Chinese rule. He is violent of temper and uncertain in action. Fortunately, he can always be made drunk and either hurried on to the next town, to worry somebody else, or cheated at leisure. His government is blind, but powerful; it strikes constantly in the dark, but what it hits it hurts. The Oross government is a great manufacturer of paper money, which should be dealt in with extreme caution; much of it is believed to be made for the express purpose of being unloaded on Chinese speculators, and thereafter declared valueless. This government is itself the result of obscure but prolonged and bloody wars between a Black Party and a Yellow Party — these being equivalent, in the Chinese nomenclature, to the Red Revolution and the White Guardists.

The point of view of simple Russian people is given better than I could ever give it by Stephen Graham,[1] who was on the Russian side of the Ili frontier in 1914; and Graham is one of the most notable among modern travelers, for his own unaffected, unprejudiced outlook, and his instinct for moving among and understanding the simplest, plainest people. He has a graphic little account of a " Chinese circus " performing at Kopal, a little town near the site of Friar Rubruck's Cailac, of the thirteenth century : —

" The public . . . numbered from 100 to 120 and were a mixture of Russians, Tatars and Kirghiz. All the Russian officers

[1] *Through Russian Central Asia.*

and officials of the town seemed to be there, and were accompanied by their smartly dressed wives and daughters. . . . There were colonists and their *babas* — open-faced, simple-souled peasant women who came to be petrified by the seeming devilry of the heathen Chinee. To them the fact that the Chinese are heathen — not Christian — is no joke, but a fierce reality. They look upon the Chinese as being comparatively near akin to devils.

" The juggling was a great mystification to the simple Russians, and I heard many amusing comments from those behind me and beside. The conjuring forth of the steaming samovar was especially troubling to the minds of the peasant women, and I heard one say to another: ' God knows where he got it from.' And the other replied seriously: ' What has God got to do with it? It 's the power o' Satan.' "

XXII

INTO THE HEAVENLY MOUNTAINS

WE went out of Kulja with a transport of pack ponies, in all the yelling hugger-mugger of the first day with pack animals, when they are fresh and devilish, whanging their loads against each other, pursuing each other into bazars, or choosing the most evil places for slinging off the most fragile boxes. In a couple of days they would lose this pride of the flesh, and plod at a pace unbelievably slow in four-footed animals; but on this first day they had not only to be controlled with oaths, clouting over the head and flung stones, but manœuvred across the Ili River. The river swung down at a rapid pace from the distant mountains, running with a smooth, deceptive speed between riparian flats on the far side and short, bluff cliffs of loess on the hither side. The crossing was accomplished in a flat scow, the owners of which, when they saw us, towed it upstream on the far side until they were well above us, then launched it and came swooping across to us on the thrust of the current. Our two ponies entered it without much difficulty, though not without trepidation, and stood reasonably quiet so long as I stayed at their heads, holding Iskander's muzzle and talking to them both. The pack ponies and loads were got aboard at a prodigious cost of blows and language, the scow shoved off again, and away we went to the far side, being swept a great distance downstream before we made the shore. The Padre and the owner of the stinkless leather factory, who had ridden a handful of miles to put us on our road, waved farewell. We slept that night on a raised platform in the courtyard of a Taranchi steading, and the next day began the ascent into the heart of the T'ien Shan and the high mountain country.

" I am a little bit doubtful about the horse business," Moses had once said to me, in the now far-off and shadowy days before our vagabondage; " but still, when it comes to horses, I am sure you can find me a good, reliable donkey." Now, however, with a white felt Qazaq cap cocked on his blunt head, and a wide grin on his heavy-jowled face, he bestrode a dun pack pony, straddling the huge saddlebags in which he had stowed all his belongings. He wore a shooting jacket of mine, and had hung on himself my water bottle and a spare camera. He lifted the lead-rope which was all he had to guide the pony, waved in the air a freshly cut switch, and brought it down in a most liberal manner on the haunches of his mount. The pony did not quicken its step, nor so much as lift its head. " This horse business has come out all right," Moses shouted to me. " After a camel, a horse is no peril. After all, when we travel, we travel. Let us try all things." He was game, too. Before the end of our travels, he could ride a yak with the same unconcern. " It will make a good story in Tientsin, when you get back," I said to him. " In *Tientsin!* " quoth Moses. " And who in Tientsin do you suppose would believe the half of that ? "

Our transport, which belonged to the regular caravan trade over the Heavenly Mountains between Kulja and Aqsu, was handled by two Turkis, one a slender, wiry, indefatigable man, with a humble, yearning face. He had an ingratiating way of crawling into our tent, and we would wake in the morning and look out of our sleeping bags to find him curled on the felts near us. After that we could hardly call him anything but Faithful Fido. He and the other man, with Moses, had a tent for themselves, but they could never be bothered to put it up. They would pile the loads into a wind-break and sleep round a fire in the open. Only when there was an extra nip in the air Fido would insinuate himself, without a word said, into our tent.

The other man was as deep in the chest as a bass drum, and about as broad as Fido was long. As he walked, he rolled his great body on short, thick, waddling legs, and bobbed his head about, muttering, crooning, and chuckling to himself. He was not so much half-witted as dim-witted. In Moslem countries, it is thought that such people have been touched by the hand of Allah. They are gently treated, and in Central Asia perhaps more gently than anywhere else. This toleration had allowed him to grow up a peaceful lunatic, no more inclined than a St. Bernard dog to misuse the brute power of his huge body. If you gave him a lighted cigarette, he frolicked about with it like a trained baboon. In fact, all of the more human actions, like eating and smoking, he performed like a trained animal rather than a man. His vocabulary was so limited that he could not even express in full such vague ideas as he had, but had to grimace and rumble in his chest. He was dressed in fluttering rags, had no bedding or any possessions except what he carried on him, and swung himself along bare-chested in rain and all weathers, and slept happily on the bare ground without covering. It seemed only reasonable to call him Sadie, the Girl Gorilla.

Sadie, when we first acquired him, was consumed with the ambition to own a phial of *nasr* — the snuff, or whatever you like to call it, of the Turki peoples, both nomadic and settled. This is made of pulverized tobacco, with the addition of lime and other ingredients, including sometimes, I believe, *charas* or Indian hemp. It is carried usually in a hollow gourd; a little is taken in the palm of the hand and scooped up between the tongue and the nether lip. There it is held until absorbed or gradually swallowed. We gave Sadie a glass bottle and money to buy nasr, and he was happy for days. He had hardly put nasr in the bottle when, realizing that bottles were commonly meant to hold liquids, he poured a little water in on top. This caked the nasr, so that it would not come out. Sadie was more delighted than ever. He could pretend all day long to be taking nasr, and yet never use it up.

We were not so fortunate in our two escorts. This was not the fault of the Chinese authorities, but of circumstance. Most foreigners who visit the Tekes valley and the high mountain country come there to shoot. They arrange for permits in advance, and, coming from India by way of Kashgar, Aqsu, and the Muzart, never see the lower Ili country at all. They are provided with escort-guides at the first military post they reach after coming over the Muzart. The soldiers at this post know the country thoroughly, know something about the strange ways of foreigners — and above all, there are men among them who are not opium sots. Arriving as we did at headquarters, and calling at the yamen in person, we were supplied with the men who happened to be on hand. They were both of the evil yamen-runner class, justly dreaded throughout China. One was a locally born Chinese, whose clean equipment, smart bearing, and knowledge of the Qazaq dialect immediately made a favorable impression, and must have recommended him as a good man. The other was a " tame " Qazaq, of the rascally kind that forsake their tents and hang around cities — useful as informers, or to send out with soldiers into the hills as guides, or to trace a wanted man. Not being a soldier, his only uniform was a large brass-hilted sword, too unwieldy to hang at a belt, which he tied on to his pony when riding, and carried in his arms when on foot. We were told that because very few Qazaqs are able to read documents in their own language, those among them who are dispatched on official business are given a sword like this — which ordinary men are not allowed to carry — as a mark of authority. By virtue of it they can commandeer transport, food, and guides. Our Qazaq had one eye, a wart on the side of his nose nearly as big as the nose itself, and a bibulous appearance. He was the cheery sort of villain, and would have made an excellent follower had we only been able to talk to him directly; but he spoke not a word of Chinese. We called him Bardolph.

We had a far greater variety of names for the Chinese. At first we understood that he was a Sibo, so we called him the Sibo. Then, finding that he was really a Chinese, we changed the name to Sheepo, partly because of the sheepish look he assumed as his delinquencies increased, and partly because of his appetite for mutton. He began excellently, found us our transport at a most reasonable hire, and made himself useful in every way. Once we got into the hills, however, the worthlessness of his yamen training became evident, making him an impossible fellow. He had no idea but how best to bully the Qazaqs, and that not for the furtherance of our plans, but to enrich himself, while his opium addiction made him lazy and dilatory. As we had no other interpreter, we were at a loss. However, I did pick up enough mingled Turki and Qazaq to get along splendidly with our pony men and with casual

people we met.   It was in the complicated negotiations that I was
defeated, for I had no adequate maps, and Sheepo, who disliked
the idea of uninhabited country where he could not smoke his opium
snugly in a Qazaq yurt, managed to edge us away (as I afterwards
found out) from the only practicable trail into the highest, wildest
country, the Qaraghai Tash.

In spite of him, I managed to butt my way by the most difficult
trail of all into that magnificent country, or the edge of it; but only
at the cost of getting so far away from a base and pasturage for our
pack ponies that it was impossible to hunt for more than a couple
of days.   We decided, therefore, simply to camp and wander among
the Qazaqs, learning as much as we could in that way, since after all
the object of our travels was not shooting, and we could not afford
the transport necessary to bring out trophies.   The luck was all
against shooting, anyhow, because it was June, the season when the
hunters are out after elk (the Asiatic wapiti), which are then in
the velvet.[1]   The best hunters were off in the forest, and could not
have been bribed away from their own pursuits except at a heavy
expense; and owing to their activities all the game had withdrawn
to the most inaccessible ground, and had turned exceptionally wary.
The stags were not only being shot, but trapped, netted, and, worst
of all, driven, by bands of hunters beating the forests.   The Qazaqs
are the most blundering hunters I have ever met.   A good Chinese
hunter, or best of all a Mongol, will take you to within fifty yards
of wild sheep — than which there is no more wary beast.   Many
foreign sportsmen have spoken slightingly of the Mongols as
hunters; a thing which I cannot understand, unless it is because
the foreigner is unwilling to place himself unreservedly in the
hands of his hunter, which is absolutely necessary.

The Mongol gets his training as a stalker (at least in this part
of the world) in the pursuit of marmots, for whose skins there is
a steady market.   He shoots his marmots at a distance of from
fifty to a hundred feet, with a clumsy flintlock or matchlock, at the
cost of endless patience and the most laborious stalking.   The
Qazaq, if he cannot catch marmots with traps, or poison them,

---

[1] I have given some description of the traffic in elk horns in *The Desert Road to
Turkestan.*

does not bother about them. His big game he either attempts
(and usually fails) to drive, or else he blunders along hoping to
come on something at close range, by accident. The best hunters
in the Tekes country are Mongols, but to get a Mongol hunter it is
necessary to go into Mongol territory and fetch out your hunter
yourself, under your own escort, as owing to the hostility between
Mongols and Qazaqs he cannot travel to you through country full
of Qazaq camps. As a hunter, the Qazaq is lazy, impatient, and
not content unless he is dashing about in the saddle. For this
reason he likes to take his game with hounds, eagles, and, for partridge and pheasant, hawks, riding with his friends in noisy parties.

My funniest bit of shooting luck was when we had camped one
evening and I found near at hand the marks of a wild boar rooting
about near a covert of brush and brake. The next morning, however, Sadie was before me, going out before dawn to see that the
ponies had not strayed. He came back wagging his head and chuckling. *"Tonguz* (pig)," he said, " very bad, very bad." He imitated a pig, rooting and grunting, to show what he meant. " Aha,
the old devil, I threw a stone at his damned hide, and he ran far
away."

Camping among the Qazaqs was just what suited our escorts.
At each halt they commandeered fresh ponies for themselves, and
a sheep for everybody. They were disgusted with what game I
shot — roe deer or ibex — because it weakened their demand for
mutton from the Qazaqs. Sheepo told us that we must not pay for
anything we received, as it represented part of the taxation paid
by the Qazaqs to their Chinese rulers, who oblige them to entertain and pass on all official travelers. This I could understand, as it
is a practice common among all nomadic people. As for the sheep
butchered in our name, there was no need to worry about them,
as our hosts always ate far more than we did. We found out later,
however, that the reason Sheepo was always insistent that a sheep,
or rather half-grown lamb, should be butchered every day was
that he exacted the skin as his perquisite; and that he always chose
the lambs himself, for the value, color, and condition of their skins,
out of which he would make a pretty profit when he got back to
Kulja.

The commandeering of ponies, if it had been reasonably done, would also have been in the usual way of things. Mongols, Qazaqs, and Qirghiz, when they travel, are accustomed to borrow ponies from day to day. This practice, however, is based on the understanding that the traveler will return by the way that he went. At each camp he returns the pony he borrowed there, recovers from the herd the pony on which he arrived, and so on, until at the camp which had been his first halt after leaving home he returns the first pony borrowed and gets back his own pony, on which he had started. As we were not going to return by the way we had come, the escorts had a chance for more peculation. First they would threaten to commandeer the ponies of the rich, and be bribed off. Then they would take the ponies of the poor, and commandeer also a man to bring them back; and Bardolph, when he felt really lordly, would even commandeer an extra man to carry the huge sword which was his mark of authority. Sheepo's word for commandeering was most expressive. He used the Chinese word *chua,* which means " to grab."

When these petty rascalities got excessive, and I protested, he always answered, " You do not know these people. You must be *yaman, yaman* — treat 'em rough. If you are nice with them, they think you are weak, and they get unruly." There was a familiar ring about this that recalled the formulæ of the dominant race in other parts of the world. Still, I protested whenever his exactions were too excessive. The year before, an American party coming from India to shoot had got into trouble; or rather, there had been trouble between their following and the Qazaqs. We had heard a lot about it at Sui-ting, and I could well imagine that the cause of the trouble had been the rapacity of the escorts, which had gone so far as to provoke wrathful resistance from the Qazaqs.

By the second night after crossing the Ili, we were among Qazaqs. This was sheep country. The pony herds were away on other ranges, and only the few ponies needed for riding were tethered near the yurts. The camps were up in the steeply sloping, rich hillside pastures. All of the camps were high above the streams, so that not only was the nearest water often a mile away, but the fetching of it meant a steep climb up and down. There are a num-

QAZAQ FAMILY GROUP

GROUP IN FRONT OF THE YURT OF A QAZAQ CHIEF

ber of reasons for keeping the summer camps so high above the streams. One is that a better watch can be kept over the flocks, and a better lookout against any raiding enemies. Another is the greater coolness — for in the middle of the day it can be very hot. Perhaps the most important of all is that the flocks are thus kept out of danger from the sudden spates and freshets with which drastic thunderstorms are likely to fill the valleys. In winter, when shelter is needed, the camps are moved down to the valleys; for there is then no more danger from floods, and raiders are kept away by the deep snow. And as for the hardship of fetching water in the summer, it is not after all so very great. A trip a day, for each tent, will do. Only a minimum of water for cooking is needed, for summer is the time of plenty, when people drink almost nothing but milk.

About an hour before sunset we reached the chief's camp where we were to spend the night. Women and girls were milking the sheep and goats, tethered in long lines, with their heads in loops which were secured to ropes laid along the ground and pegged down. Thus there would be a double line of sheep and goats for one tethering rope; each line facing the other, with the rope running between them, and each animal held with its head in a loop. The rams and he-goats were tethered in a group near by, while small boys, by dint of running and yelling, kept the kids and lambs milling in a small herd about two hundred yards uphill. When the milking was over, they were released, and came pelting down the slope, bleating and blathering, in search of supper. The youngsters thought that any mother would do, but the mothers were more particular, butting away chance comers until they found their own idiotic but beloved offspring.

The chief's yurt was unusually large, at least thirty feet in diameter. The lower wall was formed by a lattice or trellis of wood, rather more than three feet high. From the top of this circular wall of trellis-work sprang curving poles, like the ribs of an umbrella, to hold the domed roof; but instead of meeting at the apex of the dome, the ends of these rods were socketed into a wooden ring a yard across, to allow the entrance of light and the escape of smoke. A flap of felt could be drawn across this hole by ropes, either enough to control the draught, or entirely, in order to keep out rain. The dome itself was also covered with great pieces of felt, which had long bands attached to the corners of them, the bands being drawn tight to secure the felts, and then fastened on the inside of the roof; and as these bands may spring in graceful arcs clear across the inside of the dome, they are strikingly ornamental. They are woven from woolen yarn, in colored geometrical designs. In winter the lower walls are also covered with felt, but in warm weather they are simply screened with a reed matting, which is covered with a bold red and blue design in woolen yarn. The yarn is not woven into the matting, but each reed separately is wound in long and short sections with alternating red and blue yarn.

At the back of the yurt, in the right-hand half of it as one looked in at the door, was a huge bed, with carved and painted posts. When taken to pieces, it must have been a load for an ox or two. It was hung with gay curtains and piled with quilted blankets. A pole, from which the branches had been lopped to make rough hooks, was hung with saddles, bridles, and belts, all studded heavily with silver. Near it leaned an old Russian " Berdan " rifle. Around the walls were ranged two, sometimes three, tiers of chests, covered with enameled tin in angular designs, and on top of them was piled more bedding. At the back, opposite the door, were spread heavy, colored felts, some with appliqué designs in cloth, others with designs of different colors worked into the felt itself.

In the centre of the yurt a fire burned at night, but during the heat of the day the cooking was done outside, over a hole in the ground. A corner on the right-hand side, as one entered the low door, was screened off with reed matting, to serve as a pantry and at the same time to afford the only privacy the women ever knew.

A lamb was quickly butchered, cut up, and put in a huge iron cauldron to boil. The meat was kept boiling for several hours, until it was deliciously tender; moreover, the flavor was not cooked out of it, but it was as fragrant as any lamb or mutton could possibly be. The guests assembled in little groups, in a semicircle at the back of the tent, the group of honor in the centre. Before us were set pieces of dignity: the whole head, a piece of the fat tail, a section from the loin, and a thigh bone.   Those who are skillful with their fingers and a knife can strip from the head — though admittedly it has a somewhat ghastly appearance, the hair having been removed by scorching before it was boiled — such extremely delicate morsels as the ears, cheeks, tongue, and part of the palate.

When the meat has been finished, without any talking (for it is better manners to eat your host's food noisily, and keep silence toward your host himself), the water in which the meat was cooked is passed around in bowls.   It makes a soup even more delicately flavored than the lamb, unsalted, but seasoned with pepper.   The women serve the men, before beginning to eat themselves; but they do not necessarily have to wait until the men have finished, before beginning their own meal.   The children, in turn, come after their mothers; the women and children being grouped on the inferior side of the tent.   Thus it not uncommonly happens that a man will pass an unfinished bone to his wife.   She goes over it with skillful rapidity; when she has finished, there is nothing left except what must be worked for.   Then she passes it to a child.   The child goes over it with teeth and finger nails until there is nothing left but a vague smell of meat; sinews and gristle have all been swallowed. The unutterably naked bone is then flung out of the door to one of the waiting dogs; but not, of course, if it is a marrow bone, which must be cracked open and sucked by a man, resucked by a woman, and sucked a third time by one of the children (more for practice than with any hope of getting anything) before the dog gets it.

Before and after eating, water is poured over the hands from a rococo copper ewer; and after eating, all those who have any manners (which they all have, being most precise in matters of ceremony) belch heavily to show that they have been generously fed. Then the men stroke their beards, and spreading their hands palms upward they look up and mutter a grace to Allah, and the day's entertainment is at an end.

XXIII

QAZAQS OF THE HIGH PASTURES

THE Ili River is formed by the conjunction of its two main affluents, the Tekes, or River of Ibex, and the Qunguz. Parallel to
the Qunguz, on the north, is the Kash, and the valleys of the Kash
and Qunguz are the chief nomadic ranges of the Mongols on the
north side of the T'ien Shan, their most important tribal centre
being a great lama monastery on the Kash.

In traveling from Kulja to the high mountain country, we did
not follow up the Ili to the point where the Tekes and Qunguz
come together, but climbed up over the spur of a lesser range and
descended into the valley of the Tekes, where we found ourselves
with the minor range on our south and the great central range of
the Heavenly Mountains on the north. In going thus up from
one main valley, crossing over forested mountains, and descending
to another main valley, we saw all the different zones into which
the Qazaqs distribute themselves during the summer, and passed
also a number of Mongol camps, at a point where they had come
out of the mouths of the Kash and Qunguz valleys and crossed the
Ili. The sheep were congregated on the colder, steeper, unwooded
slopes, both because they were better able to climb for their food
than other animals, and because, on account of their wool, they
needed cool nights at least. In narrow, wooded valleys, where
the steep slopes would hold the least snow, we found the sites of
winter camps, with large corrals for herds and wooden huts or
yards in which yurts could be pitched. Lower down, in more
open country, were the herds of horned cattle and the immense
pony herds.

In this midsummer season the young men were picking and
trying their best ponies for the annual races which are an im-

memorial tradition among horse-owning nomads, originating in the idea of selecting animals of excellence to symbolize the fertility and power of increase of the herds; these chosen ponies (which originally, it seems, were mares) being either sacrificed or preserved as talismans. If they were kept instead of being slaughtered, then they were thenceforth inviolable, no man being allowed to ride them, and were distinguished by streamers plaited into mane or tail. The purest survival of the old custom is among the Mongols, for it has been much pruned down among the Mohammedan tribes. The holy or talisman ponies of the Mongols, which at the present day may be mares, geldings, or stallions, are distinguished. They are kept among the herds belonging to lama monasteries, and may not be ridden except by the very highest lamas, on journeys of ceremony. The races are rarely for less than two miles, and the ponies raced are three-year-olds, ridden by boys and girls; and in order to reduce the weight as far as possible, they are frequently ridden bareback, or with only a pad of felt girthed on.

In the most open valleys of all, especially those which could be irrigated by digging ditches or spillways from the streams, we saw even a little rough cultivation. The fields are never weeded, and after only a year or two of cultivation lie fallow for a long period. There has always been a minimum of rough agriculture among the Qazaqs and Qirghiz, but the slow increase of it in modern times is a most significant phenomenon. During all the centuries of recorded history these lands north of the T'ien Shan have been dominated by the nomadic culture; the temporary establishment of cities has been of little moment in comparison with the migrations, conquests, and tribal conflicts of the nomads. The tide of history turned long ago, but its force is only beginning to bear on these nomads, who are gradually being penned in by the settled peoples and brought under the coercion of new conditions which are compelling them to attach themselves more definitely to the land.

Owing to their lack of fixed centres, and therefore of rooted interests, all the nomadic peoples of Central Asia have never knit themselves more closely than by grouping themselves in hordes, or loose associations of tribes and sub-clans. They have never achieved cohesion when in a state of rest, but only when led to conquest by a chief of unusual ability, and this cohesion has never endured after the cessation of war. " Every tribe . . . resorted to arms only when the advancement of its prosperity impelled it to do so, or when the political circumstances of its neighbors promised rapid acquisition of great wealth by means of predatory attack. Marauding excursions in the unlimited steppe, the conflicts and insurrections of which the history of the Qazaqs consists in previous centuries, would have completely ruined any settled people. But for the nomads it was a period of prosperity : it was just under these circumstances that the wealth and the prestige of the Qazaqs increased." [1]

The growth in numbers of nomadic peoples depends on the capacity of their winter quarters, which can support far less live stock than the almost unbounded country over which they range in summer. Riding through the magnificent valleys of the Ili and Tekes in summer, past endless alps of high pasture and lordly forests, the traveler wonders at the scantiness of population. It seems incredible that such wide reaches of the noblest kind of land should be so scantly held. For a day's march one may see no camps ; and these great tracts may never be touched, the whole summer through, by the greedily eating herds. The reason is, that in winter the uplands and the wider valleys are buried in snow and swept by winds. Except for the animals that they sell yearly to the Russian markets, the nomads can keep only as many as have a chance of living through the winter, when grazing is limited. The great surplus territories could be colonized by a settled people, laying by grain for the winter ; but the pressure of population has not yet been severe enough to force the Qazaqs as a race to settle on the land. They prefer to wander, and to put up with the hard winters for the sake of roving summer freedom.

[1] *A Manual on the Turanians and Pan-Turanianism.* London, The Admiralty. All my own scattered information on the Qazaqs and Qirghiz, and most of that on the Mongols, has been checked by comparison with this useful handbook. It is a compilation from various sources, and probably by various hands, and not free from minor self-contradictions, but gives a unique, scholarly, comprehensive survey of all the " Turanian " peoples, with their history, courses of past migration, and so forth.

In the old days, when a tribe was made uncomfortable by the increase of its families, it made war on its neighbors.   The spoil of summer raids meant temporary triumphs, the capture of new wintering grounds meant solid success.   The increasingly rigid control of the Chinese and Russian governments has interfered with this cycle.   The international boundary is the main check, preventing free migration, for neither government will allow the tribes under its control to pass out of its territory, with their taxable wealth in live stock.   Within each country, there is a tendency also to forbid the tribes to fight each other for the possession of wintering grounds.   The Russians, even before the war, had begun to regulate matters by assigning fixed winter quarters to each family.   Thus in their summer quarters, where they had room to spare, the Qazaqs clung to the ancient system of tribal ownership of land, but were forced to recognize during the winter the alien principle of private ownership.   This in turn was responsible for a tendency among families to increase by purchase their private holdings of land, thus gradually breaking down the nomadic tribal system.   On the other hand, government interference of this kind, together with other Russian policies of a more drastic kind, started the Qazaqs migrating at that time across the border into China, where they were less strictly controlled.   This migration away from the Russians was even more noticeable, as will be seen, among the Qirghiz.

Not only do all the Qazaqs call themselves Qazaq, and recognize that all their different tribes are in fact one nation (an unusual thing in Central Asia), but they speak a common language, which does not vary a great deal from tribe to tribe, though it does have slight differences of dialect.   Because this language is a comparatively old and relatively pure form of Turkish, it is commonly assumed that the Qazaqs are a relatively old and pure stock of the ancient Turkish race.   This is not true.   They show a most erratic mixture of racial types, though the purity of their speech may well be an indication that on the average, throughout their history, the Turkish blood has predominated, the other stocks being absorbed one at a time.   A Qazaq may have a flat, Mongol, thinly bearded face, and yet have a full brother who is hook-nosed and hairy.

This diversity, occurring thus in families, proves that on the whole the mixture of races was accomplished a long time ago. Generally speaking, it is impossible to distinguish tribes by racial admixture. It is only possible to say that the Kirei-Qazaq of the Altai are probably the purest Turks of all, and that they have lived for a very long time in the Altai, preserving themselves from overmuch contact with the Mongols or other races.

The racial confusion of the Qazaqs, generally speaking, is due to the extraordinary openness, as well as the extent, of the steppes over which they range, freedom of movement over their major territory enabling them to roll up and absorb in their hordes fragments of peoples that had preceded them, or joined them later. They range from the T'ien Shan past Lake Balkhash right away to the Ural River, which flows into the Caspian from the north, and can be numbered, by a well-established division, in three hordes. The Great Horde, roughly speaking, ranges between the T'ien Shan and Lake Balkhash. The Middle Horde is north and west of the Great Horde, its extremes being on the upper Irtish (the Kirei are included in the Middle Horde), and in the neighborhood of Tashkent. The Little Horde are mostly between the Aral and the Caspian Sea. Some of them, who later migrated into Astrakhan, are sometimes called the Inner Horde. In this far western region, where bands of Russians formed themselves into a semblance of nomadic tribes, roving between the nomads and the settled Russians, they borrowed from the true nomads the name Qazaq, in Russian Kazak or Kaizak, which in its English form is Cossack. The Russian Cossacks are still known to the Qazaqs as Oross-Qazaq. The origin of the name has been referred both to some Turki or old-Turkish word meaning " free " and to a word meaning " rider "; but it is after all quite as probable that Qazaq was never anything but a tribal name, and that the Russians borrowed it because they thought it meant Riders or Freemen.

At the present time, because of the restrictions on their wanderings, there is a gradual tendency among the Qazaqs to settle down. There has always, as I have said, been a minimum practice of agriculture among them, owing to the necessity of a little grain for the people and hay for the cattle during the winter. The growth in recent years of prosperity and trade in the towns, the spread of settled farmers among the more accessible valleys, and the rise in price of all commodities, and especially of grain, which may be called the staple luxury of nomads, have begun to break down the true nomadic structure of Qazaq life.   There is an increasing tendency among those of the Qazaqs who cannot keep up their traditional nomadic life against this economic pressure to convert their casual summer tillage grounds into permanent holdings, to establish individual claims to such land, and to let their flocks and herds become a secondary interest.   The process is not without its dangers, for in the background is the threat of conflict between the Qazaqs, wishing to retain their old lands, and colonists of other races, wishing to thrust in among them; and conflict of such a sort may well come to play a bloody part in the future border history of this frontier of Inner Asia.

As things now go, the old tradition is strong among the Qazaqs. They set great store by the nomadic life, the true freeman's life. No man who can afford to live as a nomad will tie himself down to the indignity of a fixed holding, grubbing the earth for grain to sell.   In the old days, women and young men who were not heads of households were sent down from the summer pastures to tend the lowland fields and reap the lowland hay for winter provision.   In the new tendency, it is the young man not established and the man who fails to hold his own as a flock-master, herder, and raider who drift out of the nomadic life and settle on the land. The prizes of the lordly, nomadic life belong to the strong and successful men.   Yet, in the course of history, the sons of these weaklings, because they have secured a hold on the land, will have the reversion of wealth and power, and the sons of the proud men who now are looked up to as the leaders of their race, free from the indignity of ploughing and regular labor, will be only poor shepherds and cattle tenders, in the employ of the masters of the new economy.

In the New World, through pride of growth and success in such countries as America, Australia, and Canada, and a desire to glorify our pioneer ancestors, we have subscribed to the legend that the making of change and the growth of civilization are in the hands of the strong. A study of history in the making, in these buffer lands between Europe and Asia, points to a reverse process, the strong maintaining it as their privilege to live in the old way, the way of prestige, and forcing the weaker minority to serve as the instruments of unavoidable change. If we consider our own history justly, we must recognize that our own pioneers, in large number, were also men who, being unable to hold their own in the Old World, were forced into the New World; and that we, their sons and grandsons, are now in the ascendant because we were born at the lucky turn of the wheel when the new conditions were beginning to overweigh the old conditions.

The arts and industries of the Qazaqs, and of all other Central Asian nomads, have been more affected by changing conditions than any other aspect of their life. A generation or two ago, the tribe was a self-contained unit. They made everything they needed; felts, carpets, and rough fabrics, and the dyes for coloring them. The knowledge of working metals was very old among them. They not only had their own smiths, but workers in silver who made jewels for women and ornaments for saddlery. These men could not only execute very fine work, but preserved forms and designs of ancient origin. These tribal craftsmen can no longer survive in the proximity of such trading centres as Kulja. The old heavy silverwork is being replaced by brummagem stuff from the bazars, and the old saddles of wrought leather and hammered and inlaid metal by shop ware imported from Russia. They still make their own felts, though most of their carpets are bought; but even the dyeing of their wool is now done for them. Parties of Turki and Taranchi dyers from the towns go out among the Qazaqs with packets of German and American aniline dyes, dye their wool for them in horrible colors, and return with payment in the form of wool or live stock.

XXIV

MARE'S MILK

AFTER a week of wandering we came to the Tekes River. The fording of it was a matter for serious debate; that is to say, a matter for much shouting and yelling, for it was yet early in June, when all the rivers are charged to their fullest with the melting of glaciers and high snows. The river swept across our road in a flood about two hundred yards wide, so vehement that many large, rounded, water-smoothed boulders rolled crunching and grinding forward under its impetus. We had had a little rain for several days, but rainy weather, in these mountains, means less rather than more water in the streams, for the volume of water added by a day of steady rain is far less than that which rushes down after an unclouded day of hot sun on the upper snows.

There was, we understood, a bridge over the Tekes at a point higher up, on the trail usually followed by the Muzart trading caravans; but it had suffered the usual summer collapse, being carried clean away by the flood water. We had been brought to a point where a slight double curve in the river offered a chance of using the thrust of the water itself to carry us across. Luckily, we caught some Qazaqs who had just forded, and impressed them into our service. We were ahead of the baggage animals, and made the fording without waiting for them. Taking off from a point past which the water ran deep and strong, we went down with the current until we struck shoals in midstream, across which we tacked with the water no higher than the saddle-girths. Each of us had a Qazaq rider on either hand, while a fifth man rode in the lead. This was the first time that we had ridden our own ponies in such a test. Mæander, stronger but less agile than Iskander, lurched badly once and might have been carried away, but the riders

on each side half lifted my wife out of the saddle, and heaved at the
pony until he recovered. Iskander quivered at the first shock of
the water; he was intelligent enough to know the danger, and
courageous enough to face it, as a noble horse should be. His
nostrils expanded in alarm, but he gathered his legs well under
him, and picked his way cannily, never taking a step until he was
sure of his stance; with neck arched and ears alert, he yet suffered
the Qazaq ponies to crowd him on either side, without savaging
them, showing that he understood the seriousness of the enterprise.

From the shoals we crossed another channel, diagonally, with
the water over our saddle flaps, to shoal water again. The last
tack was to take us to a point of land that jutted downstream. Here
was the deepest, most rapid water, with no white riffle on the surface. After a few strides the ponies were swept off their feet
and carried rapidly down-river. I looked at my wife, and saw her
laughing; I felt under me the gallant effort of Iskander, swimming
freely, and my heart rose to it. The savage yelling of the Qazaqs
rose to a frantic pitch; but it was not frantic, for they too were
laughing boldly, and they too were exulting in the struggle and the
sense of contest, in the courage of their ponies and their own skill.
I had a better liking for Qazaqs, after that. They are lazy, they
are thieves and rascals, they are not as comradely as the Mongols,
but they can rise to an adventure.

All the while that they shouted as if out of their minds, they
worked knowingly to get the ponies across the channel of swift
water in time to strike the spit of land, beyond which the steeply
rising banks offered no landing for some distance. It seemed that
in spite of all we were being carried past the point, but when we
had been swept a few yards below it the ponies found their feet
on an underwater shoal running out from it, swung round with
their heads upstream like boats checked by a snub-rope, and heaved,
straining, out of the water, the Qazaqs grinning and chattering in
triumph.

We had a long wait while the baggage was being split into half-
loads and packed high on Qazaq saddle ponies, taller than our
little pack animals. Some of the Qazaq ponies made the fording

five or six times that morning, and we saw only one mistake, when a pony ridden by a Qazaq failed to make the spit of land, and was carried away down the channel. In a moment, the rider was out of the saddle; he twisted a hand in the pony's mane and swam beside him, edging him to shoal water out in the stream. When they found footing again, the man rose mysteriously from the water, laughing, swung into the saddle, waved to us, and worked upstream along the shoals until he could once more drift down and across the deep channel. Our loads were got across without wetting more than one or two of them, and the pack ponies, tied head to tail, were swum across in bunches. Last of all came Moses and the Chinese soldier, each of them riding pillion behind a Qazaq and supported by Qazaqs on each side. Moses was grinning stolidly, but the soldier was frightened to the verge of hysteria, and looked sick at the stomach. " I thought," said Moses, stamping on the comfortable, safe, dry land, " that I was going to be frightened, that time." As for the soldier, his teeth were chattering, and for the rest of the day he did not recover his cocksure swagger.

While we were waiting, a raft of logs, worked only by two Turkis, with a bow and a stern sweep, came careering down the main channel. A little below us it grounded on a boulder and swung across the stream, but the two Turkis went into the race without hesitation and after a little heaving and tugging got the raft headed downstream again. Then, climbing aboard to the sweeps once more, and shouting, they were swept rapidly out of sight.

That night we slept within sight of the forests of the main T'ien Shan, and the next morning made for the Kök-su, at whose headwaters are the finest of the shooting grounds. We rode most of the day over high downs, past many camps, and past warrens where marmots at the mouths of their burrows whistled at us before diving out of sight. Herds of ponies now and again stamped across our way, and riders would appear at a gallop, inviting us to their camps. Then we entered the gorge of the Kök-su over the shoulder of a high, smooth down, on the crest of which was a small camp. The far side of the gorge was a wilderness of riven rock; at the point where the Kök-su emerged into open country, the colors of these rocks were vague blotches of reds and greens and purples, the whole confused and made more magnificent by the dark-bellied shadows of roving clouds.

We traveled up the Kök-su a little way by narrow flat meadows, some of them irrigated, of wild hay, which the Qazaqs harvest for the winter. Then, at a point where the stream is enclosed by sheer rock walls, we took to the hills again, until we could return to the gorge by a scrambling slide down a watercourse, where the ponies descended by leaps and slides as if they had been monstrous goats; we, on foot below and ahead of them, dodging as nimbly as we might. We finished that hard day's march by camping at a lush meadow, under the shadow of willow scrub, by the edge of the swift gray water.

The next day we found a Qazaq camp a mile above us, and with an old hunter who lived there I went out the day after that to look over the country. The old man was the only good Qazaq hunter that I struck, but though he understood stalking he was too old to keep up the pace. To shoot in this country one must climb, and the climbing begins within a few yards of camp. The hills rise very steeply, and while the dells on the versants away from the backbone of the central range are hung with spruce forests, the slopes pitched toward the eternal snows are covered with loose rocks and scant grass.. Climbing several thousand feet, so steeply that I should never have dared the ascent alone, we got clear above the line of tree growth; but even so, we found the tracks of wapiti or elk, driven up out of their natural forests by the hunters, who were after them not only with rifles and dead-fall traps, but even with nets. We had here an outlook into heart-stirring country, incomparably savage and inaccessible mountains, peak after peak, with uplifted, guarded valleys that will long resist the advance of lumbermen and settlers. I parted from my hunter on the way back, missing his proposed rendezvous through insufficient understanding of his dialect, and got home only after a long and difficult round, in which I forded a side-stream of the Kök-su and was nearly swept away by the force of the water, which, though it was only knee-deep, surged up to my waist the moment I had waded into it. The hunter was distressed when he reached his camp by a short cut known to him and found I had not returned, and men rode down to our camp, giving an alarm that needlessly worried my wife, leading her to think that I had fallen over a cliff or committed some other imprudence.

It was now evident that Sheepo, our poltroonish guide and escort, had deliberately led us into the Kök-su gorge to hamper our further progress, because he had no liking for really wild country, apart from large Qazaq camps and profitable requisitions. The head-waters of the Kök-su cannot be reached, at least not with any sort of transport, by following up the Kök-su gorge; the only way is to strike sidelong into the hills from the mouth of the gorge, but this, with no maps and an obstructive guide, we had no way of knowing at the time. However, we pushed on one more march, to the horror of Sheepo, who turned green at the sight of the trail and refused to accompany us, remaining behind at the last Qazaq camp to smoke opium. There we also left Moses and most of our stuff, the two Turki pony men and some Qazaqs going with us, but leaving us in camp with only one man, and returning to the base until we should send word to be fetched out.

The trail is carried the first part of the way along a steep scarp of rock, partly on banked scree and partly on a three-foot ledge on the face of a cliff. At one place a side-gully had to be crossed by a precarious bridge, made of two logs with brushwood and earth thrown on them, and at this and several other places the light loads had to be taken off and the ponies gingerly led round corners, while the loads were manhandled. At last a steep ascent and a steeper drop over a mountain shoulder brought us to a pocket in the gorge. On the far side, cliffs towered unbroken for hundreds of feet, while on our side was a small bay, the foot of it all birch and jungle, in which a series of hot sulphuric streams issued from the rock. These were called Arsan Bulaq, a name common to such springs, which means, I suspect, "male springs" — Turki ar, husband, arkak, male. They are visited not only by sick Qazaqs and Mongols, but even by Chinese coming all the way from the towns of the Ili, as is proved by small shrines, fluttering rags, obos, and inscriptions in several languages, carved or painted on rocks or cut into birch trees.

Here my wife "kept camp," cooking for both of us, with one of our Turki pony men to look after her, while I went on still

further with one incompetent Qazaq hunter. Climbing above the
gorge, over still more shoulders of mountains, we looked from afar
into the true Qaraghai Tash, the Stone Spruces, at the headwaters
of the Kök-su, where the pinnacled rocks are compared to trees.
There, at the sources of the Kök-su, although the land is on the Ili
Watershed of the T'ien Shan, the country is claimed by Mongols;
whether by Mongols coming over from Qara Shahr, or by the scattered Mongols of the Qunguz, I am not sure. At any rate, it is
no use hunting there unless with a Mongol guide. The country
over which I was ranging was even more remote and inaccessible,
and with a good hunter I might have had fine sport; but the man
with me was not only incompetent, but would not sleep out at night
so as to be above the game and in a position of vantage at dawn.
Still, it was fine wandering, with no humanity within many miles
of us. We could pass from alps to bold bare down, climb above
forests, cut through copses, and come to the verge of cliffs, to look
out over deep voids. On far slopes we saw many ibex, but all of
them does. We ended up with a long traverse of a spruce forest,
taking a trail trodden only by game. In the heart of it, on an up-
lift of rock, we found the stronghold and watching place of some
old elk, whose tracks were all about it and who had there scratched
off much of his hair; for lying there in the afternoon sun he could
look over the whole great valley, screened himself by fringing trees.
It was in this forest that the hunter nudged me, while we were at a
halt, he looking in one direction and I in the other. I turned, and
there, within thirty yards, and advancing toward us quite unconsciously in the obscurity of the towering spruces, was a monstrous
boar; the size of a rhinoceros, he looked. Up went my rifle, pirouet-
ting dizzily in my uncontrollable but altogether unnecessary agi-
tation, and I missed clean at little more than twenty yards; at least
the Qazaq swore that I missed, because we could not find blood,
though I think myself that the vast pig carried off the bullet in his
thick hide. At any rate, he vanished with amazing speed, and
yet without a sound of broken twigs or stone displaced, and as he
got on to a well-trodden game trail, we could not distinguish his
spoor. It was the most ridiculous miss I have ever made, and I
am glad of it, for had I foolishly slain him we could not have

carried anything home; the Qazaq would not have touched the unholy animal.

We returned from Arsan Bulaq to the middle Kök-su, and after lingering there in camp for a few days went back to the Tekes valley and turned toward the Muzart Pass. It was during this period that Iskander gave us trouble, for the mountain breezes brought to him the scent of pony herds and mares innumerable. It was not that he turned wild or savage; but, poor fellow, he was a stallion and he could not help fretting. He yearned so ardently for the mares of the Tekes that he went off his feed a little, and lost a certain amount of condition. We shackled him at night, when he was turned out to graze, with specially made iron fetters like handcuffs, muffled with felt to keep them from chafing him; but even so, unable to move except with both forefeet together, he strayed once or twice incredible distances, even hobbling down precarious rocky trails and up the almost perpendicular watercourse by which we had entered the Kök-su gorge. If we tethered him to a stake, he pulled it up, and if we tethered him to a tree, no matter by how long a rope, he entangled himself so badly before morning that there was danger of his injuring himself.

Once we had left the Kök-su, we traveled by easy stages along the edge of the forest line, in the valley of the Tekes, but out of sight of the stream. From the forested slopes of the main range of the T'ien Shan, which we were skirting, streams issued at intervals. Like the Kök-su, almost all of them were closed by almost impassable gorges at the point where they ended their upper courses, but then, clearing the forests and the steepest fall of the mountains, flowed easily the rest of the way to join the Tekes, through open downland and broad, rich pastures. Our camps were almost always at the edge of such a stream, and one of them was just below the strangest waterfall I have ever seen. Leaving its upper gorge, the little stream struck a fault-line, where the slope was broken by an abrupt undercut ledge of rock, fifty or sixty feet in height. Instead of running over the ledge, the stream had pierced it, dropping in a straight, unbroken fall from what was like the peak of a half-enclosed vault. The roar of its plunge was so contained by the enclosing rocks that one could not hear it, except directly from the

front, looking over a boulder into the shattered spray.   Undoubtedly, this was spirit-water; in recognition of which, two or three
trees at the foot of the fall were hung with rags, for the Qazaqs retain strong traces of the old animistic beliefs that still flourish in the
practices of *kam* — the shamans or witch-doctors of remote races
like the Urianghai — and linger under the lama-Buddhism or Mohammedanism of all the nomadic and most of the settled races of
Inner Asia.

To the chagrin of Sheepo, we managed to camp several times
privately; that is to say, well away from Qazaqs, so that he had to
ride a couple of miles or more to find a yurt in which to smoke his
opium out of a draught.   Knowing that his instructions were never
to leave us, he urged us always to camp near the Qazaqs, because
of the nomad rule of hospitality, which makes it imperative to
respect the animals and property of the stranger who enters one's
camp — whereas the stranger camping at a distance is fair game,
and may be robbed by anyone who has the skill or daring.   I knew
this well enough, it having been drummed into me by the caravan
men of Mongolia; but still, we could hardly run much risk in this
territory, where our official standing was well enough known, and
the rumor of our approach had gone far and fast in advance of us.

To Sheepo's joy, however, and mine, and Sadie's, and Fido's, and
Moses', — my wife being the only one of the company who did
not especially take to it, — we had all the *kumiz* we could hold, for
we were traveling along the best milk-route in the world.   This
was the line of the summer pony-pastures, where at every group
of yurts a herd of mares was tethered, their foals near them, ready
to furnish kumiz for endless conviviality.   The Qazaqs, like the
Mongols, mix together the milk of sheep, goats, cows, and camels;
in fact, the milk of all their animals, except the mares, which is kept
for the noble drink of kumiz.   The Chinese, in their own country,
are shy of milk and all its products, for they consider it a kind of
urine.   In these countries, however, where they mix with milk-
drinking peoples, they often lose the prejudice.   Moses, ever since
we had turned toward the Ili, had been all agog to taste the celebrated " horse-milk wine," or kumiz.   We saw it made most often
in the whole skin of a colt, sewn up to make a bag, the neck of the

colt being the neck of the bag. It struck us also that mare's milk was thin and rather sour from the moment it was drawn; but perhaps we were wrong, for William of Rubruck says otherwise. I will take in full his description of the making of kumiz, partly because it shows how unchanging have been the habits of the nomads from the thirteenth century (and before), and partly in tribute to him as one of the most patient and observant of travelers.

"This *cosmos,* which is mare's milk, is made in this wise. They stretch a long rope on the ground fixed to two stakes stuck in the ground, and to this rope they tie toward the third hour the colts of the mares they want to milk. Then the mothers stand near their foal, and allow themselves to be quietly milked; and if one be too wild, then a man takes the colt and brings it to her, allowing it to suck a little; then he takes it away and the milker takes its place. When they have got together a great quantity of milk, which is as sweet as a cow's as long as it is fresh, they pour it into a big skin or bottle, and they set to churning it with a stick prepared for that purpose, and which is as big as a man's head at its lower extremity and hollowed out; and when they have beaten it sharply it begins to boil up like new wine and to sour or ferment, and they continue to churn it until they have extracted the butter. Then they taste it, and when it is mildly pungent, they drink it. It is pungent on the tongue like rapé wine when drunk, and when a man has finished drinking, it leaves a taste of milk of almonds on the tongue, and it makes the inner man most joyful and also intoxicates weak heads and greatly provokes urine. . . . It is for the following reason that mare's milk curdles not. It is a fact that [the milk] of no animal will curdle in the stomach of whose fetus is not found curdled milk. In the stomach of mares' colts it is not found, so the milk of mares curdles not. They churn then the milk until all the thicker parts go straight to the bottom, like the dregs of wine, and the pure part remains on top, and it is like whey or white must. The dregs are very white, and they are given to the slaves, and they provoke much to sleep. Nowadays they are used for tanning skins. This clear [liquor] the lords drink, and it is assuredly a most agreeable drink, and most efficacious."[1]

[1] W. W. Rockhill, *William of Rubruck,* Hakluyt Society.

A much more powerful drink, called *arraq,* is prepared from kumiz by distillation.   The kumiz itself is celebrated widely as the most healthful of all sour-milk concoctions; in Russian Turkestan they have regular health resorts to which people come to drink mare's milk.   I have heard Russians compare the taste of it to champagne.   The nomads also carry it on their saddles (where the jolting churns it), either in beautifully made bottles of stamped leather, or simply in a skin bag.   The route we were taking and the time of our approach being widely known, we received very often during the day's ride a most pleasant attention.   A man would appear at a gallop from a distant camp, carrying a bowl and a skinful of kumiz on the saddle before him.   We would dismount, and all squat round on the fragrant grass.   The man would tuck the skin under his arm, untie the mouth, and by a squeeze of his elbow project a stream of kumiz into the bowl, and we would all drink in turn.   There is no land like the high Tekes for lordly travel.

XXV

QAZAQ AND QIRGHIZ

We had been traveling almost all of the time among Qazaqs, except for the few Mongol encampments we had passed when on our way from Kulja to the Tekes. Most of the Qazaqs we met appeared to be Kizei, — who are, I think, a distinct tribe, — or else Alban, who are a clan or sub-tribe, rather than a tribe. It is extremely difficult to distinguish all the sub-tribes of the Qazaqs, not only on account of the number of their names, but because many of them appear to be known by several different names, often calling themselves by one while their neighbors call them by another. The easiest way of distinguishing the major tribal differences is by the headdresses of the married women, which vary not only in shape, but in the design and amount of the cross-stitch embroidery on them. Their names, however, are important, for by these it would be possible to study their migrations and to a certain extent their origins. Thus the Alban Qazaqs came from Russian territory, where at one time they were neighbors of the Issiq Köl Qirghiz, while the Kizei have been a much longer time up in the high valleys of the T'ien Shan, where, being much more remote and isolated from other Qazaqs, they have taken on a Mongol admixture, both of blood and manners. The Alban Qazaqs, I was told, fly a white flag only at the tent of a dead chief, while the Kizei Qazaqs fly a flag at any tent where a man has died.

At a place called Kök-terek, the Blue Poplars,[1] we came among true Qirghiz for the first time. This fine tribe is much less numerous in Chinese territory than the Qazaqs, but a few divisions

[1]*Kök*, "blue," appears to be an exact equivalent of the cognate Mongol *kuku*, and of the Chinese *ch'ing*, "the color of nature." It is used in place names not only where we should use "blue," but often where we should use "green," or "clear" or "bright."

of them are quartered high up in the Tekes valley, besides those on the south of the T'ien Shan and in the Pamirs. I say " true " Qirghiz advisedly, for these are the people most commonly called the Qara-Qirghiz. This miscalling of them is chiefly due to Russian influence. The Russians, having borrowed for a division of their own people the name Qazaq, usually call the true Qazaqs the Qirghiz-Qazaq, to avoid confusion with the Cossacks. This in turn obliges them to call the Qirghiz the Qara-Qirghiz, to avoid confusing them with the Qazaqs. In later times, a good deal of pains has been taken, rather unnecessarily, to explain why they should be called " Black " Qirghiz, and one reason sometimes urged is that they became Mohammedans a good deal later than the Qazaqs, and that the " black " is equivalent to " heathen." As a matter of fact the Qazaqs, except when speaking to Russians or other foreigners, never call the Qirghiz Qara-Qirghiz. The Qazaqs call themselves Qazaqs, and are called Qazaqs by the Qirghiz, and the Qirghiz call themselves Qirghiz and are called Qirghiz by the Qazaqs. Moreover, the Qirghiz look down on the Qazaqs as an inferior people, and resent being confused with them.

It has been claimed on behalf of many tribes that they " are the nearest to the original Turks." Probably the Qirghiz deserve this distinction more than any, unless it be those aristocrats of the Qazaqs, the Kirei of the Altai. Both Kirei and Qirghiz have been in their present mountains for a very long time, being not only mentioned by old Chinese chronicles, but mentioned without any account of their having arrived from any other place. Both speak very pure, archaic dialects of Turkish. Both of them, by reason of their hold on high, inaccessible mountain retreats, were probably able to survive with comparative immunity the turbulent centuries of the Great Migrations, when all the nomadic hordes of Asia were sweeping by from south of the Altai to north of the T'ien Shan, and on into the Russian steppes. The migrating hordes followed the easiest line of travel, high enough up the flanks of the mountains to obtain water and pasturage, but as low as possible in order to avoid difficult going; thus allowing such tribes as could withdraw into the upper gorges to escape without being either slaughtered or amalgamated.

The Qazaqs, in spite of the immense range of their territory, and of wars and raids against each other, have always preserved their consciousness of being a single people, because of the ease of communication across the plains which they for the most part inhabit. The Qirghiz also have a consciousness of belonging to a homogeneous racial unit, but owing to their difficult mountain country, into which they have for some centuries withdrawn, they have not the same ease of intercommunication. They have two main divisions, the *Sal* or " Left " Wing, in the West, chiefly on the Russian and Chinese Pamirs, and the *Ung* or " Right " Wing, in the East; that is, about Issiq Köl and on both sides of the Heavenly Mountains.

They have several legends of their own origins, of which some apply to individual tribes.[1] The central legend, applying to the whole people, recounts their descent from forty maidens — *qirq qiz,* forty daughters, forty maidens. In one version, the forty maidens became with child by the foam of Issiq Köl, the Warm Lake. In another version, they became with child by a red dog. The legend of descent from an animal is not, of course, anything unusual in Central Asia; but there is a strange echoing resemblance between this legend and one which I heard from a caravan man in Mongolia. A Chinese emperor in ancient times, he said, had a daughter who was very sick. As I remember, her trouble was boils. All remedies having failed, the Emperor proclaimed that whoever could cure the princess should have her to wife. The only response came from a large dog, which entered the palace, licked the boils, and cured the princess. This gave rise to a certain natural dismay among the court people. The Emperor, however, with a delicate sense of his high responsibilities rare in any monarch of any age, declared that the Imperial word could in no circumstances be retracted, and accordingly gave the princess in marriage to the dog. From this union, according to my informant, sprang the " race " of Mohammedans.

This legend, in turn, has an even closer resemblance to an ancient Chinese tradition concerning the origin of the P'an-hu, a barbarian tribe of what is now Hu-nan province, cited by Chi Li in his *Forma-*

[1] Schuyler, *Turkistan.*

tion of the Chinese People.[1] In this case the legends correspond so closely in actual structure that there is not even any question of common origin; I am quite satisfied that the legend I heard is a " late " or transferred version of the ancient legend. The interesting thing is the speculation that the Qirghiz legend may have been carried back toward China along the caravan routes until it reached people who knew the old Chinese legend concerning totally different barbarians in a totally different direction; whereupon these people, relying on the dog as a link, switched over their own legend to account, not for the Qirghiz alone, but for the whole conglomeration of Central Asian Mohammedans.

The Chinese do not generally differentiate between the Qazaqs and the Qirghiz of the T'ien Shan. When they do, they call the Qazaqs Ha-sa or Ha-sa-k'e (both purely phonetic renderings) and the Qirghiz Hei-hei-tze or Hei-chia, while a closer phonetic rendering, Chi-li-chi-ssu (Ki-li-ki-se), seems to have been used in the past, and may still be used, in written documents. The reduplicated form Hei-hei-tze means simply The Blacks (that is, if the characters are read for their meaning, apart from their phonetic value), while the abbreviated form Hei-chia means Black Family, or Black Tribe. In both names the association with the Turki *Qara* may be traced. It has been from of old a practice among the Chinese to give to barbarian tribes a name which, if read according to the sound of the characters, had a rough approximation to the native sound, while if read according to the meaning it had a pejorative sense. In the eighth century we even hear of an Uighur ruler who, at a period when his people were increasing in power at the expense of the Chinese, sent a request to China that the characters until then used to represent " Uighur " be changed for other characters of a similar sound but having a more flattering meaning.[2]

It has also been stated that the Chinese follow the Mongols in calling the Qirghiz *Burut;* but this is not true, at least not in com-

---

[1] Harvard University Press, 1928. The same legend is discussed by Dr. B. Laufer, " Totemic Traces Among the Chinese," *Journal of American Folk-Lore*, Vol. XXX, 1917.

[2] E. H. Parker, *A Thousand Years of the Tartars*. Parker is working from Chinese sources, but in his toplofty way does not give references to the particular chronicles.

mon practice. This name is etymologically the same as Buriat or Bur-yat, the name of an out-and-out Mongol tribe in Russian territory, about Lake Baikal, who are not in the least the same people as the Qirghiz. The syllable *ut* indicates the Mongol plural, while the syllable *bur,* as I believe, may be related to the modern Turki *buri,* a wolf. There is nothing impossible in this, as Turki and Mongol are languages of the same stock, and Mongol and Old Turkish, I understand, have something like half of their roots in common; and as for the wolf, there is an old Mongol legend of descent from a blue wolf.

I asked the very intelligent Qirghiz guide who was with us later what his people called themselves, and after a good deal of hesitation he said, " Böliq." He also told me that the Qirghiz tribe on the south side of the T'ien Shan, above Uch Turfan, were the Chirik. This I have been able to confirm, but I have never confirmed the " Böliq." I can only think that it must have stood for " Bo(r)liq " (the *r* could be thus dropped in spoken Turki). In this case the first syllable would stand for the same root as the first syllable in " Buriat," while the second syllable would be adjectival, as in *taghliq,* " a man from the mountains." In other words, the name would be simply a variant of " Burut "; just as if one were to say " the Bör (or Bur) people," instead of " the Burs." I think the hesitation of my informant was due to his pausing to find an answer that he thought would suit me; just the would-be pleasing answer that one gets so often in this part of the world. He spoke Mongol well himself, and knew that I knew a few words of Mongol; therefore he gave me a form of one of the names of his people that he thought might be familiar to me — and I, unluckily, did not recur to the matter again when we knew each other better.

Most of those Qirghiz who are in Chinese territory on the north side of the Heavenly Mountains came originally from the region of Issiq Köl, in Russian territory, and their migration and the fortunes of their fellows left behind in Russian territory are bound up with an obscure record of dark, bloody, tragic history. This Qirghiz guide of ours had come over with his portion of the tribe as a boy, " about the time of the Chinese Revolution " — say in

1912. Russians at that time were crowding fast into the province of Semirechensk, and were settling near Issiq Köl. As they were peasant settlers almost to a man (except for the Cossack villages), they picked out the best arable lands and especially those most easily irrigated. Now the Qirghiz had long been used to do a little farming, to provide themselves with winter supplies, and in their farming, as Radlov [1] testified so long ago as the eighteen-sixties, they showed no little skill. The Russians began to push them out of this arable country, and, once they were deprived of it, the summer pastures that had before been ample could no longer support the whole population. They began, accordingly, to drift into Chinese territory, and the Russians, at that time, were glad to have them go. Graham,[2] a couple of years later, in 1914, has testified to the attitude of the Russians. He has described the long slow caravans of settlers moving out into the prairies, and he has described the impatience with which they regarded the nomads. The heathen wanderers, they thought, were a nuisance. It was hard to collect taxes from them, and they did not supply satisfactory labor; for a few weeks they would be about you in swarms, then it was down tents, up loads, and off into the mountains. Let them either clear out and make way for steady-going Christian folk, or else settle down and become steady-going Christian folk themselves — for this must be said to the high credit of the Russian: he has shown less race animosity in Central Asia than any other white race would ever have shown. He might have no use for "the native," but a "native" who chose to learn Russian, wear Russian clothes, and live like a Russian was always every bit as good as a Russian to him.

The Qirghiz do not appear to have shown any hostility to the Russians at that time, for they knew too well the power of Russia. With the outbreak of the war in Europe, however, the Russian settlements, especially the Cossack *stanitzas,* were largely drained of their able-bodied men. The Qirghiz may have been docile, but could have felt nothing but resentment for the way in which their lands had been taken from them. Then, in 1916, came a German,

---

[1] *Aus Sibirien.* Leipzig, Weigel, 1884.
[2] *Through Russian Central Asia.* London, Cassell, 1916.

Dr. Werner von Hentig.[1] He had been with a German mission to Persia and Afghanistan, to raise a diversion in the rear of the British in India. The British influence at Kabul proving too strong for him, he was forced to escape into Chinese territory (which was as yet neutral), reaching Yarkand. Either then or before leaving Afghanistan, he seems to have got emissaries to work in the Ili country, among the dispossessed Qirghiz, spreading a rumor of the collapse of Russia. Believing that the Russians would never return, the Qirghiz went back to recover their lands. The rising spread rapidly throughout the Qirghiz districts in Russian territory, and Russian resistance led not only to real fighting and the slaughter of noncombatants, but to the capture of Russian women and children by the insurgents.

It was a black day for the Qirghiz when they rebelled. Russian forces were dispatched against them, and they were defeated with at least ten times the slaughter that they had previously inflicted, and lost an enormous quantity of cattle, sheep, and horses, besides having nearly six thousand acres of land confiscated to the Russian crown; though what may since have become of this land, it would be hard to say. The remnants were thrown back into Chinese territory, but Russian pressure was powerful enough to make the Chinese act decisively, refusing entry to some and disarming all the others. Those who did find asylum were heavily mulcted by the Qazaqs, who took from them not only large numbers of cattle in blackmail, but " whitemail " also of all the silver they had, besides a great quantity of tent-plenishings, metal-worked chests, and silver-studded saddles, bridles, and girths. The Qir-

---

[1] W. O. von Hentig, *Ins Verschlossene Land*, Potsdam, 1928. See also *A Manual of Turanians and Pan-Turanianism*, and a few remarks by Sir George Macartney (who at the time was British Consul-General in Kashgar) in a book review in the *Journal* of the Central Asian Society, Part I of 1929. There is a mention of von Hentig in *Secret Patrol in High Asia*, by Major (then Captain) L. V. S. Blacker, a British officer who was himself engaged on " special missions " at that time. Von Hentig has been heavily censured by British critics, because he got away, leaving the Qirghiz to pay the piper; hardly fair criticism considering that British officers were up to the same sort of tricks not so very far away; especially later on, when there was a question of keeping supplies of cotton in Russian Turkestan away from Germany; and still later, when British policy in Central Asia was pitted against the Bolsheviks. It should be added that von Hentig, in his own account of his remarkable adventures, barely mentions the Qirghiz rising, leaving it to be inferred that he had nothing to do with it.

ghiz were hipped, for the winter was on them, and they must pay for cattle room and quarters, or die; and many of them died. Qirghiz heirlooms and their choicest possessions may be seen to-day scattered among the yurts of the Qazaqs, who are accustomed to say, noncommittally, that " they came from Andijan."

Of the Qirghiz, all who could settled down in Chinese territory; but a revision of Russian policy after the success of the Revolution dragged most of them back over the Russian border. The Russians, by then, were in pressing need of food supplies and raw materials; the Qirghiz they had once thought good riddance were now a people to be desired within their borders, in what have now become the Soviet Republics of Qazaqistan and Qirghizistan. Accordingly, by the regional Trade Agreement between the Russian authorities and the Governor of Hsin-chiang (Chinese Turkestan and Zungaria) made in 1925, and independent of but locally supplementary to the renewal of diplomatic relations between Russia and China at large, a stipulation was made that those tribes or portions of tribes, both Qirghiz and Qazaq (for some of the Qazaqs also had been involved), which had migrated into Chinese territory at the time of the troubles should be returned to Russia. They went, unwillingly, herded by the Chinese, and losing portions of their live stock as they went to rapacious soldiers and rival tribes.

The latest turn of events, however, appears to have completed the cycle. The measure of autonomy granted to the native republics under Russian " advisory " government appears like comparative freedom; especially the privileges of carrying arms and policing themselves, which are ingenuously interpreted as license to revive the old-fashioned neighborly diversions of sheep-lifting and horse-reiving — so long as it is not too noisily done. The news having spread across the border in more ways than one, and the advantages of Russian allegiance being vehemently borne in upon the tribes on the hither side of the border, who chafed under the Chinese restrictions on the bearing of arms, there revived among them the ancient nomadic instinct to migrate. Nomadic tribes do not spontaneously respect international boundaries. Thus the Alban Qazaqs and those of the Issiq Köl Qirghiz, who, having removed to Chinese territory at the time of the Chinese Revolution, were not brought within the scope of the 1925 agreement which had taken their kindred back to the Russian side, determined to follow of their own accord.

The Chinese did not intend to countenance any such free roving about. To them, the nomad tribes not only meant annual taxes and tribute, but their presence, helping to fill up the strategically insecure Chinese territory in this bay of the T'ien Shan, was to a certain extent a check on the potential Russian urge to flow into an empty land. They therefore forbade the migration, and barred the passes. At the Chinese post near the head of the Tekes, guarding the most open of the passes, a long skirmishing battle was fought between the troops and the nomads. In this fight my Qirghiz informant, a conscript in the Chinese forces, was compelled to fire on his own people. At the end of the engagement the nomads, whose light-horse tactics and hampering live stock did not fit them for the forcing of passes, were obliged to desist and to return to their appointed grounds.

XXVI

THE DEATH OF ISKANDER

WE were entertained by the Qirghiz of Kök-terek with the simple, open hospitality of their people, and breakfasted with them before moving on. The chief of them not only spoke but wrote Russian, an accomplishment of great use to him in trading across the frontier. His wife was either a Russian peasant or a highly Russianized Qirghiz. His establishment was made up largely of wooden corrals, but he lived himself in a handsome yurt. In one of his corrals was a tame young *maral*. This is the name indiscriminately given to the wapiti or T'ien Shan elk; but it is in fact the name of the hind, the stag being *boghu* — whence comes the name of one of the tribes of the Qirghiz. They can be bred in captivity and the horns of the stags sawn off when in the velvet and profitably sold.[1]

We rode on across rolling country at the foot of the forest line, and more than once roe deer which had left the forest and nested down for the day in the long grass sprang up and bolted before us. Thus we came to Aghiaz (in Kashgar Turki, *aghiz*), meaning The Mouth, at the stone-gated place where the Som Tash stream issues from its upper gorge. We found here another Qirghiz trader, and camped on the edge of the forest. From the moment we camped we heard constantly the barking of the T'ien Shan roebuck, which can easily be mistaken for the barking of dogs. They seem to be even more plentiful at Aghiaz than elsewhere. We had just camped, and I strolled up among the spruces, more to look over the country than for any other purpose. One of our men was chopping wood, within a hundred yards of camp. I went beyond him, not more than a hundred and fifty yards, and in fact

[1] Stephen Graham, *Through Russian Central Asia*. See also *The Desert Road to Turkestan*.

only just out of sight. The sound of his axe was perfectly plain. I looked up, casually, and there, in a glade, saw a deer. I was taken aback, and utterly unprepared, but it stood very politely until I recovered and shot it, to the great joy of all in camp. The wild ass provides the best eating in all Central Asia. After him, one wavers in doubt between the T'ien Shan roebuck and the Tibetan antelope, and after these two comes the Mongolian antelope.

I rather suspect that the country back of Aghiaz is better shooting ground even than the Qaraghai Tash; it is extremely hard to climb in to, wondrously rugged, and nobly supplied with forest covert, out of which rise bare peaks, crags, and open fells. Just by our camp, though the forest had been scarred by lumbermen, I saw the marks of stag and wild boar, and I saw innumerable roe deer; in fact, having no need of shooting them, I amused myself by seeing how close I could approach. We decided to let the caravan go ahead the next morning and make a late start ourselves, so that I might go up once more into the forest. I climbed almost above the tree-line, until I could see far into the challenging wilderness beyond, my heart sad at the thought of passing it thus and waiving the challenge. I sat down on top of a crag, my feet over a hundred-foot drop and my back against a spruce. Fifty yards from the foot of the crag a roebuck lay in covert, but neither he nor I knew it. Then a shift of the wind bore my scent down to him, after I had sat for a quarter of an hour; he bounded into view and went flashing down a sunlit glade, leaping high over the lush grass. I covered him for fifty yards, but I should not have known how to carry his sleek red body back by the rough way I had climbed, so I held my hand. Then I roused myself from my sun-warmed shelter and plunged downhill, over slides of rock slippery with moss, and through glens almost impassable by reason of fallen and rotted timber.

I returned to disaster, the most piteous calamity of our travels. Iskander, my stallion, whom I had loved from the first moment I saw his proud head and met his steady gaze, as he stood in the dusty Urumchi lane before the gray brick gates of our quarters, died that day. He had eaten too fast and too full of the fat pasture by our camp, and then drank greedily from the little brook. Within five minutes he began to swell with a fatal colic. I have never forgiven myself. Had I been more knowledgeable in horse mastery, I might have prevented it. He should probably have had more corn-feed to mix with the juicy grass; but I had been husbanding what I had, in order to tide him and Mæander over the desolate Muzart. Probably the immediate cause of his death was my negligence in not looking to him myself, the night before. The ponies were regularly tied up, not being allowed to graze until they had thoroughly cooled off. This time the Turki pony-men, busy over their meat, neglected to turn them loose at the right time. It was past midnight when their stamping roused my wife, and I, to my shame, only then ordered them to be turned loose. Thus Iskander ate too fast in the latter half of the night. Mæander did not suffer, his T'ien Shan-bred vigor being equal to any chance or circumstance of travel.

We rushed Iskander down to the Qirghiz trader near our camp — a small, wiry, most engaging fellow. He shook his head, but set to work. I hated to see Iskander subjected in his agony to the barbarous and useless treatment of slitting the nostrils, jabbing with needles, and so forth.[1] Still, it was necessary to give the Qirghiz a free hand, and he did have some common-sense notions, trying to get rid of the wind not only by pressure and squeezing with a rope, but by trying to clear the lower bowel, from the rectum. Nothing was any good; it was too severe a case. The only trick he did not know was that of piercing the bowel from behind the ribs on the near side, to ease the gas-pressure; I knew there was such a trick, but did not know how to do it.

Iskander made a noble end. When the Qirghiz had worked over him for more than half a day, he rose suddenly to his feet, and started off at a gallop. Less than half a mile away, he wavered in his gallant run, toppled over, and lay dead.

Our caravan, having started hours before, was gone beyond recall. The Qirghiz put us up for the night in the log hut of which he was very proud. He was a good fellow, and a gentleman. He brought his children to us, he brought his wife to talk with us, he brought a little fawn that was the pet of the family, to amuse

[1] I have given a description of this treatment in *The Desert Road to Turkestan.*

us. He made a little feast, that evening, of what supplies he had, and after the feast, because we were still disheartened and restless, he played to us on his *rabab,* and sang Qirghiz ballads. The next morning he found a mount for me, and rode with us to the next encampment, where a fresh pony was found. My wife gave his wife a ring, for a present; but in the morning, when we started, it had been transferred from wife to husband, and as we rode he flashed it at all comers, swaggering so that he fidgeted in the saddle.

Thus we rode on, the people coming out of their own accord at every camp to give me a fresh pony and act as guides, and on the next day we reached the Chinese post near the head of the Tekes, where the Muzart valley branches off to the pass, on the road to Aqsu. We passed on the way many tumuli, the most characteristic of which are arranged in lines, and in odd numbers, — five or seven, — with the biggest in the middle. They have weathered into such smooth and innocent shapes that they are nowhere recognized by any people of the country to be burial places. They are always explained as " mounds of stone that have grown out of the ground " — being confused, in other words, with ancient moraines of similar appearance. Most of them, in all probability, have been robbed at some remote period in the past; but it is equally probable that they have not been touched for many centuries.

The Chinese post is called Hsia T'an Ying P'an — the Barracks on the Lower Flat; that is to say, on the levels below the Muzart. This name has been corrupted by numerous travelers, who have received it as garbled by strings of interpreters, into "Shutta," or "Shatta." We found it in charge of a burly great Chinese, Ma Ta-jen, Ma the Great Man, as he was always addressed, although his positive rank was that of major or colonel. He welcomed us with more than the usual cordiality — in fact, with nothing less than tumid enthusiasm, and showed himself during our short stay not only an understanding host but a magnificent companion. All foreign big-game shooters on their way from India and Kashgar to the Qaraghai Tash to hunt pass by this post, so that in the experience of a number of years he had a lively knowledge of them; but I was the first foreigner he had ever met who could talk with him in his own language; for which reason his interest abounded, and we yarned for hours, explaining things to each other.

He ruled the tribesmen under his jurisdiction with a heavy hand, it was evident; and for good reason, for he not only sat astride the caravan route over the Muzart, but had to keep vigilant watch over the much easier pass which leads to Russian territory and Issiq Köl, from which direction come the most formidable cattle-stealing raids. At the same time he was of a jolly, forthcoming disposition which enabled him to get on extremely well with the nomads. The advantages of his position had enabled him to amass a respectable wealth. The nomads presented him with ponies and sheep every year; and putting these under the care of neighboring chiefs, he was able to sell their increase. He had been canny enough to marry the daughter of a Tientsin merchant in Kulja, so that he had family connections for his activity in trade.

The nomads under his immediate eye were mostly Qirghiz, with a few Qazaqs and scattered bands of Mongols. Although most of the Mongols are gathered in the valleys of the Kash and Qunguz, they have also small camps in the winter in most of the high, inaccessible valleys. It seems that they not only regard the Muzart valley as a winter preserve of theirs, but also claim a special guardianship over Khan Tengri, the nodal peak of the T'ien Shan, access to which they forbid to other tribes. These Mongols, while related to those of the Yulduz and Qara Shahr, are not under the rule of the Prince of Qara Shahr. They represent fragments of the ancient Zungar or Eleuth (Ölöt) Mongols; but it is difficult to determine how far they are descendants of the Mongols of the Zungar empire, who were slaughtered and almost exterminated by Ch'ien Lung, in the eighteenth century, but of whom a few, after being driven into Russian territory, are known to have come back later into the T'ien Shan; how far they are descendants of Torguts and the few Hoshuts (Khoshod) and Durbets (Dorbot) who accompanied or followed the Torguts in migrating to the Volga, later returning to Chinese territory; and how far they represent regroupings of all the Ölöt tribes after the Mohammedan Rebellion of the sixties and seventies. They are at present, and have been for a long time, commonly known as the Four Somons and

the Six Somons, being in the curious position of having no hereditary princes. The *somon* is a military, not a tribal unit. Structur-
ally, it is related to the Manchu " banner," and for all I know it may
be a reflection of the " banner." The hoshun, by contrast, the true
Mongol unit, is the hereditary tribal following of a tribal prince.
The somon exists also among the tribes retaining the hoshun
organization, the two systems overlapping. Thus, as I understand, two men may belong to the same somon and at the same time
to different hoshun, or to the same hoshun and at the same time
to different somon. In the Four and the Six Somons of the
Tekes, Kash, and Qunguz, the somon has entirely replaced the
hoshun, just as the " banner " first overlaid and then almost entirely replaced the tribal grouping which had at an earlier period
been the social system of the Manchus.

These Mongols of the Somons of the high T'ien Shan, we were
told, are a hardy lot; the Qazaqs almost everywhere have the upper
hand of their nearest Mongol neighbors, but they do not intrude
into the holdings of the Somons, especially their winter quarters,
except under fear of death. While we were camped at Hsia-t'an,
two Mongols came riding up to us; one an old man, so blear-eyed
as to appear almost sightless, and so stiff in the bones that he could
neither mount nor dismount except by the aid of his son, himself
a wrinkled fellow in his fifties. "There's the finest old hunter
in all this land," said Ma Ta-jen. "For many, many years he has
been guide and chief hunter to all the most distinguished foreign
hunters. Now he cannot see well, and he can hardly travel at all,
but he still spends the summer in the high places. You can see
that he carries a rifle. He is weak and old, but his wisdom is in his
belly. He knows where the game goes. He says to his son, ' Take
me to such and such a place; the game is there.' Then his son
takes him, and leads him near to the game, and when the old man
has the rifle in his hands he can still shoot. He knows the secrets
of the Holy Mountain also, and he has taken me there, because I am
his friend; but if a Qazaq were to go past this fort, into the upper
glens, the old man would kill him. The old man has many, many
letters and photographs from great foreigners." The old man came
to make his salutation to us, with a high dignity; but his letters and

his pictures were at his camp, which was far off; he was returning from a round in the mountains, where he had lived on nothing but meat and slept out rolled in a sheepskin coat. His son picked him up and placed him in the saddle, and he rode away down the valley.

All of these Mongols of the now scattered clans are among those carelessly called "Kalmuks," by almost all travelers. It is worth correcting this, if only because numbers of people are so slipshod as to say that "the Kalmuks are closely related to the Mongols"; as if one were to say that "Yorkshiremen closely resemble Englishmen." The Kalmuks *are* Mongols. Furthermore, none of the Kalmuks call themselves Kalmuks, with the exception of the most remote of them all, the Kalmuks of the Volga, who have for centuries been surrounded by Turkish-speaking peoples, and by repetition have fallen into the way of calling themselves Kalmuks. It is not even a Mongol name. It has come into general use simply because the Turkish-speaking neighbors of these Mongol tribes call them Kalmuk. It is usually said that the "name is of doubtful origin," or "obscure origin." I see no reason, myself, why it should not be identified with the root which in modern Turki is represented by the verb *qalmaq,* "to remain." It is significant that *all* the "Kalmuk" tribes are remnants of the one-time great confederacy of the Western Mongol tribes, the Ölöt. Moreover, so far as I know, all the Tatar (that is, Turkish or Turkic, rather than Mongol) tribes who use the term "Kalmuk" are aware that the Kalmuks represent now one, now another branch of the Ölöts of history, whose fame has never died. Nothing could be more natural, it seems to me, than that they should begin by calling these tribes "Ölöt-Kalmuk," — remnants, or survivors, of the Ölöt, — and later simply "Kalmuk." I was extremely interested, when I was talking with Ma Ta-jen about the Six Somons and the Four Somons, to have him explain that they were "Jungars" — or Zungars. It was the only time that I ever heard this word spoken in Central Asia, although it survives, on our maps, in the name of Zungaria.

XXVII

THE AMERICAN DUKES IN CENTRAL ASIA

"Ptui! Wrong again! Will you ever be fit for official life? *Ptui!"* Thus the Great Man, pursuing his orderly with a flying gob of spittle. Ma, the Great Man, prided himself on doing foreign travelers in good style, and the ineptness of his orderlies was a trial to his seigniorial soul. "Now let us talk," said he, comfortably settling his bulk; then, bounding up again and thrusting his domed, shaven head with the round black cap on it out at window, he began to shout, "Orderly! Orderly! Horse-milk wine for the guest!" When it came, he would not take any himself — until the orderly had withdrawn. "The pure Orthodox Faith?" I inquired, thinking, especially with the name of Ma, that he might be a Moslem. "Not at all; within the Ritual," he replied, smirking a little. Having, or being within, the Ritual, or the Three Rituals, refers to the members of a secret cult, which is said to have been founded about a hundred years ago. Some say it was founded at Tientsin, others at Jehol, others in Manchuria. At any rate, Tientsin is now its stronghold. Its members neither smoke, drink anything fermented, nor use opium. They are prodigious drinkers of tea, and are said to practise retreats, or periods of fasting and meditation, during which they take nothing but tea. Moses, out of his vast curiosity, once joined the cult. "But I never got farther into the mysteries than swilling tea," he said; "the rest is too hard. I don't suppose it's much different from other faiths. It's good if you're good, and no good if you're no good." I fancy that the Ta-jen had joined more out of policy than innate spotlessness. This cult is almost a shibboleth of the Tientsin men throughout this far western dominion. Even those who do not belong frequently practise the well-known outward observances, in order to improve their public reputations.

"Those dukes, now," resumed the Great Man. "They were no end of a bother when they came through. Could n't talk. They had a Kashmir, who spoke a little Inglis, and they talked to him, and he talked to a Chanto ("Ch'an-t'ou," Turbaned Head — a Turki), and the Chanto talked to one of my men, who talked to me. And they could not eat. Not properly. You are the only foreigner I have ever seen who could both eat and talk; and you have with you your t'ai-t'ai (lady), and I have my t'ai-t'ai, so we can eat all together, just in the family. Now this is better.

"Yes," he went on, "when I heard the Ameriki dukes were coming (*Ameriki*, I may say, is a Turki version of the Russian *Amerikanski*) I sent all the way to the Temple of the Golden Roof (a colloquial name for Kulja) to order the best food to be had. Sea-slugs, and everything. And then they fought shy of my food. If they saw a dish was all meat, they would try it, and sometimes they liked it. Then, because they would not eat my food, I was afraid for my 'face.' It would never do to have dukes starving under my care. Therefore I gave them a whole sheep, to make food for themselves, as they pleased, and they were relieved. They did not slice the mutton fine and cook it thoroughly, but warmed it over the fire in great lumps, and ate it so. However, it was the hospitality they seemed to prefer." The Great Man sighed. By the traditions in which he had been brought up, the ducal degree of civilization was hard to comprehend. *Ta-jen* and *kung-yeh* of the Ameriki; but mad!

"I gave them also a pony," said the Great Man, feeling more cheerful. "I always give ponies to foreigners. They are great officials — why else, indeed, should they be sent so far from their own countries? — and give me handsome presents; but I also, I am not a small official. The Elder Duke was set on having a stallion, so a stallion I gave him. And you, too. My t'ai-t'ai shall give your t'ai-t'ai a pony." He was as good as his word, that excellent man, for he gave us a pony to replace Iskander, and refused any sort of present in return. The exchange of presents, he said, was a ceremony, and the matter ended there; but he wished me for a friend. He hoped some day to go back to the coast, if he could realize on his wealth here, and then he would claim my friendship in Tientsin. We dined in the most free-and-easy way with him and his family, and took a most pestiferous round of flash-light pictures afterward, filling the room with fumes, which delighted the Great Man, he being able to display his soldierly courage before his somewhat fluttering wife and daughter. He gave us not only delicacies procured from Kulja, which had been brought by caravan from the far coast and hoarded as treasures, — delicacies treasured by the Chinese in this land of exile much as we should cherish caviar in Timbuktu, — but local specialties; fragrant mushrooms, and the flesh of the *ular*. The ular, a kind of giant partridge (I understand it is the same bird as the *ram chukor*), is found only above forest-line, on the edge of eternal snow. The Chinese call it *hsueh-chi,* or snow-cock. Its unaccountable climatic preferences, and the strength and well-being it develops in spite of them, lead to the belief that its flesh must be a specific of great value against the rheumatism.

The Great Man, a true and natural democrat, also invited Moses to this and other feasts, and to the bosom of his family — a most signal mark of favor. Moses, however, was diffident. He passed throughout this province as a Tientsin man (except when he came upon Shan-tung men, when he was quite prepared to be a Shan-tung man). This not only increased his " face," but ours. In a province where the Tientsin men control so much of the wealth, only the most ostentatious officials can employ Tientsin servants; it is the height of extravagant fashion. Our invitations to dine frequently included Moses, but he was loath to accept. When he and I had been alone, he had not been reluctant to go swaggering with me, and never failed to add life to the party. With the t'ai-t'ai present, he felt it somehow unbecoming. Another thing which added to Moses' good standing, wherever we went, was the fact that he addressed me as *shao-yeh,* showing that he had served my father. The Chinese have a great respect for old family servants, whose long service proves them to have been honest and trustworthy. A man will often retain his father's old servants as trusted counselors. As for going in good company, Moses was a credit. Although illiterate, he had assiduously cultivated a vocabulary of ceremonial and polite phrases, and was adept in the usages of old-fashioned official society. He employed this knowledge with a droll air of jovial grace which was inimitable.

"What do you think of my soldiers?" the Great Man asked. "Not bad, for the troops of this province, are they? But I should like to see good foreign troops of to-day, for comparison. I fought against foreigners in front of Tientsin, in the Year of the Rat (1900, the Boxer year), and they were too much for us then. But man for man, with equal weapons, we can beat the Russians; and since I have been stationed here, we have kept down the raids of the Qazaqs. They don't come over the way they did."

He dropped enough hints to make it evident that he had been, not only a Boxer, but a Boxer leader, for after the occupation of Peking by the Allies, and the proscription of the Boxer leaders, he dared not return to his native province. He was a Shan-tung man, and proud of it; he had remained all his life illiterate, but was all the more proud of the literary flourish on his cards, which proclaimed him to be from Shan-tso, Left of the Mountains, instead of Shan-tung, East of the Mountains, as it is in the colloquial. In the first years of his exile, I more than suspect, he was a bandit on the Mongolian borders, near Kuei-hua. When there appeared among some photographs I was showing him an enlarged portrait of that reformed freebooter, the Fu Kuan of the corps which protects the Kuei-hua caravans against the Free Companies, he asked some very shrewd questions. He wanted to know the Mongol name of the Fu Kuan, the wealth he had amassed, and whether he was a friend of mine. The names of obscure places in the Kuei-hua hills cropped up in his speech with the hesitancy of a man remembering long-ago scenes. Above all, he wished to know whether the Fu Kuan had a son. "You can lay to it, they were thieves together," quoth Moses. "They have n't either of them got a son." Moses was always a stout believer in the Chinese tenet that lack of sons to perpetuate a man's name and honor his spirit is the vengeance of Heaven vented on the sometime sinful. "He reformed," they often say, "but too late. Look at it! No son."

The Ta-jen became more friendly than ever. He spent long hours in our tent — over which he wagged his head. "You don't get any face out of a *Ta-tze* [Tatar, Mongol] tent like that," he

MA TA-JEN WITH HIS TROOPS

THE MUZART PASS: CAMP AT GLACIER HEAD

said. " You should see the kind the dukes had ! Why did n't you bring one of *those* from Ameriki? Regular houses! " He was off again on the dukes. The son of an American President is, in Chinese Turkestan, where they take little stock in republican notions, a duke. The pure milk of the democratic doctrine that a man is a man, regardless of the rank of his father, is not for them. On the contrary, if a man has a title, his son has a title. Of course. As for Presidents, it is true they have the modern Chinese term, *tsung-t'ung;* but it is quite evident that many even of the less sophisticated Chinese, not to mention the subject races, believe that a President is merely a somewhat unstable kind of emperor. At the same time, the Chinese, as the ruling race, are beginning to be proud of the possibilities of a future for China, as well as a past. " China," according to one of the dukes, reported by Ma the Great Man, " is like a man just waking from a long sleep, and realizing his strength." The duke had made this plain by imitating a man waking from a long sleep and realizing his strength, and the Great Man imitated the duke's imitation, and I sorrowed because I could not photograph this pantomime.

From the moment we entered the shooting country, we began to hear of the dukes, their train of pack ponies that took from dawn halfway through the morning to load, and their fearsome automatic rifles, which were described as machine guns. Even the men who had been detailed from the fort to accompany them now believed firmly that they had sprayed the hillsides with machine-gun bullets, thus bagging unheard-of quantities of game. They had also a cinema camera, but perhaps the best touch of all was their dogs. They had special servants to look after their dogs! The imagination of Central Asia boggled at the thought. The legend grew until we heard that the dogs had been carried over the Karakoram Pass in sedan chairs. Not only was this true, we were assured, but because one of the dogs died a large part of their retinue was sent back to India in disgrace; although this must have originated in the harmless fact that the dukes had paid off part of their transport after crossing the Karakoram.

The appearance of our typewriters caused much chatter in the yurts of the High T'ien Shan, and a slight fall in the ducal reputation. It seemed a pity that dukes should have had to write books by hand. Could it be that they were stingy? For they certainly wrote books. They wrote books all about the gold in the country, every bit of which they detected under the ground with their thousand-li glasses, and about Khan Tengri, the sacred mountains, from which they removed a treasure of jewels. Our tinned food proved us of the same nationality as the dukes. Not only did they have food in tins, but wine in bottles, also brought all the way from Ameriki — which, we could have told them, was a mistake. They did not, it was true, drink so copiously out of bottles as certain other high officials, Ameriki and Inglis, but only in the evening, after shooting. A group of Ameriki officials shooting animals and looking for gold and " precious things " with field glasses is the Central Asian definition, used by those who cannot read a letterhead, for an expedition.

In the way of shooting, beyond a doubt, the dukes could beat all comers. They got more than any other expedition. According to the curious rule by which the assistant of an expedition is usually a better shot than the leader, the Little Duke excelled the Big Duke; but even he was not free from lunacy. He came one day on a herd of six wild sheep, rams; and what should he do but take photographs of them. The quarry, becoming alarmed, ran away. The Little Duke, though slow off the mark, got his machine gun into action in time. He shot five of the rams. The sixth, he said with a magnanimity which became his rank, had too small a head. On their way back from the Qaraghai Tash, the dukes met another high Ameriki official, who had followed them over the Muzart. He was an old man, not so high in rank as the dukes, because he was not entitled to wear the ducal uniform of shorts; but nevertheless the dukes delighted to honor him. " Why do Ameriki dukes wear short trousers? Is it a matter of ' face '? Not only in the heat do they wear them, but in the cold, ai-ya! Not only to walk, but to ride. Also in Ameriki they have strange hats. The dukes had one with them, but after leaving Ameriki, to wear it they were ashamed, so they gave it away to a lowly man. It was a high, round hat, and black. When pressed from the top it became flat, and no use at all. This is a strange matter concerning the Ameriki, who have much mechanical skill, that their hats, when become flat and useless, can be restored to shape by pressure from the inside; yet with the art to make hats like this, they do not make hats which can resist pressure from the top. Was it not true that the dukes were in time past great military officials? There, they had heard it! Indeed, it was true. Behold, another far-wandered man, also an Ameriki, but capable of speech, and he confirmed it. But why, then, should military dukes wear tall round hats obviously of no use in war?"

I was talking, now, with a humbler man than Ma Ta-jen; a soldier who had accompanied the dukes. I asked what manner of man was the old official whom the dukes had met on their homeward way. Ah, yes, that old man. He was, it seemed, an official dispatched from Ameriki to collect birds. All day long he did nothing but shoot birds, both those that were good for eating and those that were good for nothing at all. Neither he, nor the dukes, nor any other Ameriki are interested in elk-horn in the velvet, or saiga-antelope horns, although from these things the Chinese, who are more learned than the Qazaqs, have the skill to make medicines. On the other hand, it is well known that Ameriki medicines are not understood by the Chinese, and are in their own way potent and wonderful. It must be that they are made from birds, the horns of wild sheep and ibex, and other materials in the use of which the Chinese are ignorant. The old official was a man of the most profound learning. He was a scholar. After shooting the birds, he would skin them, and fill the skins with cotton until they looked like live birds. If the old men of the Ameriki are not afraid to travel many tens of thousands of li to find birds for making medicines, — nay, if their high officials condescend to such service, — then it is no wonder that the Ameriki are a mighty nation, as is reported, riding in gas-carts and using gold coinage.

When the two parties met, the joy was mutual. They all pulled each other's hands, according to the Ameriki form of greeting. That night many tins of food were opened, and bottles not a few. It is the custom of Ameriki of high rank, when entertaining each other, to laugh very loud and to sing far into the night. But it was lucky that the dukes stayed awake that night, for there was great *chadak* (trouble) in the camp, and the manner of it was thus : —

It is the practice of Ameriki to bring with them a train of Kashmirs and Indostans; and the Inglis also do this. The Ameriki have good hearts, but the Kashmirs and Indostans are crooked-hearted hellions, the whole lot of them. Coming into the land of strangers, they revile the Qazaqs and Qirghiz as bad Moslems, for drinking mare's milk and eating horseflesh — as if they themselves were not heretical; do they not wash their hands before meals all together in one bowl, instead of pouring water decently over the hands of one man at a time from a ewer? Moreover, of the wealth and presents intended by the munificence of the Ameriki for their escorts and stalkers, they intercept an undue part. Would that the frank and generous Ameriki would dismiss altogether such runagates, and take on instead leal and trustworthy Qazaqs.

The chadak? Ah, it was a great chadak. Both Kashmirs and Indostans, it is known, come from Indostan, which is that province of Inglis nearest to Kashgar. Inglis, however, is a small country, for if you travel through it you come out at the other side in Yun-nan, which is still a province of China. Now Indostans and Kashmirs disagree as often as Qazaqs and Mongols. The old official had in his train more Indostans than Kashmirs, and along the road they put upon the Kashmirs; but when the two camps were pitched together, the Kashmirs were more numerous than the Indostans. Therefore they attacked the Indostans in the night. Before the escorts could turn out, you could not tell the heads of one set from the feet of the other. They fought like dogs, all up and down and under and about. Then the dukes and the old official appeared, and with much shouting, and by beating everybody the same as everybody else, they made quiet. Then the dukes put on revolvers and walked up and down the rest of the night, in a very fierce manner. In the morning, they made inquiry, and, having cast up the account of one of the Indostans, they sent him home. It was a very good fight, and the Kashmirs won. They laid one of the Indostans out so stiff that the breath was not in him, and it took much exhortation and medicine from the old official to bring him round.

And so, all in good time, dressed in their shorts, their dogs led for them by servants, and taking with them the stallion, their trophies, their knowledge of the gold as yet undiscovered by Qazaq or Chinese, and their wealth of jewels extracted from the Holy Mountain, and having made a present of an electric torch to the Ta-jen, which he in turn discreetly presented to his General in Suiting, the dukes withdrew in the direction of Kashgar, Indostan, Inglis, and Ameriki.

XXVIII

THE MUZART GLACIER

THE Ta-jen parted from us as handsomely as he had entertained us, for not only did I ride away on a pony of his, but he gave us as escort one of his picked men — a handsome young Qirghiz called Sopu. He would have been invaluable could I only have had him in the shooting country, for he knew not only the Muzart but the passes to the Yulduz and Qara Shahr, having accompanied at least two expeditions. He spoke, in addition to his own Qirghiz dialect, the Qazaq and Kashgar Turki, good Mongol, excellent Chinese, and at least a little Russian, which he had learned as a child before his people migrated from the Issiq Köl. Indeed, he complained that he was too clever by half, because, though he had served as a conscript for ten years — since he was sixteen — and now, being married, wished to return to his yurt, the Chinese flatly refused to let him go, on account of his usefulness as an interpreter, and his trustworthiness in special work. As a soldier in the Chinese service, he had had the unpleasant experience of being forced to fight against his own people, when they attempted to migrate back to Russian territory.

Sopu, proving himself a good companion as well as the soundest of guides, was worthy of the Qirghiz pride in being the flower of the nomadic races. He had the most charming manners toward my wife; for women are in better standing among the Qirghiz than anywhere else, perhaps, in Central Asia. It may be that the arduousness of their life causes an exceptional mortality among girls; and that the consequent scarcity of women entitles them to a respect which is fortified by the independence which they must of necessity develop in breaking and making camp unaided, and in handling the heavy transport alone, when the men have gone ahead with the pony herds. However Sopu had come by his manners, they were good manners. Elsewhere in Central Asia I was often hampered by the brawny men who jostled each other trying to heave me into the saddle or hoist me out of it; to Sopu alone it did not appear unfitting to stand at a woman's stirrup to help her.

From Hsia T'an Ying P'an we rode up the valley of the Great Muzart. At our right hand the forests had been badly damaged by a great fire, started some years before by horse thieves to check pursuit. Halfway up the valley, at a level of about 8400 feet, are hot springs, the temperature of which is given by Merzbacher[1] as 48° Centigrade. He does not mention, what we were many times told by local people, that they break out every year in July, and, after flowing for several months, vanish again. They are said to be hotter than the springs in the Köksu valley, and like them are considered medicinal.

The valley, near its head and at the verge of the forest line, expands into the meadows of Köhne Yailaq, or Old Pasture, which are rich even for the T'ien Shan. Here lived, in Qirghiz yurts, with his family, the Kashgar Turki who owned our pack ponies. He was the owner also of one of the biggest caravans passing between Aqsu and Kulja; his herd of mares giving him a regular supply of new ponies and his pastures enabling him to rest them in turn. We camped here for a day, overhauling gear and replacing worn horseshoes; and as we lazed and worked by turns, we could hear the barking of roe deer in the forests.

Only a mile or two on, when we set out for the "ice pass," it seemed that the valley was closed by walls of snow and ice, at the foot of which great glaciers rotted away in a waste of ponderous boulders and stunted spruces. Here we turned west for a short distance and then south into the pass proper. We left on the west, at this turning, a glacier that formed, as we were told, a pass over to Issiq Köl. A mounted man, said Sopu, could reach Issiq Köl in five days, and this was one of the passes used by his people, the

---

[1] *The Central Thian Shan Mountains.* London, Murray; New York, Dutton; 1905. References to heights and distances in this chapter are all from Merzbacher.

Böliq Qirghiz, in their migration from Russian territory.   It is not marked as a pass on Merzbacher's map.

The upper ascent of the Muzart, on the northern side, is so gradual that the crest is hard to determine.   It seemed to me to be near a group of small marshy pools.   The height is given by Merzbacher as 11,480 feet and by Skrine as 11,450.   Mr. Skrine says [1] rather bewilderingly, that this is " an elevation equivalent in the Central T'ien Shan to about 16,000 feet in the Himalayas."   I had always thought that one foot was twelve inches, except when measured by a Kashmiri tailor.

Thus far we had not traveled on ice, but among rocks and over meagre turf at the side of a glacier.   A little way beyond the real crest, we reached a camping place with a little thin grass among the boulders.   Below us was mist, into which vanished a glacier that, coming from the east across our front, turned to the south and offered the only way down.   On the east, at our left, were superb masses of what seemed to be unblemished marble, capped with sheer ice.   We set up our patched blue Mongol tent on a scant ledge looking down into this frore desolation.   As the afternoon cooled toward evening, masses of snow and ice, which during the day had been warmed rather than melted and were now chilling again, were loosened from the mountains and slipped away in brutally clamoring avalanches to the depths.   After each avalanche the echoes were thrown across and across from hill to hill, between ice and towering stone, till the noise died slowly to a tense hush

noiseless as fear in a wide wilderness

Not far to the west, though hidden from us by lower mountains, stood Khan Tengri, Lord of the Sky, the culminating peak of the Central T'ien Shan, whose unscalable summit reaches 23,622 feet. This is the Holy Mountain of the Mongols of the Tekes country. The Chinese call it the Mountain of Pigeons and the Mountain of Precious Stones.   The Mongols, they say, shoot any Chinese or Qazaq attempting to reach it; but Ma Ta-jen of Hsia T'an Ying Pan told me that once by special favor of the Mongols he had been taken to the flanks of it.   What the precious stones may be, I cannot

[1] *Chinese Central Asia,* London, 1926.

tell, though the Ta-jen told me he had presented one to the Ameriki dukes. The wild blue pigeons are of the kind protected by superstition throughout Chinese Turkestan, and especially honored by the Turkis, at whose desert shrines they are always found. The superstition is probably connected with the fact that they are to be seen even in the worst deserts, whenever there is a little water, so that the sight of them on a desert road is a cheering omen that water is not too far away. It means also that the traveler has not gone astray from the road, near which the pigeons remain, to scratch in the dung of transport animals and to search camps for scattered grain. Chinese carters, who have, I suppose, taken over the belief from the Turkis, aver that if the pigeons were to be killed or driven away the water would dry up. They say also that to kill pigeons brings bad weather — which must be an extension of the belief that associates them with water.

Not only is it said that the Ameriki dukes carried away great treasure in precious stones from the Lord of the Sky, but since the Merzbacher expedition in 1902–03, and the Russian expeditions that have worked in the T'ien Shan for geological or geographical purposes, and have reconnoitred Khan Tengri, the tribesmen have been persuaded that foreigners believe like them in a pot of undeniable gold on the top of the mountain. We heard long yarns of Ameriki, Inglis, and Oross who had approached the mountain with " pieces of wood and other instruments," but had all failed to reach the summit. According to the Mongols, there is a fire on the crown of the peak, never lit by man, and over the fire is a pot, in which bubbles molten gold. I do not think that the story has anything to do with a legend about volcanoes, but that clouds hanging about the peaks have suggested the smoke of an eternal fire; yet this is another of the stories by which early travelers were persuaded that a great volcano would be found in Chinese Central Asia.

The Chinese believe as firmly as the Mongols that stones of price are to be picked up on the flanks of this mountain. I suppose that never a foreigner, lusting innocently for record " heads," travels across the Muzart to the Qaraghai-tash and the high tributaries of the Tekes and Ili without the report being bruited that he has carried away with him jewels from Khan Tengri and gold from Aghiaz (Som Tash), Kök-terek, and Kök-su. A high military officer said to me quite seriously in Kulja that I need not expect to get great profit in America from my reports, inasmuch as the Ameriki dukes had already taken full reports, with maps and samples of everything to be found.

At about the hour of daybreak the next morning we left the ledge above the glacier. A vague light glowed in the mists that hid the mountains, and in a few minutes we had lost sight of our pack ponies. We worked out into an almost level trough, choked with rotting glacier ice and heaped at the edges with the ruin of mountains brought down by avalanches. Falling boulders of a vast size roll sometimes far out on to the glacier, which is about twelve hundred feet in width. The surface of it, channeled by streams and pitted with wells in the ice, is largely strewn with the detritus brought down in its passage from the hills. This is the slouching glacier that Merzbacher calls the Jiparlik, the monster of those parts,[1] and an anomaly in that it thrusts down the southern face of the great range, whereas the other major glaciers are for the most part on the north. Merzbacher ascribes to peculiar melting processes the appearance along the crown of the glacier of strange masses of solid ice, like battered globes, often balanced freakishly on small stones: "like a yurt on a man's fist," as Sopu the Qirghiz put it.

The tracks taken by the caravans vary from season to season as new crevasses open or new avalanches fall athwart the glacier. Little cairns mark all the tortuous ways, the old like the new, so that one can only be sure of the right way by the freshness of the dead pack animals and the droppings along it. In the heavy mist that dripped about us, we lost our way and fetched up in a nasty maze of rifted ice and morainic heaps of stone, with deep straight-sided pits at the bottom of whose glimmering walls gurgled swirling green glacier water. The mist had obliterated yesterday's exalted world of glittering splendor, when the late sun had flickered on naked marble and stark pinnacles of ice. Instead, as the morning

[1] Although still greater glaciers are to be found on the northern slopes of the T'ien Shan.

warmed a little, a sick smell of mortal corruption pervaded the gray depths in which we labored; an effluence from the carcasses which are the toll of caravans that cross the Muzart.

Our escort, admirable young man, did not lose his head, nor even shout for Moses and the caravan men, busy with their own toil somewhere, God knew how far, in the damp shadows; for to shout might have misled them and done us little good. He made several casts, until he struck a passable trail, and skillfully led us over to it. He said that it was not uncommon, when such a mist held, for lost men to wander for several days on the glacier, without finding a way either to the crest or the foot of the pass; and his words were believable.

After several hours of slow fumbling work, often in rifts with the ice high overhead, we struck a point from which it was possible to leave the ice and keep to the foot of a slope descending to the glacier. The young Qirghiz, of whom we had already become very fond, turned in the saddle and said that he had for a while been worried, but that he was now sure of the way. He said that not only was it a point of honor for him to get us across the pass with the least possible trouble, but for his own cogent reasons he must earn no one's bad opinion on this road. His wife, a sweet girl of about nineteen, who had brought us a gift of cream when we had passed her encampment in the sunny Tekes country, was about to bear him his first child, and he had that vague but convinced belief of the man living in harsh proximity to blind inexplicable powers that if he were found lacking in skill or good-will it might be reflected on the woman in the hour of travail.

Suddenly we had the best of omens. A gap in the lazily shifting mist showed us an ibex feeding on the slope above us. It saw us, too, and trotted slowly over a descending ridge. We went cautiously ahead, and rounding the nose of the ridge had again a sight of the beast, through a funnel in the mist, grazing about two hundred yards up. It stayed there innocently while I dismounted, drew my rifle out of the sling, and loaded it. A nook in the rocks gave me a comfortable position for the upward shot. The first took it behind the shoulder, a little low. The second, as it walked slowly away, was a miss. It dropped dead just out of sight, and

Sopu and I went up the shale to retrieve it. " This is from the Old Lord of Heaven," said Sopu piously. He meant Allah, but he used the Chinese phrase that comfortably includes all ultimate deities; him of the Christians, him of Islam, him whom the Chinese peasant addresses, whoever he may be, and Khan Tengri and other half-understood gods of the wild Mongols as well.

After five hours or so on the glacier, we reached the foot of it, a scarp of ice that entirely fills the valley, between sheer walls of utterly bare rock, worn smooth in remote glacial ages. At the left hand we found a shoulder projecting, and on it, not high above the fall of the glacier, the post of Tamgai-tash; a name which, so far as I can tell, means Post in the Stones. It is protected by a little embrasured wall of uncemented rocks; and seems from what I could hear to have been built by a Turki leader during the rebellion of Yakub Beg, as an advanced post to control the Muzart passageway. Certainly there was fighting for the control of the route between the Ili valley and the Great South Road, both in the time of Yakub Beg and in the short-lived troubles at the time of the Chinese Revolution. At the back of the post a cliff of white marble goes up to a height of 1300 feet, polished as ice can polish in a geological lapse of centuries.

In the post we found two young Turki fellows, appointed by the authorities to aid caravans in the unchancy scramble between the glacier and the lower valley. It is written in a number of books that they cut steps in the ice; but I saw no sign of any such thing. The rate at which the ice melts during the day, in the hot season, would make it hard to maintain steps. The edges of them would melt until they became round and slippery; but it may be that in winter steps are used.

By the post are several obos, which have been described as graves by at least one pair of travelers. This must be wrong, though the place as a whole is called *mazar,* which is a Turki term for a burial place, perhaps because cairns like these are found in lonely Turki burial grounds in the deserts. They are in fact obos of the kind that Qirghiz and Qazaqs, like the Mongols, Tibetans, and all the folk of the inner lands of Asia, set up in all memorable places and on peaks, passes, the junction of boundaries, and holy ground. In this place they are raised to the guardian powers of the pass, and staves are set in them, fluttering with tassels, rags, and, by a peculiar custom of the Muzart, the tails of all horses and beasts of transport that have died on the importunate glacier. These cannot be taken away and sold, however high the market for horsetails, but are a witness of the toll taken by the pass, and a kind of appeal to the powers not to take more than a fair levy. Stags' antlers and the horns of wild sheep are also stacked on the cairns, but this is a general custom, not particular to the Muzart. As our Qirghiz trooper came to the obo he dismounted, added a stone to one of them, and under it an offering of hair from the mane of his pony; a propitiation symbolic of devoting the whole pony. My feeling ran with his. It was a fitting rite in the savagery of that place, one of the marvels of High Tartary.

We huddled for a while with the Turki watchers of the pass in their mean shelter, until our caravan caught up. We had then to make the descent from the glacier to the moraine, the terror of the pass, and more difficult to get down than to get up. The snout of the glacier drops away 350 feet, a spectacle of riven ice, though like most bad places we found it worse to look at than to attempt, the most uneasy bit being a slide of some thirty feet. A sudden push from behind, and a smart blow, sent each pony down in kicking panic. At the end of the slide was a slanting wall of ice; if the pony coasted too far along it, he was in danger of falling over into a crevasse. Once he has fallen into such a place, a pony rarely escapes. It takes a number of men with ropes to lift a pony vertically, and often there is no stance where the men could safely get a purchase.

We were too tired already to worry overmuch, and let our men slide the ponies down without taking off the loads. We were told that when the glissade was in really bad condition a man would hang on to the tail of each beast, to check it as far as he could. Our riding ponies fetched up in a heap at the bottom, scrambled to their feet, shook themselves all over, and were ready for what might come next. Indeed, the new pony, the gift of Ma Ta-jen, was a bit too ready, for when my wife patted him encouragingly he lashed out and kicked her badly on the shin. The rest of the descent to the lower moraine meant no more than labor and assiduity; except for one narrow ridge of ice, barely a foot wide and a matter of twenty feet long. In the crevasse on one side lay two dead animals, and on the other three.

All this time it was raining heavily, for the mist had turned to rain, after lifting a moment to afford us a farewell prospect over the last shoulders of the sprawling glacier, a howling wilderness of dirty, jagged ice, unlovely to the eye but beautiful to the heart. We saw only for a few moments the fullness of the bald cliffs of limestone and marble, the jaws of the place where the glacier ends. It is a place that I should willingly see again. It is a recognizable gateway between two worlds. We came down through it and knew that the life we had been living was a cycle of our past. We had done with the horse-riding nomads and the most delectable lands of all nomad peoples, the lands of the high Tekes.

We were glad to rest for a while in a cave where we found some wood left by a caravan; fortune of the road, since travelers by the Muzart find no fuel for between two and three stages, but must carry all with them. The fire warmed face and hands, and, though the rain felt cold enough down the backs of our necks, it was warmer than the wet glacier ice.

The day's thaw was now taking effect, and one avalanche followed another down the incredibly steep bare mountains that looked as though they had long been swept bare, and waterfalls leapt to life in every deep narrow ravine. We had to search a long time for a safe ford across the South Muzart River, which comes roaring out from under the glacier and is joined at once by another river from an equally large valley. Far below the regular ford our canny Qirghiz found a good crossing, and we rode on for hours until the ponies began to flag and to stumble occasionally among the water-worn stones across which we straggled. We had to keep far out in the floor of the valley, for the easier trail at the edge of the impending hills was being pelted with bounding rocks that shot far in advance of the avalanches.

At a place where our escort warned us to keep a sharp lookout, because it was more than usually dangerous, a man who had been sitting in the most exposed place possible, as though waiting for an avalanche to squash him, suddenly rose and stalked toward us. The Qirghiz trooper at first looked at him sidelong, for of all the escorts we ever had he alone was ready to stand on guard; but in a moment he also was reassured. The man was a Turki of at least fifty years, gray-haired and gray-bearded, but youthful and serene of countenance. As he strode over the flood-bed of the river to intercept us, he did not even turn round when a small avalanche crashed down within a few yards of the hazardous place where he had been sitting. He was dressed like a beggar, and carried in his two hands a wooden bowl of the kind the Mongols use. It was filled with ashes long gone cold; " to keep him warm," he explained with an innocent smile. He told our escort, with the same charming smile, that he was a fiend for gambling, and, having lost everything in the cities of the Ili, was making his way home in poverty toward Kashgar. It was plain, however, that he was a *sarang,* a weak-witted man, or man who has been " touched," such as are kindly treated, for Allah's sake, wherever Islam has penetrated. He had been cowering in this valley for two days, hungry and near frozen, afraid to cross one of the sidestreams that barred the way. The Qirghiz took him on our strength at once, giving him all the food he had on his person and promising him a pony for the ford.

We had gone but a mile or so forward, and had reached a little scrub which promised fuel for our fire, when we met another derelict, a Chinese with chattering teeth and clothes wetter than the rain could make them. He was a Tientsin man by his speech, and by his own account a small trader who had been over to Aqsu to collect a debt. On the way back he had rashly forded the stream of which the wandering Turki fool had been afraid, and, though he got across, the water had near drowned him and had carried away the bundled coat in which he had his food and the money for which he had made this hard journey on foot. The story sounded honest, but the man looked a scamp. He was mean-hearted besides. He began at once to vilify the Turki we had picked up, saying he was a madman, well known in the Ili valley, who begged and tramped his way from place to place, and was not to be trusted.

He said all this, perhaps, to win the sympathy of Moses, as the other Chinese in a mob of barbarians; but to no purpose. Moses liked our other men as well as we did, and, besides, one of our Turki caravan men was weak in the head, so that we were all partial to fools.

We camped as soon as possible and struggled with wet, prickly fuel. Then the Tientsin man suggested that we take the wooden bowl of the sarang, who was off grubbing fuel in a dazed way, for kindling, and before anyone could say a more generous word it was caught up and smashed, and in a few minutes we had enough blaze to dry out our sodden clothes. That night, as the caravan men, Moses, Sopu, the Qirghiz, and the two strays were thawing themselves, the sarang went into a mild frenzy, mourning for his bowl. He called on Allah to witness what men had done to him, and on the men to witness that Allah would feed the despised fool, and began to eat dust and ashes. He was, however, much comforted when we gave him an empty tomato tin to replace the wooden bowl. The rescued Chinese, now fed and warmed, sneered and jeered; but the Mohammedans, now abashed, did their best to comfort Allah's fool, and Moses looked on, his face a blank.

For Moses more than any fought shy of the Tientsin man. He and I both like the company of the hearty sort of villain and the gay kind of scallywag; " but this bad man," said Moses, pulling a doleful face, " is not a good man," and that was about the gist of it. Yet the Qirghiz, natural gentleman, though he knew of the Tientsin man by report, and that not to his good, sent him off the next morning with the gift of his own leather boots. The mountains of the Muzart, he explained, were not good mountains. The man who traveled among them without a conscience at peace was likely to be abandoned by Allah to their wrath. The Tientsin man was obviously not a fellow with an enviable conscience, and therefore it was that he had nearly been drowned. Nevertheless, in the dreaded valley of the Ice Pass, of all places, travelers must stand by one another; and so, for the quiet of his own conscience, no less than to ensure his return to his wife, and lest badness in his heart bring evil on her in child-bearing, he felt bound to make his good leather boots a free gift to a rogue who did not even thank him for them; while he went on with shoes of cotton cloth.

The descent from the Muzart on the Aqsu side is much the longer. Though we had camped far below the glacier, we had yet a good forty miles to go before clearing the mountains. All through the upper valley there is hardly a glint of green. The mountains corresponding to the great spruce-covered slopes of the Ili side are too steep to hold the tiniest ledge of earth; only rarely could we see, remote and dwarfed, what seemed no more than a copse of forest in a nick between inaccessible peaks. In the valley bed, scoured by floods and hammered by the rocks of avalanches, only a few alluvial fans are large enough to hold a little tattered scrub and a little grass. The far side of the river, where runs the winter road, was a little better, but we had no way of getting over to it. On our side we traveled half a day more before we reached the first willows and poplars. All day we went by the foot of cliffs that lifted to a stupendous height, sometimes near 5000 feet of sheer fall; and looking across the valley we could see bizarre formations of the rock — bands of purple and red porphyry, and extraordinarily looped and twisted strata.

Although the day was cloudy, the snows were melting fast, and we were never out of sight of waterfalls. More than anything else they made one realize the scale of the huge mountains at the foot of which crawled and stumbled our caravan; they came down in leaps of scores of feet at a time, one below the other, but so high and so far away that the roar of them could not be heard above the growling of the river. We had several times to ford deep, swift, narrow streams coming from the side — all of them more difficult to cross than the streams of the Tekes valley, which we had found hard enough. They came down headlong, with all the force of the cascades in which they had their sources, over big rounded boulders between which the wise mountain-bred ponies picked their way with all their craft and all their strength gathered for the struggle. It was almost evening when we camped. The valley had widened, the stream was fringed with willows and poplars, and we had long been clambering up and over vast ruinous moraines. Opposite us on a bluff terrace was a farm, with fields irrigated and laboriously cleared of stones. The crops, in July, had not nearly reached full growth, for the harvest here does not come until October, and is always threatened with destruction by frost. The place was occupied by the Turki families which are required by government to keep two men always on the Muzart glacier.

That night our sarang prophesied, and though tired with a march of about twelve hours the two caravan men and our escort sat up half the night to listen to him. During the day they spoke to him as " fool," but at night, when he prophesied, they sat at his feet in reverence and awe. Again he called them to witness how Allah fed his chosen — with dust and ashes. Then he chanted long rhapsodies, in sonorous tones ringing through the brushwood; and the red fire, leaping and falling in front of him, threw a pulsing light on his bold, rapt features. The recitals, I imagine, embodied fragments of old shamanistic incantations, garbled with phrases from the Quran, for he called much on Allah. At the end of each incantation he bent his body many times in many directions, hissing loudly " to scare away evil spirits." Then, enlarging as far as I could make out on the text he had been reciting, he would tell the fortune of one of the men; frequently requoting a verse or saying, and expounding it with measured gravity. Between each fit of prophecy he was moody and sullen, but while the fit was on him he was exalted and radiant. When at last the men had lain down by the fire, he still sat muttering, and swaying back and forth. In the morning he was gone.

We ourselves were clear of the T'ien Shan before noon. Crossing the only bridge over the river, we rode under small forests of spruce, all of them high above us and looking drier and less vigorous than the forests of the northern side. At its mouth the valley narrows, and is blocked from river to cliff by a stone wall, under the shelter of which are grouped a barracks and a tax station. The place is called Köhne Shahr, Old Town. The fortification is said to date from the wars of the Mohammedan Rebellion, and, though it could be raked by machine-gun fire from the hills at either side, is regarded locally as the last word in " strong points," an impregnable position giving absolute command of the Muzart mountain way. The maintenance of it in comparative repair is a monument to the Chinese instinct for conducting their wars from behind walls. Sir Aurel Stein bears witness to the ability the Chinese have shown, from the earliest times, for understanding strategic routes and strong points in extending their empire into the remote West. Yet their reliance at the present time on such mediæval fortifications to hold down this outer dominion, and the kind of troops maintained in their cantonments, are less a proof of the Chinese ability to conquer than of their success in pacific administration, and of the docility and lack of fighting instinct of the population they control.

We drank tea with the official in charge; we looked resignedly at the heat shimmering on the open lands before us, and rode on slowly, the deserts of the south before us.

XXIX

DOWN TO AQSU

OUR way to Aqsu went through the low barren hills that make a desert outwork between the T'ien Shan and the basin of the Tarim, the main depression of Southern Chinese Turkestan, taking us by the Hung Yen K'ou or Red Salt Pass, the same that the Turki people call Topa Dawan, or Dusty Pass — that is, of earth rather than rock. Our escort stopped at several places to attack a hill with his sword, and each time, chipping away the crust of red earth, he dug out gleaming rock salt. These deposits, according to Merzbacher, run to a thickness of twenty inches. In the lower hills of this range we saw also a few *toghraq* trees, the "wild poplar" of the books of Central Asian travel. Near the Edsin Gol, in Mongolia, the year before, I had noticed one from which grew what appeared to be an unmistakable shoot of willow. I had thought it at the time some freak of self-grafting. Here many of the larger trees had such shoots of willow springing from them, and when we got to Aqsu the Tao-yin, an observant man and a lover of trees and flowers, told me it was not uncommon. Our Qirghiz escort, as coming from the Ili country, was not familiar with the toghraq, and thought this manifestation of willow leaves as curious as I did. The first one I pointed out to him he studied for a long time, looking a little nervous. Then he said, " This is not a worthless tree. This is a good tree." If it could have been taken to the Tekes country I have no doubt that the nomad people would have hung votive rags on it, regarding it as the abode of holiness. It was long afterwards that I realized the truth, which had been observed by Miss Sykes: [1] the toghraq is a tree whose leaves vary

---

[1] *Through Deserts and Oases of Central Asia,* by Miss Ella Sykes and Sir Percy Sykes. London, Macmillan, 1920.

a great deal in shape, and the appearance of willow shoots is due only to an extreme variation, shown by the leaves when they first come out.

A full stage from these hills across an extremely droughty desert, riding almost all the time blinded in a dust storm, brought us to Jam, where we joined the Great South Road, the Road South of the Heavenly Mountains, running from Urumchi by Toqsun, Qara Shahr, Kucha, and Aqsu to Kashgar. A short march on, and we entered Aqsu, passing on the way a small oasis where was a village, and in the middle of the village a monstrous tree, its base heaped about with skulls of wild sheep. That, said the Qirghiz, was the first tree planted in the oasis at the time of settlement. We passed also a mosque, more conspicuously decorated than usual with the same kind of trophy, which may be seen everywhere in the province, as at Hazrat Apak itself, in Kashgar, the most splendidly kept-up shrine in the country. Here again the Qirghiz spoke to the point. He said that the horns " kept the river from running wild and drowning the fields." Now stags' antlers are sometimes used in the same way, and I suspect that the custom derives from a primitive association of these animals with the powers of the mountains and the springs of the rivers. I suppose that the votive horns are intended to constrain an unfailing supply of water, as well as to prevent inundation. On the one hand the use of the heads of wild animals is likely to be drawn from an origin other than ordinary animal sacrifice, which would have led to the offering of the heads of domestic sheep, and on the other hand it suggests a parallel with the bull's head, connected with springs and rivers in Greek symbolism. Rivers have commonly been regarded as manifestations of strength, and it may be that the bull was associated with them in Greece partly for that reason, partly because of the contagion of other rituals of animal sacrifice, and partly, perhaps, for lack of wild beasts of such striking nobility as the lordly wild sheep of Central Asia.

Letters of introduction to two Tientsin men, one the postmaster and one a trader, assured us a charming reception at Aqsu. By reason of our inquiring the way, we were escorted by nothing less than a concourse of the populace to the place where the sign of the trader hung out. It was only a narrow booth, open to the street, along which the swelling crowd at once made passage impossible, and stocked with pathetic oddments reminiscent of China far away — paper, porcelain, different kinds of food, cheap ornaments, and tea. The owner was overwhelmed at our coming, and took us at once to his quarters at the back, to secure us a little quiet; he could hardly speak, for embarrassed courtesy, until he had put before us little delicacies — cakes, melons, and fragrant tea.

His quarters being small, we stayed with the postmaster, and the two men, who were old cronies, did their utmost to show that the famous hospitality of the nomad does not rank ahead of the cordiality of a civilized race like the Chinese. It was a friendly stay, even more friendly than had been possible in the trading firm that had entertained us so handsomely in Urumchi, because of the family life. My wife talked with the women, while I talked for hours with the men. Their eagerness to hear of the " home country " was pathetic, for theirs was a rigorous exile, sundered from China not only by distance but by severe censorship of the mails, extending to the absolute prohibition of newspapers. The thing that made their sense of exile most poignantly plain to us was the wish of our host's old mother that they might be transferred nearer to Urumchi; at least to a place where the Tientsin people were numerous enough to have a cemetery of their own. She was resigned to death in a far country, but hoped at least for burial among her own people.

Living thus, not in official guest quarters, but with a family, we saw also something of the life led by Chinese of the educated middle classes in a town where they not only represent the ruling race but are few in numbers and deal almost entirely with " natives." They seem to have even more Turki servants than foreigners on the coast have Chinese servants. They are unlucky in one thing, that the Turki rarely masters the delicacies of Chinese cooking, so that in families not rich enough to employ a Chinese cook the women must attend to the kitchen. For a Chinese in this province to have a Chinese servant is as extravagantly luxurious as to have an English valet in India.

More than any race I know, the Chinese have admirable man-

ners with their servants.   Here, south of the Heavenly Mountains, where the Chinese population is limited to a few opium-
smoking soldiers, a few scattered traders (other than pawnbrokers and money-lenders), and a few officials, their relations
with the " natives " of their own households are, as they would
be with servants in China, a blend of democratic familiarity and
patriarchal authority.   In Aqsu we had one of our comparatively
rare opportunities of seeing the Chinese as individual masters, in
contrast with their class position as the ruling minority by right
of conquest.

The most convincing and at the same time most comical example we saw of prestige borrowed by the individual from the
prestige of the race was at an oasis where the village was so tiny
that it had no resident Chinese official.   We had been accompanied
by the Beg or minor native official of the last village through
which we had passed, who continued " in waiting," supported by
the local Beg and by another Beg, sent by the Chinese official of the
district township.   We were being accorded a " regular right-
down royal " reception, when somebody burst in among us with
a hurried announcement, whereupon we were in a moment almost
deserted.   The District Magistrate's " number one boy " (chief
personal servant) had arrived.   It was a gracious courtesy on the
part of his master to send him, but his presence totally eclipsed us.

At last our attendants came back, breathing softly that the Ta
Yeh, after refreshing himself with a pipe of opium, would call upon
us formally.   He proved, when he came, to be an incredibly provincial youth from Kan-su, that most provincial province.   The
Kan-su men are looked down on by other Chinese as backward
and outlandish bumpkins; but the old Governor, at that time, was
employing a good many of them in official positions, because he
knew they would not combine well with other Chinese in any
intrigue against him.   Hence the presence in that remote district of what Moses called a mouse official, with a mouse valet.
Moses never would call Kan-su men anything but mice; a bit of
slang he had picked up from the caravan men in Mongolia, where
the men of Chen-fan, in Kan-su, are known as sand-hollow mice.
Moses never bothered to learn the slang names for men from other

parts of Kan-su, such as Kan Chou dried donkey-skins; mouse was good enough for him.

Our "official visitor" did his best to improve matters with a really most ingratiating giggle. I nearly snickered myself to see the lowly carriage of the Begs, in their robes of gorgeous colors, their bright sashes, red leather boots, and embroidered skull-caps, before this funny little opium-smoking bumpkin with his soft giggle, his rusty black jacket and trousers, tawdry watch-chain, slovenly shoes, and shapeless foreign-style felt hat — and his all-important position at the right hand of the mighty, the District Magistrate. The breath of a hint from us, and he could and would have commandeered without payment anything in the countryside. Yet he could not even speak the language of the people to whom he gave orders. The Begs who toadied to him had to speak Chinese, and were by so much his superiors in accomplishment. That such a man should have been competent to handle any matters that might come up was proof outright of the domination of the Chinese as a racial group.

The winter before, on the North Road, I had seen an example of the less creditable sort of thing that happens when one race rules another. An escort riding in front of me had met two "native" sledges in the snow, at a place where it was impossible to pass without one party floundering into deep snow. My escort, before I could stop him, struck at both beasts and men with his whip. "Out of the way, *tao-mei i-jen!*" he shouted, using an expression equivalent to "damned savages," and quite as brutally arrogant as "damned nigger" would have been in the mouth of, say, a British soldier in India or an American soldier in the Philippines. This sort of thing, it need hardly be said, is not the commonest or most noticeable under the Chinese rule in Central Asia. It is true, however, that a pointed racial superiority is publicly maintained by the Chinese. At any sort of public reception the subject races, if they are seated at all, are separately seated. Very often they are not seated at all. None of the Turki Begs of whom I have spoken would have dared sit down in the presence of the District Magistrate's body-servant, unless invited to sit. Nor were they invited.

On the streets also the Chinese take precedence. Even children may have to look lively. I have already described how we were told, in a village in another part of the province, where some Chinese children threw mud at my wife, that we must not take it as meant in hostility; it was only children playing. The men of the village, who were a friendly lot, apologized and reassured us; but the children were not even scolded. Yet if a " native " child, getting in the way of a Chinese, were to be cuffed on the ear, nothing would be thought of it. Were a foreigner to do the same thing, say in Canton, he would risk being mobbed.

Nothing is more striking than the similarity of cant in every country where one race rules another; wherever, to use the modern phrase, " imperialism " prevails. In China, although events have moved at such a rapid pace in the last few years, there are probably still foreigners to be found who would say that the Chinese understand nothing but the firm hand. This is hardly a full comparison, because the foreigner does not rule in China; he is only doing his best to dodge being ruled by the Chinese. Yet there is, just as probably, hardly a Chinese in Chinese Turkestan who would not say that the only way to rule the Turki and the other " natives " is high-handedly. As I was going once to call on a fairly important official, I asked my companion what crime had been committed by two men whom I saw chained by their necks to the gates of the officials' yamen. " They are thieves, or debtors," I was told. " These people are not like us, you know. They don't appreciate fair treatment, and they don't know what gratitude means. Let them off lightly, and they only think you are weak, and make all the more trouble. When you punish them, you cannot think only of the just punishment for the crime; you must make them an example to others." Familiar phrases! They sound as if they came out of an apologia for the White Man's Burden.

I touch on these things, partly because it is the business of a traveler to appreciate, if he can, everything that comes to notice, partly because I think that the Chinese rule in Central Asia is, on the whole, a remarkable achievement; and praise is not salty if the man who utters it does not show that he can see more than one

side of the matter.   I think I rate the Chinese administration in
those parts of the world more highly than most people do.   The
commonest published opinions on Chinese rule are Russian and
British.   It seemed to me that as a general rule the opinions of
the Russians I met were not well balanced.   I think that in their
minds the chief difference between the Chinese and the indigenous
races of Central Asia was that the Chinese were probably more
civilized, in a mysterious way, but that they were certainly more
heathenish and more incomprehensible.   Nor do I think that the
Russians, in spite of the stout efforts they have made to carry out
new Central Asian policies, have been able to handle the Chinese
any better, or by essentially very different methods, than before
the rise of the Soviets and the change in aim of the old " forward
policy."

British opinions are much more easily found in print.   On the
whole they give the Chinese praise where praise is due, but not
in very strong terms.   This is almost certainly because the average
British visitor has behind him the background of the British rule
in India.   He must of necessity contrast Chinese methods with British methods; the venality of Chinese courts with the unrelaxing
British effort to secure impartiality and level justice; the careful
scrutiny of taxation in India with the Chinese tendency, thus far
ineradicable, to manipulate taxation for the benefit of officials; the
selective systems of recruiting and promotion in the Indian Civil
Service with the nepotism and sale of office current in Chinese
Turkestan; the British rule of requiring officials to learn at least one
and usually several native languages with the Chinese indifference
toward the languages and culture of their " barbarian " subjects;
the lavish expenditure on education in India with the indifference
toward education in Chinese Turkestan;[1] and the efficiency of the
troops in India with the unkempt soldiery to be seen in Chinese
Turkestan.   Such things, I believe, obscure a most important
basic instinct which, as I believe, the Chinese and the British really
have in common, whenever they are at their best — the pragmatic

[1] It should be noted, however, that the Chinese maintain schools throughout the
province where men of the subject races can acquire a rudimentary Chinese education, and sometimes more advanced learning, by the aid of which they can
acquire promotion in the Chinese government service, as minor officials.

instinct for doing the best that can be done on the spot with the men and materials to hand.

The success of the Chinese in the last generation in Central Asia can only be appreciated against the background of China, inchoate and ill-directed, with old standards breaking down and every possible handicap in the way of setting up new standards. Since the Chinese Revolution, especially, the Chinese in Turkestan have had in China only a background and a memory, without any genuine support; with, in fact, an increasing danger of civil war and the breakdown of Chinese rule in the New Dominion through an attack, from China, on the ruling faction. Thus the Chinese in this province have during recent years become even more isolated. Nor have they been in a position to emphasize their military control of the subject races. Any attempt at importing arms through China would be futile, as they would be confiscated long before their arrival, and possibly used in an attack on the province. As for importing arms from any other country, that would be impossible either because the other government concerned would refuse, or if it consented would demand in return privileges of trade and exploitation which the Chinese would not be willing to grant, for fear of losing their economic control. Thus they have fallen back on a policy which, in the broadest view of it, is tolerant and wise. It is true they have played off one group of their subjects against another, in order to frustrate any revolutionary coalition against them, and have deliberately retarded economic development in certain directions, lest the pace of development get beyond their control. On the other hand, they have encouraged in many ways the general prosperity of the mass of the people, and have succeeded so commendably that food and living are cheap: no man willing to do a hand's turn of honest work need be a rogue, and the people are so generally contented that they would be unwilling to revolt against the Chinese for fear of destroying their own prosperity. This policy of fostering general contentment and strictly limiting the control that could be exercised by any one group was consistently developed by the old Governor. It worked so satisfactorily that at least one plot for a Mohammedan rebellion, originating with a group of Mohammedans from Kan-su province, in China proper, was betrayed to the Governor by a conservative group of his own Mohammedan subjects, and the malcontents quietly obliterated before they had made any headway. Since the assassination of the old Governor by one of his subordinates,[1] the equilibrium he had so carefully maintained has been endangered. No equilibrium, unfortunately, can last forever. The pressure on Chinese Turkestan from the world at large, and especially from China itself, cannot be withstood indefinitely. When the frontier breaks, and new factions of Chinese invade the province, a period of rivalry and exploitation will begin. The subject peoples will be lucky if they escape miseries which they never knew under the old autocracy, and the upshot of affairs in that remote intermediary land between the Far East and the Near East is unpredictable, what with the conflicting interests of many minor peoples and the inevitable pressure, as it were impersonal and foreordained, of the two major races, Russians and Chinese.

In the meantime the foreign traveler along the Great South Road, even more than in the northern division of the province, gets more courtesy than any man really deserves for just taking money out of his pocket and going abroad to see the sights. The Tao-yin, or lieutenant-governor of the sub-provincial circuit of which Aqsu is the chief town, had himself ordered quarters to be prepared for us in a garden; but though a garden to camp in would appear to be the chief ambition of most travelers in Central Asia, we preferred the family hospitality so kindly offered us. We spent, however, a good many hours with the Tao-yin in his own garden, which he had laid out himself, many years before, during his first tenure of office. He had, in his distinguished career, been appointed and reappointed to a number of the most important lieutenancies in the province, and in each of the several great towns in which he had spent his best years he had laid out celebrated gardens. In his Aqsu garden, the kindly and scholarly old man, friend and helper of a number of foreign travelers in the past, spent most of his time, among his flowers and trees. He was known in Aqsu,

---

[1] It was not until some time after I had left Chinese Turkestan and after the greater part of this narrative, in which I have so often referred to the old Governor as still living, had been written that I learned of this murder.

Kashgar, and Yarkand as a benevolent administrator; but I think he took more pride in the thought that he had made this garden out of desert land. Never was a garden so tenderly cared for. Down the alleys where fruits were maturing skipped small Turki boys with hollow gourds and wooden clappers, to scare away hornets and other pests. We liked best the rose beds and lotus ponds, the lotus being an importation all the way from China; but I think the Tao-yin set as much store by his potatoes, cabbages, and maize, of varieties brought from Europe and America. The first potato to reach the province had been sent to a Swedish missionary in Kashgar, from his home; and from one of the eyes of this potato the Tao-yin had raised his own stock. When we lunched with him, the dish of pride was potatoes, boiled plain, in the fashion of the West to which these corners of Asia look as the home of the fabulous and romantic.

In a cage in the garden there lived a fine Yarkand stag — the stag of the lowland marshes, rather smaller than but nearly as handsome as the wapiti or Asiatic elk. Seeing the Tao-yin's interest in my interest in his pet, we thought of showing him our own — a weird desert mouse we had captured out of a cart rut, just on the outskirts of the Aqsu oasis. I think it must have been some sort of jerboa, or kangaroo rat. It had bat-ears nearly as big as its body, hind legs like a kangaroo, and a long, skinny tail that ended surprisingly in a white-tipped black tuft of hair. It bounded phenomenally, was very companionable, ate bread soaked in milk, and grieved us to the heart by dying after a few days.

The Tao-yin demanded that it be fetched, and a courier was dispatched at once on a horse to get it. Then, in front of the disdainful stag, we all inspected it. "This is the kind of thing that expeditions hope to find," said the Tao-yin. "In all my years in this province, I never knew that such a beast existed. And those American dukes! They came all the way to the Heavenly Mountains, to find animals that everybody knew were there. What would they say if they knew of this thing, which is so remarkable and totally escaped them?"

I have a pleasant memory of Aqsu, and not the least pleasant facet of that memory is the vision of that dear old gentleman of exalted rank, squatting on his heels between the oleander borders, with me, an uncouth, hairy stranger; not to mention the second highest official, the head gardener, the pipe bearer, a sentry or two, and the small boys who made noises in the garden to scare away insect pests, all bumping our heads against each other while we coaxed the desert rat to eat lucerne, and to jump and show off his legs.

XXX

THE ROAD SOUTH OF THE HEAVENLY MOUNTAINS

EVERYBODY conspired to send us off from Aqsu with comfort and decorum. The Hsien official (the Amban of travelers' jargon), who was no less a person than the son of the Governor-General at Urumchi, gave orders which ensured our finding a good cart, sound cart ponies, and a trusty carter; and all at the cheapest possible rates. The Hsien and the Tao-yin between them furnished us with escorts who carried orders that we should everywhere be treated with all honor; and these orders were everywhere carried out. The postmaster lent us his own cart-top, and his friend (and ours) the trader made us a gift of two tins of coffee, which in Central Asia is about all that a wife needs to make her more precious than rubies. He also presented us with two half-bottles of a French wine under the label of the *Veuve Amiot,* which had arrived by caravan from God knew where and was reputed to be champagne. The trader and the postmaster between them also effected some prestidigitatory banking for us. In this one province, besides the silver Chinese dollars which reach Ku Ch'eng-tze, three principal local currencies are in use, and one of lesser importance. In Urumchi and along the Great North Road to Chuguchak, they have the Urumchi tael, which is a paper money without metal backing. In Turfan there is another paper tael. The Urumchi tael is current in Turfan, but the Turfan tael is not accepted in Urumchi. In Kulja and the Ili cities there is another paper tael, worth sixty cents of the Urumchi tael. Here also the Urumchi tael is accepted, although the Ili tael is of no worth in Urumchi. The third of the important currencies is that of Kashgar, with both silver and paper taels. Each region has its own fashion in small money, which in part follows the market, but can also be altered by decree, as when at one time the Governor in Urumchi ordered that copper coins be no longer legal tender in the provincial capital.

On the South Road the Urumchi tael leapfrogs the Turfan tael and continues current as far as Aqsu, where it yields to the Kashgar tael. There is a fixed nominal standard for each kind of paper tael, so that within the province their ratio to each other does not change; or rather, in default of banks, there is no public quotation of exchange rates, which must be settled by individual negotiation. The Kashgar tael alone is backed by silver, a few silver tael-coins and many half-tael coins being in concurrent circulation. The paper quarter-tael, which everywhere else in the province is referred to as a *kou-wa-tze,* or " puppy," is in the Kashgar region respectfully referred to as a real kind of money. The Kashgar tael is worth, with little fluctuation, three Urumchi taels. It should therefore be worth $1.20 in Chinese silver; but in point of fact, although a few silver dollars reach Ku Ch'eng-tze, they remain an extra-provincial currency. As official policy maintains the difficulty of money transactions between the province and China proper, an anomalous exchange prevails. When we were in Urumchi, 2½ Urumchi taels would readily buy whatever silver dollars were available, that being the par rate. At the par of three Urumchi taels for one Kashgar tael, it should, therefore, have been possible to buy silver dollars at the rate of one for 83⅓ Kashgar tael cents. Actually, owing to the distance and lack of facilities, it took about 96 Kashgar tael cents to buy a silver dollar. If the transaction were worked the other way, the same difficulties would make the silver dollar worth only 75 Kashgar tael cents. Thus the official financial policy succeeded in maintaining stable financial conditions within the province, while hampering extra-provincial transactions.

Chinese Turkestan has always been old-fashioned. The " tael " is nominally an ounce of silver. In practice, both the standard of weight and the standard of fineness have varied according to place and time, throughout China. When, in the last century, coined silver dollars began to displace lump silver dispensed by weight, it must have appeared to the Chinese that the calculations involved would upset their alien subjects in Turkestan. At any rate, they introduced a tael coinage; the only tael coinage ever used in the Chinese dominions. The old Governor seized control of the province in 1911, at the time of the Chinese Revolution, and held on to it until his assassination in 1928. He saw what a powerful lever of control he could keep by maintaining within the province not merely one but several currencies, different from each other and from both the tael and dollar values of China. In the first place, it made it virtually impossible for a man to amass wealth in Chinese Turkestan and return with it to China. The only profitable way to use wealth acquired in the province was to reinvest it in the province. In the second place, the different regional values afforded a check on the movement of money within the province. Money could not be used within the province to finance a political coalition against the Governor-General because, owing to the lack of banks, any considerable exchange transaction must be detected, owing to its effect on the local market. In the same way an official who had made a great deal of money during his tenure of office could not quietly take it away with him to his next post; nor could he deposit it in a bank. The result, in practice, was that it was of no use for officials to amass great sums in cash through oppressive taxation, as happens so frequently in China. They therefore turned the money-making power of their official positions into trading activities, working usually through agents, their wealth thus being put, in some measure at least, to public use, instead of being drained out of the province.

The subsidiary coin of the Kashgar system is as beautifully confused as might be expected. In the first place there are pierced copper cash, with a value of four hundred to the tael. Then there are copper coins, not pierced, at the value of forty to the tael, or one for ten pierced cash. These coins are roughly equivalent in weight to the double-copper of the coast, where at least 330 single coppers, or 165 double-coppers, are required to buy a silver dollar. The value of the coastal copper increases as it travels away from the mints which flood the market in the coastal provinces, until for instance in the remote Chen-fan district of Kan-su, lying away from main trade routes, forty or fifty will purchase a dollar. It was, as I understood, an attempt on the part of caravan traders to manipulate the money market by loading up their camels with copper coin that caused the old Governor in Urumchi to refuse temporarily to accept copper coins as legal tender.

Our local difficulties were increased by the existence of a very badly pitted Aqsu-minted copper, which could not be used away from Aqsu, and by double double-coppers which were wanted in some cities but not in others. Moreover we had to cope with the *tenga,* which we found to be a value but not a coin. It represents, I believe, an old Turki monetary value; and the fact that it is reckoned as sixteen tenga to the tael indicates that it must have been adapted once to the subdivision of the " ounce " of silver, which nominally constitutes the value of one tael. We found that prices were constantly quoted in tenga but had to be paid in coin of other denominations, which made it necessary to juggle a decimal currency, with minor values in terms of 400 and of 40, into sums divided or multiplied by sixteen. We had also to bear in mind that this kind of tenga was different from the *aq-tenga,* or " white tenga," that being the popular Turki name for the silver half-tael, worth eight of the " fictitious " tenga.

When we reckoned our ready cash at Aqsu it came to about ninety Kashgar taels; that is to say, a little more than ninety Chinese silver dollars, or about $45 gold; or, at the rate of about eight and a half tenga then prevailing at Kashgar, about 170 rupees. We had cut our calculations very fine, in order to avoid loss on exchange on the various transactions between Urumchi and Kashgar, and should draw our next remittance at Kashgar. No paper being available (for the only time of our experience in the province), our Chinese friends raided the market very quietly, in order not to disturb its sleep, and presented us with a small parcel of aq-tenga (the silver half-taels), to the amount of fifty taels, and another forty taels' worth made up in strings of pierced cash and in unpierced coppers counted off in rolls and wrapped in paper. These we deposited in a sack. That sack weighed at least sixty pounds. We put Moses in charge of it, told him to look after all disbursements on the journey of more than two weeks to Kashgar, and hoped he would enjoy himself. He did. For once in his life he was able to shove his hand into a sack of money and pull out a fistful, without count-

MRS. LATTIMORE'S CART ON THE SOUTH ROAD   MARKET DAY AT FAIZABAD, NEAR KASHGAR

ing it. "Here," he would say, showering a fistful on some low-bowing and suitably flabbergasted Turki, "we give you this. Our master does not wish to be bothered with the account."

As it was far too hot to ride, we had our riding ponies led by the escorts and traveled in our cart, making night marches and lying up during the day. We found that during the day, even in darkened *serai* rooms with thick mud or adobe walls, we frequently had temperatures of 100° F.

The cart was of the kind called an *araba*, bigger, wider, and on much higher wheels than the Chinese "great cart." It had two huge wheels and was drawn by three ponies, one in the shafts and two in traces. As in the Chinese style of carting, the carter had no reins whatever, but sat at the front and controlled the team superbly by whip and voice; the whip being used much more for making a noise than for lashing the ponies. On the bottom of the springless cart we put our boxes; over these we spread felts, and on the felts our bed-rolls. Then we fitted on the top borrowed from the kindly postmaster. It was like the walls and roof of a house, with a "porch" looking out over the rump of the shaft-pony, double doors at the front, and a window at the back, all screened with mosquito netting. The one box which held cooking gear and everything for immediate use was lashed on a projecting rack behind, and inside we had ample room for the two of us, together with our water bottles and books; besides which we fixed a well in one corner, so that one of us could always sit European fashion, with legs hanging down.

Thus equipped with a cross between an English "caravan" and a Central Asian caravan, we lurched and jolted, high up in our hut on the araba, from Aqsu through Maralbashi and Faizabad to Kashgar. Because we traveled at night, we saw almost nothing of the country, and because it was too hot during the day we saw little more of the villages and towns where we stayed. The tiny, mud-built rooms in which we lodged were the coolest places to be found, but the fleas raged furiously together and the thermometer surged ominously up to 100°, where it stayed until late in the afternoon. If we had stayed in the cart for the whole march, instead of riding ahead, then the order of arrival would have begun with the

clamor of wheeling the great cart into the serai yard, the carter and
escorts shouting for the inn folk to turn out.   Each inn has usually
a " state " room, for the accommodation of Chinese officials on
their travels, and sometimes there is a whole *kuan tien,* or official
inn; but we found that usually the smaller rooms were easier to
keep clean and cool.   Out of regard to Chinese convention, the
state apartments always faced south, so that they were as hot as
possible.   Moses would find the best room he could, sprinkle water
on the mud sleeping platform to lay the dust, then sweep it and
spread out our own felts.   We would move in, to sleep and read
and write and swelter until the shadows were long and the air
faintly cooler and the mosquitoes assembled for their war-dance.
If the mosquitoes, flies, and fleas were too pestiferous during the
day, we hung from the rafters a sort of tent we had made of mosquito netting, under which we would cower, hotter than ever.   Then,
in the evening, we would bundle and go, the vast cart wallowing out
of the serai, the ponies tossing their heads and jangling their bells,
the driver cracking his whip and shouting *" Oa-oa-oa-oa, O ! "* as
though the cholera were in him.

We had our diversions.   As usual, I yarned for hours with our
escorts, learning everything I could about what they knew or
thought they knew, from the digging of dykes, the hunting of wild
pigs, and the nature of God, to technical discussions of horses'
teeth, and the allowances to be made in judging the age of a range-
bred horse from his teeth, as compared with the teeth of a stall-fed
horse.   Here, as elsewhere from Kuei-hua to the extreme West, I
found that *ya-fen* (tooth powder) stood in sovereign repute as the
remedy for sore-backed ponies.   The most commonly used is a
Japanese brand which is brought by caravan all the way through
Mongolia.   It is never called anything but tooth powder, and
rarely used for anything but saddle sores; a perfectly good idea,
as far as that goes, for it dries up the sore and helps in forming
a scab, and is at least mildly antiseptic.   Better than a poultice
of cow-dung, anyhow, which may indeed assist in drawing the
poison from a running sore, but keeps it too soft for quick healing.
Other quaint things happened to us, partly from a mistaken
notion among simple Turki folk that we were Great People.   I was

more than once addressed as *k'uang sui'rh* (a Chinese version, in the local patois, of " consul," used also by the Turki), and demands were made upon my grace accordingly. Most of the Turki people knew white men only as " sahib," or " Inglis " (Englishman), or " Oross " (Russian) ; that any such person should speak Chinese appeared to them fabulous, and they hastened to ask my intercession for all kinds of things with the Chinese authorities. Thus we found that, over a few stages where the water was notoriously bad, water was being sent ahead for us at every stage, carried in huge hollow gourds by the postal couriers. At first we thought this must be an extra courtesy, ordered as a pleasant surprise for us by the postmaster at Aqsu. It very probably was, but we soon found that the postal couriers claimed the merit for themselves, and hoped that I would present on their behalf, to the postmaster at Kashgar, a general petition for an increase in wages for the whole corps of couriers! Then, again, we fell in with a company of wandering Chinese players; all of them Tientsin people ; or at least, those who were not from Tientsin had acquired a Tientsin way of talking, because that was where the money lay. Their trouping from one isolated community of Chinese to another, among the uncomprehending Turki, brought back memories of the Treaty Ports of China, where all the foreign residents turn out in their best boiled shirts and five-year-old evening gowns to welcome a touring stock company.

One grief abode with me — the necessity of beginning to reduce to order my notes and diaries. Wearing nothing but shorts, and running with sweat, I would squat cross-legged by a shaft of light from a badly fitting door and hammer at the typewriter which had survived in triumph its journey by camel caravan and pack train. The sweat ran so fast down my face and along the stem of an ordinary pipe that it would drip on to the typewriter, so that I resorted to a contrivance which commanded a good deal of respect whenever it was displayed. It was a briar bowl, mounted on a square base, so that it could be set several feet away and smoked at long range through a flexible tube.

But that daily recension of this and that about mountains past and deserts left behind, recalling people met and things seen, re-

membering the feel of a well-loved pony going willingly on a long
new road, or the record of crossing another pass and entering
what Moses would announce to be "another empty place," did
much to bring into those stages the seeming of a dejected retreat
from lands where legends endured and time was stayed, back to
regions where the horn of the smug man is exalted and the vagabond is tied by the foot.

Once and again — usually dressed in pyjamas — we would ride
our ponies through the dusk or the moonlight, when the edges of
the world raveled into distance, at once near and without end,
thinking how wonderful it would be to be riding in the other direction.   From Maralbashi to Kashgar we had with us an escort
who, though a Chinese, knew a power of Turki ballads, being
country-bred.   He had a fine trolling voice, and would sing magnificently, the other men joining in or chanting the burden canor-
ously, all out in the moonlight flooding the bare desert or scattering tangled shadows among obscure jungle thickets of toghraq and
tamarisk.   Then, sometime between midnight and dawn, we would
ride into a sleep-stricken village, where only a few vague figures
lingered about the brooding red of a fire in the yard of a serai, and
a Turki in flapping white gown would make a bustle to welcome
the *sahib* and the *mem-sahib,* and we would curl up in some corner
to sleep until the cart should overhaul us.   "Sahib" and "mem-
sahib"!   We had entered a new orbit, for sure — where men shave
every day, people have semi-detached bath tents (as if a tent were
a villa and Central Asia a suburb), and the most fearsome circumstances are taken as a challenge to dress for dinner.

It was almost more disturbing, when the cart heaved and bumped,
staggered and jolted, too much for sleep, to sit out in front and
yarn with Moses.   The two of us up there swayed as we talked,
and the carter swayed as he slept, and my wife inside wondered if
this time we had got clear of the serai without an expedition of fleas
to explore our geography and carry back a report to fleadom em-
bellished with a map on which "the red line shows the routes followed by the expedition."   Moses reviewed our travels with no
orientation but the places where Tientsin men were or were not
to be found.   As he talked of men and marches, though, half con-

sciously he tricked out his memories with words and phrases of the camel men of our caravan days in Mongolia, and the winged words carried with them the pungency of camel-dung smoke and the aromatic savor of the smoke of tamarisk. I remembered in procession how we dodged through broken soldiery at the setting out from Kuei-hua; the last sight of my wife in the fields and the last sight of the evening smoke of the gray city, as we turned into the pass that led to Mongolia; the high grassland plateau of Inner Mongolia; the Tiger Mountains; the sands of Alashan; the red and gold of toghraq trees by the Edsin Gol in autumn; the long, pounding marches of the Four Drys Together and the Three Drys Together in the crossing of the Black Gobi. I remembered the dragging rhythm of those twelve-hour marches; the uneasiness of the men in our camp near the House of the False Lama, when they thought the ghost of the False Bogdo Khan might be on the prowl; the feeling of uncertainty in the land of the Three Don't Cares, after we had heard of the raiding of a whole caravan within a march or two of where we were; the night when our camels, belly-deep and foundered in the snow, froze from sunset to dawn in Dead Mongol Pass; captivity and uncertainty at the Oasis of the Third Stage. Then came the last struggle through the snow, with worn-out camels, when the food was nearly gone and we had no guide and could not see the road; and the day of falling snow when my camel man wept and wanted to turn back. Then came the day when, having fallen in with an unladen caravan, I, with a friendly trader, rode ahead and saw Ku Ch'eng-tze in the snow.

After that came the ten-day ride to Chuguchak, muffled in ibex-skins, on the hard snow roads of Zungaria; and the uncertain days of waiting while I wondered if my wife would ever get through the snows barring the way to that gate of the province; and at last, when she had brought off a journey that seemed incredible, the progress, now lordly and now comical, in the saddle and by cart, about and across the province, meeting rogues and vagabonds, tatterdemalion soldiers, gracious officials, open-handed merchants, Chinese, Turki, Mongol, Qazaq, and Qirghiz. I wondered if I had dealt honestly by them all. At least I had gone as much as was humanly possible by the custom of the country. As for my own customs, at least I had never called a Chinese a Chinaman or a Celestial; nor, as far as that goes, a camel a ship of the desert, nor a horse a steed. Nor had I written out in detail the menu of a Chinese dinner. Nor had I, in print, got nearer to Nature. Never, in striking camp, had I folded my tent like an Arab. I had not gone behind the back of Mongol or Qazaq to call him a child of Nature, nor insulted the sanctity of any temple by speaking of idols. And I had left poor old Marco Polo and his much misrepresented Trail alone, as much as I decently could. In fact, had I only been a cartographer, I should have drawn a large, unmistakable map to show exactly where the footsteps of Marco Polo never were.

But I had one shock. I read in *Unknown Mongolia* that one of Mr. Carruthers's companions thought lightly of the Tekes country, by reason of the jam tins left there in no small number by big-game-hunting worthies. In truth, all the way over the Muzart and on we had been coming into country more and more thoroughly traveled and " written up." We began to hear not only of recent travelers but of travelers expected. Most people at Kashgar are seeing their future in front of them and leaving their mail behind them. We were reading from the other end of the book. And so, when we left the cart one morning in the dawn, dressed this time not in pyjamas but in such respectable manner as we could accomplish in the belly of a moving cart, and rode along a wide tree-bordered thoroughfare, entered Kashgar through one engulfing gate, clattered deviously along empty streets, waking alleys and market-places in which the shutters of booths were just being taken down, out through another gate, and rode on until, at the end of a lane, we saw the solid portals of the British Consulate-General, with Lion and Unicorn all according to specification, we felt a queasy, sinking feeling, as if we had finished with travel and come to the Place Where the Books Begin.

Not that I mean to decry Kashgar. It is a noble city, and if I might approach it again, from the direction of the Pamirs or Russian Central Asia, I should go with a high heart. Our only sadness was that the presence of Consuls-General, both Russian and British, not to mention a Swedish Mission, made it for us an outpost of the known and the familiar.

Major Gillan, the British Consul-General, was away with his wife in the hills for the hottest weeks of the summer, but they had left hospitable orders for our reception, and until their return we took our ease in surroundings of more-than-Oriental luxury, among terraced gardens where rills of brown water ran by beds of bright flowers and the roots of heavy-laden fruit trees. We were delightfully entertained by Mr. George Chu, Chinese Secretary to the Consulate-General, who took me to pay my preliminary calls on the Chinese officials, and rode with us to mosques and shrines and the show places of the city. He was a shining example of the modern generation of adventurous Chinese. During the war he had gone to France as an interpreter officer of the Chinese Labor Corps, and afterward had come to Kashgar, over the Karakoram route, in the British service. Not only was Mr. Chu justly proud of his English and French, but since coming among the Turkis he had thrown himself whole-heartedly into the study of their religion and their ways. He had embraced Islam, married a Turki wife, and spoke Turki fluently. As a final cosmopolitan touch, he spent a great part of the day, during the hot weather, dressed in a Japanese kimono. We could not have had a more sympathetic and entertaining guide. We rallied each other on our knowledge of each other's language, and he had a great deal of fun in introducing me to his friends as "a fellow townsman of mine from Peking" — in spite of the fact that the Peking veneer must have been pretty well worn off my speech, which had by then reverted to its original Tientsin accent, garnished with weird acquisitions from Kuei-hua caravan men, Kan-su Mohammedans, Turkestan carters, and the soldiery of the back blocks.

Mr. Chu's prize jest was when he introduced me to a handsome young man in robes as chastely elegant as any to be seen in Kashgar, turbaned like a man of dignity and trimly bearded like a young Turki of fashion. "And now," he said, "what do you think? Here we are, the three of us, three *Ching yu-tze* together"; using a slang phrase which means "oily Peking men," or "slick fellows from the Capital." In fact, the young Turki spoke the purest mandarin of Peking — as well he might, for he was Peking born and Peking bred, and had not come to Kashgar until he was a man grown. His story entranced me, for it was the strangest thing I heard in Kashgar.

Much has been written of the shrine of Hazrat Apak, the richest and most splendid shrine and place of pilgrimage in the neighborhood of Kashgar, and a good deal of the little mosque and precinct of Islam at a corner of the Forbidden City in Peking, where was housed a lady of Central Asia who was taken into the household of the magnificent Emperor Ch'ien Lung; but until then I had never known of the connection between the two.

According to Marshall Broomhall,[1] the Moslem lady was brought to Peking after the final campaign in which the armies of the Emperor Ch'ien Lung, under the command of his general Tsao Hui, had overthrown the Zungars. The campaign resulted in the subjection of the Mohammedan petty states south of the T'ien Shan, as well as the Western Mongols north of the T'ien Shan. The Chinese had been assisted by two Turki Moslems, named Aschek and Khodjis. Broomhall further says that " in reward for their services they were both honored by the Chinese Emperor, Aschek receiving the title of Duke and Khodjis that of Prince. Palaces were built for them in Peking, where they both settled down. . . . The Chinese General Tsao Hui . . . triumphantly returned to Peking bringing in his train a number of Moslem prisoners of war. Among them was a young Kashgarian woman whom the Emperor adopted as a concubine. It is stated that for love of this concubine the Emperor, after having built barracks for the Turkish captives, built the mosque on which the tablet with an inscription in four languages was erected. The Chinese text was written by the Emperor himself and bears his own seal.

" Facing the mosque, but within the Imperial palace grounds, the Emperor erected a pavilion for his Kashgarian concubine's use, which pavilion was called the *Wang-chia-lou,* ' Tower for gazing on one's home.' This pavilion, which can be seen by anyone passing down the Ch'ang An [Eternal Peace] Street in Peking to-day, as well as the Mohammedan camp, still remains. Each male of the girl's escort received a pension. . . . The Mosque was built at government expense in 1764 A.D., and the monument, to commemorate this act, was erected at the same time. The four inscrip-

[1] *Islam in China.* London, Morgan and Scott, 1910.

tions in Chinese, Turkish, Mongol, and Manchu are all on one monument. . . .

"The Emperor, who was a great scribe and wrote more than 30,000 pieces of verse during his reign, has closed his inscription by a few lines of verse . . . setting forth some of the facts concerning Islam as known to himself. Though a great soldier and a great *littérateur*, Ch'ien Lung did not escape some serious errors." His most serious error was a confusion between the followers of Mani and the followers of Mohammed; he did the Moslems one good turn, however, in forbidding the slighting practice of combining the character for " dog " with the Chinese character for their name.

The inscription on the monument mentions the conquest of Zungaria and the cities of Turkestan, gives the names of Aschek and Khodjis, and tells of the settlement of the captives in Peking. It also summarizes the Emperor's view of the historical relation between Chinese and Western Mohammedans. It concludes in a most charming manner : —

"Accordingly among our amusements we have reserved a place for your wire dancers,[1] and those who wear the turban have had their place among the Imperial guests. Who will say otherwise. That is why we write this record, to which we add this inscription :

> " What is the Kaaba?
> What is the Heavenly Hall?
> It is the mysterious Shrine
> Of the Moslems near my Palace Gate.
> The city is Mecca,
> Their ancestor is Mohammed.
> He gave them the Quran
> And handed down justice.
> These volumes of classics
> Are entrusted to the Ahungs.[2]
> Bowing west or bowing north [3]

---

[1] There is a photograph of such wire dancers in *East of the Sun and West of the Moon* by Theodore and Kermit Roosevelt. New York and London, 1927.

[2] This word (in Turki, *akhun*, used in a manner much equivalent to " Mr.") is the only Turki word that has penetrated as far as Peking, as far as I know; it is there used for " mullah."

[3] "The Emperor always sits facing south, consequently all Chinese officials bow north. The Moslems in China bow to the west toward Mecca. The Emperor classes both acts together, and thus makes himself equal to Mohammed." (Broomhall's note, *loc. cit.*)

Alike show one respect.
These steps of marble and beams of wood
Are the work of officials of the Public Works.
As stars move round the pole,
So all nations follow us." [1]

Now as for Hazrat Apak, at Kashgar, it is the shrine of Hidaya-tulla Khoja, the most famous of the priest-kings, or Khojas. The Khoja line at Kashgar was founded in the seventeenth century by invaders from Samarqand, and at about the same time related families also established ruling houses, at others of the cities along the Great South Road, on the prodigious semicircle of the silk trade route, from Hami (Qomul) to Khotan. The power of the Khoja families was broken at the time of the Manchu-Chinese conquest in the eighteenth century, and the main branch of them then retired from Kashgar to Andijan, west of the farthest Chinese dominions. With the outbreak of the Mohammedan risings of the sixties of the last century, a number of them returned to Chinese Turkestan, endeavoring to reëstablish themselves. In fact Yakub Beg, who ended by asserting his personal rule in Kashgar and an overlordship over a great part of the province, entered it originally as a soldier of fortune in the following of one of the Khojas. He displaced his master, exiled some of the family, and reduced others to subordinate positions under him. [2] After the defeat and death of Yakub Beg and the final reconquest of the whole province by the Chinese, only two rulers of the Khoja blood were left, both of them far to the east and well overawed by the proximity of the Chinese, the Princes of Hami and Lukchun. The last of the related ruling house of Kucha took a lead in the revolt against the Chinese in the sixties, but was then overthrown himself by Yakub Beg; the family lands were taken over by the Chinese after the reconquest, but the dispossessed descendants of the last Prince have since been allowed military and civil posts under the Chinese. [3]

The story of my " fellow townsman from Peking " was like a

[1] Broomhall, *loc. cit.*
[2] Shaw, *Visits to High Tartary, Yarkand and Kashghar.*
[3] Skrine, *Chinese Central Asia.*

thread connecting all these events. To hark back to Broomhall's account of the victories of Ch'ien Lung, it appears that his "Khodjis" must have been one of the Khoja family, and was probably not so much an ally of the Manchus and Chinese as a hostage taken to ensure the good behavior of the people of Kashgar. The lady also appears to have been more than "a young Kashgarian woman"; in fact, herself a daughter of the princely family. This is the more likely, as she would be so much the better qualified for the Imperial household; besides which the honor would tend to placate the Kashgaris. At any rate, my new acquaintance was descended from the very community of Kashgaris whose settlement at Peking is recorded in Ch'ien Lung's monument, and evidently he claimed also to be a member of the Khoja family. The Mohammedan Princess of the Tower Looking Toward Home never forgot Kashgar, and it seems that those of her relatives who had not gone into exile followed her to Peking, either as hostages or to live on the Imperial favor. At any rate the family sanctuary of Hazrat Apak was left in the charge of caretakers. It was not, however, relinquished by the family. In the shrine itself they preserve a sort of palanquin in which, they say, the body of the Princess, after her death, was borne back to Kashgar. I did hear part of another story, of which unfortunately I could not get the rights, to the effect that while the funeral party halted at Turfan on the way home the body was filched. It seems that some prince of the Khoja family then ruled still at Turfan, as a feudatory of the Manchu Emperor. I should think it not at all unlikely that the Turfan prince was trying to claim next-of-kin to the dead princess, in order to get a better standing in his relations with the Imperial court. However that may be, the palanquin at Hazrat Apak does not very convincingly look its age.

This princely body-snatching does not seem to have led to trouble, probably because the members of the family at Peking were content with their position and Imperial pension there. It may even be that the body never reached either Turfan or Kashgar, but that the lady was buried in Peking, while a mourning party was sent to Turkestan as a matter of ceremonial, with a funeral "chair of state." At any rate, after the death of the poor Princess of the

Tower, her kin at Peking began to forget Kashgar, having little need even of the revenues of their family sanctuary. After the lapse of generations they forgot their Turki language and became like the Manchus among whom they lived; and, together with the Manchus, more like Chinese than anything else. My " fellow townsman " had never worried about his Turki origin, but had lived like a Peking aristocrat until the crash of the Manchu dynasty at the Chinese Revolution. In his youth, at Peking, his Turki blood was probably hard to recognize, though he might have been distinguished as a Mohammedan by his beard, which though slight for a Kashgari was heavy for a Chinese or Manchu; the kind of beard that is found occasionally among Chinese Moslems, by virtue of their infusion of alien blood from Western Central Asia.

After the Revolution these descendants of Mussulman princes became distressed, their Imperial pension being cut off. Then they remembered Kashgar in earnest. The shrine of Hazrat Apak, associated with their most celebrated forbear, had a notable revenue collected from pilgrims, and from the sale or lease of burial sites near the sanctuary. They must reassert their proprietary rights. Unfortunately for them, however, the descendants of the caretakers whom they had put in charge were now well established as proprietors; they denied any duty toward the heirs of the masters of their ancestors, and being in possession, and at Kashgar, they had the ear of the local officials. My friend, accordingly, had set out from Peking to canvass in person his rights at Kashgar. There he had lived ever since, a matter of some fifteen years, conducting a truly Central Asian lawsuit. I shrewdly suspect that the local courts allowed him enough of his claims to give him an income and so keep the case alive; the actual possessors of the shrine being too important and well established to be rudely dislodged, to the peril of local religious and political equilibrium, but quite rich enough to be freely bled in the way of bribes and fees. The comedy was therefore set for an indefinite run. Every time that a new official was appointed it had to be reopened, and it looked as though my friend would live to a great age, a mellow Kashgar age, and die highly venerated, but unvindicated.

XXXI

THE WAY OF THE FIVE GREAT PASSES

Two chief roads lead from Kashgar to India. The first goes by Yarkand, to start for the great passes of the Karakoram, whence it passes through Ladakh into Kashmir. The second goes by the tiny states of Hunza and Nagar into Gilgit, and so down to Kashmir. The first of these is the only true trade route; on the other, supplies are inadequate for regular caravans, but because it is the quicker by a good many days it is used a good deal by the British consular officers going to Kashgar or returning to India. The consular mails are also carried that way, and occasionally, when enough transport can be spared from official uses, big-game shooters get permission to use the route on their way to the Pamirs. Other ways of crossing the multiple mountain barriers can be found, but they are not routes, much less roads. Some of them were used in old days by small raiding parties, others have been used by explorers and topographers; but none of them could be developed into regular trade routes, because of the lack of transport and supply stations. Over and above these, of course, are routes that lead from the Pamirs into Afghan territory, or from Kashgar over the T'ien Shan into Russian territory; but these are not convenient routes to India.

It is not even a simple thing for a traveler to scramble over the Karakoram route into British territory, for special permits must be secured. It had not been possible for us to apply for permits in advance, because in the vague order of our travels we did not know exactly when we should be able to start for the high passes. Fortunately, I had been able to write from Urumchi to the Consul-General at Kashgar. Still more fortunately, we benefited by the tradition of British officials in far places. It verily appears that British

officials on the rim of nowhere take pride in helping out stray
people who have no claim on them whatever ; and the farther over
the rim they are, the more pains they take. Major Gillan not only
secured permits from the Government of India for us to enter
British territory by the Karakoram route, but sent orders in advance to prepare for our reception, and to assist us in getting reliable transport.

In most of the southern oases of Chinese Turkestan are little
groups of British subjects from India.   Their usual trade is money-
lending, the profits of which are partly invested in goods to be
sent to India.   The headman of each group is appointed agent for
the British Consul-General, and is known as *Aqsaqal,* a Turki term
meaning " white-beard," or " elder."   The money-lenders are both
usurious and litigious, with the result that a great deal of the
Consul-General's time is spent on tour among them, holding consular courts to keep their affairs in order and adjust their troubles
with the Chinese authorities.   For reasons of prestige, the Aqsaqals
take pride in the reception they give to all " sahib " travelers.   Their
only fault is that they like to take a commission on all business they
manage, which was disconcerting to us after we had been dealing
so long with Chinese officials who took pride in seeing that we not
only were not exploited, but were given the best available transport
at the lowest possible rates.   As a matter of fact, we should have
been less embarrassed had we known that Aqsaqals did not expect
to be treated like Chinese officials, but to receive orders, and not
only orders, but tips.   At first, overawed by their patriarchal manners and stately robes, we blushed at the idea of base financial
patronage.   Not a bit of it.   Making money was their business.
If we did not give them orders, — offhand, but at the same time
precise and firm, — and dispense condescending gratuities, we were
no true sahibs.   It was no wonder that, thinking it their privilege
to receive crumbs from the great and lordly, they could see no alternative but the extraction of " squeeze " from the ignorant and
foolish.

Once we had grasped that our " greatness " was now understood
in new terms, we got on much better.   The Aqsaqal, in truth, is a
blessing to the traveler, for he is under official supervision and he

can and does prevent transport men from forming rings to exploit foreigners. After we had been made free of the Consulate while we repacked our gear for the high passes, we said our farewells to Major and Mrs. Gillan, the engaging Mr. Chu, the Swedish missionaries, and the Chinese officials who had cordially entertained us and put our final documents in order, and set out for Yarkand in carts.

Five days brought us to Yarkand, where, being borne for a while on the full tide of tradition, we lodged in a summerhouse in a noble garden belonging to the British Aqsaqal. The Chinese are far less numerous in Yarkand than in Kashgar, and when the news went abroad that we spoke Chinese we could not pass through the streets without smiling invitations to stop and drink tea at the few Chinese shops, while respectful Turki crowds choked the roadway to watch us.

From Yarkand we went on by cart to Posgam and Qarghaliq, and then rode over long wastes of desert to Sanju Bazar, our transport once more, and for the last time, being carried on camels. The pack ponies we had hired at Yarkand awaited us here, in charge of four Ladakhis. We paid for the hire of nine ponies, including riding ponies for ourselves and Moses (having sold our own at Kashgar) ; but the caravan numbered fourteen altogether, five of them being brought along by the caravan men themselves, to carry food and forage, and at times even fuel, over the highest and most barren stages.

At Sanju Bazar we camped in an orchard of apricot, plum, and walnut trees, and took our farewell of the true Turkestan of desert and oasis. The harvest was over (it was the end of August, 1927), and donkeys and cows were trampling out the grain on mud threshing floors, in harvest-colored golden fields, near the heavy green of poplars and willows. Water carried in runnels from the Sanju River made all the fertility; where water could not be brought, the oasis ended abruptly in sandy, utterly barren hills.

After several days of sorting, mending, and chattering, the ritual prelude to our kind of travel, the end came abruptly, as it always does. We left in sorrow, with a dust storm railing at us and harrying us into the unknown. The ponies tumbled into a ravine and paddled across the waste end of an irrigation runnel, clambered up the other side, and, behold, we were in a desert of dry loess, the oasis behind us obliterated in a whirl of rufous dust.   The Turki Beg of Sanju, sometime a tailor (the Turki has a knack of going up and down in life), who had got down on his gorgeous hambones to mend our tent the day before, dismissed himself at the edge of a forlorn loess terrace.   We were in the hands thenceforth of our four Ladakhis.   On the accusation of their pigtails Moses would call them nothing but Mongols, or Tatars, but they were in fact Tibetans by race and language, although a kind of secondhand British subjects, Ladakh being geographically a western extension of the plateau of Tibet, but politically a fief of the Maharajah of Kashmir, which is an independent native state of India, under British protection.   We could speak with them only in the mutilated Turki which they had picked up in the caravan trade and we in High Tartary and along the low-lying oasis roads.   Our caravan leader, known on the routes of the high passes as a *kirakash,* was called Tashi Serengh.   He had several top teeth missing in front, and tootled plaintive, short, melodious airs on a doublebarreled flute of polished old brown wood.   All four men had the beautiful, lithe, mountain-bred walk; they grinned and laughed and tumbled over themselves to help us, and were the most willing, stout-hearted, and handy men we had throughout our travels.

The first march, conforming to ancient usage, was not long. In about six hours, having passed several parties of Turki hunters, hairy men who had gone up into the mountains with their wives and a little bedding and come back with spoil of ibex, we reached a tiny farm under tall old poplars, where we pitched our tent in front of an offering of sour milk in wooden bowls.

We had five " great " passes to cross on the way through the K'un Lun mountains and the even higher Karakoram plateaurange that lay between us and Ladakh; and between Ladakh and Kashmir lay the inner range of the Himalayas, the guarding wall of India itself.   The " great " passes are those over 16,000 feet above sea-level.   The first pass we crossed, the Chuchu Dawan, does not rank among the great; but the final ascent of it, at an altitude of about 14,000 feet, is a stiff pull.   The Chuchu is a mud pass; mud elevated to the monumental. Though we climbed and climbed, we never got above rubbly conglomerate and sandstone, clothed in great folds of loess. On the far side we went down through rocky defiles, where the ponies looked like clowns walking on their hands, and then down and down again, by lap after lap of winding path laid along the flanks of loess hills. All about us were the naked, riven hills of the K'un Lun, in which at last we struck the Sanju River — the same that flowed down to Sanju Bazar, distant about twenty-five or thirty miles. We had come three days' march instead of one, because the height of water in the gorges barred the direct way.

From camp at a ruined fortress, called Tam Qaraul, we struck for the headwaters of the Sanju. As we got above tributary after tributary the fordings were easier, until instead of having the water swirling at our saddle flaps we had it below our stirrups; then we climbed up over old moraines into an amphitheatre of snow-mantled hills, and a *yailaq*, or high summer pasture, of the Qirghiz. These were true Qirghiz, like those of the Pamirs and the related tribes of Issiq Köl, living in a small encampment and hiring out yaks for the crossing of the Sanju pass. Their yurts were pitched near dug-out storerooms, which may also be used for shelter in the coldest weather. Beside a yurt a girl was weaving one of the woolen bands which are carried in swathes across the inside walls of the yurt, stretching the felts in place. The loom was made sketchily of sticks, braced with ropes of twisted wool; but we could not watch the weaving of the colored design because the girl, who had on a high, mumpy headgear, like a goitred mitre, fled squealing at the sight of us.

The next morning the bulk of our loads was transferred to yaks, leaving the ponies with light packs only. We made a straggling start, for several of the yaks were unruly, bolting uphill as if the altitude were nothing. We headed into a bay of the vast, steep-sided hills, from which there appeared to be no exit whatever; but the men, pointing at the ragged line of rock against the sky, said, "There is the pass." They "attacked" it in superb style. We went up in a thin sunshine, breaking through thin clouds, with once or twice a thin flurry of snow whirling down past us. The men were in high feather. Tashi Serengh, the leader, brought out his flute and played as he went up the long, grueling climb, and every once in a while someone would throw back his head and howl a taunt or challenge at the gray, unanswering, echoless crags. *"Shaba-a-a-ah!"* they would yell — which I suppose was the *shabash,* "hurrah," of India. Then Tashi Serengh would shout at the pass in his broken Turki: *"Yakken boldi keldimur, O Sanju Dawan!"* — "Soon and well we are coming, O Sanju Pass!"

We took hours going up. The ponies were weak with the altitude, and I walked all the last part, to see what it was like, and got a splitting headache. In spite of the abrupt appearance of the mountain wall, we had a fairly good approach, the path tacking at the side of the grim slope; but the bones of dead pack animals underfoot, carcasses tumbled at the side of the way, and ravens wheeling on the watch for the next death, showed the Sanju to deserve its caravan reputation as the worst of the Five Great Passes. I felt as I have never felt except when "rowed out" at the end of a really trying race. My wife felt all right so long as she kept in the saddle, but had a bad headache from the reaction, after getting down from the extreme height. Our one relief was that Moses felt no trouble. We had been a little worried about him, after an evilly disposed Turki in Yarkand, coveting the job of cook for a friend, had warned us that fattish men of forty always blew up and died when it came to the high passes.

When we clambered sidelong into the crest of the pass, at an altitude of 16,500 feet, we found it no more than a nick a few feet wide in the ridge of shattered rock, too steep and wind-bedeviled for any snow to lie. There was not more than enough room for a loaded yak to lurch through without smashing his load against the rock. Under the shelter of the ridge we sat and bit at our lunch and watched the yaks come jolting down from slab to boulder with our precious boxes. A few yards below us they seemed to be swallowed in that savage, defiant wilderness of scree and rock. Then we slithered down over sliding scree for about a mile and a half, and far away below that passed through a rock gate into a larger valley, where the loads were put back on the ponies, and the Qirghiz, with their yaks, dismissed.

Yaks at the Crest of the Sanju Pass

The Sasser Pass: Tashi Mending Halter

It began to rain. We went on and on, crossing a slide of rock that had almost filled the valley, at a place called Kichik Karakoram, or Little Black Gravel. The last of our watches had now gone out of commission, so that we could only guess at the time, but we must have been a good twelve hours on the way when, at dusk, with the rain setting in more heavily, we slumped into camp; a wet camp, and a weary.

Between the Sanju and the Suget, the next of the Great Passes, we passed by Ali Nazar Qurgan — a *qurgan* being a fort, and Ali Nazar a master-robber who, in his day, took toll of the caravans. It is said that he came from the Khanate of Bokhara, and according to one account was sought out and destroyed by emissaries of the Emir of Bokhara. Another account lays his death to the Chinese, but both agree that treachery and a woman were the means to his destruction. Near the fallen walls of the fort is the Qirghiz burial place of Abu Bakr Mazar, a desolate place of cairns, with rags fluttering and yak tails hung on sticks. In the face of one of the hills are caves, which may have been used once by settlers, but were more probably dug out by gold-workers. Most remarkable of all, signs of old fields can be seen. I can answer to the impulse that sends a man scrambling into such a brutal and amazing wilderness to get a trading venture across by the strength of his hand and the readiness of his wits; but passing those abandoned fields I marveled blankly at what could lead a man, a comfortable farming man from the lazy oases, to squat on a fan of alluvium in a pocket of the great hills, just to raise barley by the half-handful for the struggling ponies of the caravans. A few such crops are grown still, at several points, strong pressure being brought to bear by the Chinese officials for the sake of the caravan trade; but if the coercion becomes unjust, the cultivators can easily decamp.

In this region we traveled for a while by the valley of the Qaraqash, the River of Black Jade, and found by it one of those men who are what the camel pullers of Mongolia call "more than mad." There is a certain place where a large mountain steps into the stream. Until recently the track ran round the foot of it, on a narrow ledge of rock hidden by eighteen inches of water; a bad place, where loads had to be manhandled and ponies were often lost. Then there came a Turki, and built himself a hut of rocks. He set his wife and two brats to herding goats, while he shoveled and grunted and put his shoulder to great stones; and behold, a kind of track, sidling round the mountain. We found the Turki sitting at one end of the track, collecting offerings. We had no money of any kind on our persons, so my wife called his wife and gave her a red ring that came from Peking.

Early the next morning we forded the Kilian River before the water had risen. In the K'un Lun, as in the T'ien Shan, the rule of water is that when the sun gets high and melts the high snows and glaciers water surges down all the valleys. In the afternoon, evening, or night (it depends how near one is to the source) the surge goes past and the streams can be forded again. In the short fullness of summer the water reaches its high marks, and most of the routes cannot be used at all. Thus the Kilian River, flowing down the Kilian pass, prevents all travel until September. Had we been able to use that approach to the main Karakoram route, we could have saved the long lateral traverse by the Chuchu and Sanju passes. The entrance to the pass is marked by the long-abandoned fort of Kilian Qurgan, the greater part of which is built up on top of one stupendous boulder isolated in a little flat field.

Beyond the fort we met a party of Qirghiz, who had with them a white pony, which there and then, after an urgent but brief exchange of loud lies, was exchanged for the black mare I had been riding. It was the quickest deal in horseflesh I have ever seen. The black mare was laboring in some sickness, brought on, I think, by the altitude, but our men switched her craftily under the belly so that she jumped briskly, and thereby they got the better of the bargain, seeing that no money passed. The white pony was old, but our men were jubilant. The pony, they said, came from somewhere on the Lhasa road, in Greater Tibet, and was bred to hard work at great heights. Moses rolled a knowing eye and said that the Qirghiz must have stolen the white pony, for which reason they were in haste to get rid of it.

We camped that day beyond the last scrap of lonely barley-field. "No more," said the men, grinning, "until we come to our country." The day after that, making our eighth march, we passed the opening of the Shahidullah valley, where are ruins of the old village of Shahidullah, famous at the time of Younghusband's explorations. British and Russians were then feinting across the Pamir boundaries, and the celebrated Russian " Hunting Detachment," so called because the officers engaged were supposed to be hunting big game, was prospecting for a potential route toward India. The Chinese sat back and worried about what might happen next. The trade route, at the same time, was being plagued by raiders from Hunza and Nagar; fantastic fellows, whose idea of a raid was a prodigious journey over crags. They harried the Qirghiz as well as the caravans, catching men to sell into slavery at Yarkand and in other oases of the plains. Nor was the raiding stopped until the Gilgit Expedition put the fear of the Raj into Hunza and Nagar.

While the troubles were on, the Qirghiz appealed to the Chinese for protection. The Chinese replied that the Qirghiz were beyond their boundaries and must look to themselves. Then Younghusband came by, and the Qirghiz appealed to him to take them under British rule. Younghusband could hardly annex them, but, being a Political Officer at the time, he detailed a few Kashmir levies to protect them for that year, and later got the Government of India to make them a grant, to build themselves a fort. It is quite clear that the Government of India had no idea of extending its frontiers beyond the Karakoram watershed, or any other motive than to protect trade along the caravan route. The Chinese, on their part, had not wanted Shahidullah until the building of the fort made them think the British did. Once the Kanjutis (the tribesmen of Hunza and Nagar) had been set to rights by the British, and there was no more danger, the Government of India paid no more attention to the Qirghiz; whereupon the Chinese imprisoned the Qirghiz headman who had taken British money, razed the fort, and built themselves another, higher up — the present Suget Qaraul.

We came to the post, or *qaraul,* the outermost post maintained by the Chinese, a couple of hours later. It was a square Chinese *ch'eng* on a flat in the valley. There was only one gate, through which all caravans must enter, piling up in the yard for inspection and then scrambling out as best they could. Great doings were to

the fore when we turned up, as caravans belonging to three great
Khotan merchants were passing through, homeward bound with all
manner of wares.   The swarming Ladakhis were all at least as
dirty as and more gorgeous than our men, with even wider grins,
and huge single earrings of silver and turquoise, and massive silver
amulet-cases slung under one arm.   The Ladakhis, an obliging race,
remove much of this finery when they reach Turkestan, in order
not to offend the Mohammedans with their heathenish appearance.
Our men, when we engaged them, wore Turki skullcaps, which
they did not exchange for their own Ladakhi caps, of a mediæval
cut coming down to protect the ears, until we were quit of Chinese
territory, and their earrings were not resumed until we reached
Ladakh.   Moses was not alone in calling the Ladakhis " Tatars,"
for one of the officials at Suget Qaraul described them to me as
"the Mongols of the English."

The two officials, one a Kan-su Chinese and one a Kan-su Mohammedan with a T'ung-kan wife, entertained us to tea and cakes
and presented us with two chickens.   We chatted pleasantly until
Tashi Serengh interrupted, howling and yelling.   First the Turki
underlings at the post tried to drag him away, then the Chinese
officials tried to explain matters to me.   It appeared, partly from
what I was told at the time and partly from Tashi Serengh's version given later, that the two *ssu-yeh,* as might be expected, were
not paid enough for a living.   They could not make a profit out
of heavy imposts on the caravan trade, because there would have
been a protest from the British side.   In this difficulty, they took
to selling barley for pack ponies, getting it up by the donkey-load
from the plains, where it is always cheap.   As any caravan man
would rather starve his ponies than pay a price set by somebody
else's needs, the business had to be turned into a kind of tax.   So
many ponies, so much feed.

The Chinese complained that it was a hard life.   They could
manage the Turki men, who were Chinese subjects, but the Ladakhi
fellows never paid up for a couple of years.   Our men ostenta-
tiously borrowed from me to pay their debts of two years past ;
if they had admitted to money of their own, they might have had
to pay more.   Then having noted the effect of their leader's yells,

all of them continued to yell until they were let off their purchase of barley for that journey — "on account of my face," as one of the officials was charming enough to remark. We were later to regret that the officials, for our sake, had been so lenient.

Two more short marches took us to the foot of the Suget. It was cold at night, and Moses woke one morning to find one of our chickens trying to die. "But I was too much for it," he said, with one of his quaint relapses into innocence. "I hurried up and got a knife to work on its neck, because if it had died of itself that would have meant there was something wrong with it, and it would n't be well for you to eat it."

Under the Suget, at a height of nearly 16,000 feet, the altitude was more than enough to be felt when walking. My wife had a headache, I panted as if I were fat, and Moses panted anyhow. He had said once that he would go anywhere with me if I did n't make him ride a horse; by this time he could not have been prised off the lean pony which he straddled like an anomalous frog, on top of his *p'u-kai* of bedding.

Our last marches had been so short that we were several times overtaken by parties of-Hajis bound for Mecca, though since the Russians have consolidated their position again in Central Asia the Russian railways are competing once more as a pilgrim route. Many pilgrims go out through Russian Turkestan, and then by steamer through the Black Sea, in order to pass by Constantinople, which they call Roum and still in a vague way consider the secular capital of the faith. On their way back to Chinese Central Asia they more usually take a pilgrim steamer to Karachi and then go up to Kashmir to take the Karakoram road. The Russian route is free of physical hardship, but the pilgrims are robbed by their coreligionists, who pretend to show them the ropes. They like the Indian route because they are less harried; for these poor fellows can be imposed on by any rogue in a railway uniform who demands their passports and a fee. One Indian regulation at least protects them — the police order which requires a list of maximum prices fixed in bazars; but in this and everything they owe their protection to the "sahib." The men of their own religion fleece them at every chance. When we came to Kashmir, the news went out that we were from Turkestan, and we were everywhere saluted by pilgrims. Then, at Rawalpindi, where we reached the railway, a group of Hajis at the station besought me to buy their tickets to Karachi, " because they did not know the price and could not trust the ticket seller." I bought the tickets and found out where their train would come in, and there and then they went into camp, on the platform. Poor fellows, they did not escape after all. A friend of ours who came down to the railway several days later found the same party still camped on the platform, still hoping for a white man to help them. Undoubtedly some railway underling would not let them get on the Karachi train without paying an extra fee.

The Mecca Haj is no light pilgrimage; it must be the most arduous journey in the world — but what a journey! It is not much less than two years before the Haji can return to ease and honor in his own oasis; and many that set out never return. When we had camped below the Suget, two red-bearded Khotanlik Hajis had come by, on their homeward road. Two men striking for home with no more provision for man and mount than they could carry on the saddle. It was magnificent, and our hearts rose to the noble feeling of what it must be to be a Haji, full of righteousness, travel, and the recollection of Mecca; and a few marches from home.

XXXII

SUGET AND KARAKORAM

WE were to have made a very early start for the Suget, but where we had camped on bare ground we woke under three inches of snow, with wet snow still falling. The day before we had looked to be not more than a few hundred feet below the pass, with perhaps a mile of climb; but we had been going several hours when at last we crawled up to the crest. There was nothing difficult about it, but the pace was dead slow because of the altitude, and the distance far greater than it looked in the thin air.

Our men did not go at the Suget as cavalierly as they had at the far more forbidding Sanju. They were all cowed by the deathly hush of the pass in the falling snow. There was not a sound but the hard-taken breath of men and ponies, and the subdued drone of Tibetan prayers from the Ladakhis, telling their beads as they labored beside the caravan. Nor did Moses grin as he usually did when he heard " natives " at their prayers. He was feeling rather sick. The altitude and the cold had brought on a touch of an old fever, and he said his " bones hurt."

We hardly knew it when we dipped over the crest of the Suget, at 17,610 feet, with all the world hidden in the gently falling snow; but when we were safely over the men yelled, right enough — an eerie ululation, but a small enough sound in that waste. We were now out of the K'un Lun ranges, having penetrated in eleven marches to the Karakoram plateau. To the east rose hills covered with snow, the Aq Tagh or White Mountains, to the west were bluffs of conglomerate, and we passed the desolate camping ground of Chibra, littered with the bones of dead animals, where we disturbed two incredibly large vultures, one so gorged that it could not fly, but only staggered drunkenly on the ground. We had been

going anywhere between twelve and fifteen hours when we turned
suddenly off the track and found a wet spot in a little sand gully,
with a thin wet streak going back into the sand hills.

This was Qum Bulaq, the Spring in the Sands, and a place of
misfortune. We found there a large number of small bales, very
heavy and solid. Our men told us that they contained *charass,* or
extract of Indian hemp, which is good for a great price in India
and a large taxation revenue to Government, being the same thing
as *hashish.* The bales had been abandoned by a caravan. One
of the Chinese at Suget Qaraul had told me that the year before the
winter had set in suddenly, weeks before time, with heavy blizzards
— the same severe winter that I had encountered in Mongolia and
my wife in Siberia. Caravans had dropped loads all along the route,
the men thankful to get away alive, and all these months later many
of the bales had not yet been salvaged. Cast loads are perfectly
safe on the Karakoram route. The travelers of the last generation
all point this out, and the rule still holds, although traffic has increased and values gone up since British action has made the road
safe from marauders. It must be partly because the caravan
traders are all known to each other, so that extra bales coming in
could be traced, even if the covers and marks had been changed.

We were much delayed in starting the next day, because two of
the ponies had strayed in the night, and two of the men ran and
walked until near noon before they brought them in. We got a
good rest, but suffered because the wind started coming to Qum
Bulaq just as we started to leave it. The custom of the weather,
day after day, was a calm morning with a wind rising after noon,
especially if the sun had been strong, heating the air and setting
currents to work. We had many Tibetan antelope in sight;
sophisticated dwellers by the road, who knew what shooting range
was, and kept beyond it. At Qum Bulaq itself we had seen antelope
incredibly tame, which must have come in for water from some
place far off the road. I had missed a number of shots at a ridicu-
lously short range, because Tashi Serengh, coming over the Sanju,
had smashed the sights off my rifle.

Toward the end of the march we found a big caravan in camp,
and called upon them to look for rupees, of which we found but

CAMP AT QUM BULAQ

LARGE MANI STONE NEAR PANIMIKH

eight. One of our difficulties on leaving Turkestan had been the conversion of our remaining money into rupees, which were at a premium in every southern trading town. In the first place, the Indian money-lenders, when unable to make up their profit balance in trade goods, bought in rupees to send to their homes. In the second place, rupees were wanted by Chinese officials, who, in default of any bank, had no way of remitting money to China. In the third place, the smaller supplies of Indian silver were wanted by pilgrims preparing for the Haj. English officers coming over to shoot in the Pamirs usually carry most of their money in rupee cheques, for which they could get a premium, if they only knew it. Usually they cash the cheques through an Indian money-lender at a slight discount, the money-lender thereafter selling the cheque at an extra profit. Cheques are coveted because they are portable, concealable, and negotiable. The signature of any totally unknown " Inglis " on a cheque is perfectly good — a nice piece of prestige. Russian money is also bought up and hoarded, but only in gold pieces — usually of the old Imperial mintage, imported into Russian Central Asia to maintain credit.

There was a bad sky when we camped, and a high wind; but the wind fell during the night and once more we woke under snow. Both of us had slept badly, with a feeling of suffocation. We had to lie with head and shoulders propped high, sometimes almost in a sitting position, and to breathe in an alternation of several long and several short breaths. Comfort in sleeping depends on acquiring the habit of this breathing unconsciously; otherwise one wakes at intervals, choking. Moses complained that the thin air " made him stupid." He disgustedly compared the road of the High Passes with Mongolia, where he had ridden a camel, a beast he thought superior to a horse, in that " sitting on a horse is more like riding, but riding on a camel is more like sitting."

Before we turned in I had urged Moses to come in and share our tent, warning him how his bones had hurt at the Suget. He refused indignantly. " You like these four Tatars," he said, still referring to the Ladakhis by the name of contempt, " because they grin all day and talk a word and a half of turban-talk (Turki). Not I ! They come from God knows where and their language is God knows what. All the time they talk with each other. Who knows what they say? Suppose they ran off in the night with all the ponies and a load or two? No! I know which loads are worth money, and I sleep beside them. Did n't I serve your father and your mother all those years in China, and shall I lose all my good name here, these two steps from India?"

The shelter he shared with our men was made by stacking the loads in a crescent, with a tiny fire in the lee. Poor Moses! He missed the exercise of his good, satisfying Chinese, which he could use no longer with anyone but me. He would grin and grimace jovially at the caravan men, all the while using the most awful language on them, but even this amusement did not last forever. His broad face would lighten when I rode along with him for half an hour and we chattered and cast up long reckonings of many roads. It was a hard road, even for caravan men, equal to anything but the worst of Mongolia, yet the whole time we saw only one caravan with a tent, or rather an awning tilted over a laager of bales. There was no profit in trade unless every pound were cut. Our men wore all their clothes all the time; they sweated on the march and lay down in their sweat at night, with no extra covering.

When we started in the snow we had to take up a supply of *burtsa,* which grew there in plenty and was the last fuel to be had for a number of days. There is, I believe, a " true " burtsa, but the Tibetan name is used for all kinds of high-altitude shrubs growing on desert mountains, in the hollows down which comes occasional water from melting snows. It includes the " lavender plant " of Shaw,[1] which has a squat growth of sage-green leaves two or three inches aboveground, and a disproportionately large root which burns with a steady heat when coaxed by the knowing. While we were on the march, one man quartered the slopes of thin snow with a pick, and another with a sack grubbed for enough to feed our cooking fires in the next few days.

Passing through small hills, we came into a long desert plain, totally free of the last night's fall of snow, bordered by superb red hills, the Qizil Tagh. Here again we saw quantities of Tibetan antelope. My wife had put back the sights on my rifle, binding

[1] Shaw, *Visits to High Tartary, Yarkand and Kashghar.*

them as correctly as possible with sticking plaster. I could shoot now with surprising accuracy in elevation, but with weird lateral divagations. We wanted both meat and a "head," and as we had put up several bands of bucks, which had run to join the scattered herd, I fired at what appeared, in the glaring sun-dazzle, to be the biggest. A doe about fifty yards to one side of it lurched, recovered, and went off at an uncertain gait. The men howled with joy. The others hesitated. I straightened the sights and fired at a big fellow who had halted after breaking away from the does. A half-grown kid, this time on the other side of him, rolled over and over. The men howled again. They had not much feeling for sport, but a wonderful feeling for meat.

Two of the men, one on foot and one on a pony, ran down the wounded doe, the runner putting up a magnificent exhibition, considering the altitude and the strain on heart and lungs. We needed the meat, but I had wanted fair game, a buck with a "head." As we went on, the plain narrowed to an entry into rough hills. At one side, through a curious portal like a gap in a dyke, we could see a mass of level ice, a prone glacier. A stream issued from the gap, but we followed a smaller stream into the hills. Then we met three Ladakhis, with three ponies, going toward Yarkand. Our men had been expecting for several days to meet them, having heard of them from other caravans, and they all squatted by the trail and chattered. Our men filled handkerchiefs from the store of parched barley meal the others carried, giving them in exchange the heads of the two antelope, which I had thrown aside as offal, but they had carried along. When we parted, Tashi Serengh made frantic signs to me expressive of joy, because one of the strangers was his brother.

Soon after we had entered the hills we climbed up at one side into a little corrie, to camp by a spring. This was the place called Balti Brangsa, the Camp of the Baltis, a name remembered from the old marauding days when a party of Baltis were captured and enslaved, or killed, or otherwise inconvenienced, by Hunza raiders. It was a gray, chilly camp, but a few blue pigeons flew about, visitors of the most waste places and followers of the caravans. A raven looked at us sourly from the rocks, disgusted at being driven away from a dead mule near which the antelope were being broken up and the men beginning to cook — although there is a belief that it is bad to eat meat at great altitudes. Moses long since had become adept at portioning game, always making an allowance for whatever followers we had. Venison he divided into " beefsteak," " mutton chop," and " give-it-to-them."

Although the men had warned us to be ready for a long pull and a strong pull from Balti Brangsa, we felt somewhat harassed at being roused about two or three in the morning. I objected that we must at least have some kind of light in order to break camp and load without leaving things behind, but Moses, busy already, answered shortly that the " Tatars " had it in mind to start " with empty bellies and a sky full of stars." We compromised on having a tiny fire nursed up so that we could get something hot into us. Then we finished packing, in a cold that was obviously below freezing, by the light of a naked candle. It was an example of our stupendous luck. Our electric flash died quietly at about the time we entered the high mountains, and not long after somebody smashed the candle-lantern. From then on, for one of the most windbedeviled journeys in the world, we managed perfectly well with naked candles. I walked about that morning ordering all things by candlelight, only hooding the flame once or twice with my hand from a flutter of the air.

The first hours of the march were savagely cold, but at last a weak dawn woke out of the darkness

> Like a soul belated,
> In heaven and hell unmated,
> By cloud and mist abated.

The valley, a gorge at Balti Brangsa, had opened up above and we found ourselves in a huge, shallow gulf, sunk between smooth-edged fells that were in fact the tops of mountains about 20,000 feet above the sea. An increasing number of skeletons and dead animals proved that we were well forward in the highest altitudes, on the stages of hardest marching and scantiest grazing. A sinister population of glossy ravens hardly bothered to move out of our way as we passed the freshest carcasses. Dunmore mentions a

famous pair of ravens which in his day (1892) used to follow caravans from the Karakoram to the Suget, where they would turn
back.

Ravens, by tradition, go for the eyes first; wolves for the haunch.
We neither saw nor heard wolves, though all the early travelers
mention them, and the caravan men said they were still plentiful.
We did see dead ponies torn at the haunch. Dunmore (though no
other writer that I remember) speaks also of " wild dogs," both on
this route and on the Pamirs.[1] I could not make this distinction
in questioning our men. Even in asking for wolves I was put to it.
The only word I knew was *koshker,* which in the Turki of Qirghiz
and Qazaqs in the T'ien Shan means a wolf, whereas a different
word is used by the people of Kashgar and Yarkand. When, however, I asked them, *"It okshash, ao-o-o-o-o, bar ma?* — like a dog,
howls, is there any of it?" they answered at once, *"Bar, bar, tola
bar!* — There is, there is, much there is!" This all goes to show
how easy it is to travel.

I suppose it was about nine o'clock when the sun broke through,
massive curtains of white cloud drawing to either side just as we
made a small turn and saw the Karakoram before us. The name,
qara qorum, means Black Gravel, but the pass, which is a low *col*
rising only a few hundred feet to close the head of the valley, is
conspicuously of a yellow clayey appearance, with an earth path
approaching the crest in zigzags. I dismounted, to go up on my
feet.

Just below the pass, on the Chinese side, is a cairn with stamped-
cotton Tibetan prayer-flags on it, and in the nick of the pass a cairn,
now falling to ruin, put up in memory of Andrew Dalgleish, the
Scottish merchant-adventurer and early explorer of Central Asia,
who was murdered on the pass by a Pathan.

The watershed of the Karakoram plateau is the boundary between the British and Chinese dominions, so that as I went over
the crest I passed out of Chinese territory for the first time in
eight years, and Moses for the first time since his boyhood adventures in South Africa. It was our fourteenth march from Sanju
Bazar. I advised Moses to get off his pony and *k'o-t'ou* on his de-

[1] Dunmore, *The Pamirs.* London, Murray, 1893.

parture from China and his entry into foreign parts. " But I *like* going to foreign countries," said Moses, stolidly. Moses, I think, is one of the last of that old-fashioned race, the body-servant.

The Karakoram is 18,310 [1] feet above sea-level, but none of us felt the height especially. One traveler after another has pointed out that the caravan men do not realize that this pass is the supreme high point of the journey. They have no way of comparing passes except by the apparent height of each climb. Thus they believe that the Sanju is the highest of all; but they do recognize, of the Karakoram, that it is the central point of the central portion of the journey, and that the most barren and arduous.

Even the caravan men, of whom the Ladakhis at least are bred in high altitudes, and who make the great journey perhaps twice a year, are not immune to mountain sickness. The effect on them is just as erratic as on other people: sometimes they get over without suffering; at other times they are very sick. I believe it may be that the effect of height varies with temperature and weather conditions, which alter the pressure of the atmosphere. Like other peoples of Central Asia, the caravan men ascribe the physical distress they feel at these extreme heights (having no way of discerning that what appears to be an irregular plateau is in fact higher than all but the highest passes) to a poisonous exhalation from the ground. Chinese caravan men who penetrate the Central Tibetan plateau from the Koko Nor region have the same tale of those parts. Garlic, I believe, is an empiric remedy for mountain sickness. Men on the Hsi-ning–Lhasa route suck a clove of garlic when at high altitudes. They say that the garlic turns brown in their mouths, which they hold a final proof that it has absorbed the poisonous gases.

The descent of the Karakoram on the southern side is longer than the northern approach, but just as easy; but the height kills. We saw many abandoned loads, among them bundles of felts coming from the Turkestan side. All of them were plain white felts of the soft, long-staple wool, one of the best in Central Asia, gathered in the Lob Nor region and marketed at Khotan. There is no de-

---

[1] Skrine, in his excellent *Chinese Central Asia*, gives 18,550 feet, which is probably a later and better figure.

mand from India for the parti-colored felts with worked-in designs
which the Turki themselves use. The plain felts are taken to Kashmir, where they are worked with stitched designs in thread. Some
of the felts are left with the white ground-color, while others are
dyed a solid color. A few of these embroidered felts even find
their way back to Turkestan. The underwool of goats is also ex-
ported from Turkestan to Kashmir, where it is mixed with similar
wool from Ladakh to make the very fine, soft *pashmina* tweeds.

At the foot of the pass proper the track debouches into a main
valley; a long, gently sloping valley, but, when one stands to look
across it, a magnificent scene. There we saw Tibetan antelope
again — very shy herds, the last we saw in numbers. We held on
and on down the long valley, passing Chajosh Jilga, the camping
ground which marks the end of the regular long stage across the
Karakoram. Dunmore [1] gives the story of the place: —

A Yarkandi merchant halted there to brew himself tea before
attempting the pass. He carried bundles of fuel on his loads (just
as we did) and started a little tea-making fire. The water, because
of the great elevation, would not boil to his liking, but he obstinately
added fuel until his whole supply was gone. Still the water was
not fit for steeping tea. Having thoroughly lost his temper, he
started on his cargo, a stock of wooden combs which he was carrying back from Kashmir. He fed the combs into the fire one by
one until, with the last comb, the water boiled just so, the tea was
made to his taste, and he was a ruined man. Therefore the place
is called Chajosh — " boiling tea," or " a teapot," I am not sure
which — and Jilga, " a valley." Central Asian joke.

A little farther down we saw three tiny beehive stone huts, the
place being called Palo, which is obviously a corruption of the
Chinese *p'ai-lou,* and may mean that at some time in the past the
Chinese advanced ·a border post thus far, claiming a frontier beyond the Karakoram. On the other hand, the post may have
been established by men from Turkestan, who borrowed the Chinese
word, which properly used does not mean a post, but a memorial
" arch " across a road. As if by omen, we met a single Turki
merchant, and a Haji and his wife, and the Haji was the sole

[1] Dunmore, *The Pamirs.*

man we met beyond the Chinese frontier who could speak Chinese. It seemed queer, to use the old speech in that place, with that shaggy stranger. Most strange of all, he knew a Chinese friend of mine, then thousands of miles away. Such encounters have the true taste of Asia.

Nor had we gone much farther when we ran upon a whole camp of Hajis, who had been primed by our pony men and were ready to sell us rupees, their baggage being handy to open and their girdles loose in the ease of camp. We made a big haul, getting rid of the bulk of our Kashgar paper. Men, women, and children were *p'a-hsia* (squatting, as a camel squats), to use the Gobi caravan phrase, without a tent among them, but sheltered by big rocks. A little fire was being jealously fed from the small store of fuel they had brought on their pack animals, and they gave us tea. They were gravely merry and pressed on us the courtesy of the good folk of Turkestan. Old men stroked their beards and youths waited on us and women fluttered about the rim of the circle to get a glimpse of the *khanum*, my wife. Hajis they might be, but they had not lost on pilgrimage the tolerance of the Turki people, giving us the greeting of the faithful, the *salaam aleikum*, as though we had not been unclean Nazarenes. As for me, I had before then learned to stroke my own beard and return the *O aleikum es s-s-salaam!* in their own canorous manner.

When we rode on, we rode heavily, the weary ponies unwilling to leave the hobbled caravan animals. Once more we came to a place with a name, but little to show for it; the camping place known as Daulat Beg Uldi, beyond the scattered streams of the Chipchak or Wujuk River. The name of the place means no more than Daulat Beg Died; for Sa'id, Khan of Kashgar, who was Daulat Beg, or Prince of the Realm, died there of a sickness brought on by the great height, on his return from a campaign against Ladakh.[1]

This in all conscience was a long enough march. We should have camped, but had failed through our delay to catch up with the caravan. We could see the dead-beat baggage animals far off in front, but our own ponies were too limp to stride out and overhaul them. Three of the men were keeping on like machines, but the

---

[1] A. von Lecoq, *Auf Hellas Spuren in Ost-Turkistan.*

headman had lain down by the track, where we found him asleep. This was not laziness, but because, being the most active of the lot, he was the most worn-out. We made him hold the ponies while we chewed in a fatigued way at the crumbs of lunch.

We started again, and went, the good Lord knew how many hours. The ponies could hardly put one foot before the other. It was late evening when we climbed slowly up a mild dawan to find, at the top, not a crest, but the almost level plateau of the Depsang Plains, the same that are higher than all but the highest mountains. In about the middle of the bare levels we struck the rift of a faint stream, and in it camped. All of us were done to the world. We had meant, knowing that the men planned a killing march, to call a halt when we saw fit, but had got too far behind. We had been something like eighteen hours on the march.

Though tired, I was drawn out to stroll in the glow of the last light. The plains of clay and gravel, dotted with large boulders, all open to the great sky and nothing else, tilted away to the east, down to barren, snowless hills. The uplifted western rim of the plateau concealed all the world except a few ice-peaks that lifted above it. One of them was K2, the highest peak in the world bar Mount Everest, but from the Depsang Plains, which are sixteen or seventeen thousand feet, K2 and its companions looked strangely truncated. On the bank above our tent were irregular squares of stones, with Mecca-pointing rocks; praying places of the pilgrims. What a faith, and what a pilgrimage; the noblest journey in the world. Beside us there camped that night a small party of homeward-going Hajis. They were haggard-eyed, and as weary as we.

XXXIII

FAREWELL TO HIGH ASIA

On the next morning, the fourth of September, 1927, we began our fifteenth march, having been able to sleep only when propped almost in a sitting position, because of the difficulty of breathing. The men had wanted to be off at the crack of dawn, but this we had quashed. We had found out by now what was at the back of all this passionate marching. The men were short of barley for their ponies. On the first stages, where there had been a semblance of grazing, they had loitered. Now, on these heights devoid of any grazing at all, they wanted to force the pace, trusting to our light loads to get their half-starved ponies over to the next grass. I wished then that I had thrown my influence to the side of the officials at Suget Qaraul, and made the men stock up with extra feed.

At the thither edge of the Depsang Plains we came to an easy slope — easy for us, going down. At the top we met a breathless pilgrim caravan. We sat and watched their stragglers coming wearily up. The men reeled as if drunk, striking weakly at ponies that hung their heads, gasping desperately. A woman sat bowed abjectly over the withers of her pony, miserable with mountain sickness. A Haji, as he reached us, slid from the mound of saddle-bags on his pony, laid aside his umbrella, turned toward Mecca, and composed himself to prayer. Eight Hajis out of ten carried an umbrella, bought in some Indian bazar. It was almost a badge of pilgrimage accomplished.

Then we went down until we came to a stream where, the water being low, we left the track and turned into a corridor of red rock. The walls of darkly glowing red were at times only thirty feet apart, soaring straight up to the height of the blue sky. We emerged from the gorge into a wide desert valley, with a flat floor of heavy shale, where the stream severed into many channels. All day we went down, down, down the slow windings of the deepening valley, and all the way was rubble and stone, shale, gravel, sand, and rock. The uppermost heights were snowless, but as we got down we began to look into wild ranges holding snow and glaciers. It was an eerie march, going all the way downhill from the plateau, to find ourselves penetrating ever more deeply into enormous hills, whose tops had been below our feet.

The last few hours of that march were the most incredible passage we had yet made, beyond all the passes in ferocious wonder of setting. The valley narrowed to a gorge, the noble and savage Murgo gorge, into which we climbed over a barrier of rock that had fallen from the hills. In the shadow of the deep cleft the track reeled and twisted over huge falls of conglomerate rock, and was carried over unbelievable sweeping slopes of detritus, climbing and falling by turns to find the most workable level. Often on a two-foot track there would be a sheer fall of many score feet under us, or a sharp glissade of hundreds; the whole in a gray light as of the Elder Gods, with a flushed peak or two striking up to an impossible height above us.

Tashi Serengh led my wife's pony. Mine, the white veteran of the Lhasa road, delighted in walking on the edge of the edge, sending pebbles and rotten rock skidding down the slopes. Then we came down a dizzy descent to avoid a gap where the track had been carried away by a landslide. There was a place where the ponies had to do a right-angled turn with head and neck sticking out over a clean drop, all their weight on the forehand at an angle of forty degrees or so, with their hindquarters high above them, and a loose footing. I swear that for one moment both my feet were hanging out over pure space and undefiled. I went round corners that I should never have believed could have been turned in the saddle; no, not with prayer. But it was too late; there was not even the chance of a leap for life, and there was my wife, ahead and below, sitting her led pony placidly and telling me not to be so reckless in my riding.

We went right down to the bottom of the gorges, where we

splashed through water for two hundred yards, Tashi Serengh on my crupper, where he had landed with a leap and a yell. We heard faint whoops, and looking up could see the trail climbing again, lap over lap, and our little black caravan at the very top, looping around a corner into the pale sky, hundreds of feet over us. We started to climb, and slowly put one level after another under our feet; then we too turned round the corner into the sky and started going down again.

Thus we came to the mouth of Murgo Gorge, choked by a confusion of wild boulders. On the flat of a terrace rose a strong spring, from which ran two streams, one plunging over a monumental rock. This was Bulaq-i-Murgo, the Spring of Murgo, the place where Stoliczka died, the Moravian missionary who accompanied the Forsyth diplomatic mission to Kashgar as naturalist, in the seventies. Because of much grass poisonous for horses on the terrace, we camped on a flat below. We had done in two marches three of the longest and hardest stages of the whole journey; a distance of sixty miles.

Even the men were by then ready for a short march, and we made the next day only the twelve miles across the Shayok to Sasser Serai. The Shayok is the first great river of the Himalayan versant of the Karakoram, and a major affluent of the upper Indus. During the high water it is unfordable, and a different route has to be used, beginning from Leh by crossing the Digger La, and coming into the main route at Bulaq-i-Murgo. We found the river flowing strongly, some twenty-five yards wide, three feet deep, and encumbered with big, round, nasty boulders.

Two men are paid by the Kashmir State government to look out at the ford of the Shayok; but they did not look out at us. We got over with the edge of a load or two wetted, and scrambled up into a corrie in the valley coming down from the Sasser glacier. There we found a pig-horrible sty inhabited by the two Ladakhi fordwatchers, this being the serai, or inn. It was the dirtiest camp we had yet experienced, but we stayed in the little hollow because of the shelter. The half-buried stone hut of the ford-watchers was ringed about with the remains of dead animals, which were attended by obscene ravens. The rest of the place was rags of felt,

YAKS ON THE GLACIER

THE ICE SLIDE

THE KHARDONG PASS

ends of rope, swathes of dry dung, and a prevailing stink of putrescence; and over all wheeled the blue pigeons of the high places, with pulsing wings.

Another fourteen miles laid the Sasser behind us, but they were fourteen miles of punishment. We started early, climbing up to the glaciers, with ice and snow in sight from the very start. Yet before we got into the ice we saw grazing camels — a good sight for those that love them. Camels come as far as this from Yarkand (as attested by their dead along the road), but the ice of the Sasser is nominally impassable to them. Their loads are taken on over by yaks, and relayed along to Leh by local transport; but we did see in the Panimikh valley a few camels, which our caravan men said were the first, so far as they knew, that had crossed the Sasser.

From glacial moraines we toiled up at the side of a bulky glacier and traversed to the watershed of the pass, at an altitude of 17,500 feet. Almost at the top we met a few returning Hajis, with whom we bargained on the ice for rupees. Then, taking the downward tilt, we picked a way first along a glacier, until we sidled off it into scree rock. The caravan went on along a glacier, but Tashi Serengh took us two among frightfully tumbled rocks at the side. After we rejoined the caravan we all flopped and toppled among glacier-heaped rocks, very slowly and painfully.

The difficulty of the pass is that several glaciers, first from one side and then the other, push out into the central valley, so that the laden ponies must crawl round their snouts, over the ruin they have heaped. Cupped in the heavy ice were several green tarns, and waterfalls plunged down the abrupt sides of glaciers. Then at last we slid down 350 feet to the zone that I like best in these tremendous mountains, above the usual range of man; the region where, just under the ice and before the mountains stand away again to unassailable barren heights, grooved with stony watercourses, the glaciers have left patches of short, close turf, growing on mud between the boulders.

All at once we were among flowers — red, yellow, and purple. We rode over them and were thankful, having " folded over," as Gobi men say, to the hither side of the worst pass we had yet faced. A little farther and we camped, in a beautifully sheltered hollow

of the tract of camping grounds and summer yak-pastures called
Tutialik, with nothing to seek but fuel, which the men gathered
in copiously, yak-dung by the sack.

The men pleaded to go " just a little far," the next day, because
they were out of pony feed. *"Tsou-che k'an,"* admonished Moses
— " look as we go," and we made that the order of march. Almost
the whole day we went by one great valley, leading down from the
huge, black Murgisthang glacier. The mountains crowded up to
the valley, forcing us up on steeply pitched slopes of soft detritus.
Below us the water rattled out of sight in a rock-sided ravine. At a
stomach-affecting depth beneath the track were stray tufts of
coarse grass, and nearer the water was brushwood. Out of call in
the depths were shepherds, perched among the boulders like ravens
in their nests, while their sheep and goats voyaged, as it were like
birds, from one blade of grass to the next. They were a presage
of places where men lived. At our own level, where now and again
solitary boulders unbelievably big slumped in the detritus, grew
wild rose bushes. The path would edge under these house-high
boulders in the most fascinating way.

All on a sudden we made a twisting descent to the camping
place gloomily called Umlung. Sure enough, as the men had
warned us, there was no grazing. There was no picketing room
for more than a donkey and a half, between the sheer slopes and
the full-throated stream, and even that room was taken up by dead
donkeys, with a gang of road-repairers camping on the top of them
with Tibetan insouciance. We agreed with the men to try the
next lodgings.

No path could come in at the mouth of that gorge, where the
water choked in a sluice of rock, and the sides were buttressed with
naked rock. In the old days, Tashi Serengh explained with a sweeping arm, men climbed around and entered this valley from the side.
This must have been by the Qaraul Dawan, or Fortress Pass, which
early travelers called the Vanguard Pass. We got out by a shored
and blasted track, a recent work, that climbed five hundred feet
over a mountain shoulder to get above the mouth of the gorge, then
sank away a thousand feet.

In some places this Quruq Dawan or Dry Pass, as the men call it, because it gets above the water and holds no ice, is built up over sheer precipices, in other places it is blasted out of the living rock over still sheerer drops. Thus at any turn we could look out over hollow voids into endless mountains in the pale clear sunlight of afternoon.

Our men, prodigious fellows on any slope at any height, had always breath to sing, or to sprint after a pony whose load had dragged askew. At the crest of the Quruq Dawan they yelled as they had not yelled yet. Away and beyond, below us, through a field-gun's pitch of empty air, was the great Nubra valley. On the far versant of that, on a spreading fan of detritus that issued from a gorge, was a village, and fields, displayed like a map. You do not know what life can hold, nor travel, until you stand in such howling mountains, and see with a feeling of discovery such a place, where men house themselves snugly among stone walls, and grub for a living in fields — and the whole still unattainably far away. We went hammering down the Quruq Dawan until we struck our own side of the Nubra valley, then pushed ahead to the edge of the river, where we camped among brushwood on the sandy flats. When the tent was pitched and the loads ranged, two of the men rode off, for they were within a ride of home.

We had made eleven marches between the last barley fields below Suget Qaraul and the first sight of fields in the Nubra valley.

When we had settled into camp I said to Moses, " Well, Moses, and what do you think of all this? "

"*Hao chia-huo!*" quoth Moses. " They told me, ' Wait till you get to the Great Sand-hollows,' and I waited, and got there. Then they said, ' Wait till you get to the Black Gobi,' and I waited, and got there. Then they said, ' Wait till you get to Dead Mongol Pass,' and I waited, and got there. But of this road, this road to India, all they said was, ' Who knows? ' *Ai-ya!* I sit on my horse (of which I knew nothing before I left home), and the horse puts his head, and his two legs which are in front, into empty air, and I shut my eyes and hold my stomach in my mouth — and yet, *hsi-lo hu-tu-ti*, by the fortune of fools, I get there. But this road, now, could you call it a road? "

"Anyhow, Moses," I suggested, "you will have a fine time talking about it all when you get back to Tientsin."

"Well said!" replied Moses. "And who" — pointing with his chin at one mountain and with his thumb at another — "and who in Tientsin would believe all this?"

The next morning we rode into Panimikh, the highest village in the Nubra valley of Ladakh, at least on our side of the Nubra, and the final taking-off point of caravans bound for Chinese Turkestan. We rode on the way over several "fans," the disgorgement of side-ravines entering the main valley. If there is a permanent stream in the ravine, it can be spread all over the fan by little irrigation channels. As much as possible of the surface is roughly cleared of stones, by building them into houses, walls, and *mani;* and behold fields, all yellow with ripe barley. Lower down on the fan are stony commons for grazing, and enclosures of thorn and brushwood from which fuel is gathered.

As we drew toward Panimikh we saw poplars and willows, the first trees for many days, either singly in the fields or clustered about the houses. The poplars were shorn of their lower boughs in the Turkestan fashion, so that they sprang tall and slim to a tufted crown. Everywhere and all about were wild roses, now past flower and hung with red pods like lamps; while thorn bushes were profuse, and every wall was topped with dead thorn. White *chorten* and slug-like mani-wall marked the piety of the people. A chorten is nothing other than the *dagoba* of Peking, but a mani-wall is a low, broad dyke of stone, littered on top with flat slabs and slates, on which are carven the *om, mani, padme hum* that runs from Lhasa to Mongolia. The people observe honor toward the mani-wall by putting it always on the right hand as they pass, the track therefore diverging as it approaches one, to give a way at either side, for those coming or those going. The length of the longest mani-wall in Ladakh is counted in a very large number of rods, poles, or perches; but in these matters I speak as a tourist.

At the very first group of houses our way was barred by the family of the youngest and handsomest of our caravan men, who came before us with offerings of flowers and *chang*. This latter is a Tibetan barley beer, said to be potent when kept, but, as we tasted it, uncommonly like what flat ginger beer might be if laced with still cider.

We had not gone much farther when we were met by the head-man of Panimikh, who called himself in hybrid style Tsetan Bai (*bai* being the Turki for a rich man, a landholder of consequence). He had robed himself notably in purple, and bounced himself on the top of a small, fat, waddling pony. He was a man of fifty or sixty, grizzled about his red chaps, and a complete illustration of a fat, prosperous, genial Central Asian villain. He led us on with something of a swagger to a camping ground in his own back yard, but, it being one of the regular caravan pitches, my wife demurred to the dirt. Later in the afternoon we found for ourselves a little green enclosure, where we rested for several days in the greatest tranquillity, except that one night a cow trod on an irrigation runnel a quarter of a mile away, whereupon the water came broadside down the hill and flooded us out of our sleeping bags.

We established ourselves in Panimikh by calling on Tsetan Bai, who was not only headman, but chief owner of our caravan. After falling over a calf on the ground floor, we stumbled up a dark stone stair and round a corner into the upper living quarters. It was dirty but lovely, with no light except what came through tiny windows in the stone, shuttered with wickerwork in default of glass and wood. We sat on Turki rugs and felts and were served with Tibetan beer out of Kashmir copperware, and blinked through the gloom at the dull, rich shine of old copper and brass, and the blue and red of a few old China plates.

The houses of the Ladakhis are a delight, built with sheer, white-washed walls of the crudest masonry and entered by obscure openings; but the savagery of them is toned down by overhanging balconies of carved wood. The Ladakhi women look more uncouth than the men, but their black grime and matted hair are set off by the wild barbaric glitter of turquoise, silver, and coral. They wear an astonishing headdress of cloth, like a long, tapering leaf, laid from the top of the head down the back, and this flat headdress is studded with turquoise.

Women were threshing barley in every courtyard, and clouds of chaff went surging up in golden dust all over the village. There was a chatter of children at every corner, and in the lanes could be heard the deep tones of men; the rolling Turki speech as well as the clacking and grating of the Ladakhi Tibetan. Their greeting is *Ju, ju, or ju, ju-lei!* When Moses first heard it, he rolled his eyes; and that evening, talking in Chinese, he made the one English joke of his career. " This journey of mine," he said, " was ordained. Many years ago, when I was a youngster, I went to South Africa to work in the mines, and there I got the name of Moses. Now, these many years later, I travel with you and come to Tibet; and what happens? The people know about it; the moment they see me, they say ' Jew '! "

On the first evening of our stay at Panimikh we heard a cheery noise of roaring and yelling, pierced by the wail and screech of strange musical instruments. We thought it might be a little timely dissipation, celebrating both the return of our caravan men and the presence of a Turki caravan going homeward to Yarkand, and as the dark fell we strolled into the village. Just then all the clamor died. As we came into the central lane we could hear only scuttlings and whisperings. Then a Turki bumped into us, chattering with fright. " Oh, Sahib," he said, *"yaman, yaman!* A stone, a man, a bang on the head, man *tashalan,* ruined, spoilt, finished! "

Going on, we found a group of villagers, their heads together and their tongues hushed but busy. Among them was one of our own men, who started to go with us, but his wife plucked him away down an alley, to make good his alibi. Then we entered a great yard, in which awed groups of whispering men surged and fluttered, Turki with Turki and Ladakhi with Ladakhi.

I demanded the what and the why with a sternness and authority I did not feel, and got garbled explanations, in Turki, that five Ladakhis and two Turkis had turned on each other in an old-fashioned way, and one of the Turkis had been killed. Where was the dead man? Over there, where he had fallen. No one had dared touch the body. I commanded a lantern, and the shadows of men flowed back and forth as we went over and found the man, lying like a half-filled sack, without seeming breath or motion. Turning him on his back, I felt his heart, while the assembly held its breath and was aghast.

He was alive, but not excessively. I proclaimed loudly that he was not dead, but on the next day would move and speak. On this a man darted forward, and who should he be but a Kashmiri, helping me to straighten the body, laying it comfortably and folding the limp arms. Then, rising, he said solemnly that *Inshallah* there was no murder done.

The Kashmiri, and another of the same folk, then took heart to reveal that they could speak, of all tongues, English. They were clerks of a sort, attached to a government station where the *corvées* that keep open roads and improve passes draw their tools and supplies. It was not copious English, but they could understand a good deal, when they did not think it would involve them in any responsibility.

Another Turki was then brought forward. He was much battered about the head, streaming with blood from scalp and chest, and with a shoulder either broken or displaced. He was man enough to be defiant, and was more concerned about the man on the ground than about himself. He said that he was headman of a caravan carrying Hajis back to Yarkand, and the man on the ground was one of those Hajis.

The English of the two Kashmiris dried up when it came to rights and wrongs. However, I was assured that the parties of the other part were under strong guard, so, ordering that the unconscious man be covered with a warm coat and left undisturbed through the night, we went away to our tent. There we read up concussion in our first-aid book, being agreeably surprised to find that we had done quite right, except that we had not followed the instructions about sending for a doctor.

The next morning, the man had not stirred. My instructions about leaving him alone had been gladly followed. He had not even been moved into the shade, much less did anyone worry about the flies beginning to gather in the cuts on his head. I cleaned out the wounds and touched them with mercury ointment. The caravan man, tough brute, had said the night before that he would wait for morning before being doctored. He was not yet ready, but stood by a huge beam scale, weighted at one end with boulders, in which grain was being weighed out for his ponies. His face and chest were caked with congealed blood, and I suspected that he wanted to keep this evidence in case he were detained for official inquiry.

Of the five Ladakhis originally mentioned, it had apparently been decided that two should not count as having been in the fight at all. One of our men explained, with eloquent shrugs, that they were by now a long way off in the hills. Another had escaped later. These were probably the men who had begun the trouble. It was plain that if the affair ever came before an Official — terrible word in all Asia! — the two men left would be those against whom the least evidence could be brought; barring that one of them had been handsomely clouted on the scalp, in a way to crack the skull of a more sophisticated man.

Local counsel was all against bothering any officials. Men came from the Turki caravan to assure me that the matter had been negotiated. Everybody had forgiven everybody else. As for the victim, they stood to it that he also would be forgiving when he woke up. They wanted to hoist him, still unconscious, across a pack pony and bear him away into the hills.

However, I was by now committed to an authority which I enjoyed by the mere assumption of it. This is called " being a Sahib." Therefore I forbade the pilgrim caravan to depart without my leave. I followed this up by photographing the " body " and the two prisoners as yet in hand. All Panimikh thereupon fluttered in subjection. If the man lived, I said, it was for him to lay an accusation or not, as he pleased; but until he lived or died the caravan must not go.

In the afternoon a deputation of Turkis came to our tent, with a Kashmiri clerk as interpreter in part. Saving my presence, they said, the man lived; and please could they all go. I went and found the Haji, who after eighteen or twenty hours had indeed come to. He was conspicuously unhappy, but anxious to be gone; and as far as I could see, in a fair way to recovery. We gave him and the battered kirakash of the caravan a stock of aspirin to appease their aches for a few days, and our blessing, and leave to go.

Bazar and Palace at Leh

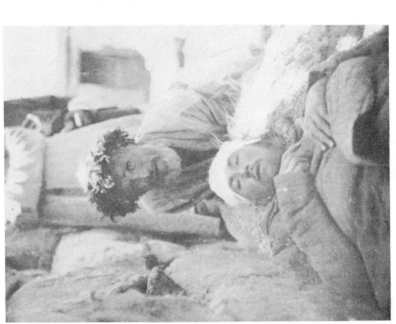

The "Corpse"

The Kashmiri asked hopefully for the gift of a dictionary, as reward for his services. A Kashmiri would.

Two days later we left ourselves, this time with a mixed transport assembled by Tsetan Bai, leaving all of our men but Tashi Serengh, who knew more Turki than any of the others and was the most handy and devoted. He had gone to his own village, on the other side of the Nubra, but caught us up at the end of a march, smelling abundantly of chang and still a little tipsy. Bundling off his pony and bowing to the very earth, he represented that his family had made him very drunk, but he was now ours truly again. What was more, he had picked up on the road my wife's whip, which I had lost from a saddlebag, so instead of reprimanding him we gave him a silver rupee.

Tsetan Bai, that prosperous old man, was doing things on the cheap. Our transport at one time consisted of a man, carrying a box on his back, a yak, a donkey, and the rest ponies and mules. Their different rates of travel scattered the procession over half Ladakh, so that we were a good deal put out, and should have been uncomfortable but for the heroic efforts of Tashi Serengh. In two days we went down the Nubra to its junction with the Shayok, which thus appeared before us again after mysterious wanderings, and followed up the Shayok to a place where the stream spilled over from its main channel, flooding a wide, shallow enlargement of the valley and making a ford possible. Then we climbed for hours up a narrow valley filled with brush, until we found Khardong Serai, the village below the fifth of the Great Passes.

There was a great accumulation of bales at Khardong Serai, because of losses among caravans in the previous season, which had made it impossible for all the yaks that could be pastured about Khardong to shift so many to the Leh side in the course of the present season. A Yarkandi caravan leader told me that he had been waiting twenty days for yaks.

On the fourteenth of September we ascended from Khardong Serai and knew again that vague but superb feeling which comes when you begin to labor toward the very rims of the hills and renew the struggle against thin air and the particularly evil cold that goes with the really great heights. When we camped, it was a cold camp, in spite of good fires of yak-dung. At this camp our solitary tin of molasses, which had been bought in Peking for no good reason and carried all the way from China without being used, was found to have bulged and voided itself over all the spare matches. Immediately after that, I dropped the last box into the washbasin. We could then get a light only by holding a damp match to a tinder-lighter and blowing fiercely. A malign wind sneaked and gnawed about the tent, and the candles guttered and went out.

We made a bitterly cold start, in eddying mists and a gray light, after a scant breakfast that put no warmth into us. We went on and up until we began the last grueling climb of fifteen hundred feet, up a slope of loose rock, reported dangerous from avalanches in the early season of snow-melting. Below us lay several glacial tarns, on which flocks of a small kind of duck were swimming in circles, gathering for migration. Then we struck the Khardong glacier, which tilts down athwart the Khardong pass. In September it was at its smallest and dryest. I had walked most of the way up the scree, and as for the glacier, there was no way that any of us could mount it, but on foot. We got on to the ice near its upper rim, having shoots of smooth ice below us for several hundred feet, and then a plunge on to crags, dark and glistening. The danger of the pass is that an animal slipping on the little, evil path will go over sideways on to the ice; from which there is no return.

We had but started when some Ladakhis came over from the other side with unladen yaks. They came down the slanting path to a point where it failed, and they had to get down to the next slant, thirty or forty feet below. They turned the yaks head-on to the slope, heaved them from behind, and sent the huge brutes skittering down on four bunched hoofs and their sterns until they struck a knoll of rocks, projecting from the ice, and came unconcernedly to a halt, nodding and bowing over the abyss.

It was not so easy for us. The track ran up at an angle, partly hewn out and partly rotted out by strewing earth on the glacier, a device which corrupts the ice and gives a surer footing. We two went up slowly by hand and foot; Moses applied himself to the surface and inched up by some trick of adhesion known to him. Our two riding ponies were hoisted by men at head and tail. Only the grunting yaks lurched up almost unassisted, except for men to steady them. Only one failed, but luckily it slipped back on to the rocks, not to the sheer ice.

After the one steep pitch the glacier was easy and safe. Marshaling the yaks again, we tacked up at one side and came abruptly to the crest of the pass — bare, splintered rock, at a height of 17,400 feet. There we rested, looking down with the sight of triumph to Leh, a star of green oasis whose points reached up to bare crags. Beyond Leh was the valley of the Indus, and beyond that again the true Himalayas, an immense and solid range, with peaks of almost uniform height, connected by curtains, so that they looked like a wall. These in truth were the ramparts of Hindostan, and it was a wonderful thing to come all that way out of the farther East and see the Himalayas, as it were beneath our feet. It was the fifteenth of September, 1927, and we were twenty-five days out from Sanju Bazar. It was in March 1926 that I had started from Peking, and my wife had set out to join me in February 1927.

There was Leh itself, below us, a place known for many things. It was anciently the capital of Western Tibet. It has a fortress on a crag, which was once the palace of kings, whose line has now been deposed, Ladakh having become a fief by conquest of the Dogras, whose ruling house is headed by the Maharajah of Jammu and Kashmir. Leh has also an abundance of monasteries. Transport and supplies between Srinagar and Leh are extremely scarce, for which reason the government authorities limit the number of travelers who are allowed to enter Ladakh in any one season.

Yet Leh has a government rest house or bungalow. It has a Moravian Mission, under a Swiss bishop, who is the most cheerful and generous of missionaries. It is the summer residence of one of the Assistants to the British Resident in Kashmir. It is the end of a telegraph line, and during the greater part of the year at least it has a postal service.

But our journey, in all truth, was at an end. We should have half a month of travel from Leh to clear the Himalayas and descend, by a noble enough series of passes, to Srinagar, in Kashmir. From Srinagar it would be about a hundred and thirty miles of motor road to Rawalpindi and the railway — Rawalpindi where, on a certain day, we were to say good-bye to Moses, when he took the train for Calcutta, to catch a boat to China, and we the train for Bombay, whence we should take shipping for Italy; and on that day we all wept.

That was all to come; but on the fifteenth of September we rested on the Khardong and looked down to Leh. Then we went down the pass.

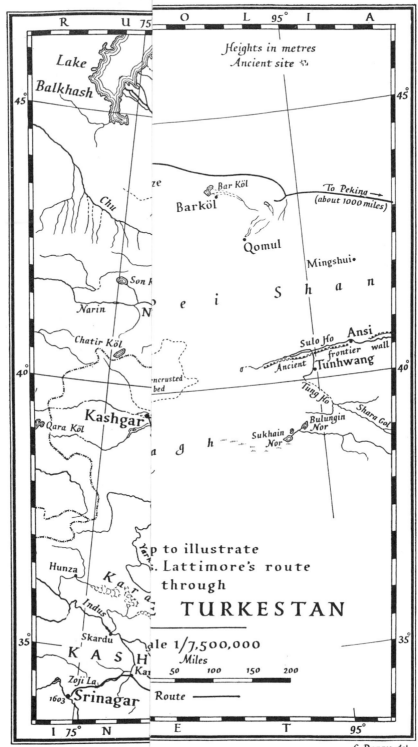

Map to illustrate O. Lattimore's route through

TURKESTAN

Scale 1/7,500,000

Miles

Route ———

C. Denny. del.

INDEX

INDEX